Women in the Inquisition

T0311371

Women in the Inquisition

Spain and the New World

Edited by MARY E. GILES

The Johns Hopkins
University Press
Baltimore &
London

.

*This book was brought to publication with the generous
assistance of the Program for Cultural Cooperation
between Spain's Ministry of Education and Culture
and United States' Universities.*

The Johns Hopkins University Press
2715 North Charles Street
Baltimore, Maryland 21218-4363
www.press.jhu.edu

Library of Congress Cataloging-in-Publication Data
will be found at the end of this book.
A catalog record for this book is available
from the British Library.

ISBN 0-8018-5931-X
ISBN 0-8018-5932-8 (pbk.)

For my husband, Paul

Contents

Introduction   MARY E. GILES   1

PART I   The Inquisition and Jewish Converts

1 · Mari Sánchez and Inés González
Conflict and Cooperation among Crypto-Jews
GRETCHEN STARR-LEBEAU   19

2 · Inés of Herrera del Duque
The Prophetess of Extremadura
HAIM BEINART   42

3 · María López
A Convicted Judaizer from Castile
RENÉE LEVINE MELAMMED   53

PART II   The Inquisition and Christian Orthodoxy

4 · Francisca Hernández and the
Sexuality of Religious Dissent
MARY E. GILES   75

[vii]

5 · María de Cazalla
The Grievous Price of Victory
ANGEL ALCALÁ 98

6 · Francisca de los Apóstoles
*A Visionary Voice for Reform in
Sixteenth-Century Toledo*
GILLIAN T. W. AHLGREN 119

7 · Y Yo Dije, "Sí señor"
Ana Domenge and the Barcelona Inquisition
ELIZABETH RHODES 134

8 · María de Jesús de Agreda
The Sweetheart of the Holy Office
CLARK COLAHAN 155

9 · Contested Identities
The Morisca Visionary, Beatriz de Robles
MARY ELIZABETH PERRY 171

10 · When Bigamy Is the Charge
Gallegan Women and the Holy Office
ALLYSON M. POSKA 189

PART III The Inquisition in the New World

11 · "More Sins than the Queen of England"
*Marina de San Miguel before
the Mexican Inquisition*
JACQUELINE HOLLER 209

12 · Blasphemy as Resistance
*An African Slave Woman before
the Mexican Inquisition*
KATHRYN JOY MCKNIGHT 229

13 · Rosa de Escalante's Private Party
Popular Female Religiosity in
Colonial Mexico City
LINDA A. CURCIO-NAGY   254

14 · Testimony for Canonization or
Proof of Blasphemy?
The New Spanish Inquisition and
the Hagiographic Biography of
Catarina de San Juan
KATHLEEN MYERS   270

Notes   297

Glossary   377

Bibliography   381

Notes on Contributors   389

Index   393

Women in the Inquisition

Introduction

The essays in this volume combine two areas of interest for the scholar and general reader: the Spanish Inquisition and the status of women in early modern Spain and the New World. A significant number of publications and conferences reflect increasing attention to Inquisition studies in recent years,[1] while efforts to identify individual women and understand the issues confronting them in centuries past have led scholars to Inquisition archives, where voluminous records entomb women from all reaches of Spanish society. The purpose of this collection of essays is to draw from these records and other historical documents portraits of women who, on a variety of charges, were brought before the Inquisition to answer for their lives. In words recorded by notaries who were present at their audiences with the inquisitors and in chambers of torture, women step forward, like ghosts in a dream, to claim existence and identity in the reader's imagination. Poignant reminder that survival on any terms is tenuous, the portraits are at the same time testimony to the creativity of scholars who, in the tedium of research, effect for these women a kind of resurrection.

. . .

The chronological presentation of essays accords with the changing concerns of the Spanish Inquisition from the early decades of its existence in modern times through the seventeenth century in colonial Mexico. Although a medieval inquisition had been established around 1232 in the kingdom of Aragon to counter the threat of the Cathar heresy, Castile did not have a tribunal until Pope Sixtus IV authorized the appointment of inquisitors in 1478 and the Catholic monarchs Isabella and Ferdinand founded the Holy Office two years later. By mid-October 1480 the Inquisition was operating in Seville, and by 1491 the kingdom of Castile had tribunals in Avila, Córdoba, Jaen, Medina del Campo, Segovia, Sigüenza, Toledo, and Valladolid. In the meantime modern tribunals were instituted in Aragon, Catalonia, Valencia, and Mallorca, and in 1483 a central office, the Consejo de la Suprema y General Inquisición (Council of the Supreme and General Inquisition), known simply as the Suprema, was organized to oversee these widely dispersed offices under the administration of three ecclesiastical members and an inquisitor general.

Theories about why the Catholic monarchs instituted the Inquisition are many and diverse, turning not only on religious issues but on political, economic, social, and racial ones as well.[2] For some historians the Holy Office was a means by which the monarchs could enforce absolute authority and ensure a religious unity that they deemed to be essential for political unification.[3] For others, the principal purpose of the Inquisition was to ensure that baptized Jews and their descendants, commonly referred to as *conversos,* not lapse into heresy by reverting to Jewish beliefs and practices.[4] A recent study focuses on anti-Semitism as the basis for the modern Inquisition and its mission to preserve orthodoxy among the conversos as well as for the decision in 1492 to expel unconverted Jews.[5] Regardless of the complexity of issues that may have informed the decision to found the modern Inquisition and the attitudes toward the Jewish and converso communities which influenced the decision, records clearly demonstrate that the target of the Holy Office was the conversos: of those tried by the Barcelona tribunal from 1488 to 1505 and in Valencia from 1484 to 1530, it has been calculated that 99.3 percent and 91.6 percent, respectively, were conversos.[6] Not only did the Inquisition direct its efforts principally against the conversos in the early decades of its existence, but the brutality and zeal popularly ascribed to the Spanish Inquisition as a whole especially characterize its treatment of suspected Judaizers. Henry Kamen notes that "it is likely that over three-quarters of all those who perished under the Inquisition in the three centuries of its existence, did so in the first twenty years."[7] "The savagery of the onslaught against the conversos," he asserts, "was without equal in the history of any tribunal in the western world."[8]

The inclusion of three essays on converso women underscores the fact that in the early years the Inquisition moved primarily against conversos on charges of crypto-Judaism and that this population suffered the cruelest treatment of any group investigated by the Holy Office. In their portraits of conversas, Gretchen Starr-LeBeau, Haim Beinart, and Renée Levine Melammed shatter a reader's illusions of detachment with haunting descriptions of community and family life destroyed by an Inquisition bent on preserving orthodoxy at all costs, including that of human life. Statistics may isolate the phenomena of torture and execution, but they fail to convey the reality of fear and pain as do the words of the defendants themselves. Through their eyes we see how thriving communities of hardworking people are undone by the intrusion of a presence that encourages betrayal and feeds on suspicion and secrecy and how ordinary people react in situations that threaten not just their way of life but life itself.

The subject of Gretchen Starr-LeBeau's portrait is Mari Sánchez, whose husband was tried and executed by the Inquisition in 1485. Her case is particularly revealing of life in the pilgrimage town of Guadalupe, where monastic authorities and the Inquisition increasingly dominated the community. Her story discloses as well how inquisitorial trials could be used by other lay people for their own ends and how even family members turned against their own.

The hopes of a converso community surface movingly in Haim Beinart's description of the twelve-year-old Inés of Herrera del Duque, whose prophecies about returning to the Promised Land inspired the converso community that had stayed in Spain after 1492, hoping for redemption and a return to the fold and beliefs of their forebears. As prophetess, Inés was dear not only to adults but also to children, who, despite their youth, were made to endure the hardships of persecution, abandonment by families, and forced "adoptions" into Christian families.

Renée Levine Melammed offers the story of María López, who was born into a Jewish family but chose to be baptized rather than join her brethren as they faced expulsion from Spain. Denounced in 1516 as a crypto-Jew, along with her daughter, María maintained her innocence even under torture, but in the end the force of adverse witnesses carried the day.

Cases involving conversos continued to be recorded throughout the sixteenth and seventeenth centuries in both Spain and Mexico, but the numbers in no way matched those of the period from 1480 to 1520, suggesting that the "success" of the Inquisition against crypto-Judaism had mitigated the need for vigilance over this segment of the population. But in the atmosphere of intellectual and religious restlessness of the early part of the sixteenth century, the Inquisition discovered new threats and with them new justifications for its work. The early sixteenth century was a time of intellectual vigor as Cardinal Francisco Ximénez de Cisneros (1437–1517) fostered humanist studies at the newly founded University of Alcalá de Henares and the writings of Desiderius Erasmus (c. 1469–1536) circulated freely in the peninsula.[9] In a climate of relative openness a religious reform took hold as well which emphasized interiorized Christianity over and against blind adherence to church ritual and belief, with spiritual writers and preachers encouraging individuals to nourish a personal relationship with God through mental prayer and quiet attentiveness to the inner presence of the Divine. Convinced that the Holy Spirit inspired men and women and illumined their way to God, both lay and religious, men and women, learned and uneducated, emerged as spiritual leaders to teach interior prayer and interpret Sacred Scripture. Prominent on the spiritual scene were charismatic women, popularly known as *beatas,* or holy women,[10] who often were accompanied by male admirers and through their ecstasies, visions, and miraculous healing confirmed the power of God to make of the most ordinary person, even an unschooled peasant woman, the channel of his will. In general, the people who followed the inner light of the Holy Spirit were called *alumbrados,* or enlightened ones, and interestingly, many of them were conversos.[11]

By 1525 the church was sufficiently alarmed at the incursion on ecclesiastical authority represented by the alumbrados to begin investigation into their leaders, Isabel de la Cruz and Pedro Ruiz de Alcaraz in 1524 and, a few years later, María de Cazalla, Francisca Hernández, and Francisco Ortiz, among others. By then Inquisitor General Manrique had gleaned enough evidence against the alumbrados from their own statements to issue an edict, on September 23, 1525, identifying forty-eight alumbrado propositions that inquisitors might consult in their investigations into the new heresy. The next two essays treat charismatic women who were alumbrado leaders, although they were not necessarily friends nor did they share the same circle of admirers. History has not been kind to Francisca Hernández: she has been stigmatized as a fraud who corrupted male companions and a traitor who gave false testimony against former friends. In an effort to reveal the woman behind the denunciations leveled against her by the Inquisition and by later scholars and perhaps hint at a rehabilitation, I build her portrait on those of two priest friends who also were tried by the Inquisition and whose motivations and character in part explain Francisca's behavior. María de Cazalla may have occupied the same prison as Francisca Hernández, but she has fared much better in treatment from both her contemporaries and later historians. Angel Alcalá offers ample evidence to support the favorable judgment of history: brought before the Inquisition on charges of *alumbradismo* and Protestantism, María de Cazalla maintained a heroic stance under the most grievous circumstances. Her story illustrates how personal enmity brought undeserved grief to an exemplary life and how personal heroism and integrity ultimately made a mockery of the charges brought against her.

The atmosphere of intellectual inquiry and spiritual innovation which fostered the emergence of charismatic women as lay teachers and preachers changed under the weight of growing concern over threats to orthodoxy from other quarters. By 1538 Erasmianism was no longer welcome in Spain, liberal humanism was suspect, and Protestantism was regarded with heightened alarm and, after 1558, relentlessly investigated by the Inquisition. In the history of the Spanish church and its increasing efforts to control cultural and religious life in Spain, the watershed year was 1559, when the Inquisition issued an index of prohibited books with the explicit intention of protecting Catholic orthodoxy. Known as the Valdés Index for Inquisitor General Fernando de Valdés, who issued the index, the list of prohibited books included fourteen editions of the Bible, nine of the New Testament, and notable mystical and spiritual treatises as well as sixteen works by Erasmus, the last entry a telling indication that the Inquisition had embarked on a policy of censorship in order to define orthodoxy and shape culture.[12] At the same time the Holy Office was acting boldly against persons suspected of Protestant leanings; on May 29, 1559, several people from a group centered in Valladolid, whose ranks included members of the prominent Cazalla family, were burned, and from 1559 to 1562 a second group met a similar fate in three autos-da-fé held in Seville. As a result of the Inquisition's swift and thorough action, Protestantism was virtually extinguished in Spain.

Unlike the Protestant threat to orthodoxy, which effectively was disarmed, the alumbrado challenge repeatedly asserted itself throughout the sixteenth century in individual women acting on their own and collectively in groups in Extremadura and Andalusia, where autos-da-fé were held in 1579 and 1590, respectively. The essays by Gillian T. W. Ahlgren and Elizabeth Rhodes portray visionary women in the alumbrado tradition whose fortunes before the Inquisition contrast sharply: Francisca de los Apóstoles was sentenced as a false visionary and possessed by the devil, whereas the vindicated Ana Domenge transformed her experience with the Inquisition into an apology for it. Both women sought reform within the church by founding or reforming religious houses, both were accused of false sanctity, and both had their reforming mission—and for Francisca her redemptive one—confirmed in visions whose nature and content the Inquisition questioned for authenticity. In their desire to effect reform through foundations and a problematic relationship with a Counter Reformation church that after the Council of Trent (1545–63) was increasingly determined to ascertain on theological grounds the genuineness of visions by which women claimed authority for their work, these visionary women recall Teresa of Avila, who had her own troubles with the Holy Office in its skeptical attitude toward women occupying center stage when they ought to be silent and obedient to the church.[13]

Like Ana Domenge, who made of her experience a heroic venture that redounded to the glory of her reputation and the Inquisition's, the "Sweetheart of the Holy Office," as she is known in Clark Colahan's portrait, demonstrates the terms and methods by which a woman, clever and educated, could transcend mere survival. The essay explores how Sor María de Jesús de Agreda, who reputedly had been miraculously transported to the New World and had written a voluminous and questionable biography of the Virgin Mary, managed to persuade her interrogators to her cause and win their enthusiastic approval.

[6]

At first glance the woman presented by Mary Elizabeth Perry is another latter-day alumbrada, but hers is a singular case among the women considered here: Beatriz de Robles was a Morisca, a Christianized descendant of Muslim lineage, and as such linked to a group of people which was forcibly expelled from Spain (1609) much as the Jews had been in 1492. Beatriz's multivalent identity as a Morisca and alumbrado invites speculation about syncretism in popular culture, how a woman in whom several Muslim traditions coalesced might subvert religious assimilation, and why her questionable status as both Morisca and visionary may have been a double advantage rather than doubled liability.

The Counter Reformation Inquisition that zealously monitored orthodoxy among conversos, Moriscos, alumbrados, and Protestants also faced the daunting task of Christianizing a largely rural population that was appallingly ignorant of rudimentary Catholic doctrine. Parallel to the teaching church that labored to educate this populace in the Catholic faith, the Inquisition concentrated on elevating moral standards by identifying and punishing sexual behavior that demeaned the sanctity of marriage, teaching, for example, that contrary to popular opinion and behavior, "simple fornication," defined as sexual intercourse between an unmarried man and woman, was a sin. Solicitation during confession, sodomy, and bestiality were other sexual acts that the Inquisition punished, as well as the widespread practice of bigamy, which Allyson M. Poska studies in her collective portrait of Gallegan women tried by the Holy Office during the period from 1550 to 1700. Her essay identifies reasons why women committed bigamy, describes life for the bigamist wife and the abandoned wife, and shows how some women defended themselves successfully against the charges while others met severe punishment.

Many of the same issues that beset the conscience of the church in Spain carried over to the colonial church, where, as in the peninsula, the Inquisition sought to protect Spanish religion and culture against heresy. Prior to the establishment of the tribunal of the Inquisition of New Spain in 1571 and the appointment of the first inquisitor general, papal bulls of 1521 and 1522 placed matters first in the hands of a monastic inquisition and friar inquisitors and later in an episcopal inquisition (1535–71), beginning when Juan de Zumárraga was given the title of apostolic inquisitor by the Council of the Supreme and General Inquisition in Spain. Hindered by ill-prepared personnel and an intrinsically defective administrative structure, the episcopal inquisition struggled unsuccessfully to meet its responsibilities. According to Richard E. Greenleaf, two circumstances in particular led to the establishment of the Holy Office of the Inquisition in Mexico: the first was "the feeling that diocesan administrators had used the Holy Office as a weapon in the conflict between the regular and the secular clergy," and the other was "the deluge of suspicious printed matter from Europe which was entering New Spain."[14] On January 25, 1569, King Philip II authorized the establishment of two tribunals, one in Mexico, the other in Peru, and a subsequent order (August 16, 1570) identified an area of jurisdiction for the Mexican tribunal which today includes Mexico, Central America, the American Southwest, and the Philippines. With an area larger than the one policed by all the tribunals in the Spanish peninsula and a population of bewildering ethnic complexity of which 75 percent were Amerindians exempt from inquisitorial control, the Mexican tribunal was hard pressed to monitor heresy and morality with the efficiency characteristic of its parent organization in Spain.

In the first portrait from colonial Mexico Jacqueline Holler presents the case of a woman born in Spain to an Old Christian family and moved at the age of three to Mexico City, where she later adopted the lifestyle of the beata and became famous for ecstasies and visions. Like the Spanish beatas, Marina de San Miguel suffered the negative repercussions of a fame severely tested under inquisitorial scrutiny; finally, in a startling turn of events, she admitted to scandalous behavior long blamed on women who sought authority outside ecclesiastical channels.

Other issues the Mexican Inquisition handled were unique to the society it policed, although, as in the case of the African slave woman portrayed by Kathryn Joy McKnight, the formal charge might mask the true menace. Blasphemy was the charge, but the circumstances in which María Blanca renounced God and his saints reveal that the purpose behind the Inquisition's action was not only to extirpate heresy but to suppress slaves whose unrest endangered social and economic well-being.

Just as the Inquisition in Spain feared syncretism in terms of Christianity, Islam, and Judaism, so its Mexican counterpart guarded against the blurring of boundaries between Catholicism and folk piety. In her essay on Rosa de Escalante, Linda A. Curcio-Nagy demonstrates that even devout Catholic women in Mexico City undermined orthodoxy in the practice of erecting in their homes private altars where they hosted lengthy ceremonies, or *oratorios,* featuring dance and ritual objects. With mestizo, mulatto, and African women engaged in similar practices, oratorios became so widespread that edicts against them were issued on four occasions from 1626 to 1707. Organizing popular religious rituals that mixed the profane and the sacred, these women compromised the success of a male establishment to model society on its terms.

The Inquisition's function of ensuring orthodoxy and shaping society to conform with Counter Reformation ideals affected women not only in their lifetime but also after their death, when the possibility of living on in popular memory as exemplars of Catholic piety depended on the construction of biographies in accordance with a typology approved by the church. Kathleen Myers identifies and analyzes the difficulties in making a case for sanctity when the subject was a visionary laywoman originally from Delhi, India, and revered as a saint by the people of Puebla, where she came to live for almost seventy years. Fear of a popular piety that would subvert ecclesiastical authority as well as issues of race, gender, and class resulted in the direct and complete censorship of one biography of Catarina de San Juan and a censorship by misrepresentation in another text whereby the author sacrificed the real woman to the ideal paradigm. In either case, the essay illustrates how the Inquisition could reach into the grave to silence a woman much as it had done countless times in the past when it condemned the dead and exhumed their bones for burning.

· · ·

In an effort to hear women's voices from the past scholars are turning to convent archives for letters, poetry, plays, accounts of foundations, biography, and autobiography[15] and to Inquisition files where the hand of the notary leaves record of a woman's existence while her own narrative, which initiated the examination, may still lie tucked between folios. A few women like Teresa of Avila, and among those in this collection, Sor María de Agreda and Ana Domenge, were able to bequeath testimony of their lives in a form that was appropriate to literary and theological convention, but as analysis of Teresa's writings reveals, such success was the exception; Teresa negotiated acceptance for her visionary authority because she was uncommonly intelligent, rhetorically skillful, cognizant of the larger religious scene, and theologically adept.[16] Few Spanish women in the sixteenth and seventeenth centuries had the space for self-expression which Teresa achieved for herself. Even for women of the middle and higher classes, access to education was limited, and the formal theological studies that could have legitimated their spiritual teaching were foreclosed to women. The general view that women were inferior creatures subject to the vagaries of flesh and emotions was pervasive in Spanish society, as evidenced by Fernando Valdés's scathing denunciation of women in his *Excelencias de la fe* (Excellences of the faith; 1537):

> No matter how learned a woman may be, put a padlock of silence on her mouth in matters of the mysteries of faith and the Church. For it is certain what the ancients said, that the jewel which makes a woman prettiest is the padlock of silence on the doors of her lips for all conversation, and particularly for the mysteries of holiness and so she is not to be a teacher of the doctrine of the Sacred Scriptures.[17]

Restrictions on self-expression by women became even more stringent after the Council of Trent set firmly in place tenets that promoted obedience, humility, and service as ideals for women. Even the illustrious humanist Juan de Vives (1492–1540), writing earlier in the century, had encouraged education for the purpose of forming the ideal wife, and Fray Luis de León (1537–91) continued that project in his treatise *La perfecta casada* (The perfect wife). Whether in or out of the convent, women faced standards for behavior which emphasized submission to male authority and celebrated the ideals for women which the visual arts reinforced in images of the penitent Magdalen and Mary as sorrowing mother or the Immaculate Conception. Enclosure extended throughout society, sealing women in their homes, nuns in convents, and even prostitutes in brothels.[18]

In such a restrictive atmosphere the woman who invites friends for a private ritual in her home, involuntarily denounces God and his saints as she is whipped by a mistress fearful of her slave's disobedience, or commits bigamy rather than endure ten more years of abandonment broadcasts seeds of disorder in a society carefully tended by the Holy Office.

Even in death a woman confident in her inner authority is a threat subject to eradication by censorship. If all the women whose portraits appear in this collection tested the jurisdiction of the church in some way, the women who as a group consistently challenged ecclesiastical authority in both Spain and the New World and who subverted gendered roles were the alumbradas with their claims that God himself was the source of their spiritual authority.[19] The authority of these "little women," as the church derisively called them, did not rest in theology dispensed by professors but in the Spirit that illumined individual understanding beyond the reach of reason. The role of the intellect was diminished further in the matter of verifying the truth of visions and inspired understandings; since no theology could be the inclusive standard against which the many individual experiences were registered, each visionary experience was ultimately self-referential and as such outside the purview of rational validation. When María de Cazalla and Francisca Hernández were visionary stars early in the sixteenth century, the religious climate encouraged spiritual individualism, and the women found ready support among the ranks of the clergy, especially Franciscan reformers who subordinated doctrine to mystical prayer and advocated personal relationship with God over reliance on priests, rituals, and sacraments. Certainly the women pushed on boundaries of gender roles in creating atypical modes of living as they traveled from town to town, mingling freely with lay and religious, married and unmarried, male and female, and publicly proclaiming matters that were the province of learned men. Women's bid for authority on the basis of visions and other extraordinary gifts proved to be the major point of contention with the Inquisition, although charges of sexual impropriety, and for later visionary women, delusion, fraud, and demonic possession, also figured in the denunciations and proceedings against them. In effect, all the women introduced in these essays who insisted on the right to an individual identity realized through visionary experience found themselves at odds with the criteria for female behavior sanctioned by the church.

The issue of authority which the visionary experience raised was further complicated by the fact that the woman's body was the means by which she received and communicated to other people her divinely inspired understandings. As the subject of an embodied experience the visionary and frequently ecstasized woman was caught in paradox: the effects of ecstasy on her body could validate her experience as genuine and at the same time be condemning of it. In the eyes of witnesses who were inclined to believe that the woman truly was infused with the Holy Spirit and for devotees already convinced of her spiritual authority, the sight of a woman's body suddenly and beyond her control turned rigid or strangely contorted and the sound of her voice in colloquy with heavenly personages were perceptible signs of God's presence, but the theologian or inquisitor bound to the dictates of reason would just as readily decry her flesh as rebellious against reason or condemn the woman as a cheat and fraud. How this paradox unraveled depended on the credibility of men who witnessed her ecstasies and their perception of the effects her embodied experiences had on her and other people. If humility, charity, and obedience flourished in both the visionary woman and those around her, the judgment might be favorable, but let her be seen as proud and arrogant, as was the case with Francisca de los Apóstoles and Marina de San Miguel, and misfortune was hers.

The centrality of the body was everywhere apparent in the alumbradas and beatas, whether in ecstatic and visionary experience; miraculous healing with the touch of the woman's hand or an item of her clothing; bilocation, whereby the body occupied two separate spaces at the same time; or spontaneous bleeding from areas of the body where Christ had been wounded in his passion. In a religious tradition that valued the intellect at the expense of the body, these experiences were suspect, especially when they occurred in women who by misogynist standards embodied sexuality. Even in the early sixteenth century the charismatic woman was the center of controversy that inevitably involved the subject of her sexuality and occasioned such charges of sexual misconduct as seducing male companions and cavorting with the devil. The erotic content of visions in which the woman caressed and kissed Jesus did little to assuage the suspicion of an Inquisition that after the Council of Trent more fiercely than ever frowned upon a woman's referring to her sexuality except in the confessional for the purpose of repentance.[20]

A feminist reappraisal of these women who mediated love for God and by God through the body interprets the embodied experience from a radically different perspective. Elsewhere I have analyzed the power of embodiment in the charismatic Sor María of Santo Domingo, and many of those observations apply as well to the women portrayed here: "Because the text that Sor María creates in ecstasy is the reality of God's love that she experienced in her body and also her love for God that she expressed through her body in ecstasies, penitence, devotion and good works, it is fitting that the medium of her art is her body."[21]

The importance of the body in a woman's spiritual life further suggests that in assessing how she wrote her life we may need to adjust our definitions of "text." Although the majority of women portrayed in this collection did not write in the sense of setting pen to paper, the records of their trials constitute a kind of text. Consider the woman who appears before the Inquisition for interrogation, presents witnesses on her behalf, refutes the prosecution's witnesses; consider, too, her words and actions under torture, at sentencing, during punishment. Obviously there are profound differences between this oral text-in-process and the writings that Sor María de Agreda and Ana Domenge constructed for the Inquisition. Their texts were the result of a conscious process that allowed time for reflection and even for consultation with authorities outside of themselves. Whereas the author of the written text could shape her account according to a controlling design, theme, or image that she selected or perhaps received through divine inspiration and develop its intrinsic elements to serve a determined purpose, the author of an oral text was at the mercy of external conditions and procedures. The policy of not informing a defendant of the specific charges against her, for example, made it impossible for the woman to prepare her story in such a way as to support her cause. She was left floating in space, as it were, with no aim other than to survive; since the conditions for survival were unknown to her or were changed from one moment to the next, she was helpless to form a text whose details advanced the cause of survival. Nor did she have time to reflect on the text-in-the-making and revise it with an eye to coherence and aptness relative to the specifics of her survival. When the woman altered her story, she did so not as an author in control of her text but as the author-protagonist made to react to oscillating external conditions in the fragile hope that somehow she knew what she was doing. The situation of Francisca de los Apóstoles illustrates the futility of the process: when the Inquisition examined her about why she believed her visions came from God and she had to answer on the spot and without the defense of theological argument, not surprisingly she finally faltered under the insistent questioning. Given time to consult with theologians, as did Teresa of Avila; to read theology, like Sor María de Agreda; and to think about her experiences, like Ana Domenge, she might have produced a text that met with approval from the Holy Office.

In considering the written text and issues of gender, it is clear that the visionary women who constructed an embodied, oral text during their encounter with the Inquisition were at a disadvantage relative to an Ana Domenge, who was able not simply to read and write but to employ the written word with sufficient deference to religious and theological issues as to win validation. How much more of an advantage did Sor María de Agreda enjoy with her lively intelligence, ability to read Latin, and enough command of theology to describe and identify her visions according to the Augustinian precepts that guided the Holy Office in discerning the nature and genuineness of visions. The persuasive power of theological justification which Sor María de Agreda mustered was enhanced by her remarkable ability to adjust the content and mode of her oral and written discourse to the occasion at hand. Hers was an acute intelligence that served her admirably under informal interrogation by officials of the Holy Office.

Although the oral text-in-process did not hold up as well as the written text under inquisitorial scrutiny, its value is without price for scholars and readers bent on discovering evidence of a woman's existence and how she wrote herself into history. Inquisition documents reveal a process whereby the woman created her story in the pain of the moment, each stroke of her voice and body executed in the darkness of not knowing if and how that stroke would fit into and carry forward her text-in-the-making, which was her text of survival—or extinction. The value of that text is not contingent on its adaptability to our criteria of literary criticism but rather on our willingness to listen in a new key.[22]

Ultimately, all the portraits of women subject to incarceration, interrogation, and sentencing raise the specter of misogyny. While it is obviously true that men as well as women suffered the pain of extensive interrogation, torture, public scorn, and death at the stake, there is in the experience of women an element suggestive of unspeakable terror and shame entirely absent or significantly mitigated in the men's ordeals. The arrested woman enters a world ordained and populated by men; she is subject to their laws, their punishments, their judgments. Everywhere she looks, she sees faces of men: inquisitor, attorney, jailer, notary, torturer, executioner. Everywhere she sees men looking at her. Imagine for a moment the woman—or a girl of twelve just coming to awareness of her sexuality—brought into the chamber where torture is administered: stripped nearly naked, she is surrounded by men—looking at her. Somehow the word *pornography* seems appropriate to a scene in which men masked in the attire of institutional respectability look at the female body bent and twisted, listen to and record the moans, the cries, the pleas for mercy as cords fastening the body to the rack are gradually tightened and pitchers of water slowly poured down the throat. No quick torture here but a tantalizing, prolonged application of pain. The male apologist may explain that the purpose of torture was to elicit confession for the sake of the woman's eternal soul, but to the reader who from the outside gazes at the female victim the word that strikes through to consciousness is *rape*. The woman—the girl—raped by the male gaze.

· · ·

Because the focus of this volume is on individual women who were subject to inquisitorial scrutiny rather than on explaining the history and inner workings of the Inquisition, this introduction does not cover procedures by which the tribunals operated. The policies and procedures of the Inquisition and the context in which they were carried out will become familiar to the reader during the course of the portraits. Terms that refer to the procedures of the Inquisition are defined in the essays as well as in the glossary. The selected bibliography is arranged according to major areas of interest; it is intended as an introduction to the subject matter.

PART I

The Inquisition
and Jewish
Converts

Mari Sánchez and Inés González

Conflict and Cooperation among
Crypto-Jews

GRETCHEN STARR-LEBEAU

Until the year 1485, Mari Sánchez was an unremarkable, longtime resident of Guadalupe in western Spain. Mari's husband, Diego Jiménez, provided a comfortable living for Mari and their children and hired a few servant girls to take care of the home. As one of the village's butchers, Diego served Guadalupe's permanent residents as well as the many pilgrims who visited the town and its shrine to the Virgin of Guadalupe. Since the discovery of the image of the Virgin in the thirteenth century, the "Dark Lady of the Villuercas mountains" had become one of Iberia's most powerful patrons, aiding numerous petitioners, especially Christian prisoners of Muslims. Thousands of visitors from around the Iberian Peninsula made the pilgrimage to the small, out-of-the-way site to visit the Virgin, to ask for her aid, or to thank her for miracles she had already granted. Shoemakers, tailors, and hostelers all flourished at the shrine site, together with other villagers like Diego, who helped provide food and drink for residents and visitors.

Diego Jiménez and Mari Sánchez lived along Seville Street, the main route in town by which pilgrims traveled to the monastery and the Virgin. In the fifteenth century, Seville Street bustled with pilgrims, friars, and shopkeepers selling shoes, clothes, and other goods to the tired and newly arrived. The din of pot makers filled the streets, as artisans noisily fashioned the copper containers for which Guadalupe was also well known. Some distinctions of wealth were evident in the buildings and among the villagers on the streets of Guadalupe, but most residents were artisans who shared social attitudes and economic status.

Mari and her husband enjoyed the comfortable but ordinary lifestyle of many artisans in Guadalupe, but the scribes, lawyers, and luxury merchants whom they numbered among their friends were the most privileged residents of the village. This difference in status does not seem to have troubled the couple, but it certainly provided them with an unusual perspective on relations between the monastery and the village, for almost all Guadalupans were united in their resentment of the monastery that both maintained the Virgin's shrine and governed the village itself. In the conflict between monastery and village the wealthy merchants played a central role, since the friars had decreed long ago that nobles were not permitted to live within the village. As a result, most residents were artisans or beggars, neither of whom had the wealth or influence to challenge the monastery's political, spiritual, and economic dominion over the village. Mari and Diego frequently witnessed bitter conflicts between the friars and merchants and artisans, as the villagers struggled to extend their autonomy from the friars.

As the fifteenth century drew to a close, however, Mari Sánchez's life changed. Her children grew to adulthood, and at least two daughters married and moved from Guadalupe to other villages in the region. Relations with one of the daughters, Inés González, grew strained, but it is possible that Inés's move away from Guadalupe helped quiet any conflict between them. Meanwhile, Mari's husband, Diego, fell ill, and for a year and a half, as he became increasingly incapacitated, Mari cared for him, sometimes preparing special dishes in an attempt to whet his appetite. Her efforts were in vain, however; after many years of marriage Mari was left a widow and was forced to quit her home on Seville Street for smaller quarters. By the beginning of 1485 Mari had quite recovered: she had even found a new lover, Albornóz. But Mari Sánchez was not destined to live out her years quietly. On Christmas Eve, 1484, a mule train of inquisitors and their functionaries arrived in Guadalupe, bringing with them the Holy Office of the Inquisition. Mari's life as she had known it was over.

Although previously Mari Sánchez's life had been typical of women in Guadalupe, in one facet it was strikingly unusual: Mari was widely believed to be practicing Judaism. Mari Sánchez was one of many Jewish converts and descendants of converts known collectively as *conversos,* or New Christians. Despite manifest differences among individual New Christians, conversos gained a collective identity separate from that of the Christian community in general.[1] The distinct practices of some New Christians, together with the attitudes of some Old Christians, generated a deepening and self-perpetuating climate of suspicion during the middle decades of the fifteenth century. Soon, some Old Christians demanded the establishment of an inquisition that would investigate the beliefs of New Christians and punish those people identified as heretics. By 1483, just two years before the inquisitors arrived in Guadalupe, clerics acting as inquisitors in Seville and Córdoba held the first modern Inquisition trials, in which hundreds of conversos were executed for secretly practicing Judaism.

A popular shrine site dedicated to the Virgin may seem like an unlikely host for a visit from the inquisitors, but the Holy Office in Guadalupe cited more than two hundred New Christians for lack of fidelity to their chosen faith during 1485. Guadalupe was one of the first cities on the Iberian Peninsula to witness the handiwork of the Inquisition, and the warm welcome afforded the inquisitors in Guadalupe can be traced in large measure to the support of Guadalupe's local officials—the friars. In frequent acts of resistance to monastic rule, Guadalupans had complained bitterly about the monastery's attempts to remove their traditional rights, and Guadalupe's conversos participated in those acts. Not all of Guadalupe's New Christians actively resisted the rule of the friars; in the years immediately preceding the Inquisition the mayor, bailiff, public defender, and some lay monastic scribes in Guadalupe were all New Christians. Other conversos were common among the shoemakers, tailors, and other artisans who served Guadalupe's pilgrims.

Most troublesome to the friars were a small group of conversos who dealt in luxury goods. These merchants were among Guadalupe's wealthiest and most politically ambitious citizens. Many of the luxury merchants whom Mari counted among her friends had loaned the friars money during the economically devastating civil war between Isabel the Catholic and Juana la Beltraneja (1474–79). Their economic influence in town was unquestionable, and that income, combined with the regional elites they included among their customers, gave these merchants a power in Guadalupe which far exceeded their numbers. The luxury merchants' most direct challenge to the authority of the friars—an attempt to form a monopolistic trading bloc—was rebuffed, but challenges to monastic authority, together with attempts to influence individual friars, continued into the 1480s. These machinations culminated in the attempts of one friar to gain control of the monastery through an alliance with wealthy converso merchants. When the time came to elect a new prior in 1483, the friar's merchant allies presented a large gift to the monastery; in return, the converso luxury merchants expected that their candidate would be elected. In fact, the friar lost the election, and it was the new prior, Fray Nuño de Arévalo, who petitioned for the presence of the inquisitors. Prior Nuño became the only secular official ever named to preside over an inquisitorial court in his own jurisdiction, and from that position he singled out political opponents as well as heretics.

Mari Sánchez was not an early target of the Inquisition, but she and her friends occupied the attention of the inquisitors for the better part of 1485. The converso luxury merchants who had challenged monastic authority were among the first to be tried by the inquisitors. These men were almost certainly not devout Christians, but it was the combination of political opposition and religious heresy which sealed their fates early. Later in 1485 the inquisitorial gaze shifted to lesser folk, to the New Christian tailors, scribes, and shoemakers who were Mari's old neighbors on Seville Street. Shared religious beliefs, economic attitudes, and resistance to absolute monastic lordship had reinforced social cohesion and encouraged solidarity among all Guadalupe's residents, Old and New Christian alike, but now that cohesion was threatened by the actions of the Holy Office.

Not all Guadalupans—or all conversos—were united by religion, economics, or politics, and Mari Sánchez had her share of detractors among Old and New Christians alike. Many of Mari's former servants, for example, did not remember her fondly. Servant girls in Guadalupe generally came from small villages in the region which lacked a Jewish presence, and for most servants Guadalupe provided their first introduction to New Christians and Jewish practices. Not surprisingly, they resented any attempt on the part of their employers to compel them to participate in Jewish rituals, work habits, or days of rest. Servants like Mari's witnessed Jewish practices in the home and resented those occasions when they were compelled to participate, even when participation meant not working on Saturday, the Jewish day of rest. Years later these same servants returned to explain to the inquisitors what they had witnessed in the homes of Mari and others, and Old Christian neighbors also reported their observations and suspicions to the Holy Office. Yet Mari's accusers were not exclusively Old Christians.

New Christians also spoke out against Mari Sánchez. Mari Jiménez, the wife of the converso mayor Andres González, roundly criticized Mari Sánchez for her Jewish practices. Mari Jiménez's comments may indicate a personal dislike of Mari, or she may have been forced to testify by the inquisitors while she herself was imprisoned, but it is also possible that her testimony hints at local political conflicts as well. The mayor was one of several New Christians who worked as lay functionaries of the monastery by appointment of the friars.[2] A small number of Guadalupe's conversos held a disproportionate number of these appointed positions in Guadalupe and were often put in the position of defending the monastery's opinion against others in the village, including the Old and New Christian artisans and merchants who had challenged the monastery's authority during the previous twenty years. Mari was a friend to several of these converso merchants, and it is possible that the testimony of the mayor's wife reflected the political differences that divided the two women.[3]

Most startling, however, was the testimony of Mari Sánchez's daughter Inés. Inés González had long ago married Fernando Montalban and moved to Valdecaballeros, a nearby village inhabited almost entirely by Old Christians; but when the inquisitors moved through Guadalupe's converso community, Inés returned, perhaps in response to a summons by the inquisitors. Through her mother, Mari, Inés had witnessed the crypto-Jewish practices of several women in Guadalupe, but she seems to have held Judaism in lower regard than did her mother or her mother's friends. Many people in Guadalupe remembered that Inés had complained openly that her father was a good Christian but her mother was not.[4] Differences had apparently existed between Mari and her daughter long before 1485, although it is difficult to know whether religious beliefs were at the root of that conflict or whether their divergent attitudes toward religion reflected a disagreement whose source lay elsewhere. In either case, the tensions between them may have contributed to Inés's move away from Guadalupe, and their relationship remained strained in 1485.

For Mari Sánchez and her friends, January began on a bleak note as the inquisitors initiated a month-long "period of grace" during which conversos submitted written confessions of any heretical or Jewish practices they had engaged in. Most of Guadalupe's conversos, including Mari Sánchez and her New Christian friends among the shoemakers, tailors, scribes, and merchants of the village, submitted statements of reconciliation. Adherence to the "law of Moses" among Christians, as the inquisitors referred to crypto-Jewish practices, was a profoundly troubling heretical act meriting strict penance, but anyone who fully and freely repented of heretical activity during the period of grace could not be tried for those acts by the inquisitors. As a result, almost all conversos confessed to crypto-Jewish activities they had engaged in, expressed their penitence, and begged for forgiveness.

Mari Sánchez was one of those New Christians who confessed during the period of grace called by the inquisitors, and her statement of reconciliation is preserved in her Inquisition file. The reconciliation records Mari's first statement to the inquisitors and hints not only at Mari's character and personality but also at the way she hoped to avoid the attention of the inquisitors. "I appear before Your Reverences," she dictated that January, "with very great shame and contrition and repentance for my sins which I committed and did against Our Master and Redeemer Jesus Christ and against our holy Catholic faith, which grieve me heavily and for which, by repenting them greatly, I desire contrition. I state my sins asking penitence of my lords."[5] From the beginning of her encounter with the Holy Office, Mari seems to have recognized a need both to acknowledge her wrongdoing and to obscure the extent of her participation in Jewish practices. Her opening, though largely formulaic, suggests the depth of Mari's fear and the possible extent of her wrongdoing by its unusually strong protestations of contrition and by the broad acknowledgment of crypto-Jewish acts in the reconciliation itself.

In her reconciliation, Mari Sánchez expounded upon her sins and pleaded for forgiveness. She admitted that she had observed the Jewish

Sabbath by dressing in clean clothing, lighting candles on Friday evenings, and avoiding all work, even spinning. She had mourned the death of her husband, Diego Jiménez, with traditional Jewish practices, such as eating on the floor for nine days. She had also kept kosher and observed Jewish fasts like Yom Kippur. At the same time, Mari had frequently neglected to observe Christian fast days and had used illness as an excuse to consume meat on Fridays. Furthermore, she added, "I say to you, Sirs, that all the other feasts and ceremonies of the law of Moses that I could observe and knew how to observe I did by my own will, thinking that by them I would be saved. I repent, and renounce this belief with great contrition asking that my Lord Jesus Christ pardon me and that you give me penitence, my Lords."[6]

Most unusual in Mari's reconciliation were the descriptions of her encounters with Jews. Old Christians were suspicious of conversos who maintained close ties with their former co-religionists, and New Christians hoped to avoid situations that would lead onlookers to doubt the converso's devotion to his or her professed faith. Christians considered eating with Jews or permitting Jews to enter one's home particularly suspect, since according to Jewish ritual observance Jews were forbidden to eat with gentiles. Mari made an attempt to hide some Jewish acts from the inquisitors, but the public nature of her contact with Jews may have compelled her to confess her acts before the Holy Office.

On at least one occasion, Mari spoke with a Jew named Mose Arrovas from Trujillo. The friars in Guadalupe forbade Jews to dwell at the shrine site; but Jewish merchants frequently visited the village, and Guadalupans were familiar with Jewish communities in nearby towns. Once, when Mari visited Trujillo, Mose called out to her and invited her to view his synagogue, which she did. Either on that day or on another occasion, Mose also invited Mari into his home, where she ate cheese tarts with him.[7] Her contact with Mose suggests more than a random encounter in a city some 40 kilometers from home. Rather, Mari's description, circumspect as it is, hints at a friendship with Mose Arrovas which would have been unwise and suspect at best and heretical at worst. Indeed, Mari recounted that Mose called out to her by name, which would indicate that he knew her before these encounters.

Mari Sánchez's confession of her encounter with Mose also reveals the way in which Mari obscured information from the inquisitors even as she confessed to perceived wrongdoings. In her prepared reconciliation, Mari described her visit to the synagogue as simply as possible, portraying herself as a passive participant. "A Jew of Trujillo who was named Mose Arrovas, once when I went to Trujillo and was walking down the street, he called out to me, 'Come here, wife of Diego Jiménez, you will see the synagogue that we have here just as I have seen your church there.' And I entered it with him. For this, Lords, I ask penitence."[8] Upon further questioning by the inquisitors, Mari revealed that she had not been alone in Trujillo. A later writer added in smaller script, "And the wife of Lope García and other Old Christian women entered with me."[9] Mari was careful to note the presence of Old Christian women in the group, people who presumably entered the synagogue out of curiosity rather than heretical intent. Yet Mari's evasive answer about "other . . . women" suggests a desire to conceal the identity of the other women rather than to reveal it. If Mari had visited the synagogue with a group of exclusively Old Christian women, her reputation might have been protected to some degree; she could have engaged in little Jewish activity under the watchful eye of Old Christian companions. Her initial reluctance to mention her friends may have been an attempt to protect converso women who were present with her in Trujillo. Long before Mari's confession, rumors had swirled through Guadalupe that some New Christian women donated oil to the Trujillo synagogue, and this event would only have furthered that suspicion.

The apparent exchange that occurred between Mari Sánchez and her confessor and inquisitorial scribe also provides an insight into the extent and limitations of inquisitorial methods of gaining information. The scribal addition, which named one specific woman who had visited the synagogue with Mari, was the first instance in which Mari was compelled to provide additional information to the inquisitors—notably, the name of another woman involved in suspicious and possibly heretical activity. Mari was not the only penitent who was asked to provide additional information in her statement of reconciliation; Alonso the teacher, for example, was required to explain his mother's role in his crypto-Jewish activities.[10] For Mari Sánchez, this small incident emerged as the first in a series of encounters with the inquisitors in which she struggled to defend herself and protect her companions, while the officials of the Inquisition attempted to learn as much from Mari as possible about the potentially heretical Jewish activities of her and her friends.

Mari Sánchez confessed in January and was publicly reconciled with some two hundred other New Christians on February 14, 1485. For eight months, Mari waited with trepidation as one by one her friends were called before the inquisitors. During the spring and summer of 1485, scores of New Christians were tried by the Holy Office, from the luxury merchants who had challenged the friars to former monastic officials and impoverished shoemakers. No converso, it seemed, was immune. Even the deceased were tried and their corpses exhumed and burned at the stake as family members watched. Most living New Christians were sentenced to death or exile, although some suffered perpetual imprisonment and others were absolved of all wrongdoing. The statements of reconciliation which Mari and her friends had so carefully prepared were soon turned against them, and any hopes of answering the inquisitors' questions while shielding themselves from more serious or specific charges were dashed. Ironically, the reconciliation formed the basis of the charge that a New Christian's penitence was "false and simulated" [fingida y simulada]. The ultimate use of the statement of reconciliation, in effect, was to detail a penitent's wrongdoing. As spring gave way to the heat of summer, the first of seven autos-da-fé was held in town to sentence the guilty and carry out punishments. For those not yet tried, days were filled with increasing dread as the scope of the investigations became apparent. By summer's end, the realization must have set in that no one might be spared.

For Mari Sánchez, summer brought the first death of a family member by the hands of the inquisitors. A son-in-law, Oro Blásquez, was burned at the stake on the last day of July. With the coming of fall, the inquisitors turned their attention to the deceased, and Mari's family again was not immune. Although they were not sentenced until November 21, the posthumous trials of Mari's husband, Diego; her daughter Inés, wife of Oro Blásquez; and her aunt Elvira González the Frenchwoman had apparently begun long before.[11] As the trial began against her deceased husband, Mari must have known that it would not be long before she, too, was called before the inquisitors.

Mari's long wait ended on September 7, in the midst of the feast celebrating the Virgin of Guadalupe, when the Inquisition's prosecution lawyer, Diego Fernández de Zamora, accused Mari before the inquisitors. Despite its present-day reputation, the Spanish Inquisition operated in much the same way that secular courts in Europe operated at that time, as is apparent from the outset of Mari's trial. The inquisitors were concerned with seeing true heretics punished, but they recognized that it would be difficult to identify correctly who was a heretic and who was not. Highly ordered and bureaucratic legal proceedings, based on canon law and ultimately Roman law, assured the Holy Office and the Crown that the truth would be revealed. As a result, the inquisitors demanded that the accused participate in all the legal forms of the Inquisition. The defendants were assigned a lawyer and solicitor (*letrado y procurador*), who argued the case before the specific inquisitor assigned to oversee it. A prosecution lawyer (*promotor fiscal*) was associated with the court and argued the case against the defendant.

The substance of the prosecution's charges must have given Mari pause. Diego Fernández claimed that Mari had taken other measures to maintain a kosher kitchen besides those specified in her reconciliation, including beheading animals according to Jewish law, avoiding wild game such as hare, and preparing a traditional Jewish Sabbath dish known as *adafinas*.[12] In addition, the prosecution charged that Mari had observed the Jewish Sabbath in ways that she had not confessed previously. Fernández stated that Mari cooked on Fridays for the Sabbath and observed the Jewish Sabbath "as wholly and completely as Christians do the holy day of Sunday" [muy entera y complidamente según que los cristianos el día santo del domingo]. Furthermore, Fernández said, Mari Sánchez worked on Sundays and made others work on Sundays as well. Mari also allegedly engaged in other, specifically Jewish practices. She received Jews in her home, honored them, and ate with them; she sent oil to the synagogue in Trujillo; she listened to her husband read from a Jewish book, raising her eyes and hands in prayer when the name of Adonay was mentioned; finally, Mari washed the oil and chrism off the head of her son after his baptism. Diego Fernández also stated that Mari had forced her daughters to maintain Jewish practices as well. Ominously, Fernández closed his statement by adding that Mari was "an apostate in

[28]

other means and cases that [he intended] to specify during the course of this trial" [apóstata en otra manera y casos que protesto especificar en el progreso de este proceso]. The latter statement was a formulaic means of hinting at damning evidence that prosecution witnesses would offer but which was not sufficiently substantiated to be presented as a formal charge.

For Mari Sánchez, as for many others tried by the Holy Office, the accusation marked the beginning of a descent into a complicated mixture of divination, calculated revelation, and concealment. The prosecution lawyer spoke to his witnesses and prepared his case before making the formal accusation. To whom had prosecutor Diego Fernández spoken? How had he learned about the charges he made? Who might have had reason to condemn Mari before the inquisitors, whether justly or unjustly? The prosecution mentioned that Mari had forced her daughters to engage in Jewish practices as well. Did this mean that one of her own children had spoken out against her? With the help of Juan de Tejeda, a local monastic functionary who acted as solicitor, and Doctor de Villaescusa, a lawyer brought to Guadalupe by the inquisitors to provide legal counsel for the defense, Mari also began to consider how she might respond to the charges. Could the accusations be refuted? Were there any new charges that Mari might admit to, or should she boldly deny them all? In her reconciliation, Mari had closed with the petition that she be forgiven for any misdeeds she might have forgotten to include. Perhaps some of these charges could plausibly be confessed and forgiven with an explanation that she had "forgotten" to confess them previously?

Mari's legal counsel was available to provide some advice for the defendant, and both promotor Juan de Tejeda and letrado Doctor de Villaescusa apparently made an attempt to perform their functions responsibly. Inquisition records from Guadalupe not infrequently reported prison meetings between Doctor de Villaescusa and his clients, in which the letrado explained the current phase of the trial and asked how the defendant wished to proceed. Whatever their intentions, however, there were limits to what Mari might learn from Villaescusa and Tejeda. Both men were officials of the Holy Office, and Villaescusa had even come with the inquisitors from their headquarters in Ciudad Real. Villaescusa and Tejeda provided legal counsel, but they could not offer personal or private suggestions on how best to meet the accusations of the prosecution. Some of Mari's most pressing questions—which accusations to admit and which to deny—were shared only with fellow prisoners at the crowded prison on Bailiff's Street.

Like most conversos, Mari chose to deny all the accusations presented by the prosecution lawyer. After Diego Fernández, lawyer for the prosecution, had presented his statement, the judges gave the defense six days to receive a transcript of the accusation and prepare a reply. Often the defense and prosecution were quite lax in observing the deadlines set by the inquisitors, perhaps because of the volume of cases heard by the Holy Office in Guadalupe, but Tejeda wasted little time in preparing a response for Mari Sánchez. On September 16, just nine days after Diego Fernández had made his accusation, Juan de Tejeda issued a formal reply to the judge assigned to the case. Mari Sánchez was innocent of the additional charges made against her, he argued. She ate hare when she had it available, he claimed, and she did not avoid it for reasons of Mosaic law. Mari did not observe the Jewish Sabbath, except in the ways that she had confessed previously, and she observed the Christian day of rest. If she ate meat on Fridays, it was due to illness and not disobedience to the church. Nor, claimed Tejeda, had Mari attempted to wash away the baptismal oil and chrism from her children's heads. Tejeda vehemently denied that Mari had listened to Jewish prayers or had shown reverence when the word "Adonay" was spoken. Mari's husband, Diego Jiménez, had read from a psalter, Tejeda claimed, which was entered into evidence and presented to the inquisitor.

Some of the most damning charges stemmed from Mari's alleged contact with Jews, particularly since she herself had already confessed to some such contact. Since Mari had participated in the trial of her deceased husband, she may have already gained some experience before the inquisitors; whatever the reason, however, Mari was prepared with a response to the charge. Through her lawyer, Mari Sánchez told the inquisitors that "if some Jews came to her home, it was because they were estate administrators . . . and toll collectors for the monastery, and the friars ordered the Jews to stay with her husband Diego Jiménez, as was proved by the sayings and depositions of the witnesses presented in the trial of the aforementioned Diego Jiménez."[13] Mari also insisted that she did not make *adafinas,* noting that "if in her house some [*adafinas*] had been prepared, which she denie[d] that they were, they were made by the aforementioned Jews at their own fire and apart [from the rest]."[14] As the first phase of her trial drew to a close, Mari presented herself as an innocent woman, free from any additional charges leveled by the prosecution lawyer. Mari had freely confessed her wrongs before the court, she claimed, and was not responsible for any of the claims made by Diego Fernández in his opening statement.

Four days later, on September 20, Mari Sánchez and solicitor Juan de Tejeda followed this statement with the presentation of their witnesses before the court. Tejeda brought together seven men and women to speak in Mari's defense, including several business associates and assistants of Mari's late husband, Diego, the butcher, and others who had lived in the home as servants. All had agreed to speak in Mari's defense, but their testimony offered only lukewarm support of Tejeda's claims. Several witnesses had lived with Mari as many as ten years before and claimed to know little about her current practices or beliefs. In only a few cases did witnesses elaborate on evidence of Mari's innocence beyond a simple yes or no. Indeed, witnesses often could not even confirm the version of events depicted in Tejeda's questions, offering little endorsement of the defendant. In all, the brevity of their remarks suggested their unwillingness or inability to defend Mari before the Holy Office.

Although the statements for the defense were not promising, the mere fact that seven defense witnesses came forward provided some support for Mari Sánchez's case, especially since all seven seem to have been Old Christians. Old and New Christians are indistinguishable in written records, but since none of Mari's witnesses or their families were tried by the inquisitors, and since many worked in professions that were largely composed of Old Christians, it seems likely that the witnesses were Old Christians. It also seems reasonable to suppose that Mari and her lawyers would select as witnesses only those people whose devotion to Christianity was unquestioned. The statements of witnesses such as these served an important role in Mari's defense, despite their sometimes weak support of Mari's strong protestations of innocence.

Mari's bold stand was soon challenged, however, by the witnesses for the prosecution. Unlike modern trials, witness and accuser did not meet in a courtroom; instead, witnesses' testimonies were taken privately, and a written copy was provided later for the defense lawyer and solicitor. In addition, prosecution witnesses remained anonymous throughout the trial, and their names were not included in the transcripts provided to the defense. The Crown and the inquisitors believed that this procedure would protect prosecution witnesses from vengeful actions on the part of the defense, but the tactic also limited the defense attorney's ability to counter the statements of prosecution witnesses. In some cases, witnesses speaking for the defense might also testify before the prosecution, a situation that could only help Diego Fernández and the prosecution. Defense witnesses were permitted to provide the Holy Office with a list of enemies—names of people who might testify against the accused solely for personal vengeance—and the testimony of those found on the list was stricken by the court. Few in Guadalupe took advantage of this slim opportunity, but many defendants must have wondered at the identity of those who testified against them.

On September 28, almost two weeks after Juan de Tejeda's witnesses testified before the Holy Office, prosecution lawyer Diego Fernández presented the testimony of his own witnesses. Fully twenty people testified against Mari Sánchez, including former servants and Old and New Christian neighbors. Not surprisingly, many of Mari's longtime detractors took advantage of the trial to speak out against her. Some, like Mari's servants, testified in particular to Jewish practices in the home, especially those occasions on which they claimed that they were required to cease work on Saturdays or to work on Sundays. The motivations of other witnesses may have been more complex. Possible political conflicts among New Christians, such as between Mari Sánchez and Mari Jiménez, the wife of Andres González, the mayor, may have encouraged Mari Jiménez to testify. Pressure from the inquisitors also led many a converso to testify against his or her fellow New Christian. Some converso witnesses, such as Mari Jiménez and Alonso Ruiz, son of Alonso Ruiz the merchant, may have been forced to testify against others during their own inquisitorial trials.[15] Even Mari Sánchez had identified the wife of Lope García in her reconciliation before the inquisitors.

By far the most serious and most damning testimony came from Inés González, Mari's own daughter. Mari had at least one son living, but only

Inés testified against Mari.[16] Tensions that had long smoldered between mother and daughter were rekindled in 1485 with serious consequences for both. Long before the Holy Office arrived to punish crypto-Jews, Inés had complained of her mother's lack of devotion to Christianity, but the arrival of the inquisitors allowed Inés to present her claims before a sympathetic and powerful audience. Indeed, Inés spent six weeks in 1485 testifying against several converso women she had known as a child and young woman. One by one, she identified what she claimed were the particular Jewish practices and attitudes of her mother's friends, neighbors, and fellow crypto-Jews. Fewer than 40 of the 220-odd Guadalupe trial records remain today, but of those 40 trials Inés appeared as a prosecution witness in 10. Inés claimed to be a devout Christian, and the court believed her. Some native Guadalupans who had moved away from the area were tried by the Holy Office, but only Inés escaped serious punishment, lending support to her claim. Inés may have testified against these women as a form of retribution against her mother, but it is also possible that her testimony was the response of a devoutly Christian converso to a childhood surrounded by people who had secretly observed Judaism. Whatever her motivations, Inés's claims against her mother were not unique. Several residents of Guadalupe remembered with approbation Inés's opinion: "Certainly my father is a good Christian, and I for one take him that way; but my mother Mari is not."[17]

Modern readers should be cautious not to take Inés completely at her word. Even though many elements of Inés's testimony—that her mother observed several Jewish practices following her baptism into Christianity, that she provided oil for the synagogue in Trujillo, and that she washed the baptismal chrism from her son Diego—were verified by other witnesses and, to a degree, by Mari herself, not all the specifics of Inés's testimony should be assumed to be accurate. True to the dictates of secular and canon law, Inés's uncorroborated charges did not appear in the accusation of the prosecution lawyer, since that testimony was insufficient to prove guilt. Whatever the veracity of Inés's account, however, the specifics of her testimony provide insights into both her relationship with Mari and the kinds of practices which could be accepted or even confirmed by the inquisitors. Ultimately, Inés's claims had what was presumably the desired effect—additional suspicion was cast on Mari Sánchez, and increased pressure was placed on Mari to corroborate the accusations of her daughter.

When Inés first spoke to Diego Fernández, lawyer for the prosecution, her comments were brief, as was typical of prosecution witnesses; but the substance of her testimony was highly unusual. In addition to brief comments that Mari kept the Jewish Sabbath and observed Jewish fasts, Inés added that fifteen years before, her father "brought home a drawing of the crucifixion of Our Lord drawn on a piece of paper. Then Mari Sánchez took it and threw it in a latrine saying that she did not have need of that in her house."[18] The shocking nature of this statement seems to have caught the attention of Fernández, for her testimony then continued in a new paragraph with the words "She said moreover" [Otrosí dijo].

Inés's statement before the inquisitors was subtle, neither exculpating her mother nor flatly condemning her. Inés began by defending her mother in part, stating that Mari "was willing to ask for pardon before she asked it" [estaba en voluntad de pedir penitencia antes que la pidiese], that is, that Mari's desire for penitence was unfeigned. This claim was important because the inquisitors were especially interested in determining the sincerity of the accused's reconciliation and confession. From this assertion of her mother's genuine repentance, however, Inés continued by noting that her mother was willing to confess "except for three things [that were] more serious and central, which [Inés] had come to know, which were how Mari had washed the chrism off of Diego her son, and how Mari had given oil for the synagogue in Trujillo, and how her deceased father, Mari's husband, had bought a crucifix . . . which Mari had thrown in their latrine."[19] Inés was careful to specify where the house and the latrine were, who had been the neighbors at the time, and who lived in the home in 1485. In addition, Mari's daughter carefully detailed each of the other "more serious" charges that she leveled against her mother, describing minute physical details and explaining how she had determined the truth of her statements. In closing, Inés noted that Mari had not wished to confess to these acts because they could not be proven.[20]

Notably, Inés took as much care to explain her motivations for testifying against her own mother as she did to corroborate the accusations themselves. Inés probably hoped to allay any suspicion that her testimony was motivated by a family conflict. Furthermore, if Inés's testimony was based in genuine religious concern, it would bolster her own status as a devoutly Christian converso and further distinguish Inés from her crypto-Jewish family. Despite Inés's willingness to testify she, too, may have feared the attention of the inquisitors. Finally, it is also possible that Inés was a devout Christian who was unwilling to condemn her mother wholeheartedly but fervently wished to see Mari confess her sins. The following conversation, which Inés reported to the inquisitors, suggests that she may have been influenced by several of these multiple and even conflicting motives. The only witness to this conversation was Inés herself, and the retelling almost certainly reflects her personal interests as much as it does any genuine concern that Mari repent and confess. The rich details Inés included suggest at the least that she drew on Mari's attitudes and experiences, even if the specifics were invented; but whether the account is true or false, the conversation provides a believable image of life for Mari in the inquisitorial prison. Because the testimony was recorded by a scribe, the event is retold in the third person.

> And at that time Doctor de Villaescusa, Mari's lawyer, went to be with Inés's mother and to show her the witnesses who had made a statement against her, after which she confessed the truth about the oil and about the chrism, but not about the crucifix. And then Mari entered the room in the prison where this witness [Inés] was, looking very yellow and half-dead, and she said to this witness, "Now I shall die for what I have confessed," and Inés said to her, "Did you tell him about the crucifix?" And the mother responded, "Daughter, nobody knows about that but you; so tell me if you told them about it," which Inés took to understand that for no other reason would Mari confess it, and then Inés responded that she had told them so that Mari would confess it. And then her mother, because she knew that this witness had said it, attempted to speak with the bailiff, and with Albornóz her lover, so that she could confess it.[21]

Whatever Inés and her mother may have spoken about during Inés's visits to the prison, it is clear that imprisonment and the trial were beginning to take their toll on Mari Sánchez. By the end of September Mari had confessed to increasingly grave deviations from Christian practice; she knew that her own daughter had testified against her; and Inés may have correctly reported that her mother feared for her life. As September drew to a close and Tejeda and Diego Fernández prepared closing statements for the defense and prosecution, Mari's prospects looked grim. With her daughter's damning testimony, the tide had turned against Mari, and her ability to defend herself became increasingly limited.

By October 7, when Juan de Tejeda presented his final statement before the three inquisitors, his defense of Mari had profoundly changed. Gone were Mari's assurances to the inquisitors that she had done nothing wrong apart from what she had confessed in January. Instead, Tejeda reported, his client acknowledged that everything that the prosecution witnesses had said was true, adding that "she did it and committed it in offense of Our Lord, as a bad Christian, and as a fine Jew" [ella lo hizo y cometió en ofensa de Nuestro Señor como mala cristiana y como fina judía]. Furthermore, Tejeda reported that Mari had responded to additional questions about her activities, revealing the names of all the conversos who participated with her in bringing oil to the synagogue of Trujillo and in washing the oil and chrism from her children. In particular, Mari told the inquisitors that her deceased aunt Elvira, who was soon to be sentenced by the Holy Office, had aided in washing away young Diego's baptism. Mari also provided the inquisitors with the names of the Jews with whom she had eaten. She revealed that the Jews who had stayed with her in Guadalupe, Mose Arrovas and Mose Follequinos, had kept a Jewish book among the cushions. Both men had been in the house when Mari's husband had brought home the drawing of the crucifix, and she recalled that they said to her, "What is this devil doing here? Throw it in the latrine" [¿Qué hace este diablo aquí? Echadlo en la necearia]. Mari also admitted, through her lawyer, that her daughter Inés had testified correctly in every detail, even though Mari had not confessed it to any official of the Inquisition before the deadline set by the court. Her only remaining defense was the remorse she felt. Tejeda reported to the inquisitors: "For all that my client has given her breast many great beatings in repentance for having committed such great errors and offenses against Our Lord, of whom she demanded and demands mercy and pardon, [she asks] penitence of Your Reverences."[22]

Diego Fernández, lawyer for the prosecution, sternly refuted Tejeda's pleas and advocated strict punishment for Mari Sánchez. He questioned the sincerity of her repentance because she had not confessed until she heard the statements made by the prosecution witnesses. Fernández reminded the court that confessions made after the publication of witnesses were not allowed, since the accused could confess merely to avoid punishment. The prosecutor argued that instead of lenience Mari should face the stiffest penalty for her misdeeds—execution at the auto-da-fé.

October found Mari Sánchez a changed woman. The indirect but inevitable confrontation with her daughter, the array of witnesses willing to testify against her, the depressing conditions of the prison, where those awaiting trial and those awaiting execution conversed and attempted to console one another—all left Mari increasingly isolated and fearful. Even family could no longer be trusted. Meanwhile, the lawyer for the prosecution asked Mari to testify against several women she knew, both living and deceased. As a prisoner, Mari had little choice but to obey, especially since her own repentance might be judged by her willingness to identify the misdeeds of others. During the month of October Mari testified against at least seven fellow New Christians, and possibly more.[23] In almost every case, Mari Sánchez stated that the accused observed the Jewish Sabbath, lit oil lamps on Friday evenings, and participated in Jewish fasts.

Even as she was testifying for the prosecution, however, Mari also attempted to aid friends who were still under investigation. The close quarters of the inquisitorial prison provided an opportunity for those who were accused to compare experiences and attempt to formulate a more effective defense. Most such conversations were never recorded on paper, but one encounter did attract the attention of the Holy Office. Catalina Sánchez, no relation of Mari Sánchez, had just met with her chief lawyer, Doctor de Villaescusa. Doctor Villaescusa apprised Catalina of the testimony offered against her as it appeared in the opening statement, and he asked her if she wished to confess to any additional Jewish activities.

Particularly damning was an accusation that Catalina and her family had occasionally dressed their youngest son in large clothes and called him Jacobito. The accusation seems nonsensical to a modern observer, yet to Old and New Christians in Guadalupe such an activity indicated Jewish intent. Jacobito, or "little Jacob," was considered a Jewish name and seemed alien to Old Christians. Similarly, the game, by reason of its unfamiliarity to Old Christians, was assumed to be Jewish in origin. For the inquisitors, and especially for Old Christians generally, cultural differences, political differences, and religious differences were inextricably linked. Even a game with no immediately apparent religious significance could take on suspicious and heretical significations in the context of the Inquisition.[24]

When Catalina Sánchez heard the accusation, she laughed at her lawyer and responded disdainfully that she had nothing she wished to confess. Presently, she finished her interview with Doctor Villaescusa and returned to her shared cell, but once there her confidence vanished, and she asked Mari Sánchez what she ought to do. Only a family member or intimate servant could reveal such information, Catalina reasoned. Mari, the memory of her own daughter's testimony certainly still fresh in her mind, urged Catalina to confess all and plead for mercy. Mari's own experience served as an example that Catalina would wish to avoid. Immediately, Catalina called out demanding to see her lawyer again, and when he returned, Catalina followed Mari's advice and confessed all. Catalina was not completely forgiven; the sudden, striking shift in her attitude caught the attention of the bailiff, who mentioned the incident to the prosecution lawyer, Diego Fernández. Both the bailiff and Mari Sánchez were called to testify against Catalina in regard to this incident, but Catalina's confession saved her life. Her testimony was accepted as sincere, and she was not executed but sentenced to exile, a sentence that was at best poorly enforced.[25]

Mari Sánchez did not prove so lucky. Her closing statement might have indicated a penitent heart and willing submission to the inquisitors, but Mari still refused to cooperate fully with the Holy Office. In Juan de Tejeda's final statement Mari named several people who had participated with her in crypto-Jewish activities, and she had testified for the prosecution, particularly in cases tried posthumously; but Mari's seeming willingness to cooperate with the inquisitors masked her continued resistance to inquisitorial demands that she identify the crypto-Jews whom she knew in town. The inquisitors had announced that they would pronounce a sentence on October 14, yet October passed without the Holy Office making a judgment. The inquisitors frequently delayed in their decisions, and the wait may have signified nothing. Yet it is clear that the inquisitors had not forgotten Mari Sánchez. By November 3, the inquisitors decided to impel Mari to identify local crypto-Jews; the judges ordered that the bailiff and his assistants take Mari from the prison "to the house where they were accustomed to administer torture" [la llevase a la casa donde se acostumbran dar los tormentos].[26]

In the early modern period, torture emerged as a common feature in courts of law created by newly emergent states. Confined to legal spheres, torture remained a highly regulated tool of the judge and prosecution, and the Inquisition in Spain exercised greater restraint in the use of judicial torture than did many secular European courts of the period. Strict limits existed for inquisitors on when and how torture could be administered, and although these regulations might be stretched at times, they were rarely ignored. For the inquisitors, the purpose of torture was to learn the truth about the accused's intentions and religious beliefs, yet the Holy Office realized that torture might also drive the accused to lie. For this reason the inquisitors generally observed conventions that limited the extent of judicial torture and helped inquisitors to presume they had learned the truth.

In Guadalupe and elsewhere, the inquisitors followed an elaborate procedure designed to convince the accused to speak before he or she was tortured. In this way the inquisitors hoped to ensure that the accused spoke honestly. Like other New Christians tortured in Guadalupe, Mari Sánchez was first brought to the door of the torture chamber and asked formally to tell all she knew. If she chose to speak, the torture session would end. Instead, Mari refused and was brought inside, where she was tied to the *escalera*, the only torture instrument used in Guadalupe. Once tied to the *escalera*, the accused could be tilted with her head toward the ground and her feet in the air, while the torturer poured water into her mouth to simulate drowning. The bailiff, Anton de Castillo, "took and bound [Mari] in the said house, and admonished her to say fully everything that she knew; then, without any other torment or any injury or anything received by her, she spoke."[27]

Almost a year after her family and friends were first called before the

Holy Office, Mari finally lost her will to resist. She responded to all the questions of the inquisitors, speaking at length about the alleged misdeeds of her family and friends in Guadalupe. Mari accused her deceased husband, Diego, of occasionally observing the Jewish Sabbath with her, and she described the crypto-Jewish practices of her husband, children, mother, and aunts, including aunt Elvira González, who was sentenced that November. Even her son, "little Diego" [Dieguito], was not immune. Mari had washed off Diego's oil and chrism after his baptism, with the help of Elvira and other relatives; now she revealed that her son, a nineteen-year-old student at the university in Salamanca, fasted in the Jewish fashion and observed Yom Kippur. Mari continued by naming several New Christian residents of Guadalupe and their Jewish practices. Even at this lowest moment, however, Mari attempted to protect her fellow conversos as much as possible; most of those she testified against were either deceased, living outside the village, or already condemned by the inquisitors. Strikingly, two women stood out by virtue of their absence from her testimony: Mari herself, who had already confessed to her Jewish acts and who held out little hope of survival; and her daughter Inés, whose testimony had condemned Mari.

After her confession in the torture room, the inquisitors left Mari in peace until her guilty verdict was read at the auto-da-fé on November 20. It is unclear when Mari first learned the sentence of the Holy Office. Certainly she knew of her impending execution before the public sentencing of the guilty, although nothing could have prepared her for that grim November day. On that day, she and the other prisoners walked in a procession from the prison on Bailiff's Street down to the plaza for sentencing. The prior, in his role as chief inquisitor, stood at the doors of the monastery and looked downhill at the crowds filling the plaza. In the cemetery to his left stood the town crier, where from the highest point in the plaza he read out the sentences of the guilty. One by one the condemned, Mari Sánchez among them, filed before the crowds until the prior, now acting as lord of the village, sentenced the guilty to be burned at the stake. There is no record that her family witnessed her death. Her husband, Diego, aunt Elvira, and daughter Inés, wife of Oro Blásquez, were all deceased; they would be sentenced posthumously and their corpses burned the following day. Mari's son-in-law, Oro Blásquez, had already been executed in a previous auto-da-fé, and her son Diego was safely away in Salamanca. Inés González, Mari's surviving daughter, returned to Valdecaballeros without being charged, and it is unknown whether she remained in Guadalupe long enough to see her mother's execution.

. . .

The joint histories of Mari Sánchez and Inés González demonstrate the unity and division that existed among New Christians and the changing relationship between New and Old Christians. Not all New Christians defended Christianity with the zeal of Inés González, nor did all conversos practice Judaism with the diligence of Mari Sánchez. Religious, personal, political, and social differences divided conversos as much as they helped distinguish New from Old Christians. At the same time, the Inquisition was itself an institution that could be manipulated for widely differing personal ends. Its presence in Guadalupe was due in part to the political and religious agenda of the monastery's new prior, while Inés employed the Inquisition for her own personal or religious ends; even Mari managed to influence the actions of the inquisitors to some extent. Yet the presence of the Holy Office in Guadalupe foreshadowed a changing attitude toward conversos which would soon envelop the peninsula. Mari, like many conversos, had lived in Guadalupe for decades, and her own reconciliation suggests that she participated in at least some Jewish rituals; but none of the Old Christians who spoke out against her testified at length. Not until tensions between the monastery and Mari's converso merchant friends reached the boiling point did her crypto-Jewish behavior become unacceptable to the village and the friars. Later generations proved to be less indulgent. By 1500 Guadalupe's large New Christian community of shoemakers, merchants, tailors, and other artisans was gone, exiled to other cities in Spain, leaving clearer than ever the distinctions between New and Old Christians.

CHAPTER TWO

Inés of Herrera del Duque

The Prophetess of Extremadura

HAIM BEINART

In the fifteenth century Extremadura in western Castile harbored many Jewish and *converso* communities.[1] The expulsion of the Jews from Spain did not completely extirpate Jewish life; in fact, crypto-Jewish life went on in various converso centers, even without the guidance of Jewish spiritual leaders and advisers. When the Inquisition spread its net all over Spain, it became necessary to found a special court that would act in Extremadura as early as the eighties, in Puebla de Alcocer and in Belalcázar.[2] The institution of the Inquisition was a serious blow to the conversos, but unexpectedly they found comfort and hope in a young girl who, as if rising from the ashes, appeared with the promise of redemption. In March 1500, she proclaimed, the Messiah would come and redeem the conversos, carrying them, as in Exodus, to the Promised Land.[3] Inés was the name of this child, and her prophecy was to spread far beyond the borders of Extremadura to solace the hearts of conversos to the west in the central plains of La Mancha and as far south as the city of Córdoba. It is my intention to examine the girl's prophecies, especially those she expressed in her hometown, and the way in which her influence grew to become a movement.

Inés, the daughter of Juan Esteban, a shoemaker and leather tanner, was born around 1488 in Herrera del Duque. Her mother, whose name is unknown, died while Inés was still a very young child, and her father then married his second wife, Beatriz Ramírez.[4] Inés's visions and proph-

ecies were intimately connected with her mother's death: the girl claimed
that it was her deceased mother who accompanied her in her ascent to
heaven and travels through the celestial realms. It all started in autumn of
1499, and the girl's arrest by the Inquisition took place not earlier than
April 1500.[5] Juan de Segovia, one of her devoted followers, confessed in
the court of the Inquisition that in September 1499, while he was on his
way from Toledo to Herrera to buy tanned leather, he met another shoemaker,[6] Lope Donoso by name, who told him of Inés's ascent to heaven.[7]
Subsequently, Inés was duly arrested by the Inquisition, brought to Toledo, and questioned by the court during the period of May to July 1500.

The trial documents of Juan de Segovia, inhabitant of Toledo,[8] as well
as others are the source of rich information about the child prophetess
and the strong effect she had on men, women, and children who believed
in the genuineness of her visions and endeavored to change their lives in
accord with her prophetic counsel. For example, a cloth weaver by the
name of Pero Fernández from the neighboring town of Chillón testified
at length about Inés.[9] According to Pero Fernández, Inés recounted how
she had seen her dead mother:

> In Herrera, on the twenty-first day of the month of May in the year
> 1500, before the Lord Inquisitors in the General Inquisition.
>
> Inés, the daughter of Juan Esteban, resident of the town of Herrera,
> a sworn witness, etc., said that in the year just past, three days after All
> Saints Day, this witness dreamed about her mother who is dead, and it
> seemed to her that she had seen her, visibly, and it seemed to her in the
> dream that she had said: Daughter, tell them that they did well for my
> soul and tell them to give alms and other things that were not placed
> here.

Another time Inés told Pero Fernández how a clarity had appeared to
her, one time advising her that Elias was to come by God's command to
preach to the conversos that they were to leave Spain for a land of bread
and fruit:

> Also he said that at a certain time near Christmas, the one just past,
> there came to her a clarity that she said had come to her before, and
> this witness asked what was this coming that came so many times, and
> she responded and said that it came to tell her that Elias was coming

in the year 1500, and that for this to happen they were to fast and give alms and act the best they could. And this witness asked: Who was this Elias and for what reason was he coming?[10] And she was told that he was to come by God's command to preach in the world and the conversos were to leave and they were to go to some lands. And this confessant asked: What was there in these lands? And she was told that there were people and the sustenance of bread and fruit and all the things that they needed. And then it disappeared. But first she was told to tell what had been told to her.

Pero Fernández was not alone in receiving this encouraging news; many conversos and neighbors in town listened to the child:

And after this this confessant spoke of this to Gonçalo Bichancho and many other conversos, residents of the same town. And it seemed to this witness they listened to what she said, and it seemed to this witness that they believed it, because they listened eagerly and willingly. And he said that this witness had asked the clarity in what way they were to do the said fasting and alms giving, and she was told that the fasting was to be done until night. Likewise the said clarity told her they should observe the Sabbath and wear clean clothing on the Sabbath and do it for the love of God and to attain that happiness that they hoped for and which was to come. And this the witness told the said Gonçalo Bichancho and whatever conversos went to see her in her house.

Pero Fernández's testimony sheds light on Inés's response to the clarity as she fasted and observed the Sabbath:

Also, he said that they said that at home this witness [Inés] fasted from then on each week for one or two days, or the most she could, on Mondays or Thursdays, not eating all day until night and the stars were out, and at night she ate fish, and observed the Sabbath from the said time until she was imprisoned, dressing herself [in clean clothes] and adorning herself willingly until now.

She was asked: With what intention and belief did she keep those fasts and observe the Sabbath? She said that it was to reach that good which had been told to her. And that she had been told to believe what had been told her when that clarity came.

[44]

And likewise this witness said all this, like the other, to the same Gonçalo Bichancho and all the other conversos from the town who asked her about it. And she said that one of the people to whom she had told the above and with whom she shared and communicated everything she has said about how they were to believe in the Law of Moses and give alms and how Elias was to come and take them to abundant lands, and everything else as she has told it, was Pero Fernándes of Chillón, the weaver, and he believed whatever this witness told him and whatever the witness could know and feel as God gave her to understand.

To this confession, additional information may be added from the confession of Juan de Segovia:[11]

. . . how her mother who was already dead came to her and took her hand and told her not to be afraid because it was God's will that she ascend to heaven to see the secrets and to see marvelous things. And in like manner another young man who had died a few days before took her other hand, and the Angel who was drawing them upward thus said that they were taking her up to heaven where she would see the souls who were suffering in purgatory. And in like manner in another place she would see other souls in glory seated on chairs of gold. And likewise she told me that there seemed to be another higher place above her head where there was much murmuring, and that she asked the Angel: What is that sounding above? And the angel said to her: Friend of God, those that make sounds up there are those who were burned on earth and now are in glory. And in like manner she saw three kinds of angels and other things that she told me but I don't remember.[12]

These testimonies of Juan de Segovia and Pero Fernández of Chillón give a fair idea of the prophecies of Inés and of her dreams, which reflected not only her own thoughts and afflictions but also the atmosphere prevailing among the conversos after the Expulsion.

The impression of these prophecies on the conversos must have been tremendous, because under some pretext or another many conversos made a pilgrimage to Herrera to find out the truth of the girl's prophecies and talk with the prophetess in person. Many of the visitors, who were shoemakers and leather tanners, went to Herrera under the pretext of buying leather,[13] but once there they would meet with the shoemaker Juan Esteban, himself a shoemaker and leather tanner, who then would invite them to his home to meet his daughter.[14] Rumor had it that the girl brought special tokens from heaven: "A corn ear, an olive and a letter."[15]

Inevitably, these goings-on caused a great commotion, and conversos began to fast and observe the Ten Commandments and the precepts of Moses' law. On the Sabbath they would put on their best attire and stop working in expectation of the miraculous advent of the Messiah. All these people believed that they would be taken soon to the Promised Land, wearing the very dress they had on.[16] For those conversos who would be taken to the Promised Land God would lower to earth the wonderful city he had created for them, where they would live in joyful abundance.[17] Elvira Núñez, the wife of Ruy Sánchez, elaborated the description of the city; she saw an affluent city with tables laid out and baked bread for the repast of the conversos who would be going to that city.[18] Small wonder that a poor population's dreams of abundance were of great importance. They finally believed that this majestic repast would be served on the advent of the Messiah.[19] We may find here an allusion to the whale (the "Leviathan") caught in those days on the shores of Portugal.[20]

The prophet Elias, who announces the advent of the Messiah, figures not only in Inés's mystical dreams but also in the visions of yet another prophetess, one Mari Gómez of Chillón, a village in the neighborhood of Herrera.[21] She also claimed to have ascended to heaven, where there were angels and the prophet Elias was preaching. Furthermore, the prophet was walking hand in hand with the granddaughter of the patriarch Jacob. There, too, she saw Inés, the daughter of Juan Esteban, and another woman from Córdoba.[22] This prophecy is arresting in its resemblance to the form of a Midrash:[23]

> And it is said there were people who ascended alive to the Garden of Eden. He said: Who are they? He said: Enoc and Serach the daughter of Asher and Bitya the daughter of Pharaoh and Hiram the King of Tyre, etc. . . . Serach, the daughter of Asher, was in the Garden of

Eden because she had announced to Jacob: "Joseph is alive." And Jacob
said to her: "The mouth who uttered this good news that Joseph was
alive shall never taste death."

In the case of the prophetess Inés, it is worth examining the company
with whom she was strolling in the Garden of Eden and whether the
members of the company had anything in common.

As is well known, the prophet Elijah ascended to heaven in a chariot
of fire,[24] as did Serach, the granddaughter of the patriarch Jacob (and all
the above named). What is most striking in the account of this vision is
the evidence it offers that knowledge of the Midrash was alive in such a
God-forsaken place in Extremadura after the expulsion of the Jews from
Spain. The account is a unique testimony to how deeply rooted was the
knowledge of Jewish tenets among those conversos as a result of their
Jewish education.

The conversos believed firmly in their immediate redemption, and
they imagined for themselves a future life of joy and abundance. The case
of Fernando de Belalcázar, a resident of Herrera, illustrates how firm was
this conviction in the hearts of the conversos. It seems that Fernando had
gone to Siruela with news for the conversos of that community that Inés
had been in the Promised Land and had returned from there with carna-
tions and a bunch of green rye.[25] In Spanish the word *alcazar* is the green
part of the rye used as food for the herds in Extremadura. Possibly the
connection of this particular grass to domestic animals contributed to the
popular image of Inés as a shepherdess who would not abandon her flock
of conversos.

The trial documents of yet another converso, Rodrigo Cordón of Siruela, furnish the date of the expected redemption. It was believed that
the redemption would occur in March 1500.[26] The angel who would announce the redemption was to appear on March 8,[27] and on the next day
they all would be on their way. This event would take place, for, as testimony revealed, "There was time and half a time and the time was already fulfilled" [E que avia tiempo e medio tiempo e que ya ha tiempo
cumplido]. That is, the date is of a millennium and half a millennium, in
the reckoning of the advent of the Messiah.[28] With the advent of the
Messiah a general pardon would be issued to "the people of the conver-

sos" [este pueblo de conversos] for having sinned while being forced to lead a Christian life; despite their sins, the Messiah would have great compassion for their suffering, and they, too, would go to the Promised Land.[29] The word "people" [pueblo] had a special significance for the conversos, linking them to the tradition of a chosen people.

Another statement made in the trial of Rodrigo Cordón shows that Inés told the conversos that God himself would lead them to the Promised Land and that all conversos would have to go whether they wanted to or not. On a Monday, a heavenly voice would announce the coming of the Messiah, and on the next Thursday they would all go to the Promised Land.[30] But they would have to cross a river, where they would have to leave behind all the jewels they had and pass on wearing white garments. Once again, the testimony suggests a thorough knowledge of the Bible among the conversos, in this case the story of the Exodus from Egypt, which thus provides biblical authority for the envisioned crossing of the river to the Promised Land.

According to Rodrigo Cordón, on the day before the Messiah comes and the conversos depart for the Promised Land, a disputation will take place between two friars in which one friar represents the Christian faith while the other, who is to emerge victorious, defends the Jewish faith. How intensely this wishful disputation mirrored the hopes of Jews in Spain! Rodrigo Cordón adds that "the conversos will leave behind all their businesses and the old Christians will quarrel and kill each other in the fight to possess them."[31]

An abundance of signs from heaven confirmed for the conversos the truth of their expectation. Rodrigo Cordón told the converso Diego García of Siruela[32] that a shining angel in his full splendor stood above a bed in the house of his neighbor without uttering a word.[33] For another converso in Puebla de Alcocer an "image of a person appeared on the moon holding a golden rod in his hand: this was the scepter of the Messiah" [Que en la Puebla avyan vysto en la luna on onbre con una vara de oro en la mano, e pensaron que era señor].[34] There and in Talarrubias, conversos would gather dressed in their best attire to gaze at heaven for signs of the advent of the Messiah.[35] Many dreamed of having seen stars in heaven at daytime. These were months of excitement and commotion in the villages and places where conversos dwelled in Extremadura as

each person tried to live according to the precepts of the Mosaic Law insofar as it was possible. It would be out of place at this junction to describe everything the conversos did to prepare themselves for the expected event, but clearly the keeping of the Sabbath and refusing to eat
nonkosher food were the most important actions.[36] Certainly, too, their
actions came to the attention of the Inquisition, and many conversos
were arrested and brought to trial while many others managed to flee to
Portugal, their hopes for redemption dashed.

Men and women were not the only conversos to believe the prophecies of Inés. Many children joined the movement Inés had created, hoping to be taken to the Promised Land, where thousands of young boys
were awaiting converso maidens for marriage. Their young age did not
protect them against the Inquisition, and like their elders, boys and girls
were arrested and brought before the Court of the Inquisition of Toledo
for questioning. One child was Inés García Jiménez, who was arrested as
late as September 30, 1500, but had to wait until March 8, 1501, for a
guardian to be appointed, because she was only nine or ten years old.[37]
This Inés was the third daughter of Marcos García, a smith in Puebla de
Alcocer, and his wife, Leonor Jiménez. Her father was a witness for the
prosecution in the trial of another Marcos García, a cloth dyer from Herrera, who would read to conversos from books, probably the Bible and
perhaps other works. This little girl fasted with her sisters, and together
they awaited the coming of the Messiah. Under the direction of her
guardian, Inés confessed and on March 16 was sentenced: she was condemned to do penance and take part in an auto-da-fé and then be
handed over to a faithful Christian family for reeducation.

Another youthful follower of Inés the prophetess was Rodrigo, the
son of Juan López, whose age is unknown at the time of his arrest and
trial in 1500.[38] Rodrigo confessed to having fasted after being ordered to
do so by Inés. He told the court that the shoemaker López Sánchez, husband of Elvira González of Puerto Peña, had convinced him that Inés
truly had journeyed to heaven and that he was promised his deceased
mother would rise from the dead if he fasted.[39] Rodrigo obeyed Inés's injunction to fast, joining as well the group whose members kept watch for
signs of the Messiah in the sky. The court's judges accepted the boy's
confession, but he nevertheless was condemned to life imprisonment.

The third child, also from Puebla de Alcocer, was Juan González, the son of Juan González Crespo.[40] He was persuaded to believe in Inés by his elder brother, Alvar González, while on his way to Herrera to buy leather, around Christmas of 1499. Alvar González told him of Inés's ascent to heaven and the angel she met there. After staying for a while in Herrera, he returned to Puebla de Alcocer and started to keep *mitzvoth,* observing the Sabbath, putting on a clean shirt on that day, eating matzoth during Passover (of 1500). The boy fled after the Inquisition's first arrests in Herrera, but later he returned, only to be arrested and put on trial. On March 4, 1501, the court appointed as his guardian Diego Tellez, the famous attorney who defended many conversos in Toledo.[41] It was he who persuaded the boy to confess. The *consulta de fe* convened on March 12, 1501, and decided to accept him back into the fold of the church, requiring him to do penance, which indicates that he did not suffer the sentence of life imprisonment as had Rodrigo, the son of Juan López.

Whereas these children were linked to Inés primarily as onlookers on the deeds of parents and elders in their homes, the youngsters in the prophetess's hometown of Herrera were involved more immediately in the excitement generated by Inés and her visions. They would gather around Inés, play, sing, and dance.[42] Rodrigo, who testified to the playing, singing, and dancing, was the son of the smith Fernando Sánchez and María García, his wife; on the opening folio of his trial documents is found the sentence administered by the Inquisition: the boy was to *abjure de vehementi* (renounce his errors and promise to return to the faith) and be imprisoned for life. Beatriz was an orphan whose mother died while she was very young; she was given to be educated, work, and live with Luis de Toledo, the secretary, and Juana García, his wife.[43] Beatriz was a relative of Inés, and at the time of the latter's prophecies Beatriz was about fifteen or sixteen years of age. Inés promised her that she would meet her deceased mother and go to the Promised Land.[44] She also instructed her in the tenets of Moses' Law and taught her Jewish rites and precepts. After her arrest Diego Tellez acted as her attorney, and she was admitted back into the church, probably after abjuring and doing penance.

Four more girls from Herrera between the ages of ten and thirteen were tried for adhering to the tenets of the prophetess: Isabel, daughter of Alvaro Ortolano and Catalina López;[45] Beatriz, daughter of Rodrigo de Villanueva and Isabel de la Fuente;[46] Isabel Bichancho y González;[47] and Beatriz Alonso.[48] Two of the girls were related to Inés: Beatriz, the daughter of Rodrigo de Villanueva, and Isabel Bichancho y González. Isabel's case is particularly startling in that her own mother denounced her to the Inquisition. Her attorney, Diego Tellez, succeeded in pleading her case, for in the file, which lacks a sentence, a note appears on the first folio to the effect that the girl was to do penance according to the court's decision, itself proof that she was accepted back into the Christian fold.

The same outcome held in the case of Inés's other relative and close friend, Beatriz, daughter of Rodrigo de Villanueva. Possibly the two girls grew close in friendship because they shared the dream of finding a groom in the Promised Land from among the young men waiting there for converso brides. To marry within their own religious and cultural community was surely a desire the girls cherished but knew could not be fulfilled so long as they remained in Spain.

The other Isabel was a mere child, ten years of age, when she found herself denounced by one of Inés's own followers, Inés López, and on January 5, 1501, arrested. Like the two preceding girls, this Isabel was accepted back into the church, her fortune more favorable than Beatriz Alonso's, who at thirteen was the oldest in the group. Perhaps the inquisitors dealt more harshly with this Beatriz because of her parents, who were among Inés's most dedicated followers and who, to save themselves, had left their daughter behind and fled to Portugal. Urged by her parents, Beatriz grew stronger in her beliefs and more committed to Judaizing practices. The young girl even had visions of her own, experiencing on one occasion as she entered a room in her home a clairvoyant presence, which, when she described the incident to her mother and another conversa woman, Elvira González, they identified as a visit from the patriarch Abraham.[49] Pleading on her behalf that the girl had been abandoned, Diego Tellez kept her from the stake, but not from a sentence of life imprisonment.

I have tried to bring to life the story of a child prophetess, who in her misery succeeded in instilling hope in the hearts of her converso brethren, first in Herrera del Duque, her birthplace, but later in many towns, villages, and localities. How widespread the movement was in Castile and Extremadura, and perhaps beyond their borders, I do not know. My sources of the movement are the files of the Inquisition, which extirpated it with great cruelty. However, the files serve as a true mirror of life for the conversos, including their beliefs, their hopes for redemption and for a return to the fold and the belief of their forebears. After the expulsion of the Jews from Spain, all that remained for the members of the converso community who stayed in Spain was the cultivation of a hope for redemption with the advent of the Messiah, who would lead them home to the Promised Land. The girl who instilled hope in the hearts of the conversos did not see that hope fulfilled. A marginal note made by the court's notary on the trial documents of Juan González, dated August 3, 1500, states that by that time Juan Esteban's daughter, the child prophetess of Herrera, had been burned.[50]

CHAPTER THREE

María López

A Convicted Judaizer from Castile

RENÉE LEVINE MELAMMED

María López was a *conversa* of Jewish origin who witnessed the expulsion of the Jews from Spain; her parents and grandparents had lived and died as Jews, but María, already a mother herself in 1492, chose to be baptized rather than to leave her native soil. She was fated to die as a convicted Judaizer, an unfaithful Catholic whose soul was lost to the church because of her heretical activities.

This conversa and her family lived in the village of Cogolludo, where they became active members of the community.[1] However, as of 1516, their lives were to be drastically changed. As soon as ample suspicion and corroborating evidence existed regarding the sincerity of the fidelity to Catholicism of any New Christian, the Holy Tribunal felt compelled to prosecute the alleged heretic.[2] Consequently, María and her daughter Isabel were arrested and imprisoned in September 1516, and her husband, Pedro de Villarreal, was incarcerated two years later.[3] All three were condemned to death during the course of twelve months (1518–19), although the parents' trials were not officially over until April 15, 1521.[4]

The defendant under discussion was accused of Judaizing; once baptism had taken place, the baptized was expected to behave in an appropriate Christian manner. Any observance of Jewish laws or customs by a baptized Catholic was tantamount to heresy. A look at María's accusation reveals nine counts, although only six of them relate to Judaizing. The final three were generic heretical charges, such as having withheld the fact that she participated in heresies, having perjured herself by covering up her own as well as others' activities, and not confessing or reporting her actions or the knowledge she had of others.[5]

The more specific charges began with observing Jewish law by not eating pork or anything cooked with it because it is prohibited by the Law of Moses; she also knew of and had seen others who did likewise. In order to determine whence this contention arose, one must simultaneously examine the witness accounts. There were six testimonies utilized by the prosecution in its case against María, and two of them mentioned abstinence from pork in varying degrees.

The second witness, Mayor, had lived with Pedro and María in 1507 for about half a year; during this time, she claimed, neither of them ate pork or anything cooked with pork.[6] Another maidservant, Madalena, the wife of Martín, *cabronero* (goatherd), who was the third witness cited, testified that she had worked for this couple about four years earlier. "During the said time [a year], she saw that her said employers did not eat pork or throw any in their pots," that is to say, cook with it.[7] These two declarations clearly provided the prosecutor with the grounds for his first claim.

The second charge consisted of having removed the fat of the meat or having had it removed with the suet and the like, cleaning it thoroughly, and washing it many times in order to remove the blood; this was often done together with others. Once again, information provided by the second witness, Mayor, proved useful to the prosecution, for she had seen her masters, Pedro and María, remove the fat and the suet from meat prior to cooking it; sometimes they would order a different maidservant to perform this chore.[8] The latter statement clarified the claim that at times they had the fat removed (by others) rather than having done it themselves. The aforementioned Madalena alluded to removing fat with a knife when her masters determined that their meat was not sufficiently lean.[9] The fourth witness, a former servant of Isabel's named María, had also had contact with Isabel's parents in 1513. She specified that she had seen her mistress's mother and sister Catalina cleaning and removing the fat and washing meat.[10] The sixth witness in this trial, Francisco Yague, had worked for Pedro and María as a youth, from the age of eleven until fourteen (1511–14). He explained that in this household, "this witness saw how the said María López washed the meat that was brought from the slaughterhouse a great deal prior to cooking, far more than Old Christians were accustomed to washing." He did not know if she or one of her kitchen maids had removed fat or something else by hand, but he was certain that the meat-cleaning process in his mistress's household was quite different from that which occurred in other homes.[11]

The third count stated that she had continued in her false beliefs, transgressing and making matters even worse. For example, when a leg of meat was brought to her house, she opened it or had it opened lengthwise so that the sciatic nerve could be removed; again this was done in the company of others. This was the main contention of the first witness, Juan Ropero, a smith who had apparently visited the defendant's home in 1504. He recalled having entered María's kitchen, where he saw a leg of meat cut open and then consumed by Pedro and his wife, their son-in-law Francisco de Murcia, and two sons named Francisco and Pedro.[12]

In Madalena's testimony, which has already been cited in both counts above, there are details pertaining to this activity as well. Her employers, Pedro and María, would slit open a leg of lamb lengthwise with a knife after having cleaned it thoroughly.[13] Francisco Yague noted some activity in the kitchen when there was meat or leg of lamb involved, but his description was not precise enough to stand on its own as an indictment of koshering meat. He referred to seeing the leg cut up into many pieces that were the size of a fingertip.[14] However, the two prior references were specific enough to have enabled the prosecutor to include opening the leg of an animal and removing the nerve.

The fourth contention in the accusation maintained that María prepared Sabbath stews or had given instructions to have them or other Jewish cuisine prepared; these had been eaten together with others in a "Jewish way." The only reference that seems to pertain to preparing stews is in the above description by Yague; after cutting the meat up, it was thrown into a stewpot to cook with spices for a very long time. Although there is no reference to the Sabbath or to a Sabbath meal per se, it is clearly a communal meal, for in addition to his employers, their two sons as well as their younger daughter shared in this meal; the assumption might have been that communal meals took place on the Sabbath and holidays.[15]

Next was a charge that concerned refraining from eating conger eel, rabbit, hare, eel, octopus, spotted dogfish, or other fish without scales because the Jews do not eat them. The same Madalena (third witness) who had worked for Pedro and María for a year stated that during this time she had never seen them eat rabbit, hare, conger eel, eel, octopus, or spotted dogfish.[16] The fourth witness, María, claimed that during Lent, she had seen conger eel cooked in their house but had never seen her employers eat it; on the contrary, they included it in their servants' diet.[17]

Sixth in María's accusation was the claim that she had eaten meat on Fridays and on other days forbidden by the church on occasions when she had no apparent health problems;[18] again, she had been in the company of others. Judaizers who ate the traditional Sabbath evening meal would have transgressed in this manner, for it usually included meat; however, there were no direct claims made concerning María and Sabbath observance. In Madalena's description of processing meat, she mentioned being told to keep an eye on certain meat, sometimes raw and sometimes cooked; this task was generally performed on Thursdays or on Friday mornings. Subsequently, she would be sent out of the house on errands to places such as the vineyards; upon her return, the meat was invariably gone, presumably having been cooked and eaten or cooked and saved for Sabbath meals.[19]

As mentioned above, there were no direct references to Sabbath observance in María's accusation. Only one witness account is explicit about Sabbath activities of both the defendant and her husband, and these activities did not appear in the accusation. Closer examination reveals the fact that this particular account was copied and transferred from the list of charges in the trial of Pedro and thus dated May 20, 1518,[20] well after the presentation of the charges in María's trial. According to the prosecution, the Judaizing activities attributed to María concerned the dietary laws, in particular which foods are forbidden to eat and the koshering of meat as well as of the leg of permitted animals. María nevertheless refuted the claims made in this testimony despite the fact that the prosecution did not confront her with them. As will be seen, they resurfaced at the close of the trial when the tribunal concluded its case.

María López vehemently denied being a Judaizer throughout her trial and responded to each and every count.[21] For example, this conversa denied the charge of not eating pork, insisting that she had eaten pork and the meat of male pigs; she pointed out that she could tolerate neither fatty meat nor fatty pork but that there was no connection between these personal habits and Judaizing.

In response to the second charge of koshering her meat, she said that the meat that went in her pots was lean but had not been purged or cleaned ceremonially. She then denied having removed the sciatic nerve of leg of lamb and the like. Regarding the reference to Jewish foods and stews, the defendant said she had not made or eaten them since her conversion to Catholicism. As for the fifth count, she claimed she had eaten rabbit and spotted dogfish and hare and fish without scales. In response to the accusation of eating meat on days forbidden by the church, she explained that she had indeed done so, but always with the permission of either her physician or her priest. As for the last three counts concerning general heretical activities and affiliation with heretics, she denied and negated them.[22]

In the course of the trial, there were additional opportunities and ample time to prepare a response to the prosecutor's claims. On February 9, 1517, María again negated the first contention, explaining that the contrary was true, that she had eaten pork and cooked with it, although perhaps she had once stopped eating it because of illness and poor health rather than per Jewish rite and ceremony. The second and third charges were also negated, for she had never removed anything from meat in compliance with any ceremony; if she cleaned her meat or removed the fat, there was no heretical motivation behind it. Besides, men, and not women, traditionally remove the sciatic nerve; thus this claim was obviously erroneous.[23]

The clear-cut denial by the defendant continued as she emphasized that she ate all the nonkosher fish mentioned as well as hare, rabbit, drowned birds, and other foods not permitted to the Jews. In addition, she never ate meat on forbidden days, which, had she done so without the permission of her priest or her doctor, would have been a sin rather than a heretical act. On the contrary, she had lived her life as a good loyal Catholic Christian and could not comprehend the reason for her denunciation.[24] Later in the trial, on August 6, 1518, when the actual testimonies were read to María, she asserted that they were false and that she had never done any such thing.[25] As was the custom, the defendant was given six days in which to prepare a detailed response to these claims.

Thus, on August 12, María made a statement attesting to her innocence, that she was being wrongly detained and that the witnesses based their statements on hearsay and idle beliefs that were all without any basis whatsoever. After this rather long statement of her innocence, she once again dealt with each charge individually. Most of her claims were identical to those already presented. She insisted that she had not kept the dietary laws of the Jews and that often the meat from the slaughterhouse was disgustingly dirty, hence the need to clean it properly. On the whole, these witnesses were committing perjury. At the same time, it was by no means an act of heresy not to eat pork at times or to cook lean meat in a pot with chickpeas and spices. The witnesses were simply attempting to damage the defendant's reputation; they were unreliable, and her defense would prove her innocence by means of the *abonos* (evidence) and *tachas* (list of hostile witnesses prepared by the accused) to follow.[26]

On August 25, 1518, María made two detailed objections to the last set of witness testimonies, which were synopses of the statements given by Madalena, wife of Martin Simon, and by Francisco Yague. In the first clause, María contended, "God never intended for there to be lamps in my house on Fridays or on Saturdays or on any other days."[27] If she had entered the underground cellar referred to in the testimony, she was tending to the functioning of her household, that is, obtaining wine and not performing Jewish rites or ceremonies. At the same time, God never wanted her to dress up or to wear different clothes on Friday nights or Saturdays; she made no differentiation between her mode of dress on one day or another unless it was a holiday. Besides, wearing a clean blouse on Fridays was never a ceremony, and if she attended anything on Saturday mornings, it was mass. In addition, "God never wanted me to light or to order lamps, namely, oil lamps, to be lit with new wicks nor to throw what they call dough into the fire. And washing one's meat well is no Jewish rite or ceremony but rather cleanliness and proper diligence."[28] In the second clause, María claimed that this last witness did her no damage because, as she already pointed out, cleaning and cooking meat is not a rite. When he said that she removed mounds (of fat) from the meat, it had been done for the sake of cleanliness, and this activity was not prohibited by any law. Therefore, it was obvious that these perjurers were her mortal enemies who spread falsehoods when, in actuality, she should be absolved by the Holy Tribunal.[29]

On the following day, the defense began in earnest with lists of abonos and *indirectas*; the latter were questions to be asked of various character witnesses whose names were supplied by the defense. After establishing the fact that the witnesses on the stand indeed knew the defendant personally, they were asked if she had behaved as a good Christian after her baptism, if she had gone to hear mass and sermons and other divine offices and had observed Sundays and Easters and other holidays as would a good Christian. Next they were questioned as to whether she had confessed and received the sacraments annually as required by the church and if she was a clean and neat woman who took pride in her actions, such as preparing food, wearing clothes, and decorating and cleaning her home. The question that followed dealt with her eating habits, namely, if she had eaten the various animals and fishes that were prohibited by Jewish law. "Also, did they know if the defendant was a woman who provided proper doctrines and good advice to her male and female servants and made certain that they were properly instructed in the things that concern our holy Catholic faith?"[30] Could they verify the fact that when Don Alonso de la Cerda, the lord of the manor, had been ill, the defendant cared for him in her home and cooked meat daily for his meals as well as for those of his hawks and hunting dogs?

On October 16, 1517, four more questions were added to the list to be posed to the character witnesses. They dealt with situations when either the defendant, her daughter, her husband, or her grandchild was ill. In each instance, permission had been granted to go for medical help, to find a parish priest, or to set forth on a pilgrimage in search of a cure; special masses were subsequently recited.[31]

As one might imagine, the replies to the above questions which were given by the various witnesses were diversified; the list of names provided by the defense usually specified which questions were to be posed to which witness. The first list included thirteen names, among which were clerics, chaplains, sextons, servants from Don Alonso's estate, and even one of the prosecution witnesses, Juan Ropero.[32] Some testified that María had requested special masses or had confessed and taken the sacraments regularly and did the works of a good Christian. One recalled seeing pork roasted in the defendant's home and then eaten by her and her family. Juan Ropero, the Old Christian who was acquainted with the defendant for thirty years, responded to two questions. First, he ascertained that María was a very meticulous person who prepared food well; however, the rest of his answer, he pointed out, had already been submitted to the court. He only added that sometimes upon entering the house, he had seen the defendant roasting a partridge or a hen and that once she seemed to be tending very diligently to some sick person in her home.

Another witness named María Gaytan revealed that the defendant's son-in-law Francisco de Murcia had approached her that very week; "he told her that if the Inquisitors should call upon her, that they beg of her to reveal whatever she knows and that she should say no more [than that]."[33] She verified the claim that María's household and person were very clean and well kept. For more than seven years, the two women had lived next to each other, and the witness felt welcome in the household and free to come and go as she pleased; she often ate at María's, a clear sign she was at ease in this home.[34] The final witness in this group was the wife of a sexton who had once accompanied the defendant on a pilgrimage to Santa María de Caritas.

The defense did not rest but rather continued to compose new lists of abonos and indirectas. This time, witnesses were asked if they knew if the defendant had entered the cellar in her home in order to give wine to the wine butlers and if she went there for other purposes as well. In addition, could they ascertain that there was no aforesaid lamp in her home and that there was often a great deal of activity and talk there that could have been distracting? In addition, did they know if María went to Saturday morning mass religiously and if on that day, as well as on Fridays, she dressed no differently than any other? Lastly, did they know if the cellar in her home was without doors or closures or, at any rate, always remained open?

The defense then nominated fourteen people who might have been able to verify some or all of the above statements. This list included Don Alonso and a number of his servants, two former wine butlers, and assorted others, some of whom were New Christians and were, nonetheless, allowed to testify.[35] As it turned out, most of these people were unable to respond to the questions posed. One of Don Alonso's valets mentioned that some of María's household help would wash meat before cooking, but he knew no more than that. On September 23, an Old Christian named Catalina, who had been a neighbor of María's from 1508 to 1515, testified. She was often in the defendant's home and had seen her as well as her maidservants bake and cook on Fridays as well as on Saturdays; she saw María boil the bread in preparation for the kneading board. Catalina recalled being there one Saturday night when a pair of suckling pigs were slaughtered because guests were due to arrive; the witness herself had suggested waiting until Sunday morning. She pointed out that this was not the only time this family had partaken of meals of this sort. Further, on numerous occasions, this neighbor had seen no difference whatsoever between kitchen activities on Fridays, Saturdays, or other days of the week. In addition, Catalina never saw special cleaning of meat or preparations or the cutting open of legs of lamb. "Once, by-and-by, as she began to enter the house, she saw the said María López and Isabel, her daughter, wife of Francisco de Murcia, opening the leg of beef in half in preparation for cooking, but she did not see anything whatsoever removed from the middle."[36] Lastly, she never saw the defendant wear a clean blouse on the Sabbath.

A household servant named Juana had worked in the defendant's household for six years and had prepared food for her employers. She testified that there was no noticeable difference between the way in which she or her mistress washed, prepared, or cooked meat. Juana had never seen a leg of lamb cut open or a clean blouse donned on Saturdays; on the contrary, María often asked her servant to prepare a clean blouse for Sunday mornings.[37]

The defense continued in its attempt to prove that María was a good Christian and had not been engaged in the activities of which she had been accused. Additional questions intended for the defense witnesses referred to the defendant having eaten and cooked sucking pigs, especially on Sundays, and how people had come to her house on the Sabbath eve or during the day to conduct business. Witnesses were also asked about her servants, who knew nothing of preparing meat in any special ways or of dressing up on the Sabbath.

On September 19, none other than María's son-in-law Sancho de Horozco, an *hijodalgo* (man of noble descent), obviously an Old Christian,
testified. He said he had seen his mother-in-law enter her cellar frequently, especially when she removed wine that was for sale. He himself
had entered the aforesaid wine cellar and home of the defendant and had
never seen a lamp lit or unlit. In Sancho's opinion, "she was nothing but
a stingy woman who did not trust anyone."[38] In addition, he never saw
her differ in her mode of dress on any day but Sundays, when she dressed
appropriately. He contended that there indeed was a door and a key to
the cellar, which was necessary in order to protect the household goods,
for this was the norm in houses in which there was a wine cellar.[39]

Other witnesses had less information to offer. Two attested to the fact
that María attended mass on Saturday mornings. Two others each spoke
about having entered the cellar often, never having seen any lamps there,
a sight that would have been easily perceived, and having seen the defendant enter the cellar to see what was happening there. One commented
on the lively conversation and level of activity often found in this household. Don Alonso's page appeared before the tribunal again and ascertained the fact that his master had often been in María's home. A steward
employed by Don Alonso stated that the defendant did not dress differently on any particular days of the week and that there was both a cellar
and a wine cellar in her home. He was of the opinion that the cellar had
no door or lock but knew that the wine cellar in front of it had doors,
which he had seen María open and close. It turned out that this family
had resided in two different houses, a fact that would account for various
discrepancies that appeared in testimonies concerning the cellars.[40]

At the same time, one learns about the lifestyle of the defendant from
the defense questions, the abonos, and the indirectas. Personal habits are
discussed, including the way in which the defendant behaved in her role
as mistress of her servants. There is a distinct awareness that the life of
the defendant was dependent upon and constructed around her status.
Although servants were built-in informers and thus dangerous to have
living side by side with a Judaizer, there was no means by which a middle-class converso could avoid employing them. The very act of not doing so would be incriminating, for only one conclusion could and would
be drawn if servants were absent in the household.

An analysis of the tacha lists that follow in the file of María López reveals even more about her life as a middle-class conversa in sixteenth-century Cogolludo. It becomes clear that María, as a member of this class, not only employed but also discharged numerous servants. As is already quite obvious, a servant in a crypto-Jewish household was a built-in witness to Judaizing activities. While he or she did not necessarily understand the significance of various idiosyncratic household activities, an accurate report was all that was required by the prosecution. The descriptions already presented in the accusation attest to this fact; it was the prosecutor's job to interpret the significance of these activities.

In addition to learning about various details of daily life, one cannot but note the complexity of the relationships in a small village, even prior to the appearance of the Inquisition on the scene. María apparently was not an easygoing woman, yet she seems to have run a tight ship. In addition to her own household duties, she was involved in her shop, in her daughter's household, and in her husband's diversified activities.

There are many potential areas of tension and conflict which emerge naturally in village life. The fact that Cogolludo had a large converso population would have exacerbated these tensions because of the very nature of Old Christian–New Christian relationships in sixteenth-century Spain. Because both María and her husband were deeply involved in village life and, individually or jointly, made many decisions or carried out orders that affected many lives, one is not surprised to find a myriad of potential candidates who might have rallied to the cause of the prosecution.

The tachas reflect these tensions par excellence; while sitting in her cell, María had more than ample time to reflect upon her life and to assess numerous encounters with individuals which did not result in satisfaction on the part of those involved. Thus she as well as other members of her family continually suggested names of people who might have been cooperative witnesses for the prosecution. At the same time, it is mind-boggling for the outside observer to consider the number of unpleasant incidents that she and her family were able to recall which dealt with the defendant and her fellow residents; perhaps it is even more overwhelming to consider the number of servants unable to provide satisfactory service to the López-Villarreal family.

The tacha listing process in this trial was long, exhausting, and exhaustive. Almost half of the recorded proceedings of the trial involve this process; nearly one hundred different individuals are named as suspects by the various members of the family. Included in this rather large list are members of every class of society, but the overwhelming number of them, just under half, were former servants of the family. The second-largest category includes people with whom Pedro had unpleasant dealings in his various capacities; some were named because they had been evicted from houses by Pedro, sometimes along with María, and others were implicated because of property feuds with this couple. A number had unsuccessful business dealings with them or unpleasant neighborly encounters; some were simply cited as being hopelessly corrupt or unpleasant people, and the remainder seem to be isolated cases of social, familial, or economic tensions.

María began her defense with three group tachas and then, on October 16, 1517, added a formidable list of fifty-one names. One particular figure immediately stands out, for he appears in both of these lists as well as in a third one drawn up by Pedro de Villarreal and Francisco de Murcia two months later. Pedro de Murcia, Francisco's brother, was, in the family's estimation, capable of testifying against and incriminating his own family. He is described as a thief and a drunkard who wasted his time in taverns. He was angry with María because she and her son-in-law refused to support him; at the same time, he was castigated by both María and Isabel, who each clearly expressed to him her detestation of his vices. He had even threatened them and, while in the home of Pedro the tailor, announced that he would incur as much damage as possible upon these women.[41] The defense had already found a prospective hostile witness ever so close to home.

As it turned out, Pedro de Murcia did not usually live in close proximity to María, yet there were many individuals named who had been in very close daily contact with her, namely, servants or, more likely in this case, former servants. One discovers that some of the maidservants were discontent because they had not received certain goods from their mistress. For example, a number of them claimed they were promised skirts or blouses that they never received; this type of situation was viewed as sufficient cause for enmity.[42]

A servant fired because his master or mistress considered his service to have been unsatisfactory would be apt to take vengeance upon the former employer either because of anger and resentment or because of the reputation subsequently acquired. For example, Madalena quarreled with her employer after being told that she was being released because her service was unacceptable.[43] At the same time, Catalina had been reprimanded numerous times by her mistress in a vain attempt to make her an honorable woman.[44]

Usually there was a more specific reference to the grievance involved. Juana, the daughter of Juan Yague, resident of Jocar, a former servant, "was . . . the enemy of the said María López because she had wounded her and castigated her so that she would become a good woman and not dirty her bed and for this reason, she left the house."[45] Juana de Membrillera's name appears three times in these lists. She and her mistress had fought and insulted each other, and María had beaten her because of her wine-drinking excesses as well as her lack of responsibility. Pedro had also beaten her and claimed that she was lazy and a liar.[46]

Unacceptable behavior included lack of sobriety, wanton sexual behavior, theft, lying, and generally dishonest comportment. Madalena of Corlo, who actually testified for the prosecution, was cited as having provided poor service, having been castigated verbally as well as physically punished by both master and mistress, refusing to wear shoes in María's home, and having been thrown out of the house a number of times.[47] A servant of Isabel's also named Madalena, the wife of Martin Simon, had also provided testimony for the prosecution. Both Pedro, the father, and Isabel, his daughter, had attempted in vain to improve her behavior. "I castigated her and [so had] even my said daughter in order to make a good woman of her, so she should not be the wanton woman or thief that she is and for this reason, at times, I gave her her share of beatings." In addition, her husband owed Pedro a quantity of wool for which he had been paid by Pedro, but he never delivered the goods; it seems that he had also stolen some sheep.[48] All of the above are convincing motives for enmity between Madalena and this family.

A resident of Arvancon was singled out as being "a maidservant, who had been the said María López's, who was . . . one who [spread] falsehoods and [was] an enemy of the said María López because [María] hurt her and castigated her frequently so that she would become a good woman."[49] At least two female servants were beaten because of their loose lifestyles. Another Juana from Membrillera, "a former servant of María López's, had . . . hatred and enmity for her because she was wounded and castigated and beaten so that she would be an honorable woman and she was called a whore with a sweet tooth who cavorted with Don Alonso's male servants, asking them for 'tidbits.'"[50] The wife of Fernando Pablo was also considered hostile because she had been admonished and beaten. This woman had purportedly cavorted with Don Alonso's male servants and with other men who passed through the household. After retiring to her chamber at night, María often had to descend to the servants' quarters with a lamp in search of the peripatetic Juana.[51]

Theft was also common, and three former servants who were indeed prosecution witnesses are cited as thieves. Both mother and daughter had employed one woman who had stolen from both of them, was thrown out of both houses, and had been punished excessively.[52] Two male servants, Vicentico and Francisco Yague, were singled out as having stolen walnuts from trees adjoining Pedro's property. The former also owed María's husband a ducat; the latter, a witness for the prosecution, had a complaint lodged against him, and as a result, he left without completing the period of service which had been negotiated.[53] Many other former servants were cited as having stolen from their masters and mistresses.

As can be deduced, beatings and castigation were extremely common; the employers hoped to improve or correct unacceptable behavior or to punish outrageous antics. María usually claimed to be trying to make the servant honest or to convince him or her to behave decently, but the servant rarely appreciated the so-called effort on his or her behalf. Consequently, the most common outcome of such discipline was considerable anger and bitterness on the part of the servant.

The list of former servants who were physically beaten is rather lengthy; the fact that wounds were inflicted was mentioned by the defendant herself. The daughter of Alonso Escudero was wounded so seriously by María that she remained crippled.[54] María of Carrascosa was often wounded and once fell from one of the corridors, presumably as the result of a beating.[55] Although physical reprimands were considered to be acceptable, there was always the possibility that the recipient would hold a grudge that might later become a powerful weapon for motivation.

Outside the house, both María and her husband had a great deal of contact with numerous members of the community. Some of the tachas reflect unpleasant neighborly interactions such as lawsuits over property claims which, of course, the defendant had won or refusals by her or her husband to grant loans; others involved services rendered or not rendered by certain professionals and tradesmen. For instance, Martín de Fraguas owed María money that he reluctantly gave her; he then sued for the sum paid. Needless to say, he lost the suit and resented this fact, claiming that his payment was inappropriate.[56] In a tacha that dealt with the purchase of a farmyard and subsequent tensions regarding the sale, it turned out that there had also been an argument with the wife of the suspected individual, who was a midwife by profession; this row concerned the service or lack thereof provided to María's daughter.[57]

As for tradesmen, one carpenter was angry that he had not been employed by this family; in addition, his son-in-law was supposed to examine some cloth and had fled, presumably with the goods on his person.[58] Juan Perez Tronpeta, presumably a baker, had quarreled with Pedro over negotiation of revenues; apparently payment was to be made by supplying baked goods.[59] Juan the tailor was annoyed because María did not give him work, and, in turn, he and his wife boycotted the purchase of cloth from María's store.

In other trade-related issues, García the redhead and his wife and children were enemies as a result of business hostilities between the tailors in this particular family and the defendant, in whose shop fabric was sold. Because of the animosity between the two families, María would not give them anything to sew; consequently García and kin did their utmost to prevent everyone from buying cloth from the defendant.[60] A miller who had worked for Pedro "fought with him often because as his miller, he abandoned his post at the mill and left it poorly guarded."[61]

At the same time, Pedro, owing to his numerous official capacities, held a certain level of sway and power in the community. Many of his decisions were resented, and some individuals or families might even have had more than one reason to attempt to undermine his position. Juan de Vella had been subjected to public humiliation because he denied Christ;

he was marched through town with a bit in his mouth.[62] Alonso de las Navas was the miller for Don Alonso, by whom Pedro was employed as a steward. Apparently he caused major financial losses to the estate; in addition, one of the women in the family unsuccessfully served in the Villarreal household, and third, after serious rows, Pedro was obligated to evict the de las Navas family from one of the lord's houses.[63] Judging from the number of evictions that Pedro executed, this was one of his requisite but less glorified tasks. One group is mentioned because all of its members openly opposed Pedro's candidacy for the aforementioned stewardship;[64] Juan González, the smith, fought with the defendant and her husband when he was appointed as overseer of Don Alonso's estate.[65]

One must consider the fact that since María and Pedro owned real estate in the village, they also engaged in similar activities on a personal level. For example, a neighbor named Gerónimo and his wife were evicted from a house the conversos had purchased; in retaliation, the injured party broadcast throughout the village the claim that the offenders owed them money.[66] Francisco de Torres and his family were furious when they lost to Pedro in a competition dealing with the purchase of some stores.[67]

Many residents of Cogolludo were in debt to this couple and often resented this fact. In his role as a city official, Pedro collected payments and sometimes had to force the debtor to sell assets. One of the tachas listed two individuals who, because of money they owed, engaged in physical fights with Pedro.[68]

Juan Ropero was a prosecution witness. According to Pedro, Juan owed him money but did not want to pay his debts. María listed him as well, claiming, "He owed me money and has ill-will toward me because he asked for [the money] and went around saying that I asked him for what he did not owe me, and because we sold some houses in order [to cover] the debt, he harbors ill-will, he and his wife and his son Pedro."[69] Pedro de Burgos was unwilling to take out pledges to cover his debts to Don Alonso. Catalina *la botera* and her family resented Pedro when, as magistrate, he did not permit them to sell their estate.[70]

Little more than basic human nature was responsible for the final set of hostile relationships. Catalina de Cervantes, who was indeed a witness for the prosecution in Isabel's trial, had fought with María; the two women were verbally abusive to each other and simply remained antagonistic. A different Catalina, the wife of Hernando Cavallero, was known to the Villarreal family because she had an extramarital affair with Pedro. However, in a tacha list compiled by Pedro and his son, she was cited as having committed adultery not with María's husband but with Pedro de Brihuega. "Catalina, the wife of Fernando de Cavallero was and is licentious with Pedro de Brihuega and has had and has hatred and enmity toward the said María López and her husband because when she was their neighbor, they would not lend her what she requested nor did they want to rent her a house which they had."[71]

As can be seen, the suspicions that arose as the result of less than felicitous interactions covered the entire gamut of possibilities. Problems were rampant when servants were employed in the home as well as when the master or mistress worked outside the house in official or unofficial capacities. If one had assets or liquid funds, complications were bound to evolve; likewise, problems could arise whether or not one utilized the services of other working members of the community. Last, but not least, human nature itself played a significant role here; interpersonal tensions ensued, whether the result of resentment of a parasite of a brother, inability to cope with a cantankerous neighbor, or the social aftermath of an extramarital affair.

Eventually, the defense rested, and although all of the prosecution witnesses had been correctly named in the tachas, victory was still elusive. The court required two corroboration witnesses per tacha to attest to the suspected cause of enmity between witness and defendant. Had knowledgeable witnesses materialized who remembered the incidents or motives cited, the prosecution would have had to remove each one from its list as he or she was invalidated. Both in theory and in practice, the entire prosecution could have been nullified. Unfortunately and devastatingly for María, the failure to provide reliable corroboration sealed her fate.

The impressive number of tachas attests both to the nature of the lifestyle of the defendant and to the family's determination to disqualify those who had betrayed them.[72] The court allowed the defense to engage in elaborate guesswork as to who the enemies of the defendant might be. Only potential corroboration witnesses were summoned by the court, in this case, those who might shed light regarding the six persons who actually testified against María. The tacha lists dominate this trial but ultimately were of no value to the defense. At this late stage in the trial, there yet remained the fact that the conversa had not confessed. María probably still hoped that this fact would save her as the tribunal weighed its alternatives.

On November 18, 1518, the nine members of the tribunal voted to condemn María López and to confiscate her goods. However, the defendant would first be subjected to torture because she had consistently denied her guilt, and it was hoped that she would reveal names of accomplices. This was a final attempt to corroborate the prosecution's stance. On November 24, the notary recorded the following:

And then the said Lord Inquisitors ordered the said María López to be taken to the torture chamber and to be undressed and to be placed on the rack of torment and to be tied with some hemp ropes. She was undressed and placed on the said rack and tied with the said ropes and was required and admonished by the said Lord Inquisitors to tell the truth: Who were those persons whom she had seen commit those heretical crimes of which she is accused because the intention of your Graces is none other than to know the entire truth, and if she dies during torture or receives an injury to any limb it will be her fault and not that of your Graces. The aforesaid said, "Oh, Holy Mary of Monserrate,[73] protect me, Lord Jesus Christ, for I have been a good Christian. Oh, look, Our Holy Lady Mary, why did you consent to such a thing? Your Lord Reverences, I entrust myself to you." The order was made to pour water with a pitcher that contains up to four pints and [to put] something additional upon her face on top of a silk headdress that she had on her face. It was ordered for the ropes to be tightened with a tourniquet and it was tightened with two tourniquets.[74]

Even though this conversa insisted that she was a good Christian, at the end of the trial, the court maintained that the defendant was guilty.[75] The members of the tribunal possessed testimony that had convinced them of the prosecution's claims. There was no reason not to accept these statements. In the court's opinion, María had believed in the Law of Moses, did not eat pork or other foods forbidden to Jews, prepared her meat so that it would be kosher, dressed up in honor of the Sabbath, lit oil lamps on Friday nights, baked *hallah* according to Jewish law, and ate meat on Fridays and on other days when meat was forbidden by the church.[76] The fact that the defendant did not confess did not faze this particular court; she was stubborn, as they knew, and obviously desperate to save her life even if she sinned while insisting on falsehoods.

Thus the court declared:

> Given and pronounced was this sentence by the Reverend Lord Inquisitors, the licentiates Sancho Velez and Juan de Mendoza in the city of Toledo on the thirtieth day of November in the year 1518, being in the Plaza of Zocodover on a scaffold where the auto-da-fé takes place. Present are the very reverend and magnificent Lord Don Diego de la Ribera, bishop of Segovia and Don Francisco Ruíz, bishop of Avila and the licentiate Alonso de Mariana and Pedro Fernandez de Yepes, canons of Toledo and Pedro López and Juan de Padilla his son, and many other people who are residents of Toledo and of other parts.[77]

Thus was María executed by the secular arm at the described auto-da-fé.

Here is a case of a woman convicted of Judaizing on the sole basis of witness testimonies.[78] Again, it must be emphasized that María never confessed and consistently denied having engaged in heretical activities, even after being subjected to torture. Her defense via tachas was unsuccessful because the witnesses named to corroborate her claims were unable to do so and thus vindicate her. In the course of the trial, María provided very little information about her family background, for she had not been asked to present a genealogy. Yet one can learn a great deal about her not only from her trial proceedings but also from those of her husband and daughter.

Pedro was the only one of the three to confess, albeit only partially. He had witnessed the deadly results of his wife's and daughter's defense tactics and chose what he hoped would be a more successful line of defense. Pedro hoped to appease the court by presenting a limited list of offenses. The fact that he named his deceased wife as an active Judaizer in his confession served to validate the tribunal's condemnation of her. His statements essentially dispel any doubts concerning the veracity of María's crypto-Jewishness which might have lingered pursuant to a reading of only María's trial. Pedro admitted to removing fat and nerves from meat, seeing his wife prepare food and then eating it, and wearing a clean shirt once on the Sabbath, but not necessarily in honor of that day. He was very vague about what his wife prepared, but presumably the reference was either to Sabbath meals or to dishes cooked without including non-kosher ingredients.[79]

María López was an active member of the community of Cogolludo. In addition to raising four children, she ran a shop where fabric was sold and had numerous business dealings both on her own and together with her husband. There are even examples of money lending by this conversa which come to light in the tacha lists. This crypto-Jewish woman described herself as clean and diligent, but she was also exacting and demanding of her employees, servants, and business associates. When the need arose, she did not hesitate to carry out unpleasant tasks such as evicting tenants and castigating her servants or those working in her daughter's household; she was clearly a woman of conviction. Her strength emerged during her trial; for two years, she consistently and adamantly denied the charges presented to her despite the fact that the descriptions of Judaizing activities in her household were both numerous and detailed.

In the end, this conversa was condemned to die as a heretic in the eyes of the church, a woman whose soul was deemed not to be saved because she did not repent before being burned at the stake. The truth of the matter is that she was condemned to be burned at the stake by the Inquisition because she was a crypto-Jewess. María López had taught her daughter to observe the religion of their ancestors, and together mother and daughter experienced martyrdom as the result of their loyalty to Judaism.

PART II

The Inquisition
and Christian
Orthodoxy

Francisca Hernández and the Sexuality of Religious Dissent

MARY E. GILES

By 1530 the Holy Office at Toledo had a celebrity on its hands—and in its prisons. The celebrity was no prince of church or state but a woman of humble origins reputed to have extraordinary healing powers and divinely inspired gifts to interpret Sacred Scripture and guide souls to intimacy with God. Among her followers were well-known priests who insisted that the woman had rid them of sexual temptations with a single touch of her sash and righted their spiritual course with wisdom infused by the Holy Spirit. But fame was not without a price: detractors were spreading rumors that the spiritual gifts of Francisca Hernández were a sham and her relations with men a scandal.

Francisca was born in the latter part of the fifteenth century in the town of Canella near Salamanca to parents who were of scant economic means but could claim the honor of a lineage unsullied by Jewish or Moorish blood.[1] The family's status as Old Christians did not automatically open doors to religious life for the young Francisca, who since childhood was said to receive remarkable favors from God. When her plans to enter a convent were thwarted by lack of an education her family could not afford and perhaps by persons of ill will as well, Francisca had to rely on her own resources to fashion a religious mode of living outside the convent. A model for such a life was already in place with the *beatas* (women who dedicated themselves to God) who lived by themselves at home or in communities—*beaterios* they were called—much as the Beguines and other *mulieres sanctae* had done in previous centuries. But Francisca eschewed enclosure, whether in the convent or outside it, nor was austerity to her liking: her apostolate was in the world, and her critics would say, of the world as well. For comforts she had servants, excellent food, a soft bed with fine linen, and the company of men to whom she generously extended hospitality. Prominent among the men who benefited from her hospitality, and in some cases financed it, were the licentiate Bernardino de Tovar, brother of the learned doctor Juan de Vergara; the priest Antonio de Medrano; the Franciscan preacher Gil López de Bejar; and a certain friar, Juan Hurtado; these men were the nucleus of an ever expanding circle of clerics, friars, and lay people attracted to Francisca for her charismatic teaching on prayer and interpretation of Sacred Scripture. Their enthusiasm for the beata reached such heights that when Francisca's taste for gracious living exceeded her funds, Medrano persuaded a young man by the name of Antonio de Calero to sell his property and donate the proceeds to Francisca's empty coffers.

Francisca did not hide her lamp under the veil of discretion. Discrediting rumors reached the Holy Office in Salamanca, and by 1519 the inquisitors had heard enough about the charismatic woman and her men friends to authorize her arrest. Alerted to the impending danger, Francisca fled to Valladolid in the company of Tovar, Medrano, and the bachelor Diego de Villareal, themselves under scrutiny for improper behavior with the beata. The move to Valladolid did not remove Francisca from harm's way; on December 15, 1519, the Valladolid office undertook an investigation of Francisca and Antonio de Medrano, the man who by then had emerged as her most ardent follower. Thanks to efforts of friends in high ecclesiastical places and support from the nearby Franciscan monastery, Francisca managed to come through the encounter relatively unscathed: she and Medrano were to sever all communication with each other and live at least five leagues apart. Perhaps their intense attraction to each other or an arrogance bred of popularity explains the subsequent actions of Francisca and Medrano: in bold defiance of the Inquisition they carried on their meetings clandestinely.

Neither the move from Salamanca nor her brush with the Inquisition dulled Francisca's palate for fine living. In Valladolid she occupied a suite in the residence of the royal accountant Pedro de Cazalla and his wife,

Leonor de Vivero, where she held spiritual court, enlisting disciples from the ranks of the nobility, the Franciscan monastery, and a group of men at the university town of Alcalá de Henares who were dedicated to the reformist agenda of Erasmus. Among the Erasmian enthusiasts who aligned themselves with Francisca were Juan del Castillo, a professor of Greek; Diego López de Husillos, a priest from Toledo; and the printer Miguel de Eguía, who in 1525 began to print Erasmus's main works in Latin. Francisca's growing popularity among men and women in the Valladolid area who were seeking the benefits of a spirituality that depended less on external practices and adherence to church dogma than on nourishing a personal relationship with God through prayer and immersion in Sacred Scripture did not protect her from scandal, even within the home where she was granted hospitality. Leonor Cazalla is said to have harbored such acute suspicion about Francisca's behavior with her husband, Pedro, that she denounced the woman to the Inquisition, while outside the domestic scene the lay spiritual teacher Pedro Ruiz de Alcaraz wrote a letter on June 22, 1524, to the Inquisition denouncing Francisca.

By this time Francisca already had come under renewed suspicion by the Inquisition. Having learned about her secret meetings with Medrano, the authorities had taken action on May 14, 1524, ordering the priest to break off all connection with Francisca and return to his hometown of Navarrete in the region of Logroño. After Medrano's exile Francisca suffered a further setback to her popularity when a change of administration at the Franciscan monastery, where she had a coterie of admirers, brought to leadership one Father Guinea, who wasted no time expressing grave doubts about her chastity. On March 31, 1529, the blow fell. Francisca was arrested and imprisoned by the Holy Office at Toledo. Her arrest did not go unnoticed. Within days, on April 6, the acclaimed preacher of the Franciscan order Francisco Ortiz, himself a relative newcomer to Francisca's inner circle of male admirers, mounted the pulpit of the church of the monastery of San Juan de los Reyes in Toledo and publicly denounced the Holy Office and the inquisitor general, Don Alonso Manrique, archbishop of Toledo, for the grievous act of apprehending Francisca Hernández. Francisco Ortiz's arrest was soon to follow.

Francisca's questionable friendships with men were not the only reason for her arrest. Like other men and women imprisoned at that time by the Toledo authorities, she was suspected of promoting *alumbrado* beliefs, which the Edict of Toledo of September 23, 1525, had identified as being heretical in terms of forty-eight propositions formulated by the inquisitors from statements made by defendants and witnesses during Inquisition trials. Alumbrados encouraged interiorized Christianity in the spirit of medieval *devotio moderna,* the ideas of Erasmus, and Lutheranism, which by 1529 was making inroads into the peninsula. A sampling of the propositions from the edict demonstrate that at the heart of *alumbradismo* was the belief that personal relationship with God overruled the authority of the church and nullified the need for its mediation: Proposition Four stated that if the creature did what he ought to do, God came more completely into the soul of man than in the host, for the host was a bit of matter whereas man was in God's likeness. Proposition Eleven: After one abandons himself to God, abandonment alone is sufficient to save his soul; it is not necessary to fast or perform works of mercy.[2]

During the early sixteenth century, when Spain nourished a Christianity of the heart, whether or not in the form of alumbradismo, charismatic women had appeared on the spiritual landscape who in ecstatic teaching and preaching demonstrated the power of the Holy Spirit to enlighten the lowliest of God's creatures without benefit of priest, sacrament, or institution. Holy women like Sor María of Santo Domingo and Madre Juana de la Cruz were visible signs of God's presence for both clergy and laity and a challenge to the orthodox position that salvation was possible only through the church.[3] When Francisca enters the scene in documents of the time, Sor María of Santo Domingo already had undergone informal questioning by the Inquisition. The nature of the accusations against Sor María is reminiscent of charges brought against heretical groups of the Middle Ages and scripts the trials of beatas examined in the 1520s and 1530s. Adopted as their oracular holy woman by reform-minded Dominicans, Sor María traveled from town to town in the company of her brethren and through public ecstasies voiced prophecies and divinely inspired understandings. Her image as a visionary holy woman was bolstered by accounts of strenuous fasts and penitence, miraculous communion, and bleeding from her side. Despite public support from the king himself, Cardinal Cisneros, and the duke of Alba, Sor María was questioned about the genuineness of her ecstasies and stigmata, rumors that her confessor spent nights in her room and even on top of the bed, and the appropriate-ness of wearing ribbons and fancy hats and crimson skirts. Suspicion about sexual impropriety and religious fakery ultimately took its toll; though never formally tried and sentenced, Sor María was ordered back to the monastery and forbidden the company of male companions. Al-though Sor María's career did not coincide with the high point of alum-brado activity in the 1520s and her own letters and ecstatic utterances strongly indicate that she was not an alumbrado as such, her case did set the stage for later action by an Inquisition that mistrusted the integrity of attractive, charismatic women and discredited their teaching as being the-ologically unsound, if not heretical.

Francisca was an alumbrado in the general sense that she believed the Holy Spirit directly enlightened the soul, thus relegating the church to secondary status in the spiritual life of the individual. In nourishing rela-tionship with God, Francisca concurred with alumbrados that mental prayer was more efficacious than the rote recitation of words known as vocal prayer, and she specifically taught *recogimiento* (recollection), by which a person inwardly gathers his or her physical, emotional, and intel-lectual energies while quietly awaiting the infusion of God's grace and wisdom. A firm assessment of Francisca as an alumbrado is not possible because the beata left no letters or autobiographical accounts as did Sor María of Santo Domingo, nor is the written record of her trial available. Information about her teachings and details of her relationships with men are limited to trial documents of other people in which she appears as witness or by allusion in statements that defendants and other wit-nesses make. Given the prejudicial nature of the Inquisition process and the probability of scribal error or intervention in the recording process, documents in which Francisca somehow figures are necessary but not ab-solutely reliable sources of information about her beliefs and character. Documents of trials of Francisca's male companions are insightful, how-ever, and together with analyses by historians and theologians they pro-vide a basis for interpreting Francisca. The interpretative task implicit in studying the two sets of documents requires an examination of the men who most enthusiastically supported the beata and as such were espe-cially vulnerable to charges of improper conduct with her. The task is especially challenging when the men involved differ sharply in character from one another and are problematic within themselves as well. Francisco Ortiz and Antonio de Medrano illustrate the complexity of interpretation; at first blush they are a study in contrast, the one intellectual, ascetic, principled, the other selfish, ordinary, sensual, but under scrutiny those certainties yield, allowing for a finely nuanced, if not ambiguous, portrait to emerge, which in turn generates a problematic reading of the woman who "saved" them in times of crisis.

The Men in Her Life

Antonio de Medrano entered Francisca's company seven years before Ortiz arrived on the scene. Born in 1486 to an Old Christian family of upper-middle-class standing, Medrano left his native region of Rioja at the age of fifteen to study at the University of Salamanca. The young priest who fell under Francisca's spell at their first meeting in 1517 had suffered for years from excruciating guilt and excessive penitence occasioned by lapses into sensuality. Evidently he had been unable to control his sensual impulses in a healthy way until Francisca assured him that he could enjoy God and spiritual things without exaggerated penance. With peace of conscience his at last, thanks to Francisca's intervention, Medrano thus became convinced that his happiness depended on the beata, and he became her constant companion. In the trial of 1530, witnesses testified that in his excessive devotion to Francisca, Medrano had made claims for the beata's holiness which were so extravagant as to border on idolatry: that God had revealed the mystery of the Trinity to her at the age of three; that she could not sin mortally; and that she had infinite grace.[4]

Medrano may have praised Francisca's wondrous power to heal torments of the flesh, but when deprived of her companionship his actions demonstrate how fleeting was the conversion he attributed to her. After returning to his home region as an exile pursuant to the sentencing of May 14, 1524, he served as parish priest for two years, exercising what he believed to be a God-given gift to console feminine souls. Not surprisingly, his attitude toward women penitents, together with a legal mess involving himself and other clerics, led to excommunication and yet another turn before the Inquisition, this time in Logroño in 1526. By now the Edict of Toledo was in circulation, and several of the items defined therein as alumbrado heresies informed charges against him, principally that he believed himself to be inspired by God and as such superior to the sacraments and that he deemed himself free from carnal temptations and hence immune from sin. The last statement was particularly unsettling for the inquisitors, who read into it the double implication that he regarded himself as free from temptation on the one hand and free to indulge his sexual appetite on the other. The Inquisition's concern that Medrano viewed himself as well as Francisca as being above the church's moral and religious law was an issue that did not go away. During his trial after arrest in 1530, he was asked about his alleged belief that Francisca was infallible in her teaching: "He was asked if he said that Francisca Hernández did not say anything in which she might err because she was an enlightened person. He said that this witness did not say that she could not err but rather that he saw her speak such words that he believed she could not err in them."[5]

The reasonable tone of this response carries forward to the next day of interrogation (May 23) as he continues to defend Francisca's holiness and the purity of his own intentions:

> He was asked if he has read everything St. Paul says in Holy Scripture. He said he has read much of it. He was asked, since he has not read all of it, what has he not read yet. He said that he has read the epistles and that there is nothing in the epistles that he has not read and that he has read them many, many times. He was asked what are the things that he has seen in Francisca that he has not seen in Saint Paul. He said that he does not remember having said anything about Saint Paul; but that if he said something it was that he saw in Francisca an exceedingly great humility and that he saw his mother [Francisca] have a respect such that he never saw anyone have, and that he saw in her a simplicity and a childlike quality that he never saw anyone have; and that many people he saw who communicated with her were changed from being evil to servants of God, and that he saw in her a most marvelous wisdom, which he saw manifested many times with great theologians and this witness, who is a theologian and canonist, and this witness saw many other things in her.[6]

On May 24, 1531, the inquisitors advised Medrano of their dissatisfaction with his failure to reply candidly to their questions and informed him that he would be subject to torture so that he "might say and declare the truth about what he had been asked and about his intentions in his conversation with Francisca Hernández" [para que diga e declare la verdad cerca de lo que ha sido preguntado e de la intención que tuvo en la conversación de Fca. H.] (279). Objecting to torture on grounds that such treatment was not befitting a person of his lineage who was "learned and a priest and director of souls" [letrado y sacerdote y cura de almas] (279), Medrano "knelt down and with his hands together he said: 'Oh My God, you know that my intention has been to seek you and serve you in my work . . . That I gave up learning and pomp and I took refuge in charitable work wherein I consoled the disconsolate and counseled and gave strength to the afflicted and cared for their needs.' And he said other similar words, and getting up, he said: let it be done as they wish; that he pardons all who offended him, and may the will of God be done."⁷ Under repeated interrogation, Medrano insisted that his intentions toward Francisca were always good and consonant with his desire to honor matters of God and the Holy Catholic Faith.

When the sentence for torture was read, Medrano protested the decision as being unjust: had he not endured already fifteen months in prison, was he not a noble person and a priest, and besides, ill as he was, how could he survive the ordeal? His protestations in vain, Medrano was taken down to the torture chamber and undressed, all the while imploring God's mercy: "He was put on the rack of the said torture and warned always to tell the truth. He said that he never approached that woman except in service to God and he began to say 'into your hands, Lord, I commend my spirit.' And he began to confess to God. They began to tie his legs, from the thighs to the ankles with other cords and he was warned to tell the truth, and he said many times: 'How can such a thing be done among Christians? Have pity on me, Lord.'"⁸

At each tightening of the cords he protested his innocence and with the first pitcher of water poured down his throat insisted that "his intentions were never bad" [que nunca tuvo mala intención] (281). Another pitcher of water and the accused still did not relent. The cords were tightened on his left arm and leg. Again he declared that his intentions had always been good. But when another pitcher of water was ordered, he cried: "Take it away, take it away, I'll tell the truth." He was questioned further. If they wanted his intentions to be bad, he said, so be it, and he asked them to remove the cloth. The cloth was removed, and he was warned to tell the truth. Were he to communicate with Francisca Hernandez now, he said, he would do so in a different manner. Asked what would be the different manner, he said that he would act more prudently.[9] Medrano's answers still did not satisfy the examiners: "They resumed pouring water from the third pitcher and he said many times, 'Ay, they're killing me.' When they finished pouring the water from the third pitcher, he said: 'Have them take away the cloth.' And when it was removed, he said: 'Ay, Lord, so you want me to confess.' And he said besides: that everything I said was true and that I did have bad intentions; for you say it, and that they did not give such cruel torments to the martyrs."[10]

Finally Medrano confessed to the charges of improper behavior with the beata, admitting that "all communication with Francisca Hernández was carnal" [que toda comunicación de Fca. H. fue de carne] (282). When asked if he had caressed and kissed the beata, "he said that he had" [dixo que sí], and responding to questions about where these encounters had taken place, he identified "Salamanca and Valladolid in the house of Bachelor Bernardino and Pedro de Cazalla and that the nights he slept in the same house as the said Francisca Hernández he would get up some nights and lie down, dressed, on her bed and he would caress and kiss her and touch her all over lasciviously" [Salamanca e en Valladolid en casa del licenciado Bernaldino e Pedro de Caçalla y que las noches que durmió en su misma casa de la dicha Fca. H., se levantava algunas noches y se echava en su cama vestido y la retoçava y besava y tentava lascivamente todo] (282). Asked if she enjoyed his attentions, he answered that she did, but he insisted more than once that "he never had access to her" [no tuvo acceso a ella] (282).

On May 26, 1531, Medrano was brought before the Inquisition to hear read and have confirmed by him the confession he had made under torture. On April 21, 1532, he was sentenced: he was to appear in a public auto-da-fé in penitential attire and *abjure de vehementi*; he was condemned to perpetual confinement in a monastery, suspended from priestly ministry for two years, and forbidden any communication whatsoever with Francisca. Antonio de Medrano remained in prison until 1537, when the duke of Nájera successfully petitioned his pardon.

Until recently scholars were unanimous in their condemnation of Medrano as a lecherous scandal. Serrano y Sanz is nothing if not adamant that Medrano was a monster of obscenity and licentiousness,[11] while Bernardino Llorca shares this assessment, if not its strident tone, noting that "the actions he permitted himself with Francisca Hernández were too coarse for us to even understand how he could have good faith or good intentions toward her" [las acciones que se permitió con Francisca Hernández eran demasiado burdas para que ni siquiera podamos comprender cómo pudo tener en ellas buena fe o buena intención].[12] Román de la Inmaculada modified his assessment of Medrano, mindful that the confession was extracted under torture and attributing to the accused a complex psychology.[13] In granting latitude to Medrano, Román de la Inmaculada may have been influenced by the interpretation of Angela Selke, for whom Medrano was not a monster but a man struggling against his natural inclination to enjoy life and know God through all of his creation, including the beauty of the human body.[14] As a young man, that struggle had impelled Medrano to such arduous penitence that his health was severely impaired and his conscience gnawed by guilt and remorse. It was Francisca who released him from the prison of guilt when she persuaded him that God and spiritual things could be enjoyed without excessive penitence. Selke does not categorize this complex man as an alumbrado or an Erasmian but rather a follower of his own school of spirituality, for which a better name than alumbradismo would be *medranismo,* meaning that as an epicurean by disposition and drawn to carnal pleasures, especially eating, he viewed life as an immense banquet brimming with pleasures and delights to thrill the flesh as well as the spirit. This sensual way to find and penetrate the things of God was heresy for the inquisitors.

Serrano y Sanz may have relied on the testimony of many "impartial and trustworthy" [imparciales y fidedignos] (109) witnesses to reach the conclusion that Antonio de Medrano was a monster of lasciviousness, but alleged impartiality notwithstanding, his judgment is inadequate, if not untrue, for its failure to acknowledge the psychological complexity of the man. In my reading of the materials, I cannot dismiss the fact that

Medrano confessed under torture and then not until he had suffered several tightenings of the cords that bound his body and head to the rack and already had forced down his throat several pitchers of water. For a man of ill health and a supposedly weak will, Medrano demonstrated surprising fortitude in maintaining his innocence and insisting that if they, the examiners, said his intentions were bad, then so be it, but he, Medrano, never had bad intentions. To read the record of the torture is to see a man undone by pain to the point that he probably would have said whatever was demanded of him. As prison literature from other times attests, innocence is no guarantor of immunity from pain, nor is confession under torture the ratification of guilt.[15] A fairer assessment in that it allows for human frailty suggests that Medrano was a problematic man: weak yet strong, sensual yet spiritual, devoted to Francisca yet spurred by self-interest.

With respect to the portrait of Francisca Hernández which is in the making through the study of her relations with men, the significance of Medrano's being problematic rather than fixed in his moral and spiritual character evokes the possibility that she, too, was a problematic figure. If in her relationship with Medrano she can be seen as having good effects on him, which is the position of Selke, then a judgment of her as either slut or saint is dubious, especially when the problematic of her character intensifies in light of her relationship with the eminent Franciscan priest Francisco Ortiz.

Whereas Antonio Medrano's moral character nettled the Inquisition, Francisco Ortiz's reputation presented no comparable dilemma for the Holy Office. His reputation as a man of moral integrity was such that during his three years of imprisonment the empress herself requested his release or at least a shortening of his trial, as did the pope in a brief to the inquisitor general.[16] These actions account in part for one scholar's conclusion that Ortiz "apparently was a saintly but misled man" who "always acted with the best of intentions."[17] The inquisitors must have shared this view of Ortiz, for their original intent in arresting him was only to have him retract statements he had made in the scandalous sermon attacking the Holy Office's actions against Francisca. In the eyes of the Inquisition Ortiz's culpability lay in his insistence on the authority of his own conscience, which convinced him beyond any doubt that Francisca was innocent of the charges against her and thus placed him in direct opposition to the authority of the Inquisition and, from his perspective, perhaps outside its jurisdiction. Francisco was not charged with immoral behavior with Francisca as Medrano had been, although, ironically, he had sought her help for reasons similar to Medrano's.

Francisco Ortiz was born in Toledo in 1497 to a family of *converso* lineage. After his studies in theology and philosophy at the universities of Salamanca and Alcalá de Henares, he entered the Franciscan order and by 1520 was teaching logic to the monks at the Franciscan monastery at Pastrana. With Pastrana at that time a center of alumbrado activity and many Franciscan monasteries already linked to alumbrado teaching on prayer, it is likely that Ortiz came into contact with both *recogimiento* and the radical prayer of abandonment known as *dejamiento*. Despite a shy, retiring nature, Ortiz was named preacher of the order in 1521, a post that accorded him honor but did nothing to ease the anguish of an unruly flesh and wretched conscience, which earlier during his novitiate at the monastery of Cinfuentes had driven him to attempt suicide by throwing himself into the garden well, leading fellow monks to call him crazy and his superiors to transfer him to the Franciscan house at Salceda. For a young man of Ortiz's sensitivities and moral integrity, a sexual ordeal lasting four years and marked by a *fluxu seminis*[18] and pollution, meaning masturbation, must have been a kind of hell. The trial documents reveal Ortiz's gnawing despair:

> I say that for almost four years I suffered from a most painful and shameful temptation, which is that entirely against my will (even though I might cry out and hit and pinch myself), miserable miserable man, I would fall into pollution when I was awake. And though I know very well that my will was far from blame . . . I was sad and unhappy that by God's mercy I felt no remorse from such guilt, in my great misery I was filled with very great pain and sadness because of such a difficult and almost continual war that I saw within me.[19]

During his years at Alcalá another friar to whom he had admitted his troubles advised Ortiz that a certain Francisca Hernández had healed many monks of the same problem by granting their humble request for a sash of hers to tie about their body. In June 1523 Ortiz left Burgos, where he had been preaching, and headed for Valladolid and a meeting with Francisca. He was cured immediately. Understandably, he was as thoroughly persuaded as Medrano had been that Francisca was the channel for the Holy Spirit, and like Medrano, his allegiance to her was immediate and profound. According to Francisca herself, Ortiz became her most devoted follower, honoring her so deeply that whenever he came into her presence, he knelt, kissed the ground where she stood, and kissed her hands, careful not to squeeze them in unseemly fashion. Neither physical separation nor his superiors' disapproval of the beata loosed the ties of friendship between the priest and the beata during the years from his miraculous cure to the fateful sermon on her behalf. Ortiz depended so heavily on Francisca as his mediator with God as well as counselor in affairs of the order that he even declined the post of court preacher on her advice.

Once he was in the hands of the inquisitors, Ortiz's extravagant praise of Francisca Hernández must have instilled fear in the examiners' hearts that this woman had lured a priest of his education and stature from the path of orthodoxy and endangered his immortal soul. Undoubtedly they were appalled to hear Ortiz describe the so-called seven marvels of Francisca: (1) that without any formal study whatsoever, she could interpret Sacred Scripture, especially the Song of Solomon and the Sermon on the Mount; (2) that she had cured him with her sash; (3) that to become absorbed in God he had only to think of this spouse of God; (4) that he had been given a vision of her; (5) that she had discerned another monk's evil thoughts of her, which he then confessed and was cured; (6) that he had been able to compose and deliver sermons much better since he had known her; and (7) that despite his delicate health, he would gladly suffer martyrdom for what he knew to be true.

The fourth marvel, which is the vision he received of Francisca, illustrates the nearly idolatrous nature of Ortiz's admiration for the beata.

> Once when this holy woman was physically absent from me, her unworthy son, and being where it was impossible for me to attain to seeing her desirable presence, I saw her by her mercy, with these sinful and corporeal eyes. . . . While I was watching, I saw her, I say, raised above the earth and very near to me with a marvelous beauty looking

at me with the prettiest and kindest of eyes, like one who kept watch over me; such a thing awakened in my spirit a great admiration such as to render me stupid, not allowing me the liberty to go or to turn to go to her mercy, and a blessed joy on seeing such a something new that was so new.[20]

In testimony in which Ortiz compares Francisca to the Mother of Christ and, according to Selke, seemingly sings a hymn to Francisca which in effect identifies her with the Blessed Mother, he unhesitatingly admits that without Francisca his efforts to know God personally were futile.[21] These feelings and beliefs Ortiz did not hide but expressed openly in four letters that he wrote to the inquisitor general between April 7 and April 28 in defense of both Francisca's holiness and his public criticism of the Holy Office's actions against her.

During his ordeal as a prisoner of the Inquisition, Ortiz remained firm in his praise of Francisca and the purity of the friendship, even in face of potentially damaging testimony from Leonor de Vivero, who stated that the priest had visited the beata frequently at their residence in Valladolid, staying in her quarters for as many as two days at a time.[22] Not until the summer of 1531 did Ortiz have a change of heart about his beloved spiritual mother. On May 27, 1531, Francisca apparently had received a visit in her cell from Inquisitor Vaguer, who read to her Antonio de Medrano's full confession in which he had admitted to a carnal relationship with Francisca. Shortly thereafter, on June 2, 1531, Francisca herself confessed to improper behavior with Medrano. Selke conjectures that Francisca's statement about her relationship with Medrano and their secret meetings after the Inquisition had forbidden further communication between them was shown to Ortiz, a speculation that would explain at least in part why the Ortiz who had insisted on Francisca's grace and beauty and steadfastly refuted the charges against him would have a change of heart and ultimately retract all sixty-three statements that the Inquisition had attributed to him and branded as false, erroneous, blasphemous, rash, proud, contemptuous, and injurious to the Holy Office and its ministers.[23]

The judgment of history has been far kinder to Ortiz than to Medrano. As Tapia notes, Ortiz was sincere but misled;[24] Hamilton observes that his principal crime was devotion to Francisca;[25] and Serrano y Sanz is enthusiastic in praising Ortiz as "a noble ascetic, whose letters are worthy of praise, and a man of good understanding," though he does admit that Ortiz was "simple and too gullible" [ascético noble, cuyas epístolas son dignas de alabanza, y hombre de buen entendimiento, pero sencillo y crédulo en demasía].[26] However, evidence exists to suggest that Francisco Ortiz was not without his flaws. Testimony from companions like Gil López de Bejar indicates that Ortiz was a man who failed to obey his superiors,[27] while the record of statements ascribed to him reveals a man who in upholding the value of individual conscience devalued the church and the Inquisition as ultimate arbiters of divine will. Selke observes that Ortiz's attitude in finally retracting the statements and professing total submission to the Holy Office was arrogant and self-serving: rather than humbly acknowledging his errors and obediently accepting the judgment of the Inquisition, Ortiz rationalized his actions in asserting that he had delayed retracting his statements until God granted him the gift of "wanting to deny himself purely for God" [el querer del todo negar a sí mesmo puramente por Dios].[28] As Selke notes, "this total negation of himself . . . presupposes a total disdain for the reasons and arguments of his judges, and this is the greatest pridefulness he has shown in all the trial" [esa negación total de sí mismo . . . presupone un total desprecio de las razones y argumentos de sus jueces, y es la mayor soberbia que mostró en todo su proceso] (297). Ortiz's ultimate judge, then, is not the Holy Office but God, and the only testimony of merit is that of his own conscience. In rationalizing his retraction and act of submission, Ortiz is no obedient son of the church but a man intent on salvaging his honor much as Francisca was on saving her skin, if not her immortal soul.

On April 21, 1532, sentence was passed in the city of Toledo: Francisco Ortiz was to proceed from jail to the city's principal church, without cloak, bare headed, candle in hand, where the sentence would be read and he would retract all the propositions. He was not to preach for five years, would be confined to a monastery for two years, and was prohibited from celebrating mass publicly. Of course he was forbidden any communication whatsoever with Francisca Hernández.

If Francisca's relationships with men were ambiguous, it may be for the reason that their behavior and motivations were other than simple and straightforward. True, she seems to recognize in Ortiz a sincerity, integrity, and loyalty that she honors by testifying to the Inquisition that he treated her with unfailing respect and by not implicating him in scandal as she did other men. Perhaps Francisca was a woman who consciously or otherwise tempered her relationships with men to accord with their individual needs and character and with her own ambitions as well. Whatever may have been her motivation in friendships with men, the evidence is that she reciprocated Ortiz's honorable intentions; in so doing she belies the image of seductive and corrupt alumbrada conveyed by both her contemporaries and later scholars and suggested in documents that refer to her activities in prison.

Francisca in Prison

As trial documents of other men and women incarcerated at the same time reveal, Francisca was not idle during her imprisonment. She figures as a witness for the prosecution in trials of former associates, in some cases, even dear friends, which suggests that she was trying to save herself from a harsh sentence or perhaps death by turning "state's evidence," as it were. As close as she and Medrano had been for years, loyalty did not bring her running to his defense; on the contrary, she answered questions about her behavior with him in such a way as to deflect guilt onto him and other people. When questioned about clandestine meetings with Medrano after the Inquisition had forbidden them to communicate with each other and ordered them to maintain a distance of five leagues between them, she explained that other people had arranged the meetings without consulting her and without her consent. Asked why she had not confessed previously to disobeying the Inquisition's orders, she replied that "since she had not willingly spoken with Medrano, she was not obliged to mention it" [creía que en no aver hablado al dicho M. de su voluntad, que no era obligada a lo dezir].[29] In other instances she invoked the defense of good intentions to justify the embraces and kisses they had exchanged or that of illness and the need for solace to explain Medrano's lying on her bed: "Asked if it was true that some person would lie on the bed of this witness [Francisca] some nights, she said that some times when this witness was ill, Tovar and M. Cabrera y Villareal would go where she was lying down and sometimes the said M. would lie on the bed on top of the covering on the bed where she was lying and sleep a while."[30]

Another approach she took on her own behalf was to turn the spotlight of guilt onto an alleged perpetrator; the inquisitors themselves opened the door to this tactic when they inquired if there were men other than Medrano who had tried to have their way with her. In reply, she identified a certain Cabrera as well as Pedro de Segura of the Hieronymite order and the Franciscan Pedro de Mena, in each case painting herself as the heroine who discerns their evil intentions and thwarts their unwelcome advances. Cabrera, for example,

> came one morning where this witness was in her own home in Salamanca, and this witness [Francisca] was in bed, and he went to kiss this witness's hands and this witness went to kiss his hands, and then the said Cabrera squeezed her hands very cunningly, and as this witness discerned his bad intentions, she responded rigorously and he told her he would give his soul to the devil to have a child by this witness and he tried to fondle her breasts and kiss her and this witness resisted him and pushed him away.[31]

The trial documents of Luis de Beteta, a priest from Toledo accused of alumbradismo, illustrate how freely Francisca undertook the business of testifying against former associates; not only does she respond to inquiries about Beteta, but she speaks at length about her one-time devotee, Bernardino de Tovar, as well as three other people who allegedly constituted an alumbrado or, as Llorca suggests, a Protestant cell: María Ramírez, servant to Miguel Eguía; the bachelor Diego de Villareal; and one Ina López.[32] The inquisitors must have prompted Francisca's answers by reading to her propositions from the Edict of Toledo so that she could recognize the implicit alumbrado offenses in their questions and fashion answers that were correspondingly condemning. For example, when Francisca testified that Tovar scoffed at indulgences, vocal prayer, and the need to confess evil thoughts, she clearly was answering to implied charges that he espoused both alumbrado and Lutheran beliefs.

Francisca's strategy of "proving" her innocence by demonstrating guilt in others was turned against her by such defendants as the noted humanist Juan de Vergara, who was arrested in June 1533 on charges of insulting the Holy Office, being a Lutheran, and teaching alumbrado errors. Francisca and Vergara came to know each other only too well in a duel of accusations which lasted four years. She took the offensive in 1530, accusing him of Lutheran beliefs on four occasions in the period from July to October. Vergara retaliated four years later, on January 29, 1534, painting her as a hostile and thus unreliable witness because she bore him, Vergara, ill will for his efforts years before to free his brother, Bernardino de Tovar, from her clutches. According to Vergara Francisca was "a woman publicly notorious for giving false testimony" [muger públicamente infamada de testigo falso], while he was a man "who never frequented beaterías nor had gone to extremes in devotion" [ni he andado jamás en beaterías ni extremidades de devoçion].[33]

In some cases Francisca's testimony against former colleagues originated in rivalries that had been simmering long before imprisonment shattered whatever illusions of solidarity remained among the alumbrados. The rancor that gripped the rivals was obvious in Alcaraz's earlier trial, from 1524 to 1529, when he implicated Francisca in the alumbrado heresy, raised questions about her chastity in accusing the cleric Lope de Rueda of undue familiarity with her during her stay in Valladolid, and vehemently denounced what he regarded as her pernicious influence on such men as Francisco Ortiz and Bishop Cazalla. Alcaraz's resentment of Francisca probably was rooted as much in personalities as religious beliefs. The three women who were most prominently linked with alumbrado and Lutheran belief and who inspired a discipleship among religious and laity were Isabel de la Cruz, María de Cazalla, and Francisca Hernández. Isabel had been María de Cazalla's mentor before envy spoiled their friendship, and she already had undergone trial by the Inquisition, beginning in 1524 and ending five years later with her appearance in an auto-da-fé. Alcaraz regarded Isabel as his spiritual mother, and he took advantage of his travels supervising his employer's vast estates to spread the alumbrado beliefs she had instilled in him as well as to ferret out competing groups of alumbrados. The most threatening competition he discovered was Francisca and her disciples. Alcaraz was also wary of Francisca because praises of her which he had heard from Ortiz's very lips convinced him that her hold on the priest was dangerous. In

1524 Alcaraz had traveled to Valladolid to meet with Francisca for the specific purpose of converting her; when Francisca refused to see him, not only were his plans thwarted, but an outrage enkindled which smoldered until he had his day in court many years later.[34]

Francisca's role as witness for the prosecution reached a high—or, better said, a low—point in the trial of María de Cazalla, sister of Pedro Cazalla, whose hospitality Francisca had enjoyed in Valladolid.[35] Gratitude for hospitality rendered lost out to the more pressing concern for survival: on three occasions, in July, September, and October 1530, Francisca testified against María de Cazalla, casting the net of implication wide to snare not only María's two brothers, Pedro and the bishop, but a veritable host of other men, including the printer Miguel Eguía and the master Castillo from Alcalá. Francisca identified María as the leader of the alumbrados at Pastrana and Guadalupe, alleging that both María and her brother the bishop had denigrated exterior works, vocal prayer, fasts, penitence, and reverence for images. She further testified that she knew of letters María had written in which she denounced virginity in favor of the married state and claimed to have experienced no pleasure in the sexual act.

In addition to her role as witness for the prosecution, Francisca stars in an intriguing tale embedded in the trial documents of María de Cazalla which tells about prison officials who befriended alumbrados by facilitating the flow of letters from one prisoner to another, leaving doors unlocked so prisoners could visit from room to room, and accepting gifts and money in exchange for services. The jailer, Juan Sánchez, figures prominently in the tale, and he was made answerable to such charges as that "he leaped about and danced in the cells, in the prisoners' rooms with them and sang popular songs in three parts and other things and left some cells unlocked" [Que saltava y bailava en las cárceles, en las cámaras de los presos con ellos y cantava villancicos a tres vozes y otras cosas y dexaba algunas cárceles por cerrar].[36] And why, it was asked, "had he kept silent about what Pareja told him about how Francisca Hernández went to Fray Ortiz's room to talk with him" [Que por qué a callado lo que Pareja le contó de como Francisca Hernández yba al aposento del frayle Ortiz ablarle].[37] The possibility that Juan Sánchez was smitten with Francisca is not far-fetched in light of the long list of men claimed by her

[93]

charm and reputed sanctity. To what extent Francisca benefited from a favored status in prison is not clear. What is known is that by the end of 1532 she was confined in a convent of the beatas of St. Benedict, where, according to Serrano y Sanz, it was not long before she moved to the house of one Pérez de Montalvo and effectively disappears from the pages of history.

Francisca and the Judgment of History

Just as a final judgment of Francisca by the Inquisition is not existent, so there is no consensus among scholars that she was either harlot parading as holy woman or saintly creature unjustly maligned. The latter position is taken by the German scholar Edward Boehmer, who, in his 1865 study on Francisco Ortiz and Francisca Hernández based on examination of the Ortiz trial documents in the Kaiserllich-Königliche Bibliotheklich in Halle, portrays Francisca in glowing terms as the precursor of a true re-form movement in Spain akin to Lutheranism on the continent.[38] Span-ish historians with access to trial records for such defendants as María de Cazalla, which disclose Francisca testifying against former associates in the alumbrado movement, do not share Boehmer's enthusiasm, although they fall short of agreeing with Serrano y Sanz, who accuses her of pride, hypocrisy, and false testimony and challenges her chastity. According to this historian Francisca had a love affair with Bernardino de Tovar at a time when she was revered as a holy woman, and she subsequently se-duced Ortiz.[39]

Bernardino Llorca is nearly as virulent as Serrano y Sanz in calling Francisca a licentious woman and "a model of the seductive and corrupt alumbrados" [un modelo de los alumbrados seductores y corrompidos].[40] No doubt Llorca and Serrano y Sanz assessed Francisca in light of the testimony of such contemporary detractors as Juan de Vergara, who, in the defense he presented before the Inquisition on January 29, 1534, stated that Francisca's testimony ought to be discredited "for one reason because she [was] a woman and for another because she [was] a lying, slanderous, hypocritical, false and sham of a woman" [lo primero porque es muger; lo otro porque es muger criminosa, perjura, hypocrita, falsa, e simuladora],[41] a woman, moreover, who had borne him enmity since the first day of her friendship with his brother, when she realized how deeply he, Vergara, disapproved of her. María de Cazalla was equally adamant in her opposition to Francisca: even if Francisca were Saint Clare herself and Saint Francis among her followers, she, María de Cazalla, still would be suspicious of the woman's loose behavior with her devotees.[42] Angela Selke seems open to the possibility that Francisca was not quite the despicable woman portrayed by Vergara, María de Cazalla, and later scholars of the Inquisition, though she does not side with Boehmer in singing the beata's praises as a true reformer.

Given the uncertain reliability of Inquisition documents and the problematic nature of confessions exacted under torture, readers of trial records are hard pressed to make categorical judgments about any of the characters in the trial documents, whether they be the accused, witnesses, attorneys, officials of the Holy Office, or prison personnel. Moreover, the fact that the reality of torture or threat of it persuaded some people to "confess" while others successfully held their ground and maintained innocence is no reliable indicator of a person's character, certainly not of guilt or innocence. María de Cazalla has fared well at the hands of scholars and theologians in large part because she clung to her innocence despite being subjected to excruciating torture. In this respect she obviously was unlike Francisca Hernández, and the outcome of her trial was different as well: whereas Francisca was forced into retirement, as it were, María de Cazalla was allowed to return to her home and family after paying a fine.

Perhaps the scholar's assessment of Francisca today must take into account the problematic situation of women in the early decades of the sixteenth century and the paradoxical relationship that Francisca and other "holy" women of the period experienced with men who were themselves rent by contradiction and paradox. Francisca lived in times that were heady with the lure of opportunities for women to escape the confines of poverty, ignorance, prejudice, and obscurity into the limelight of spiritual fame. The religious climate fostered a rush to sanctity among women from all social classes, but women from the lower classes may have had the edge in attracting attention because their gifts might seem to redound more splendidly to God's glory than those of highborn women. Erasmian-flamed spirituality was in the air, and the examples of holy women like Saint Catherine of Siena, whose life the eminent Cardinal Cisneros himself had ordained be translated into Spanish for the edification of his flock, were on lips everywhere.

Spain called for its own holy women. Sor María of Santo Domingo, among others, had answered the call. Francisca was soon to follow. Though not associates as such in reforming movements, both Francisca and Sor María endured the same rumors and recriminations that haunted women who left the safety of home and convent to forge their spiritual identity in an arena where the bounds of religious respectability were blurred. The margins that Francisca, Sor María, and other women occupied afforded them exhilarating opportunities to create ways of being a woman but at the same time exposed them to perils unforeseen. As Francisca and her "sisters" in reform and adventure became increasingly visible in exercising their spiritual authority, accusations of sexual impropriety, whether founded or specious, were sure to befall them. Could these women, moving in a society accustomed to strict notions of sexual behavior for women, have escaped sexual innuendo as they traveled about the country in the company of male admirers?

So if on the one hand Francisca suffers the brand "opportunist" for taking advantage of the moment to become independent in spirit, even if still dependent on the economic largesse of men; to be famous, though of obscure parentage; to be acclaimed a wise and inspired woman, though without formal education, on the other hand, is it not to her credit that she claims her own identity from out of the faceless crowds of women for whom the patriarchy of church and state dictated the terms of their existence? Some valor must have been required of Francisca to push against the bounds of decorum and convention and fashion a life for herself. Intelligence and perspicacity were hers as well as she employed to advantage her natural gifts of charm, good looks, and the wit to discern and care for the needs of men who sought her help.

If Francisca can be reproached for testifying against former associates and for flattering the jailer into making prison life somewhat comfortable, she nonetheless deserves admiration for finding within the system of the Inquisition the means to protect herself from the deleterious actions of an institution and its officials which violated her very person in order to determine if she was a virgin. When a system is by nature prejudiced against the accused, as was the Inquisition, then perhaps the criteria by which just-minded people render moral judgments are put in question. Francisca Hernández was no saint, but neither was she a slut. Such categories falter before the human problematic wherein survival may be not only its own reward but its moral justification as well.

CHAPTER FIVE

María de Cazalla

The Grievous Price
of Victory

ANGEL ALCALÁ

María de Cazalla is one of countless people who would have passed
through history without a trace had it not been for her appearance before
an Inquisition tribunal that was scrupulous about record keeping. The
simple fact of her appearance demonstrates the sociological value of an
institution that was concerned with common folk as well as the rich and
powerful and at the same time raises perplexing questions: Why was an
ordinary woman who, after her trial, disappeared into the hollow of the
unknown called by the tribunal in the first place? What ideological con-
fusions prompted the Inquisition to believe it had sufficient reason to intervene in cases like hers, which had nothing to do with the original
charge of looking after purported "heresy" of Judeo-converts? While trying to answer such questions in the process of summarizing María's trial
we may be in for some surprises, but we also may come to see why she has
won the admiration of those who know her, if only through the documents, and why her trial is appreciated as one of the most compelling in
the long duration of the infamous tribunal.

A Climate of Confusion

Some explanation for María's entanglement with the Inquisition lies in
the climate of reform and innovation which characterized Spain in the
first third of the sixteenth century, when the three movements of *alum-*

bradismo, Erasmianism, and Lutheranism coincided at the same time and in a geographical circle formed roughly by the cities of Toledo, Guadalajara, Alcalá de Henares, and Valladolid.[1] Given the ideological similarities among the three movements, it was only natural that the watchdogs of the Inquisition confused the movements in the belief that a person who was inclined toward even one aspect of a movement necessarily advocated all its practices and ideas and had to be contaminated by the worst of the lot—Lutheranism. Roland Bainton, among others, identifies similarities in the movements:

> The *alumbrados* had in common with the Erasmians the view that the rites of the church are valueless as external performances. They agreed with the Lutherans on the worthlessness of good works for the attainment of salvation and on the denial of purgatory and indulgences. The big difference was the focusing of their piety on God the Father and the Spirit rather than on God the Son. The Lutherans, in turn, were not as remote as is often assumed from the Erasmians. The main point of difference was that Erasmus was still in the church whereas Luther had been cast out.[2]

Although scholars and historians have struggled with the legacy of confusion about the relationship of the three movements, recent studies seem to agree that the interiorization of Christian spirituality is one of the trademarks of alumbradismo and a point of connection with Erasmianism.[3] Embracing the Erasmian belief that Scripture was the repository of authentic Christian doctrine, the alumbrados believed that the Holy Spirit illuminated their understanding of Scripture and guided their spiritual lives, thus rendering ecclesiastical hierarchy useless and prejudicial. The church was understandably alarmed at this attitude of the alumbrados, but it tended to leniency in cases in which piety more than dogma was the issue. Such may have been the case of María de Cazalla, which would explain in part the ultimate disposition of her case.

The critical difficulty in studying Spanish alumbradismo stems from the fact that the alumbrados were not writers; their words were kept for posterity through the depositions of adversaries or the proceedings of their trials. Other than their answers to interrogation during trial, the only extant writings by the alumbrados themselves are two letters dated

June 22, 1534, and October 1, 1534, written by one of the leaders, Pedro Ruiz de Alcaraz.[4] From Alcaraz's confession in Toledo in 1527 we learn that his "conversion" to the attitudes and ideals of the *beata* Isabel de la Cruz, who supposedly started the alumbrado movement, took place around 1509, several years before any influence from Luther or even Erasmus could reach the academic community in Spain.

Isabel de la Cruz was a beata of the Franciscan Third Order who, from around 1509, had been practicing and teaching from her residence in Guadalajara a kind of prayer called *dejamiento,* or abandonment (to God's will). A seamstress by profession, Isabel taught embroidery to daughters of the nobility. Franciscan friars of Toledo and other convents, as well as pious lay men and women, were attracted to Isabel's form of religiosity with its emphasis on seeking God in the inner depths of the soul through total dependence on the light of the Holy Spirit. One of Isabel's disciples was Pedro Ruiz de Alcaraz, who served as accountant for the duke of Infantado in his palace in Guadalajara and later entered the service of the marquis of Villena in the castle of Escalona near Toledo. The father of several children, Alcaraz was himself a lay preacher and propagandist, in some respects even a systematizer of the movement.

Not until 1519 did the Inquisition receive a written accusation that suggested the possibly heretical nature of alumbradismo. The accusation was the work of one Mari Núñez, herself a beata and, before a rupture in their friendship, a disciple of Isabel de la Cruz. The tribunal waited more than four years before turning its attention to the denunciation.[5] After Alonso Manrique, archbishop of Seville, was appointed inquisitor general on September 10, 1523, one of his first actions was to heed the written denunciation that had lain dormant for several years. The immediate result was the imprisonment in 1524 of Isabel de la Cruz, Pedro Ruiz de Alcaraz, and a priest from Pastrana by the name of Gaspar de Bedoya and the ensuing publication of an edict granting a thirty-day grace period to people who would accuse themselves or others of "heresy" according to the newly publicized criteria. A subsequent edict dated September 23, 1525, summarized the doctrine of alumbradismo in forty-eight articles and threatened any person found guilty according to the dictates of the articles with prosecution, imprisonment, confiscation of properties, and other punishments. In Toledo on April 21, 1529, Isabel de la Cruz, Pedro

Ruiz de Alcaraz, and Gaspar de Bedoya appeared in an auto-da-fé and were sentenced to prison for several years. In addition to the edicts, Alcaraz's two letters, and confessions by him and Isabel, the most important documents regarding the inquisitorial interpretation of alumbradismo are the eighteen folio summaries in Latin of the propositions attributed by witnesses to the three defendants and appended to the manuscript proceedings of Alcaraz's trial.[6]

In this atmosphere of mounting concern about the alumbrados, María de Cazalla comes into view. Sister of the well-known Franciscan bishop Juan de Cazalla, María was married and the mother of several children when she came under Isabel's influence. Isabel and María became such close friends that when mysterious events caused María and her family to move from Guadalajara to the small town of Horche, "where her daughters could not learn" [donde las dichas sus fijas no podían asy deprender], María arranged for Isabel to educate her daughters in Guadalajara and "teach the daughters of the said Maria de Cazalla how to embroider with other girls, daughters of noble men" [mostrar labrar sus hijas de la dicha María de Caçalla juntamente con otras donzellas, hijas de honbres de bien].[7] María's trust in Isabel as an educator would have been out of place had the two women not found themselves in intimate spiritual agreement.

María de Cazalla was not arrested and tried with the others despite her association with both Isabel and Alcaraz and even though her name appears in Mari Núñez's letter of denunciation as well as in depositions of 1525 and later by witnesses in Pastrana against their own priest, Bedoya. Several years would elapse before María herself would have her turn in the court and prison of the Inquisition; by then her relationship with mentor and friends in the alumbrado circle had cooled.

The Charges

María's inquisitorial proceedings open with the February 28, 1532, text by the official prosecutor of the Toledo tribunal, Diego Ortiz de Angulo, to its chief inquisitor, Alonso Mexía; in this text the prosecutor had asked for María's imprisonment on the basis of depositions against her by Diego Hernández (a foolish cleric who liked to dress as a woman but had several women lovers) and by the dubious beata from Valladolid Francisca Hernández and other "sayings" [dichos] attributed to alumbrados and set down in what was called a "book" that served as a reference for the inquisitors in determining alumbrado heresy. The subterranean phase of her trial had been under way for several years. On April 16, 1531, the prosecutors had presented the evidence to theologians in Toledo and Avila for their assessment; judging the propositions to be injurious to evangelical doctrine, fatuous, scandalous, suspicious, arrogant, risky, heretical, or damned by the Holy Office, the experts voted for María's imprisonment, but not without first asking the opinion of the members of the Supreme Council of the Inquisition, which at the time happened to be in Medina del Campo. This step was mandatory in cases of alumbrados and as such speaks eloquently to the alarm that the movement had provoked. The Suprema sent its instructions on October 26, 1531, but several months elapsed before the local Toledo tribunal sent María to prison: the order was signed on April 22, 1532, and María immediately entered prison next to the church of San Vicente. On May 3 she would appear before the court for the first time.

At this moment we learn of two sets of accusations against María going back as far as 1525. The first set of accusations originated in Pastrana and Guadalajara and was ratified later, in 1533; the second set consists of more specific and damaging accusations by Mari Núñez, Francisca Hernández, Pedro de Alcaraz, and Diego Hernández, all of them extracted from the trials of Francisca, Alcaraz, and Diego, together with their ratifications eight years later.

In the first set of accusations the four charges were based entirely on hearsay: (1) People *say* they heard María say that she would give more authority to Isabel than to Saint Paul and all the saints. (2) She said that when she was in the so-called carnal act with her husband, she felt all divine, more united with God than at the highest level of prayer. (3) When one witness looked at some sheets of paper that María had, the witness did not find anything about Catholic truth but alumbrado things like not having conceived her children with pleasure, despising virginity in favor of matrimony, and not bowing her head at mass. (4) She said that a person commits mortal sin by loving somebody or something for the love of God. In view of Mari Núñez's questionable moral character—and she was the main witness in the trials of Isabel and Alcaraz—the Suprema recommended looking at her *tachas,* perhaps hinting at a possible disqualification of her testimony, and ordered clarification of the third proposition because it appeared that she meant something else. However, the Suprema also gave instructions to examine her with care. In an atmosphere of gossip and an instinctive popular fear of the Inquisition, the charges multiplied until by the end of the long trial they numbered thirty-six.

Although the texts of the accusations and ratifications fill many gaps in our knowledge of details and circumstances, they basically support charges that to the modern reader seem ridiculous. We learn of Bishop Juan de Cazalla's frequent visits to Pastrana; of witty sayings by María, as when she questions going on pilgrimages when God's only food is our heart; of gatherings attended by pious men and women drawn by María's religious reputation where she read and commented on passages by Saint Paul. Two general charges were typical of the times: some people observed that María omitted ceremonial and external signs of piety during mass—a sure sign of alumbradismo—and several others spoke of the abominable scandal of a woman preaching and people going to hear her.[8]

In the serious charges brought by Mari Núñez and ratified by other witnesses, it is not hard to discover deep misunderstandings and selfish motivations. A certain Francisco Carrillo, for example, explained María's comments on love as meaning that it is necessary to love everything out of love of God, and Mari Núñez believed that Isabel and María agreed with Alcaraz when he expressed regret for not having sinned more—a possible misunderstanding similar to that implied in the saying attributed to Luther, "pecca fortiter, sed crede fortius." The damage to María in the depositions by Francisca, Alcaraz, and Diego Hernández was based on their tendency to link her religious attitude to the teachings and preaching of her brother the bishop, who was already dead at the time their ratifications began in 1530. Clearly Francisca and Alcaraz intended to blame the entire alumbrado movement on Juan and María de Cazalla for the purpose of exonerating themselves.[9] In his lengthy deposition the cleric Diego Hernández not only strove to exculpate himself while charging others but also vented an irrepressible urgency to gossip and place himself at the center of certain events. However, he did mention concepts that must have been discussed in learned circles interested in new forms of piety: prayer, sacraments, Erasmus, monasteries, hierarchy, the value of papal bulls. Speaking of her five daughters, María had told him once: "People don't love each other but for money and beauty. I don't see any Christian man to whom I'd give my daughters since marrying them now is but placing them in a whorehouse. . . . I prefer them to be whores than nuns."[10] Furthermore, María had advised him to consult with Juan in order to overcome certain religious fears: "For the Bishop, her brother, to make me lose my little fears, I understand that he would have given me freedom to proceed anywhere, with eagerness and joy, since this was his job, to free Christians from servitude and grant them evangelical liberty."[11]

While Diego attributed the religious attitude of the Cazallas to either frequent contact with Isabel or Erasmian influences, García de Vargas, the family tailor and a good friend of Diego's, was the first to state, in April 1532, that María had read and praised the *Diálogo de doctrina cristiana* by Juan de Valdés, which had been banned by the Inquisition early in 1532, just after its publication. He added another charge, that María used to receive communion without having confessed her sins because "everybody took her for an alumbrada" [porque la tenían por alunbrada] (89). It is astonishing to discover that the Inquisition paid careful attention and gave credibility to statements from persons of questionable integrity like Francisca Hernández and Diego Hernández, but their charges proved to be most damaging to María and most enduring.

María's real trial begins with her appearance before the tribunal on May 3, 1532, for the reading of a "confession" she had presented earlier to the inquisitors, on March 2, 1525, in response to the publication of the edict of grace. In that confession she humbly acknowledged a possible sin of pride in inviting others to serve Jesus Christ with the same liberty she had with her confessors and brothers, and she spoke of "a distressing desire to see God without veils and without my body" [un deseo congoxoso de ver a Dios ya sin velos e sin mi cuerpo] (99). In her counsels to clerics and lay people she insisted on Christian liberty, that they not serve God out of fear of hell but only because he so deserves service. In conclusion she stated: "I don't know anything else about those errors charged to those called alumbrados."[12]

Following the format for the first hearing, María was requested to speak freely about herself and to guess why she was there. She told of her birth in Palma del Río (Córdoba) and of her parents, Gonçalo Martínez and Isabel de Cazalla, both baptized Jews who had been reconciled after some lapse into Judaism. María pretended not to know anything about her grandparents, which is a clear sign that they were still Jews. On May 8 she was asked again to inculpate herself and others, but she seemed to recall only a couple of trifles; she begged for time and promised to say more if asked appropriately. On May 14 she persisted in her silence. Only in a series of hearings between June 7 and June 12 did she start to give some answers to questions stemming from the accusations. Although these answers were not written by María, the supposed exactitude of the transcriptions by inquisitorial scribes was such that the answers they put in her mouth might be taken as her own words. With extraordinary precision in wording and with intellectual clarity she replied to the prosecutor's barrage of questions and at the same time stated the doctrinal grounds for her religious behavior. A sampling of her replies:

She said that she doesn't remember having said that she would only receive the sacrament of confession or go to mass to comply with the mandate, but she does remember having said sometimes that we should look for God in the living temples though she didn't deny that God was in the temples and in his sacraments and that we must go to material temples.

. . . if we cleaned our conscience and got rid of bad habits as diligently as we clean and adorn altars, God would rejoice much in it.

. . . it might be that she said that this was a hard thing that God had obliged us to tell our sins to another man, but she didn't reject it for that reason but rather thought it was good.

When asked if she said that when her husband paid her the marriage debt she was all divine and that being with him in the carnal act she was closer to God than when she was in the loftiest prayer in the world, she said that she never said such a thing.

When asked if she said that she conceived her children without carnal delight and that she didn't love them like her children but like her neighbors' children, she said that she often asked her confessors if it was possible to conceive her children without carnal delight because it seemed to her that she didn't feel those pleasures that she used to in carnal delight. . . . When asked what is the reason why there was a difference . . . she said that the reason was because she was busy in acts of penitence and in observing and restraining her senses the best she could.

. . . since she has been weak and tempted by the flesh . . . she forced herself and with great pain paid her debt, and in order not to fall into disorder and delectation she made herself think of some step of the Passion or of the final judgment.

When she was asked if she taught some persons not to cling to the accidents of the exterior works and acts of adoration and prayer and humiliation, she said that what she said many times was that exterior works must be taken as a means to reach the interior ones.[13]

María displayed courage in admitting that she always thought well of both Isabel and Alcaraz, who already were serving their jail terms in the same prison. She was courageous, too, when questioned about her views of Valdés, Luther, and Erasmus, openly admitting that she often had praised the book *Doctrina cristiana,* which someone sent her from Alcalá de Henares, although she noted that some matters in the book could have been stated better and without scandal. Adding an interesting point, she remembered that "bachelor Tovar reprimanded Valdés for publishing such a book so quickly without correcting and emending it" [bachiller Tovar reprehendía al dicho Valdés porque avía publicado el dicho libro tan açeleradamente syn más le corregir e emendar] (118). With respect to Luther, in the beginning she had heard he was very religious, but she attributed to him only the appearance of being religious because when he criticized vices and disorders among prelates and ministers of the church, he had used the occasion to say bad things.

All her explanations notwithstanding, prosecutor Ortiz de Angulo officially accused her of "believing Lutheran errors and errors of those who call[ed] themselves alumbrados, who should better [have been] called blind, and other kinds of heresy" [creyendo los errores luteranos e de los que se dizen alunbrados, que mejor se llaman çiegos, e otras espeçies de

herejía] (127). María answered the detailed justification for these charges
with both an oral and a written reply, the latter dated June 17 and consisting of three folios torn from the original bundle and now preserved in
the archives of Halle University. Apparently written in her own hand-
writing, the reply is a model of good Spanish, revealing a cultivated, sincere, and courageous personality. In striking contrast with Alcaraz, who
was always determined to blame everybody else, including María, she refused to accuse others: "I state that I don't know anything more about
suspect persons than what I have said."[14] An official defense attorney,
Gabriel de Quemada, was then appointed by the tribunal with the agreement of her brother-in-law, Pedro de Rueda. According to the format of
the Holy Office, Quemada presented a stern defense, pointing to formal
flaws in the prosecutor's accusation, mainly that the time of the crimes
and the place where they were committed were not identified, and reaf-
firming the Catholic faith and determination of the defendant.

The bulk of the trial followed the usual pattern of inquisitorial as well
as civil procedure when the weight of a case rested on the credibility of
witnesses who had to be called to ratify or rectify their sayings; the tribunal pronounced its enlightened sentence according to the testimony of
the witnesses. On September 11 and 22, respectively, Francisca Hernández and her maid, María Ramírez, ratified and elaborated all their former
accusations; Pedro de Alcaraz was asked for a new testimony months
later, on February 20, 1533. On October 17 the "publication of witnesses"
took place, which is the systematic presentation of charges without identification of the witnesses. According to the noted historian Juan Antonio Llorente, this action amounted to "an incomplete copy of the testimonies that [kept] out anything favorable to the defendant and what
might [have helped] to identify the witnesses, as well as those who confessed their ignorance of what they were asked about."[15] This procedure,
therefore, meant cruelty and lack of due process for countless people and
for anonymous accusers the opportunity to take hidden revenge. Some
historians, however, see in this secrecy a convenient means both to en-
hance objectivity, on the grounds that false witnesses could be prosecuted, and to preclude possible retaliation by defendants or their relatives. The publication of María's accusers summarized the depositions
of nineteen witnesses. Again she answered orally and then in writing

with the assistance of her brother-in-law, Pedro. It was already March 1533. In her answers we may admire the same qualities that have made María so appealing to modern scholars familiar with these proceedings: while first struggling to guess the identity of each individual witness in order not to misfire in her reply, she differentiated gossip from truth, re-affirmed her spiritual position, and even dared to clarify it with new theoretical formulations. Again, a sampling of her responses:

> Possibly . . . when having a Book of Hours in my hand, I read a verse or two but not in any way as to teach in public or pretend authority as [the witness] says . . . and anyhow the witness doesn't point to any error I might have stated

> If one should be accused of a crime or of preaching for reading an Epistle in the vernacular, few devout women able to read would not be guilty; especially since what these said witnesses say that I said is "we are to love God," which is more in my favor. . . . Those who give good advice deserve praise rather than having it suppressed, for the world doesn't lack for people who give bad advice.

> . . . I say that it is possible that I said that it was a higher thing to contemplate Christ our Redeemer in the divinity than in the humanity . . . and this is not to be doubted for Holy Scripture says so.

> . . . I have grumbled about some preachers who preach coldly and not with as much doctrine as I'd like for the profit of my soul and of other faithful Christians.

> . . . what I said perhaps would be that our love for our children should be grounded in charity, not in carnality . . . and from saying that I had more merit in matrimony it does not follow that I despised virginity. It is possible that in the eyes of God a good married woman is more deserving because of the burdens and hardships of matrimony than are some who are virgins in the body but dissolute and corrupt in their soul, as demonstrated in the parable of the foolish virgins in the Gospel.

> . . . although preaching is forbidden to women, learning or reading or speaking of things of God is not.[16]

Considering the time and detail that María devoted to answering the attacks from Alcaraz, Francisca, and especially Diego Hernández, she obviously realized the seriousness and potential damage of their accusations. She tried to defuse the attacks by stating that for various reasons she had distanced herself from all three people before the Inquisition had begun to prosecute and imprison them. She did not hesitate to call Diego Hernández a "heretic and apostate" [erege e apóstata] (215) and all the witnesses in general "vile, mean, perjurers, infamous and capital enemies" [viles, çeviles, perjuros, ynfames e mis enemigos capitales] (232). From a juridical point of view the rejection was based on the Inquisition's own requirement, enacted in 1532, that all testimonies be presented only after complete ratification and that time and place be explicitly stated.[17]

The reader must be spared the details of the long *via crucis* that María, like most defendants before the Inquisition and civil tribunals, had to endure until her case was ready for sentence. She and her official defense attorney presented to the tribunal petitions, series of questionnaires for the unknown but suspected accusers, other questionnaires for people who might discredit the accusers (*interrogatorios de tachas*), and as many as fifty-six witnesses who knew María well and possibly would be favorable to her cause. Humble people of various professions in Pastrana, Guadalajara, Horche, and other towns appeared on the roster next to priests, professors, servants of the nobility, and even members of the nobility, like Leonor de Quirós, Doña Brianda de Mendoza, and other persons of the Infantado family, descendants of the famous marquis of Santillana. When this cumbersome judicial obstacle seemed to have been overcome, new testimonies from additional witnesses again necessitated María's and her attorney's attention and response. The entire year 1533 passed in these procedures. Finally, on December 22 they asked the members of the Toledo tribunal that the case rest and that María be entrusted to her husband and the city be her prison should the case not be settled promptly.[18]

Interlude and Torment

While the tribunal took its usual leisure to reach a decision, something happened that forced a delay. Very possibly the tribunal would have voted and pronounced its sentence not long after the conclusion of the procedures had it not been for an obstacle for which María was truly, though understandably, responsible. The prosecutor intended to reopen at least some parts of the trial because of formal irregularities incurred when María and the bachelor Tovar, who had been imprisoned in 1530, had communicated several times within their respective prisons. It seems that Tovar had written several letters and received replies from his half brother in Toledo, the cathedral canon Juan de Vergara. Vergara slipped his letters in with the food brought into prison, writing them on the paper that wrapped the food with an invisible orange or pomegranate ink that with proper lighting was not too difficult to read; the food was then passed through the cat's hole [*gatera*] in the door of María's room. By this ruse María had been warned about the identity of some of her accusers as well as other details of the proceedings. The deception had gone on for about one year with the help of several servants whose loyalty unraveled when the ruse was discovered and they ended up declaring against the prisoners.

On May 14, 1533, María, like the others involved in the deception, was called before Dr. Vaguer and made to confess. She tried to steer a safe course by not denying the already known facts, concealing that which was still not detected, and at the same time not betraying her friends. Her astute recourse was as ancient as it is modern: "She said that she doesn't remember and if she wrote anything to [Tovar], it must be what she already confessed or denied, telling the truth and denying the contrary."[19] The prosecutor then asked on April 28 that "she be punished according to the law" [que sea castigada conforme a derecho por ello] (429). The "crime" was not a minor one: as Ortiz de Angulo said against María more than a year later, on December 17, 1534, she was accused as an "accomplice of heretics and hamperer of the Holy Office" [fautora de hereges e inpididora del Sto. Officio] (491), and he again asked that she be declared guilty, deserving the punishments and censures established by law for these crimes.

The torment María experienced in this painful interlude was nothing compared with the physical torture she had to endure in order to reach the end of her imprisonment. The immediate cause of her ordeal was the stubborn ratification given by Mari Núñez to her testimony; again, one cannot but wonder how it was possible for seasoned inquisitors who should have differentiated between credible and incredible witnesses to rely on the words of a woman who, as we will see, was of suspect character. It should be remembered that in their December 22, 1533, petition for conclusion of the case, María and her attorney asked for ratification of all witnesses. The Toledo tribunal sent to the Suprema all the documents of the trial for instructions, and the reply of April 28, 1534, cannot be more explicit: "Since the trial of this woman is concluded . . . it should be seen and formally voted upon."[20] The infractions in jail, that is, the illicit communication, were to be added to the main business so that they could be reviewed together and voted upon.

The infractions in prison had occupied the attention of the tribunal for most of 1533. By July 1534, the Toledo tribunal still had not asked the tribunal in Seville, where Mari Núñez was now living, for the ratification of testimony from that woman, she who had written the original letter of denunciation in 1519 and whose presence passed like a shadow through María de Cazalla's life. The Toledo courier reached Seville with the appropriate order on July 17 at three o'clock in the afternoon. The situation was that Mari ratified her original accusations against Alcaraz and María on two occasions, first in Toledo on March 15, 1526, and then in Torrijos on November 6, 1526, but later, in Seville on May 9, 1533, she had reversed her testimony regarding María. The prosecutor could not accept the validity of that reversal and insisted that María's relatives must have bribed the witness with gifts and promises. The inquisitors in Seville were asked to review and compare Mari's original statements, and if she persisted in denying them, she was to be put to torture.

On July 18, 1534, Mari was summoned to the Triana castle, where the testimonies were read and their disparity demonstrated to the witness. Apparently Mari was let go, but she reappeared two days later at nine o'clock in the morning, and after scrutinizing her conscience, she maintained her reversal of the previous year, explaining that it was Alcaraz rather than María de Cazalla who had said that more authority should be given to Isabel than to Saint Paul and the saints. She was informed that since the disparity in her testimony had not been erased on the grounds of faulty memory, she must be put to torment. "My lords," cried Mari, "do I deserve this for having defended the honor of Jesus Christ, for were it not for me half of the kingdom would be damned and now you wish to pay me this way."[21]

She was undressed except for her shirt and thrown on the torment ladder, and "after several turns of the rope on her legs" [dadas unas bueltas de cordel a las piernas] (455), she confessed what the inquisitors wanted: "Sir, what I said in Toledo and Torrijos that is the truth . . . that Pedro de Alcaraz and Isabel de la Cruz and María de Cazalla are heretics and María de Cazalla even more because this witness felt in her greater blindness than in the others because her infatuation with the alumbrados was greater."[22] The inquisitors had heard what they wanted. Noting that Mari Núñez was "somewhat blind and sick," "fearful of God and full of zeal for her soul's salvation and her conscience, although scrupulous," [algo ciega y enferma . . . temerosa de Dios y zelosa de su ánima y conciençia, aunque escrupulosa] (456), the inquisitors suspended torture. The following day at four o'clock in the afternoon she was summoned to ratify the truth the torture had uncovered. Two hours later the courier left for Toledo. He arrived there on August 3, 1534.

On August 21 María was notified of Mari Núñez's ratification, though naturally not of its outcome. María's response? She had nothing to declare. On October 10 she was questioned repeatedly about each and every one of the thirty-six charges, but her answers never faltered, and she reaffirmed her previous testimonies without any change whatsoever. Acting as usual on the presupposition that they knew the truth, the inquisitors informed her that according to the requirements of the law she had to be put to torture. Her reply, recorded by the scribe, was astonishingly stoic: "She said that she says what she has said."[23] The tribunal had already voted unanimously on May 8, 1534, in favor of moderate torture for María, but since the local tribunal's vote for torture had to be approved personally by the Suprema and the inquisitor general, the entire documentation of the trial had been sent to Madrid. The sentence was immediately pronounced in the same terms authorized by the Suprema, that she be subject to torture "until she [told] the truth or until there [were] purged the evidence or suspicion against her of the crime of heresy" [hasta que dixiese la verdad o fasta que purgase los yndiçios e sospecha que ay contra ella del crimen de la heregía] (469). The sentence read, María did not waver: she had told the truth.

Maria de Cazalla's torture on October 10, 1534, is one of the most famous cases in the entire history of the Inquisition for its significance, for
her courage, and for the happy end to the long nightmare. It is well
known that, contrary to popular misunderstanding and the macabre mis-
conceptions spread by the so-called black legend, only about 2 or 3 percent of all *procesos* included torture. In the case of María, as in dozens of
similar cases, the very words of the prisoner under torture are preserved
in the records of the Inquisition. María's cries and utterances still move
us today after all these centuries. The inquisitors warned her many times
to tell the truth, and her answer was always "I've already told it" [ya la
tiene dicha] (469). When ordered to undress except for her shirt, she lamented, "They must undress even women!" [y a las mugeres han de des-
nudar] (470). But she faced her tormentors boldly, stating, "The affront is
much more to fear than the pain" [mucho más se teme el afrenta que la
pena] (470), that they did not know her, that she had told the truth from
the very first day and had nothing else to say. She asked to have her eyes
covered so that she would not see herself naked and cried out to her God:
"Oh, King of heaven and you, fastened to a column."[24] When her arms
were fastened with a rope, she said that she wanted to die as a Christian,
whether there or elsewhere. Then she was placed on the ladder of torture.
The scribe in attendance recorded the scene and her words:

> "Redeemer of the world, Jesus, be adored on your cross and I adore
> you. You were born in a manger for me; no more, I am weak! Be
> damned all of you, so much force against weak people," and she cried
> out and said, "so it is for the innocent and the guilty alike" and with her
> arms tied she was warned again to tell the truth. She said, "I have said
> it." The order was given to put her on the ladder of torment and there
> she said: "Ay, lords, why do you believe liars," and she said, "Lord, help
> me as you usually help us in our needs. I do confess and adore you and
> give me strength in my distress. I did not do it, lords, and you'll have it
> on your conscience."[25]

Asked whether she wanted to hear the propositions again, she replied
that she had studied all of them very well and since God knew they were
false, he would free her. The propositions were read up to the twenty-first
one; to each one she replied that she had told the truth. The ropes were

tightened on her hands and arms, first the right, then the left. She screamed:

> "I did not sin My Lord, you know that, St. Stephen, St. Lawrence, St. Simon, and St. Judas, to whom I have promised myself . . . and this you do to the innocent . . . and what innocent person will confess what he has not done . . . good riddance, Gaspar Martínez [the torturer, doorman of the Holy Office], how very strong you are . . . do you want me to lie" and she said "use such strength on boors but not on the innocent. I'm suffocating, I'm sick."[26]

The order was given to tighten the ropes on her legs, to hold her head in place with a rope and pour a jar of water on a cloth over her face and nose. The water was poured until the first jar was emptied. They were killing her, she said, an innocent woman. Another jar was ordered, and she was warned again to tell the truth. "I have told the truth" [que dicha tiene la verdad] (471) is her reply, over and over. "Cruel executioner" [Cruel verdugo] (471), she cried out, and the second jar was emptied. It was getting late. The inquisitors ordered the torture to be interrupted, admonishing her that if she persisted in not telling the truth, they would repeat the torture. The inquisitors left the chamber of torment. The notary ended his record of the lamentable affair by noting that after the inquisitors left the chamber of torment, the said María de Cazalla "in my presence" [en presencia de mí] said, "Better crippled than condemned" [que más valía manca que condepnada] (472).

Conclusion

María had won. She would live. She would be free, but not without suffering consequences of her long trial. On October 10 a team of inquisitors and advisers examined the whole *proceso* and unanimously agreed that "she be absolved *ab instançia judicii*, submit to a penitential fine of fifty ducats, be warned not to associate with persons whom she had recognized as alumbrados or were suspected as such, and do public penance at her parish church in Guadalajara." "For the other infractions that had to do with the communications she held in jail with other prisoners . . . a penance of fifty more ducats is imposed."[27]

The final sentence, pronounced the following day, summarized the prosecutor's charges against her as a presumed Lutheran but omitted the strongest traces of alumbradismo with the exception of statements that she had insisted on interior religiosity, read and praised Valdés and Erasmus, criticized certain aspects of clerical behavior, and written letters to as well as met with persons sharing the errors and opinions of the alumbrados. The sentence stated that the prosecutor's intention had not been proved, but it said nothing about the torture that María had endured without betraying herself. The details of the penance were set forth: María had to stand in her church in Guadalajara in front of the altar on a Sunday or holiday during mass with a lighted candle in her hand, recite the Pater Noster and the Ave Maria seven times, and listen to the sentence read right after the offering, which was a time when everyone would be there and thus know why she was condemned. On December 19, 1534, María de Cazalla abjured *de levi,* her hand on the Holy Gospels, and after promising not to leave the city of Toledo, she was freed.

María de Cazalla's heroic stance before the Inquisition, especially in the torture chamber, is poignant reminder that she paid a grievous price for other people's fear, suspicion, and failure of character. Certainly fear and suspicion motivated the Spanish authorities to check the movement of alumbradismo, about which very little was known but which showed frightening similarities with Lutheranism and, in the late 1520s, with a Spanish Erasmianism already in official disrepute. Failure of character refers not to María, of course, but to another woman whose name has appeared over and over in this story, her fortunes sadly entwined with María's, her pettiness, malice, and jealousy filling María's cup of suffering. That woman is Mari Núñez, she who set in motion by her letter of denunciation in 1519 events that would ensnare María and others in the labyrinth of inquisitorial actions.

In or around 1519 an obscure episode took place which seems not to have drawn attention from scholars, even the meticulous editor of María's *proceso.* The episode helps explain why María broke with Mari Núñez, decided to leave Guadalajara, and thereafter sent her daughters back to that city to be educated by Isabel. One of the questions in the *interrogatorio de tachas* prepared by María's husband and children concerns an incident in the home of María and Lope, where at the time (c. 1519)

Mari was residing. The questions and replies from witnesses indicate that Mari Núñez had been the cause of a quarrel that involved weapons and seems to have required intervention by outsiders before it was settled. After the quarrel María and Lope moved to Horche, where the husband held some small properties, while Mari Núñez was said to have gone off with the cleric Hernando Díaz. More than one witness said that María and Lope had left "to get away from Mari Núñez and flee from her" [por dexar a la dicha Mari Núñez e huyr della] (341). One witness said that "Mari was separating the said María from the said Lope with her alumbrado business" [la dicha Mari Núñez . . . hazía, con sus alumbramientos, apartar a la dicha María de Caçalla del dicho Lope Rueda] (379), while a certain Alonso Hernández, parish priest of San Gil in Guadalajara, who might have known the situation even better, testified on April 3, 1533, that Mari Núñez had had intimate relations with the cleric Hernando Díaz and that Mari had been the cause of the rift between María and her husband. Evidently the situation became so messy that María told the other woman "not to go to the bed of the said Lope de Rueda" [que no se acostase en la cama del dicho Lope de Rueda] (380). Apparently the marriage of María and Lope had its ups and downs, provoked at least in part by the husband's taste for pleasures outside his marriage bed.

While studying the almost six hundred published pages of the proceedings of María's trial, one cannot but feel a certain kind of psychological distance between María and her husband; his role and lack of support for María during the long four years of her inquisitorial troubles seem rather strange and reveal much about their relationship. His only assistance to his wife was to draft, together with their children, two short lists of questions for friendly witnesses to be used to discredit adverse witnesses. That action was taken too late, in 1533. The minimum one can affirm is Ortega's wise remark: "It is to be supposed that in effect the husband does not seem to have shared his wife's religious anxieties."[28]

On November 3, 1533, Mari Núñez testified in Toledo that some years before 1520, when María had asked her advice on how to become closer to God, Mari had advised her not to have sexual relations with her husband unless for the purpose of procreation. María seems to have taken that counsel too much to heart: her confessor reprimanded her for not being a good wife, whereupon she changed her ways, "doing all that

[Lope] wished" [haziendo todo lo que él quería] (448). María later reproached the other woman for having given her bad advice. Such testimony about events and relationships in María's household suggests that the aforementioned quarrel was due to some sexual indiscretion on Lope's part which involved Mari Núñez; if such indiscretion did occur, we are better able to understand why Mari persisted until the very end in her accusation that María was an alumbrado.

Further evidence about Mari Núñez's character also comes under scrutiny in this attempt to sort out motives and understand why María was attacked for so long by the beata. Although Mari once enjoyed a reputation as a devout woman, by 1519, the year she wrote the fateful letter of denunciation to the Inquisition, her character was in public question and her popularity obscured by her rival, Isabel de la Cruz, to whom she had lost both Pedro Ruiz de Alcaraz and María de Cazalla, the latter having abandoned both the beata and Guadalupe on advice from Isabel. Mari's reputation was also eroding under rumors of sexual liaisons not only with the priest Hernando Díaz but also with the duke of Infantado's cousin, Don Bernardino Suárez de Figueroa y Mendoza, count of Coruña. In the aforementioned *interrogatorio de tachas* Mari was described as a "lying woman and a shaker of towns and troublemaker of homes, who under the appearance of virtue and holiness was vicious in many respects" [muger mentirosa y alborotadora de pueblos y rebolvedora de casas e que debaxo de color de virtuosa y santa era viçiosa de muchas maneras] (371). At the peak of María's trial, when Mari Núñez was asked how she found out that the other woman was an alumbrado, her answer, "because I saw her talk secretly with the said Isabel de la Cruz and Pedro de Alcaraz" [porque la veya conversar en secreto con la dicha Ysabel de la Cruz e P(edr)o de Alcaraz] (449), reveals a hidden motive—to condemn María by association with both Isabel and Alcaraz. Mari admitted that it was only "by conjectures" [por coyunturas] (449) that she thought María was an alumbrado. María's alumbradismo, therefore, was a slanderous construct born out of Mari Núñez's jealous revenge, with no more factual basis than her own resentment that María cut short what was most certainly an illicit sexual relationship with her husband.

No records of what happened in Guadalajara after María's release were left, or at least they have not been published yet, but the grievous ceremony must have taken place literally, since the sentence stipulated that an official of the Holy Office must be present at the public punishment, at María's cost, and take back to the Inquisition evidence that it had been carried out. Poor María, having defeated the Inquisition with her exemplary integrity and courage, disappeared into the mist of history from which she came. In the words of the fifteenth-century poet Jorge Manrique, who immortalized his father in the famous *Coplas*, María left us as consolation only her good fame: "Nos dexó harto consuelo su memoria."

CHAPTER SIX

Francisca de los Apóstoles

A Visionary Voice for Reform
in Sixteenth-Century
Toledo

GILLIAN T. W. AHLGREN

Francisca de los Apóstoles, a visionary *beata* and reformer in the city of Toledo, was condemned by the Spanish Inquisition in 1578, after a four-year trial. Inspired by a series of visions of the final judgment, Francisca attempted to found convents in which women could offer their prayers and penance on behalf of human sin. Francisca's monastic reforms were intended to address the serious social, economic, and ecclesiastical problems experienced in Toledo during the 1570s. Unable to secure civil or ecclesiastical support for her reforms, Francisca awaited the liberation of Toledo's archbishop, Bartolomé de Carranza, from the Roman Inquisition, and in 1574 she experienced a vision in which she understood that he would be vindicated and returned to Toledo to oversee the reform of the church, to which her religious houses would contribute. As the major source of her religious authority, Francisca's visions became the focal point of her inquisitorial trial. A fascinating story in its own right, Francisca's case also exemplifies inquisitorial challenges to women's religious authority and the shifting role of visions in vernacular theology.

A contemporary of Santa Teresa, who was undergoing inquisitorial investigation in Seville in 1575–76, at the height of Francisca's trial,[1] Francisca provides an example of what the women in Teresa's shadow might expect to encounter—women who had similar desires to reform female religious life but who were not as well connected or as rhetorically skilled as Teresa.[2] The scant attention paid to this singular woman, Francisca, has tended to agree with the Inquisition's judgment of her as "foolhardy, impudent, and arrogant" [temeraria, atrevida y arrogante].[3] Born in the town of Noves about 1541, Francisca left her parents' house at age sixteen to live as a beata at the church of Santa María la Blanca, where she remained until she was twenty-four.[4] After leaving Santa María la Blanca she attached herself to the church of Santo Tomé in Toledo, where, "having understood the way in which many young women lost their virtue, she devoted herself to bringing some of them together and teaching them needlework."[5] At first, Francisca's idea was to establish a *beaterio*, or house for beatas, and develop her own rule for the women, but the approval of ecclesiastical officials was not forthcoming. Nonetheless, by November 1573 at least six beatas were living together under a rule Francisca had written, and her sister, Isabel Bautista, had set off to Rome for a patent to found the new convent. As her vision of reform developed, Francisca decided to found a seminary for priests as well and to place both foundations under the auspices of the Hieronymite order. According to the cleric Pedro Chacón, who had supported the sisters' reforms, Francisca desired to found Hieronymite houses because they would be heavily oriented to prayer and penance as redemptive activities.[6]

Francisca's vision of the convent was to house young women and widows who might otherwise turn to prostitution for economic survival. Toledo's ecclesiastical system of poor relief had suffered since Carranza's imprisonment, and Francisca believed that women in particular had borne the brunt of this shift in priorities. In a letter she wrote on August 25, 1574, Francisca explained, "There are many young women and widows who would have occasion to offend God out of [economic] necessity." Indeed, she continued, "If I did not have the faith which I have in God that He must bring [the archbishop] back to improve this situation, I don't know what consolation would be enough for me, since things are so horrible that it seems God has commanded the churchmen to spend their incomes on their own enjoyment and to let the poor perish and the young women be lost."[7]

Although it is difficult to assess Francisca's commentary on the state of high church officials, there are several indications of economic hardship. Toledo's *pósito*, or grain reserve, used by the city to provide cheap bread for the poor, was unable to keep up with demands in the 1560s and 1570s.

During these decades poor harvests, higher taxes, and increased population took a toll on everyone, but especially the poor. In June 1575 Toledo's *corregidor* (chief magistrate) expressed his concern that more than three hundred sick people had been left to die on the street because the city hospitals were filled to capacity.[8] Francisca's religious houses constituted a religious response to very real social problems: not only did she seek to provide women with a safe haven; she also suggested that, through their prayer and penance, they would ultimately be the salvation of the corrupted church, signs of which were evident in the poverty of many of its members and the relative wealth of higher church officials. Francisca's appreciation of these inequities is reflected in the figure of Saint Peter in her vision of the final judgment. Standing at the door to heaven, Peter was inclined to deny entrance to the city's priests, complaining, "Eternal Father, may there be a harsh punishment for the priests who have followed [you] so poorly, for naked I followed the naked Christ, but these men go about weighed down by their incomes and vices."[9]

Providing shelter and subsistence for lower-class women necessitated endowments. The daughter of a painter, Francisca was from a comfortable but by no means wealthy background—and thus she would have had to acquire significant financial support for the houses. Raising this capital was supposed to be a joint effort shared by many women of the city. In a letter to her sister dated August 25, 1574, Francisca wrote with excitement that several young women, who had been enthusiastic about the convent, had begun to recruit other, "very rich young women as well as widows of such great devotion" that it moved her.

> And all tell me that they have wanted to become religious, but since they have seen such corruption in the convents they believe it is better to remain in their homes. They have understood that this convent will be a very holy place, and they beg me to assure them that they will be able to enter, and I tell them that I can do nothing more than leave everything in God's hands. . . . The poorest [of these women] has three thousand ducados, and if we were to get started there would be a great response from the people who would enter with their inheritances.[10]

Initial enthusiasm slowly turned into frustration as the sisters' plans proved difficult to enact. Isabel returned from Rome unsuccessful in her attempt to gain approval for the beaterio, but she continued to pursue various avenues of official approval. Several nobles approached Sancho Busto de Villegas, the *gobernador,* or official who served as archdiocesan administrator during Carranza's imprisonment, to get his permission to found the convent. Others turned to Philip II's confessor to get the king to order the *gobernador* to approve the foundation. However, even though the Royal Council wrote the *gobernador,* he continued to withhold his approval because of the "scandal" already associated with the convent.[11] The sisters took in a few poorer women but were reluctant to admit other women who asked to enter the convent, since the foundation still had not received formal approval.[12] After several months, and in consultation with Fr. Juan Bautista, a discalced Franciscan, Francisca and Isabel received María de Jesús, responding to the pleas of her aunt, Juana Ximenez, who desired María to be safely enclosed. As Juan Bautista took up their cause, the sisters grew more confident that they would eventually gain permission for their foundation and began to receive more beatas until they became a community of twelve.[13]

Several other clerics, Alonso Lopez de la Quadra and a Fr. Porras, offered their help in securing a license, but they were so heavily criticized by other clerics in Toledo that they began trying to remove some of the women from the beaterio. The tide had turned definitively against Francisca and Isabel. Word spread throughout Toledo that the *gobernador* was beginning a formal inquiry. Leonor de Mendoza, a noblewoman who had once supported the convent and even allowed her maidservant to enter, now pulled her out. The community dwindled to six members and waited tensely to see if any condemnation was forthcoming.

In December 1574 the initial accusations against Francisca and Isabel were presented by two women, Catalina de Jesús (a beata in the convent) and Luisa de Aguilera (a supporter of the convent). A forty-seven-year-old woman married to a sailor who had been absent for some time, Luisa had been bedridden for four years at the time of her declaration.[14] Dissatisfied with the beaterio and able to support herself with her own resources, Luisa denounced the sisters to the Inquisition, explaining that she was afraid that her association with them might put her soul in jeopardy. It is at least as likely that Luisa had committed money to the beaterio and was concerned that her two daughters would not be well provided for there.

Luisa's testimony consisted essentially of accusing Francisca of taking pride in her sister Isabel—"she said she was holier than many of the saints in heaven"[15]—and of being an *endemoniada,* a woman possessed by the devil. According to Luisa, Francisca claimed to have had visions from God regarding the manner of life the beatas were to follow, what their habit should look like, and other details. On the basis of these visions, Francisca also described how Archbishop Bartolomé Miranda de Carranza would be freed miraculously from his imprisonment in Rome. Finally, Luisa gave the first relation of Francisca's apocalyptic vision of the "Majesty of God," which would become an essential part of the inquisitorial trial against Francisca.[16]

Despite the public scandal, the inquisitorial tribunal initially took little notice of the beaterio, as Inquisitor Juan de Llano de Valdés later explained in a letter to the Suprema: "In this city there live three sisters, all beatas, who are devout and associate with good Christians who praise them, and they told other beatas about their revelations and the things they saw, and they were trying to found a convent. . . . When the Holy Office received word of this it was of the opinion that this was still spiritual activity, and because of lack of information we did not pursue the matter."[17] There was also the problem of jurisdiction. Once Francisca began to gather other beatas together without formal permission, she would have been subject to punishment by the acting diocesan representative, Busto de Villegas. And indeed, according to the witness Luisa de Aguilera, this is what happened initially: Busto de Villegas sent the vicar of religious orders, a man named Serrano, to investigate the three sisters, and when there was no official response from the governor, Luisa spoke with Padre Sebastián Hernández of the Society of Jesus, whom she asked to appear before the Inquisition on her behalf. The cathedral canon Alonso Velazquez, who was Teresa's confessor a few years later, was also consulted.[18]

The inquisitors decided to proceed with a prosecution after receiving the *calificaciones* (theological assessment) of some twenty-four propositions taken from the witnesses. According to this report, Francisca was

more of a blasphemer than a heretic; that is, the judgment of her theological views was more that she spoke disrespectfully regarding matters
of faith, rather than that she taught erroneous doctrine. More frequently,
the theologian described her propositions as both "arrogant" and reflective of *alumbradismo*. What characterized Francisca's alumbradismo, for
the *calificador*, was her claim that she had spiritual visions or was "taught
things in her spirit." For example, the theologian wrote: "Believing with
great readiness what is offered in one's interior, understanding it to be a
teaching from Our Lord and believing in dreams pertains to the heresy
of the alumbrados."[19] The inquisitors responded to the report by ordering Francisca's imprisonment in the inquisitorial prisons.

In December 1575 Francisca appeared before the inquisitor Juan de
Llano de Valdés. While inquisitorial officials may well have been suspicious about the beaterio, Valdés spent most of December asking Francisca about the content and manner of her visionary experiences. The
length of time devoted to this issue is not surprising, as the discernment
of true and false visionary experience was a major concern in sixteenth-
century Spain. Indeed, an inquisitorial campaign against the so-called
alumbrados of Llerena led by the virulent Alonso de la Fuente was taking
place at the same time as Francisca's trial. Teresa of Avila was not immune to the suspicion provoked by visionary experiences; although the
inquisitorial inquiry in Seville appears to have blown over, Teresa was
confined to her convent in Toledo in 1576–77 and temporarily forbidden
to found more discalced Carmelite convents. Although both Teresa and
Francisca justified their reforms on the basis of visions and divine edict,
their visionary experience was certainly their point of most acute vulnerability. Teresa switched strategies, relying less on locutions and divine inspiration when justifying her foundation of later convents,[20] but Francisca never had that chance. Discrediting Francisca's visions would
ensure the failure of her reform efforts, and the inquisitor's questions
plunged right into the heart of this issue.

Repeatedly asked to explain why she believed her visions came from
God, Francisca at first replicated in her answers much of the orthodox
teaching on visions represented in sixteenth-century treatises. First, she
said that they almost always occurred right after receiving communion.[21]
To this Valdés replied, "At that time and before communion and even in

the moment of receiving communion—indeed, at all times the devil searches for ways to deceive people," and he asked for other signs that Francisca's visions were of divine origin.[22] Francisca replied that she knew her experiences were from God because they were accompanied by a form of sweet rapture which left her soul in a peaceful state. The transcript records her testimony:

> It was clear that this [experience] was from God and not the devil first because her spirit is enraptured with great sweetness and in this time she felt no bodily thing with her senses nor was her soul in any way disturbed but everything was great sweetness, and within her soul there was great light and a deep recognition of her own lowliness and as a result the person returns to herself and finds in herself great humility and obedience in everything that concerns serving our Lord so that it performs virtuous acts with ease and it feels great disgust at sinful things and it embraces with delight all things which are difficult and tedious for the love of our Lord. And because of this certainty in which her soul remained she could tell that it was good and given by God.

Francisca went beyond the internal signs of authenticity, however, and sought out her confessor to confirm that her visions were real.

> But not trusting herself the prisoner spoke about [her experience] with Miguel Ruiz in order to be reassured and the said Miguel Ruiz told her that since following uprightly the ways of our Lord and keeping the commandments had been imprinted in her soul she could be sure it was not from the devil and that she should focus on her lowliness because she was obliged to despise whatever was an offense against our Lord and to love all work done for love of our Lord.[23]

This answer seemed to the inquisitor to indicate spiritual pride, and he reminded Francisca that the saints who had experienced visions were loath to publicize their experience, since they knew they should be wary of being deceived. But, he argued, it was clear that Francisca had made her visions known to others. Francisca replied that she never believed she had received any spiritual gift through her own merit. Further, the effects of this kind of spiritual experience—such as the intensity of the soul's desire to bring other souls closer to God, their great pain at seeing others sinning and "offending our Lord," and their commitment to virtue—were all signs that could not be hidden from others.

The inquisitor was dissatisfied with this answer. His concern, it seems, was the frankness and familiarity with which Francisca discussed her experiences. He asked her to reflect further on her answer "because these things of God [were] of such great weight and importance that one should not dare to speak of them so palpably even if what she said were true."[24] Francisca described how she had repeatedly begged God in prayer to help her understand if she had been deceived by the devil and that in response she heard an internal voice reassuring her that these were not the devil's deceits.[25] Pressing her on this point, Valdés asked how she knew that this internal voice was not demonic. Francisca responded that it left the soul "in peace and deep humility."[26] When the inquisitor suggested that these could just as easily be signs of the devil, who would not enter into a soul in a violent way because "one would certainly know who he was and run from him, and for that reason he comes gently," Francisca's responses began to falter.[27]

It was not only the manner of Francisca's visions which was on trial but also their content. Particularly disturbing to inquisitorial officials were two visions that were apocalyptic in character. The first vision, called the *juicio* [judgment] vision in the trial transcript, focused on the last judgment and the intercessory role of Christ, Mary, and the saints. In this vision Francisca was invited to take on their redemptive role in order to make satisfaction to God for the sins of the world. She was asked by God to allow the demons who torment sinners to come into her own body and torment her instead. In submitting herself to this process, Francisca would learn from the demons how they tempted sinners and how they could be overcome. Thus Francisca testified that the devils "gave an account of the way in which they had made creatures live and thus the prisoner after receiving communion made a vow which Our Lord inspired in her soul which was to satisfy [God] for the vices which sinners had committed through this particular sin."[28] In the second vision, known as the *ejecutoria*, the emphasis was placed on the actual execution of the sentence against the damned. In this vision, Francisca had fulfilled her duty of taking the sins of others into herself and had experienced six months' worth of torments. God's wrath was appeased, and Our Lady promised to support Francisca's convents, which would be dedicated to continual penance on behalf of others. This second vision was a powerful, embodied experience that Francisca underwent while enraptured: her head and heart nearly "burst" from its force, and she was ill for many days afterward. The two visions were interpreted and reinterpreted during the trial.

Francisca herself, in a letter addressed to her sister Isabel Bautista but dictated to Miguel Ruiz, described the first vision of divine judgment. Directly after receiving communion and in the state of rapture, she heard Christ saying, "Renew the face of the earth." At this point, she wrote, "I saw a great majesty who responded, 'It is a great thing you ask of me, Son, that I renew all the earth because many offenses have been done to me.'"[29] Then Christ revealed to God his wounds and all the signs of his suffering in order that God would pardon the world anew. Additionally, the Virgin Mary interceded, offering up the foundation of two monasteries in which she herself would dedicate people "of great spirit" to satisfy God for all the world's offenses. At this Christ turned to Francisca and said, "What do you think, daughter; the world has offended me, especially the church because it offends me with its words and crucifies me with its masses?" Francisca was not sure how to respond; with tears in her eyes she begged for mercy. When she looked up, she saw Christ present the imprisoned archbishop of Toledo, Bartolomé de Carranza, to God, saying, "Our Father, you see here Bartolomé who will be [strong] enough to reform the entire church. Rejoice in him, for I am very pleased with him, and I will be his bondsman [*fiador*]. He will lose his life for the honor of your majesty and the reformation of your church." As the vision concluded, "the Eternal Father received [Carranza] in his arms, very pleased with him, and after having held him he gave him many benedictions."[30]

In his testimony Miguel Ruiz, the priest to whom Francisca dictated the vision, introduced a different dynamic into the judgment vision, one that the inquisitor would follow throughout his questioning. On trial himself, Miguel Ruiz prefaced his comments about the judgment vision by explaining that he recorded it for Francisca more to make her happy than because he actually believed it. His doubts, he explained, were "based on this illness that Francisca ha[d]," a reference to Francisca as an *endemoniada*.[31] Ruiz claimed that it was actually a demon identifying himself as Lucifer who spoke through Francisca, saying that Christ had ordered him and all his cohorts to return to hell if Miguel Ruiz and Francisca committed themselves to found the monasteries, in which people would live in perpetual poverty, fasting, prayer, and penance. When questioned further, Ruiz reiterated that "this vision was told to the witness by the said demon through the mouth of the said Francisca de los Apóstoles after she had received communion."[32] Francisca did not, in fact, deny that demons had spoken through her body. When questioned about this part of her experience, she stated that the demonic torments she accepted on behalf of the church were so debilitating that, when trying to explain her internal state to Miguel Ruiz, she herself was unable to speak, and eventually one of the demons spoke for her. Francisca was clear, however: these demons entered her body a full month after the judgment vision in which she accepted demonic torments within her own body so that the devils would stop tormenting the rest of the world. In fact, she explained, although at first she was concerned about her experiences, she took comfort from Raymond of Capua's *Life of Catherine of Siena,* which described how Catherine, too, offered her body to the demons on behalf of human sin.[33]

These visions spoke clearly of Francisca and her beatas taking on an intercessory and redemptive role within the church which in effect elevated them to the position of the saints. Other women, such as Catherine of Siena and Angela of Foligno, had assumed such a role, as Francisca knew from her own reading.[34] But Francisca's claims to embody an important aspect of the medieval mystical tradition in sixteenth-century Toledo—in which mystics offered up their prayers and penances on behalf of human sin and received divine favors in exchange—were considered too bold and prideful. The Inquisition's rejection of some aspects of earlier mystical traditions illuminates an important dynamic present throughout Francisca's trial. As she defended her own mystical experiences, Francisca seemed perplexed and even overwhelmed by the inquisitor's rigid scrutiny of her reasons for trusting her visions and revelations and his growing insistence that demonic involvement at any stage in her experience demonstrated the falsity of her experiences. Only partially aware of the mystical tradition and not having integrated this tradition into a theological framework, Francisca was unable to defend herself within the framework of the vernacular mystical treatises that had circulated earlier in the century.[35]

When the fiscal (prosecutor) finally put together his formal accusation against Francisca and read it on January 5, 1576, he had amassed 144 points. Within this broad range of accusations, four concerns seem central. First, the Inquisition viewed Francisca's revelations and visions as inherently suspicious, and they were particularly problematic when defended stubbornly (as in the last several accusations, in which the fiscal claimed she continued to defend their authenticity) or shared in a way that demonstrated "spiritual pride." Second, Francisca's claims of an intercessory or redemptive role for herself and her reform movement were unacceptable. These claims violated ecclesiastical orientation to clerical authority in addition to providing an implicit critique of existing sacerdotal and monastic structures. Third, the fact that Francisca justified her reform efforts by claiming they had been affirmed in her visions was similarly unacceptable because the nature and content of her visions raised suspicions about their authenticity. Fourth, Francisca's reforms themselves were not seen to contribute significantly to the religious climate of Toledo. Additionally, the Inquisition disputed Francisca's adoption of a teaching role, although this would have been her responsibility as abbess. Although less numerous, the accusations concerning Francisca's support of Carranza and her condemnation of clerics could not have helped her case. Among the many accusations against Francisca, accusation number 84 encapsulates many of the Inquisition's concerns: "She has said and confesses that, because of the interior calling from Our Lord that she received, she made certain obligations to suffer on behalf of the church of God as many torments as God was served to give her. And in exchange His Majesty would grant satisfaction for all of the offenses done to him, and this is the reason that nuns would join the monastery she was to found."[36]

The fiscal concluded his accusation by asking that Francisca be turned over to the secular arm for burning, a harsh sentence indeed for an *embaucadora* (fraud). Additionally, he asked for permission to use as much torture as he deemed necessary in his inquiry of problematic issues. Francisca was overwhelmed by the fiscal's formal accusation: all of her previous conversations had been twisted around, and her case looked hopeless. The scribe recorded, "She fainted and came to, sobbing, and saying ‘how can this trial come to this?' Then she said she was not able to respond to the said accusation and asked the inquisitor to leave [her response] for another day."[37] The following day Francisca asked for a lawyer to help her prepare her defense. The inquisitor summarily denied her request, explaining that she could consult with one after she had made her formal defense. Francisca repeated the request, explaining that the accusation was extensive and beyond her ability to counter: "And then the said Francisca de los Apóstoles said that she is a woman of very weak spirit and the Inquisitor is a person of such severity in his questions and all the other things and she does not have the strength to respond to his complicated and intimidating arguments and she still asks that she be given a lawyer in whom she could trust."[38]

In her point-by-point response to the accusations, Francisca did not deny the bulk of them. She complained only about the way in which her spiritual experiences had been misconstrued so as to imply some kind of malicious motivation on her part. Throughout January and February 1576 Francisca maintained that her experiences had been genuine, but by mid-February, she was losing ground in the defense of her visionary experience on several levels. She had difficulty replying when the inquisitor said, "What she says and has said demonstrates the falsity of her affair because it is clear that when the majesty of God decides to give such great revelations it would have to be [to] a person who was already well versed in prayer, discipline, fasting and other virtuous practices."[39] The inquisitor also pointed to Carranza's continued imprisonment as a sign of the error of Francisca's visions; ironically, however, Carranza would be liberated within the year. Questioning was suspended while Francisca struggled with fever and stomach pains. When it resumed, Francisca was apparently tiring. She told the inquisitor that it was her sincere desire to serve God, and if she was indeed confused or deceived, she wanted guidance.

On February 14, 1576, in an excruciating exchange, the inquisitor forced Francisca to commit herself to declaring whether she still believed her visions were from God or whether they were from the devil. "She could not decide whether to say they were from God or from the devil until the inquisitor told her and taught her, and that is what she would believe" [Dixo que no se determinara a dezir si heran de dios o del demonio mas de q(ue) lo q(ue) (e)l s(eño)r ynq(uisid)or la dixere y le enseñare eso crehera]. The inquisitor responded, "It is very certain that none of these revelations was from God; to believe anything else would be a grave error" [cosa muy çierta fue y aberiguada que ningu[n]a de aquellas Rebelaçiones fue de dios y que creher otra cosa seria grandisimo engaño]. Francisca replied that she had stated what truly happened, but if the inquisitor were to tell her that this was an error, she would believe that it was an error, and she would believe it to be an error even though she could not stop believing what she saw. When the inquisitor pushed Francisca harder, suggesting that to believe in her visions would be an offense against God, Francisca finally acknowledged that she would "believe everything" that the inquisitor said: "Because he is a person who has more illumination from God to understand such things and that she has never said nor intended to do anything that would offend God and that if she understood something to be [offensive to God] she would not do it for heaven or earth."[40] This concession of guilt insofar as her visions were concerned signaled the end of Francisca's defense. She spent the next year contemplating her future.

In early 1577 the fiscal added several more accusations to those already discussed, all of which were sexual in nature, alleging that Francisca had consorted with a fellow prisoner and planned to abscond with him. As the fiscal laid out the new accusations, they were intended to confirm the false and fraudulent nature of Francisca's claims to holiness. The first article of these new accusations reads:

> First that the above-mentioned pretending and presuming to be a saint, and saying and publishing [that] she had revelations from Our Lord and that God had pledged himself to her and that God had asked her father for her hand and that he had said that [in Francisca] he had found a just and holy soul who could satisfy for the sins of others and that he had given her virtues in order to be saintly or resist temptations and having asked for her dowry to pledge herself to God—having said all this publicly and discussed these and other things as [if she were] a saint, in these prisons she has secretly been in

contact with and planned to marry a certain person and they call themselves husband and wife and she has tried to see and talk with him as she has in fact done.[41]

In a carefully written response to these new allegations, Francisca revealed the toll of three years of inquisitorial trial. In her statement Francisca continued to deny the fiscal's portrait of her as proud and deceitful. "I have never considered myself holy," she wrote, "nor have I done works to seem so; rather [I know myself to be] a great sinner, but because I have been an imprudent woman with little experience in spiritual things, I spoke with my friends about my experiences . . . and these friends turned these things into the opposite [of what they were]."[42] Addressing the new allegations, Francisca vigorously denied that any dishonesty had passed between her and fellow prisoner Pedro Velasco. Her trial had convinced her that she had been "deceived in a way [she] thought was clearly in the service of God." She continued, "So I have decided to ignore my understanding of what I have experienced and only to believe what this Holy Office has taught me, and if an angel were to tell me the opposite, I would not believe it, but rather would think it was the devil trying to deceive me. Seeing myself now in such a difficult situation because of all this business, and seeing my freedom in such danger, I have decided to change my way of life and get married; perhaps I will save myself better in this way."[43] We do not know how Francisca fared as wife and mother. The inquisitorial documents record only that she was condemned as "an arrogant, bold and miserable heretic, blasphemer and perjurer." On April 14, 1578, Francisca received her sentence, one hundred lashes in the streets of Toledo and three years' banishment from the city.

Francisca de los Apóstoles inherited a problematic church. On the local level for fifteen years prior to her arrest by the Inquisition, the see of Toledo had been vacant. Corruption characterized this church, and poverty characterized urban life. Francisca understood Toledo's disintegration to be an important sign of the end times. Her apocalyptic visions affirmed the need for radical reforms that would save the church from destruction. Disturbed by the crisis she saw around her, the young beata introduced a monastic reform that would address these problems through its orientation to penance but also through its recruitment of women at moral risk.

As her vision of reform expanded, so did the challenges she encountered. Francisca's critique of ecclesiastical corruption, her support of Archbishop Carranza, and, most important, the visions integrating social and historical circumstances with the apocalyptic tradition alarmed secular and religious authorities alike and ultimately clashed with the larger orientation of the Counter Reformation in Castile.

Although Francisca's reforms in theory would have served to integrate lower classes into the various manifestations of Tridentine reforms within Spain, to her contemporaries they probably seemed either superfluous in light of other religious orders already in existence or, worse, threatening to the new ecclesiastical order in Toledo established in the absence of Archbishop Carranza. Within Toledo and Castile more generally the reforms of religious orders like the Hieronymites, Carmelites, and others received ecclesiastical priority. Further, the bias against the visionary epistemology incarnate in women like Francisca reflected the extent to which visions embodied prayer, and the charismatic authority of women who experienced such phenomena challenged the theological orientation of Tridentine Spain. Recent studies of Teresa of Avila have observed and analyzed how her visionary experiences were a significant challenge to the acceptance of her authority as a Christian mystic;[44] women who lacked Teresa's theological background clearly could not justify the validity of their experiences and visions.

The Spanish Inquisition was an excellent filter for movements like Francisca's, which clearly differed from other examples of Castilian Tridentine reforms. As suspicions about Francisca's reforms increased on all fronts, the inquisitorial tribunal of Toledo seemed the logical place to suppress her reforming activities. Francisca was eventually denounced by the very women around her and by the men who had counseled her in better times. Once the fiscal and the inquisitor took over, it was relatively easy to discredit Francisca and her agenda for change. The inquisitor could ignore the social and ecclesiastical validity of Francisca's reforms by raising questions about the theological validity of her visions. And Francisca, disheartened by both her religious community and the larger church who would not hear her message, fell silent.

CHAPTER SEVEN

Y Yo Dije, "Sí señor"

*Ana Domenge and the
Barcelona Inquisition*

ELIZABETH RHODES

According to her own thirteen-folio account, Ana Domenge, a Third
Order Dominican, spent seven long months in a dark, damp jail cell of
the Barcelona Inquisition, from June to December 1610. Until her trial
documents come to light, the charges against her can only be deduced
from the record of her visions, extant in a single manuscript: false sanctity
or unorthodox prayer practices, or both. Dictating her recollections of
her inquisitorial experience to a scribe some time during the next year,
she rendered her imprisonment dramatically:

> I went to the Holy Inquisition on the Saturday of the week of Corpus
> Christi; the deputy went to find me at Santa Catalina and he took me,
> and I was in the house of said deputy until the eve of the visitation of
> St. Elizabeth. And that day at three o'clock, the deputy and the sec-
> retary called me to a hearing, and I went happily and said, "Do I need
> a cloak?" and they told me, "No, where we must take you, you do not
> need a cloak." And having said these words, they took me to a very iso-
> lated, very dark prison, and such was the stench of the prison that it
> seemed like an outhouse to me, very humid, so that when I sat down I
> felt the roaches and spiders scurrying around me. And the white habit
> I wore in, from so much humidity, turned black.[1]

So opens the first section of the manuscript collection of visions dictated by Ana Domenge, a 167-folio assortment of first- and third-person

accounts collected at the orders of Domenge's confessor, Fray Antonio Darnilés.[2] The manuscript, probably a copy of the originals, consists of a first-person account of Domenge's visions while in the Inquisition jail; a third-person description of her visions from 1611 to 1613; a memoir in first person plural, composed by one of Domenge's companions, probably one of her nieces, relating Domenge's attempts to found a convent of reformed Dominican nuns in Perpignan during 1611–15; selected passages from what were probably Domenge's preferred meditational treatises, including a copy of the "Avisos de Santa Teresa";[3] and a third-person recording of Domenge's visions of 1615. The main body of the manuscript (not including the notorial documents inserted at random) was written by two different hands and dates from the seventeenth century.

As vision literature, whose purpose is to reveal God's use of Domenge's voice, these collected documents reveal almost nothing about her as an individual in human history and focus instead on her performance as an intermediary between heaven and earth. A rubric on the manuscript cover provides what little information is available about her, and even that is vague: "This religious woman, about whom this book speaks and which she herself dictated, is named Sor Anna Domenge, foundress of the Convent of Dominican Nuns in Perpignan, who, although she was called into the Inquisition, was released and found innocent."[4]

The manuscript provides but a nebulous outline of Domenge's life during the five years represented by visions. In the section relating her attempts to found a convent, she is described as a *beata profesa* (74r), meaning a holy woman who had taken vows and was affiliated with a specific order but was not a professed nun; this status would have obliged her to be under the control of a superior but not live in a convent, and she is indeed described as residing in people's houses at various intervals between 1611 and 1615. Evidence in the manuscript dictated by Domenge as well as details provided in sections about her indicate that she was an itinerant holy woman whose exuberant prayer scandalized her companions (whether nuns, neighbors, or someone else is unknown). After her seven-month residence in jail, Domenge moved to a convent, and then to a relative's house in Perpignan, while God told her in visions to found reformed Dominican monasteries. When the resistance against that enterprise became overwhelming, God changed his mind and suggested a wide array of other alternatives, from Franciscans and Carmelites to Hieronymites, for Domenge to join. She rejected these suggestions, maintaining that she was destined to be the Teresa of Avila of the Dominican order (a notion confirmed by Teresa herself in Domenge's visions [5v, 80v, 87v]).

In 1612, Domenge took vows of an undefined type, as did her servant and two nieces, at the Dominican convent in Perpignan whose foundation she had arranged; because of later problems in Domenge's relationship with that institution, the foundation was not celebrated as her idea in the manuscript. At the bishop's insistence, some nuns from Valencia had been brought up to join the community and had been assigned the positions of authority in the convent (there were apparently too few nuns to justify its opening without them). These women, to whom Domenge referred as "the Valencian nuns" [las monjas valencianas], were unsatisfactory to Domenge and her God because of their lax observance of the Rule. When Domenge tried to introduce them to the practice of flagellation, they laughed at her demonstration; when she tried to convince them to pray during long hours, "they refused to go along, saying that was not what their Order did, that it was the business of discalced religious and Franciscans" (78r).[5] While Domenge—as related in her visions—prayed on their behalf, God threatened to "grind them to bits" [amolarlas], and, so the manuscript says, only thanks to Domenge's intercession were they saved from death.

On August 20, 1613, God instructed Domenge and her followers to abandon the convent, which they eventually did, moving into the home of one of Domenge's relatives and in so doing scandalizing the local community, whose members evidently believed that proper religious women should be as cloistered as the Council of Trent had dictated. At that point, Domenge's healing and visionary activities intensified, sufficiently to compensate for the ignominy caused by her abandoning the cloister. Her exaggerated humility and willingness to use her abilities in the service of others convinced her neighbors that she was not only a good person but a holy woman with considerable gifts, and people began to travel to Perpignan from other parts of northern Spain to seek her intercession, particularly in cases of illness and domestic abuse. Several bilocations were attributed to Domenge by the nun relating the history of these years, in which individuals under duress saw and spoke to a woman they believed was Domenge when Domenge herself was somewhere else.[6]

In 1615, God delivered to Domenge what were presumably his definitive instructions regarding what sort of subsequent foundation she was to undertake: "a convent of the third rule of Father St. Dominic, as St. Catherine of Siena practiced it" [monasterio de beatas que siguiesen la tercera regla del Padre Santo Domingo, como la guardaba Santa Catalina de Sena] (139v). Specifically, that foundation was to observe "much cloister" [mucha clausura], even though its members were not officially required to do so. Likewise, God instructed her to have them live in accordance with Domenge's stated religious ideals: poverty, long hours of prayer, and great abstinence, the typical features of the reformed religious order of the early modern period. The rubric on the manuscript cover suggests that Domenge did found a convent, but whether it refers to the one dominated by the antireform nuns or whether she managed to found another is unknown. The specification is difficult to make, in part because most of the convents mentioned in the manuscript are not named, and also because Rosellón, whose capital is Perpignan, became part of France in 1659 as one of the consequences of the 1640 Catalan revolt, and convent records from the region are now scattered. Only one of those identified convents, of La Mare de Déu del Àngels i Peu de la Creu, founded in 1497 in Barcelona, still exists (now in San Cugat del Vallès, although the Plaça dels Angels, with the convent building there, still stands). For reasons unspecified, Domenge's manuscript does not conclude, but rather simply ends with a vision of 1615.

Although what is revealed to Domenge by her God is interesting as a microhistory, it is not extraordinary, rather quite typical of the visions being had by women of her day, visions that display a complex, baroque celestial hierarchy reflective of the one with which human beings were simultaneously grappling on earth. Most of Domenge's visions were reportedly generated by the Eucharist, but many were triggered by a wide gamut of liturgical events and ceremonies, symptomatic of conservative seventeenth-century piety in Spain, which accentuated ritual and institutional practices over spirituality: the third chime of a certain hour of the office, for example, sufficed to send Domenge into a close encounter with the Virgin. Domenge's visions followed the liturgical cal-

endar strictly and served to reinforce devotion to specific saints on specified days; her visions of individual saints always coincided with their
feast days.

All of the messages Domenge received from supernatural sources confirmed and reflected the terrestrial anxieties with which she was struggling at the time she had them. For example, during the period when she
was battling with the bishop in Perpignan for authorization to hold mass
in the convent with which she was affiliated, God harped relentlessly in
her visions about the decadence of the clergy, which he threatened to de-
stroy in the same fashion as he planned to annihilate "the Valencian
nuns" (75v).

Domenge's visions confirm Antonio Márquez's notion that the mystical literature studied today is only that which the Inquisition permitted
to survive,[7] and they are a study in conservative religious practice that
supports the power structures of the Catholic Church. Her document's
major interest lies in its relationship to the institution of the Inquisition,
for unlike the great majority of religious women and men accused of
heresy by the Holy Office and subsequently silenced, Ana Domenge's inquisitorial trial actually instigated her self-representation. Where others'
records end, hers begins.

In 1610, being tried by the Barcelona tribunal of the Inquisition was a
mixed blessing.[8] On the one hand, the long history of Catalan resistance
to the institution's establishment in Catalonia, loud resistance that
started as soon as it was founded in 1491, assured a sympathetic public
outside the Inquisition itself and guaranteed at least an attempt at civil
protest to any excesses that reached the public ear. The basic posture of
the Catalans toward the Inquisition was virulent antagonism (Lea calls
them "intractable"), an attitude bound to have an effect on the workings
of the tribunal; perhaps for this reason, the Holy Office of Barcelona was
infamous for its sloppy procedures and grossly inefficient record keeping.[9] In the 1630s, family members of the Barcelona *familiares*, the Inquisition's civil officers, were being murdered and their houses burned, and
by 1677 the relationship between the Inquisition and the Catalan people
had deteriorated to the point where the inquisitorial *alcalde mayor*, or
chief deputy, asked to be relieved from carrying his scepter of office (elsewhere considered an enviable symbol of authority) because no nobles

would be seen with him while he had it. At least in part because of the incessant insistence of the Catalans that the Inquisition was a violation of their statutes, the famous Catalan *estatuts*, the Barcelona tribunal was decidedly less active than its counterparts, certainly less than those of Toledo and Seville. Consequently, it may have been more permissive.[10]

On the other hand, 1610 was not a good year to be locked in the cells of the Barcelona Inquisition. It was then that the tensions were building which culminated in the October Catalan protest of 1611 against the continued presence of the Holy Office in Catalan lands, marked by the dramatic decree by the Catalan Council banishing the inquisitors from Catalonia, Rosellón, and Cerdanya; the inquisitors ignored the order and resolutely stayed put, under royal orders to do so.[11] The Generalitat, the Catalan governing body, had arbitrarily jailed one of the inquisitor's servants early in 1611, and much hue and cry arose over the incident, which eventually found its way to King Philip III, who dutifully sent an official to resolve the conflict. Domenge was in the cells of the Inquisition ten months before the decree of banishment, when the stress was mounting; how or if the events affected her case is unknown.

The only historical events related by Domenge are those that impinged directly on her celestial communications; true to the type of text she was producing, she was completely focused on what God's messages to her were and how those messages were delivered. The two opening folios of the manuscript provide the only seemingly concrete information in the entire document, and even they contain suspect details. For example, the so-called secret cells of the Barcelona Inquisition, which Domenge called "isolated," were neither secret nor isolated; from the time of the tribunal's founding, city citizens knew that they were located in the cellars of the buildings that adjoined the north side of the cathedral, forming a long block that, even until the last generation of Barcelonians, was popularly known as "Inquisition row" [el carrer de l'Inquisició].[12] Domenge's dictations, then, pertain to a mode of representation whose blended types of reality are true to spiritual as well as physical existence, and the moral objective of her text overrides all others.

Having initially represented herself as happily marching off to persecution like a martyr, Domenge continued her holy memoir in that hagiographic vein, transforming her jailers into experts on *Flos sanctorum* and reluctant, teary officers of an invisible but potent power. Such are the metamorphoses that the vindicated Domenge, recalling her own tribulation with the confidence of hindsight, could effect in what was surely a frightening, intimidating experience:

> When the *alcalde* and the secretary had me inside the prison, they burst into tears and said to me, "For a woman, very cruel and lonely is this prison, but the gentlemen inquisitors have ordered us to use this prison." And they consoled me and told me that Father Ignacio [de Loyola] had been to the Inquisition twice and St. Peter the Martyr, and that he would get me out. Finally, they showed me the charity of consoling me with the lives of saints. And the secretary said to the deputy, "Sir, bring a chair here, for it is shameful to leave a woman here amidst so much filth." And this he said with tears. And having said these words, they left said prison and they closed me behind two doors. (2v)[13]

After recalling how she was brought in, Domenge then spun off into autohagiography. Never again did her account set its feet on earth.

Where God closed two doors, he evidently opened many windows, for no sooner did she find herself enclosed in damp darkness than Domenge—so the manuscript says—began to experience a litany of visits from innumerable members of the heavenly host, who descended upon her, singly and in small groups, to console her in her time of trouble. By the time Domenge actually undertook the task of remembering the long moments she spent in her cell, sufficient time had passed for her to work the entire experience from the very difficult interval it doubtless was into a heroic trial whose great dimensions were signaled by the hundreds of holy illuminations with which God, Christ, the Virgin, and a multitude of angels and saints regaled her. She represented her entire jail term as one long rapture in which some prominent celestial celebrity or another whisked her out of her dark, smelly, threatening environment into an inversion of that same environment: ethereal zones of light, perfume, and self-affirmation.

First to arrive, or "call her," as she said, was her celestial spouse:

> And I, seeing myself thus locked in, raised my eyes to heaven and said, "Lord, you want it, and since you want it, I want it, for greater than

this is my desire to suffer for you. I'm not talking, Lord, about being in this prison amidst so much filth, rather being in the middle of a wheel of knives, if it be your pleasure and contentment [so] shall I be for my sins." This I said with many tears, for I felt that I deserved more than this for my sins. And when I said these words, Jesus Christ, my spouse, called me and told me these words: "Sor Ana, religious of Father St. Dominic, why are you so distraught? Am I not in the jail with you?" (3r)[14]

With Christ beside her, how could she be anything but orthodox? In her cell, she turned to gaze upon a faded crucifix that a former prisoner had evidently scratched on the wall in ink. Thereupon, she said, she was suddenly able to see the figure in all its original detail, and the dark cell was suffused with "more light than the sun," as she was swept into rapture, an ecstasy whose most immediate and salient quality was a heavenly scent. In that rapture, Christ "called her" again and took her to task: "'Say it, are you not my spouse?' And I responded, 'Yes, Lord. I am the spouse of Jesus of Nazareth.' He said to me, 'Since you are my spouse, why are you so upset? Have you not told me many times that you wished to suffer for me?' And I responded, 'Yes, Lord" (3v).[15] Domenge thus used Christ not only as a vehicle to confirm her posture of humble submission before authority but also to remind her reader of her longing to earn the blessings earned by those who suffer persecution in God's name. This is the opportunity the Inquisition afforded her.

This privileged position, however, called for some adroit management, since being called in for examination by the Holy Office did not exactly suggest divine approval, much less divine favor, and the apparent lack of both made it difficult for Domenge to present herself as one suffering for God rather than a woman beguiled by the devil. Aware of this dilemma, Domenge set about transforming the Inquisition's challenge of her orthodoxy into a process designed to celebrate her as the innocent one who willingly submitted to suffering in God's name, at God's will. In using the Inquisition as the instrument to assign Domenge the suffering for which she had long pined, Domenge's Christ transformed the Holy Office from a despicable place for heretics to a holy forge where God's chosen were pounded into shape, where would-be martyrs were tested, as

Christ himself reminded her, asking: "'Have you not asked me to make you a martyr many times?' And I replied, 'Yes, Lord" (11v).[16] Such idealized recollections were clearly an extension of the examination process itself, a transformation of the procedure that challenged Domenge's orthodoxy into an experience destined not for the mere orthodox but for God's highest elect.

Domenge's rendition of her brush with the Inquisition is unique, for unlike most who were so imprisoned, she did not silence her experience but rather transformed it from an event in human history into a dramatic proofing of her merit as a spouse of Christ, evidence of her superiority, not her error. She wrote her account after she had been released and, she said, at the insistence of her confessor: "Because my confessor ordered me to, I am having this written, when I went to the Holy Inquisition, in the year 1611" (1r).[17] Insistence on her confessor as the motivating force behind the dictation of her Inquisition memoir was not merely Domenge's invocation of a standard humility topos but also her protection from the grave error of violating the oath of secrecy demanded by the Inquisition of all those it interrogated.

There were other reasons for her not to talk about her visions. Women in general were expected to be silent, which, compounded with the expectation that all religious keep God's blessings strictly to themselves, produced a doubly potent injunction against her speaking out: as Saint Juan de Avila (1500–1569) reminded those who received particular blessings from God, "true humility asks and desires to hide God's gift" [la verdadera humildad pide y desea esconder la dádiva (de Dios)]; only when the Holy Spirit specifically ordered one to speak (or write) could the mandate be suspended, the saint said.[18] Not surprisingly, this is what Domenge, as most early modern women whose visions were recorded, said happened:

> I was fearful because I did not want to write the mercies which the Lord showed me because I saw I was not worthy to receive them and although my confessor had ordered me to do it, even then I was afraid and wanted to keep them to myself.[19] And the Lord said to me, "My spouse, fear not. You shall tell your confessor when he comes that it is my will that you write my mercies and that to those who set out to

serve me and love me perfectly I shall grant even greater mercies than I have to you." (45v)[20]

Interestingly, the confessor's mandate, which Domenge already had, gave her insufficient justification to proceed with the enterprise, which she said she was unwilling to undertake without Christ's own prodding. Only Jesus was able to confirm the ultimate benefit of Domenge's visions being made public: their usefulness to others. Implicating Christ in the process of self-representation allowed Domenge, and a host of other women in the same position, to present herself as both helpless and submissive (in that she was only repeating what God had told her) yet simultaneously important (she was repeating God's own words and had been chosen as God's messenger). The posture, a perfect blend of resistance and compliance, satisfied the mandate for female modesty and also allowed these women to voice their own concerns by seamlessly joining them to God's.

Reconstructing her experience from a temporal distance, Domenge was eager to flaunt her vindication but not the process that had redeemed her, and she logically provided no information about the interrogation to which she was subjected and offered but cryptic references to the reasons that had brought her to the depths of the Holy Office, insisting instead on how many saints, from Thomas Aquinas to Teresa, confirmed both the orthodoxy of her faith and her destiny as one of God's select few. Tucked in these conversations, however, was indirect mention of worldly challenges of that orthodoxy and flat-out denials that she was as close to the saints as she claimed to be. She recalled, for example, that she complained to Saint Dominic in a visionary conversation, "I don't know why they are keeping me here. [If it is] because of the kind of prayer I practice, preachers preach it" (4v).[21] Christ himself, she said, confessed to her in an earlier vision that the visit to the Inquisition had been his idea: "It has been my will that people persecute you and gossip about you and thus likewise my will that you have come to the Holy Inquisition" (3v).[22]

"Recalling" that it was Christ's will that all this happen was an able move on Domenge's part, for by insisting that Jesus engineered her imprisonment, she obligingly melded divine will with that of the Inquisition, indicating that both operated in harmony in arresting her. Such creative acts of memory fit into her larger agenda of justifying what Jesus called "my Holy Inquisition" [mi Santa Inquisición], where he, in his divine omnipresence, arranged for her to be sent, as he explained, "so that my secrets and heavenly treasures be declared in my holy tribunal, where truths are declared and my person represented" (12r).[23] Defining the Inquisition as the place where the Divine is made manifest and the truth brought to light made Domenge's trial a revelation *for* the inquisitors, turning her into the instructing subject, not the instructed object.

The nature of the written testimony by and about Domenge contained in the manuscript at hand, considered with the cases of other women tried for false sanctity during this period, makes it likely that this willful woman's rigidly orthodox, radically observant practices and frequent, easy conversations with the heavenly host led some of her less conservative sisters to suspect her motives as well as her means, and they turned her in to the Inquisition, perhaps in the hope of having her removed from their midst. The identity of whoever turned her in was protected by the anonymity guaranteed to all inquisitorial informants. In trials of false sanctity, the rubric under which uncontrollable, often ambitious, women were tried, the would-be saints were usually reported to the Holy Office for indecorous bragging about the mercies of God they received and for lesser offenses, such as provoking the jealousy of a female neighbor, all of which the unfortunate inquisitors had to sort out.[24]

The individuals who are said to have visited Domenge in her cell also served to confirm her status as well as sanction her intentions. Not surprisingly, her most frequent visitors and those who "stayed" with her the longest were prominent Dominicans: Dominic himself, Catherine of Siena, Vincent Ferrer, and Thomas Aquinas. Of the latter, Domenge maintained: "These saints [referring to Dominic, Thomas, Raimundo, Jacinto, Vincent Ferrer, Luis Beltrán, Catherine of Siena, Teresa of Avila] disappeared, but St. Thomas Aquinas remained with me and stayed the entire time I was imprisoned, for he never abandons me, and always was there with me" (4v).[25] Domenge represented Thomas Aquinas as very much with her throughout her examination because his presumed presence bolstered the weakest point of her case: her doctrine. He was evidently a temporary necessity and by no means as dear to her in the long run as his female counterpart and Domenge's own alter ego, Catherine of

Siena, whose behavior, as reported in Raymond of Capua's much read *vita* of Catherine, served as a model for Domenge's own. In the 154 folios of vision accounts which follow, Domenge scarcely "saw" Aquinas again, whereas the closer she came to planning a house for Third Order Dominicans, the larger Catherine—a Third Order Dominican herself—loomed in her visions and the more obviously influential Catherine's *vita* became on her own.[26]

Members of the heavenly host who supposedly visited Domenge in jail, whose rank and file first appeared to her in two long, tidy rows, eventually became so numerous that she confessed she could not identify them all (6v). The sheer quantity of all these personalities necessitated an elaborate means of message passing and shared responsibilities, reflective of baroque Catholicism. For example, Domenge related how the Virgin—ever accompanied by her faithful spouse, Saint Joseph—consoled her in prison and was able to negotiate a promise of Domenge's release by interceding with Jesus, who then consulted with God, who acquiesced because of Domenge's devotion to Jesus' mother (4v). Clearly by 1611 Spanish Catholic devotional practice had developed from Teresa of Avila's intimate, binary relationship between her soul and Christ into a rich panoply of florid personalities and presences, next to whose domineering presence the worshiper pales in comparison.[27] There is an abundance of religious writing by women which reflects this trend, most notably the spiritual life story of Marina de Escobar (1544–1643), who was reportedly attended by a host of guardian angels and members of every order of the angelic hierarchy, as well as the more standard celestial company.[28] By 1611, the humanistic moment of the exalted individual was well on the wane.

Although she pretended toward an orthodox purpose, the methods Domenge is documented as employing often tottered precariously on the limits of acceptability. She was believed to cure even deathly ill people in God's name with her mysterious power to lay on hands and is described as working tirelessly as an intermediary who supplicated to a wrathful God on behalf of the sinful world. In 1614, however, an unbelieving nobleman insisted that she cure one of his relatives on the spot. When she could not perform the requisite miracle, he turned her in to the Inquisition as a false saint, although God, so the document reads, "responded for his [and her] honor" [respondió por su honra] (95r). Domenge is described as gifted with the standard features of the holy woman of her age: she could ascertain who among the dead was in heaven, purgatory, or hell; she knew about certain events, particularly those related to death and illness, before they happened; and she articulated God's will with greater facility than most voiced their own.

Most of these qualities are made clear in her rendition of her inquisitorial encounter. Although the content of her visions varies across the years, their fundamental nature, particularly their transparent relationship to the problems Domenge encountered in her daily life, continued unchanged throughout the four years covered by the manuscript, and there is little evidence of spiritual growth across the same period (which is quite short, in any case). This consistency makes it possible to hypothesize with some certainty that the practices described in the manuscript were similar, if not identical, to those for which Domenge was tried by the Inquisition. In all likelihood, it was not the fact that she was having visions which was problematic but their peculiar nature, too close to earthly concerns, too facile, and often bordering on superstitious practice.

Domenge's mission was to bring the faithful back to the practice of a ceremonial, orthodox faith whose ritualistic parameters she felt were clear and very important. Her activities during a drought in Perpignan are revealing of Domenge's determination to reestablish the vigorous practice of Catholicism's most minute formalities. Not for her the sixteenth-century belief in generous, forgiving faith and emphasis on inner piety over outer works. Domenge insisted repeatedly on the nuts and bolts of observance and the abnegation to accompany it. She represented departures from the dictated procedures as incurring divine wrath (and necessitating her Virgin-like intercession), as occurs in this rendition of a 1611 problem:

> There being here in Perpignan a great need for water, there were many processions, and they did one with the holy crucifix of St. John, which is said to be one made by Nichodemus, and they say that they had never taken this statue out without it raining forthwith. They did this procession at night. Our Lord did not see fit to give water. To all appearances, the procession was performed very devoutly, and the Orders

and many disciplinants went and people had come out for it. We asked our mother what was the reason why Our Lord did not show us the mercy of rain. She said that the procession they had done had not been properly performed, that Our Lord had told her that they had been complacent about it and that they had not carried the holy statue along the route it was supposed to follow, rather they had twisted the way out of complacence and that Our Lord had also told her it was important that the disciplinants shed blood to the ground if they had not confessed and that after they had returned from the procession, many had gone on to offend his majesty mortally.[29] . . . Our Lord told us [saying to her], "My spouse, I shall not open the heavens until they do another procession of my holy statue and they pass along where they pass the procession of the holy sacrament, and that after it shall have rained, they do another, giving me thanks." And thereafter St. Thomas Aquinas spoke to her and told her the order they were to follow so that Our Lord should show mercy to Perpignan. (37r–v)[30]

This message was passed to the appropriate secular judge (*jurado*), who refused to reroute a second procession, whereupon Saint Nicholas evidently appeared to him and instructed him in no uncertain terms to do so. The *jurado* responded, "We're already performing plenty of devotional acts" [que ya se hacían hartas devociones] (38r). He died a few days later. After another conversation with a rather petulant Jesus, Domenge repeated the precise instructions for the route and conditions of the procession to her confessor, who relayed them to the new *jurado*. The story ends there, unfinished, but it suffices to provide an impression of the tactics employed by Domenge to bring her town to more godly ways and the type of issues with which she had confronted the Inquisition in 1610.

Equally telling of the period during which Domenge was experiencing God is the way in which she described her relationship with Christ. Always introduced as "my spouse" [mi esposo], he never failed to address her as his spouse as well; the pair thus reinforced their holy union at every turn. The matrimonial relationship between nuns and Christ intensified in religious literature written by women after the turn of the seventeenth century; Teresa of Avila, for example, rarely referred to herself as Christ's bride, and God almost always addressed her as "my daughter" [hija mía]. Domenge, on the contrary, *only* perceives herself in terms of a wifely function in relationship to Christ. This domestication of spiritual experience reflects the increasing enclosure of women in the home and convent, their concurrent exclusion from public places and activities, and the growing emphasis on women as wives, a female role exalted by both Protestant and Catholic ethics.[31] The distinctions between earthly wives' responsibilities to their house and husband and nuns' duties toward their convent and celestial spouse became blurred.

Emphasis on the wifely functions of nuns was a trend that, in a narration of the homespun variety like Domenge's, produced a Jesus who approached her frustrated and tired after what was implicitly a long day's work, needful of the reviving contact only his life companion could bring him: he complained to her of the human race, saying, "Look how distressed they have me, my spouse. I'm coming to find some rest in you" [Mira cuán afligido me traen, esposa mía. Yo me vengo a descansar contigo] (51v). The timing of the scene is important: it occurred during the battle of wills between Domenge and her "husband," in which she wanted him to forgive the people of Perpignan for their sins and let it rain, but he believed they did not deserve it and held out with the drought. In the scenes preceding his tired turning to her, she represented herself as having begged him repeatedly for mercy to no avail.

Like a knowing wife, she waited to catch Christ in a moment of fatigue and repeated her entreaty with particular fervor, which induced Jesus to reveal the real reason why he would not let it rain: the misbehavior of priests. This revelation, in turn, produced a difficulty for Domenge, which she resolved by impugning her confessor and thereby protecting this critique of the clergy: "I did not want to say that business about the priests and the Lord told me, 'My spouse, do not fear, and you shall tell your confessor, "Father, Jesus Christ my spouse has told me not to fear rather to write,"' and that just as I believe in the articles of faith and in the Holy Church's commandments, so Your Reverence must believe that Jesus Christ my spouse has told me to write this" (52r).[32] The intimate companion of the Divine, Domenge was represented as privy to information brought to light by her able manipulation of her celestial spouse for the benefit of humanity.

The Holy Office evidently found what any reader can ascertain today from the 167-page manuscript account of Ana Domenge's visions: although an unsophisticated believer, Domenge was not a heretic but rather a zealous woman whose interpretations led her, a religious Don Quixote, into literal practice of a largely symbolic faith. Since 1215, a heretic had been defined in canon law as one who obstinately refused to conform her or his beliefs to the teachings of the church.[33] Orthodoxy was a question of submission, and Domenge provided no threat on that count, as she repeatedly made clear her desire to do God's will as it was manifest to her through the Inquisition, whose power and rights she soldered to those of Christ himself. Of the inquisitors' request that she consider taking up residence in the monastery of San Jerónimo so that a superior could supervise her prayer activities, she reported: "I wanted to obey the gentlemen Inquisitors because I saw it was Our Lord's will that that Holy Tribunal represent the person of Our Lord" (13r).[34] Domenge's Inquisition was her ally in Christ, in her mind (or at least her words as recorded here) a far cry from the evil institution constructed by subsequent histories. This attitude, particularly when considered next to Teresa of Avila's insistence that she would seek out the Inquisition herself should she doubt the orthodoxy of her own experience, suggests that people considered the Holy Office not only as a menace but also as a resource.[35] Not surprisingly, the extant female religious authors of the late sixteenth and early seventeenth centuries represent themselves as its supporters. The ones who did not support the institution can be read about only in trial documents.

Domenge described herself emerging from the depths of her cell cleansed and more convinced than ever that God was with her. The radiant self-assurance that it took Teresa of Avila years of painful doubt and longing to attain was replaced, in Domenge's case, with an official stamp of approval by the church bureaucracy. Teresa of Avila knew in her soul that God was with her and claimed to be unintimidated by the Inquisition; Ana Domenge, who represented herself as a willing participant in the examination process, used the sanction she obtained from the Inquisition as her passport to bigger and better proofs of her position as the chosen one for the reform of the female Dominican order in Spain, a dream she was unable to fulfill, at least by 1615. The two women differ radically in the depth of their expression, and the essence of that difference is what most confirmed their respective positions: Teresa representing herself completely justified by God, Domenge rendering herself as justified by the Holy Office.

One of the principal discrepancies between the saint and this holy woman, whose account has rested untouched for centuries in an unlikely archive, is their effectiveness with words, as Domenge's voice—reaching us through her female scribe—reminds us repeatedly, particularly in the opening folios that describe the time she spent in jail. Domenge's syntax is redundant, her lexicon extremely limited, and either her scribe was inept, or she was unable to articulate her most important experiences in anything but the most basic of terms, using flat modifiers when any and leaving the reader aware that something had been shared with Domenge but that she was unable or unwilling to reveal what that was: "He [Christ] showed me all the mysteries of his sacred Passion, all in glory and blessing" [Me mostró todos los misterios de su sagrada pasión, todos en gloria y en bien aventuranza] (46v-47r); similarly, when Christ transported Domenge to Mount Tabor, all she could report from the supposedly exhilarating experience was that "the Lord worked many miracles" [el Señor hizo muchos milagros] (47v).

God was represented as effecting divine will relentlessly through Ana Domenge, and her exhaustion over being the vehicle of these repeated interventions became clear as the years progressed. But no one was able to render a moving, convincing account of those miracles, with the result that they failed to produce their intended effect of inspiring others to the virtue attained by Domenge. In texts like this—and there are many of this nature from this period—one realizes that the success of Teresa of Avila and John of the Cross was as much a function of their ability to express themselves in human language as to experience the Divine. Curing others with the touch of her hands and speaking to saints with the ease of someone now picking up the phone, Ana Domenge was a woman of action, not words. Mere textual representation does little justice to her and individuals like her.

Without the colors and contours of an expert wordsmith, ecstasy is reduced to hollow hyperbole that makes it impossible not only to enter the text empathetically but also to believe what it says. Thus, when Domenge confused the voices of her narrative, the reader is tempted to attribute the confusion not to the total transformation of herself into the Divine but rather to her inability to finish an utterance without losing track of who is the speaker, who the voice, and who the listener—for example, "Our Lord said to me, 'My spouse, you shall say to your confessor, "Father, Jesus Christ my spouse has told me that he was transfigured . . ."'" [Díjome Nuestro Señor, "Esposa mía, dirás a tu confesor, 'Padre, Jesucristo mi esposo me ha dicho que se transfiguró . . .'"]. The sentence crumbles a few clauses later, as the distinction between speakers fades into simply what Christ said to her confessor: "that they always offend me, that Your Reverence, who is a preacher, preach it" [que siempre me ofenden, que a Vuestra Reverencia, que es predicador, que lo predique] (47v-48r).

The confusion of narrative levels reveals rather transparently what was surely Domenge's frustration at not being able to deliver her reform-minded message to the public herself, frustration over the need to take recourse in representing herself as God's microphone, who merely passed God's message to a man of authority, who would be the one to say what Domenge herself wanted transmitted. Virtually every vision recounted in the manuscript, even those related in third person and recorded by a sister without Domenge's dictation, opens with the same declaration: "My spouse, you shall tell your confessor . . ." [Esposa mía, dirás a tu confesor . . .]. The reader is reduced to a voyeur of a somewhat pathetic, confused circumstance:

> The Lord told me, "My spouse, do you want to play?" And I said, "Yes, Lord." "Do you not see how much I love you? Do you not see how much I care for you, that I come to play with you and you play with me? I regale you with those heavenly games. And you will tell your confessor, 'Father, Jesus Christ my spouse has told me to tell Your Reverence that my spouse Jesus played with me with those heavenly games.' And you shall tell him that they are games so gentle and so sweet and with such gentleness that 'my soul emerged very happy and very spirited to serve and please his Divine Majesty more.'" (39v)[36]

The speaker is lost in the sticky web of messages woven by God for her confessor, messages she was expected merely to transmit. It was a role women carried out with particular efficacy, that of the willing, passive vessel of the Divine, a role clearly modeled on the silent submission of the Virgin, who provided the body through which God was manifest on earth.[37]

At the same time, the influence of Domenge's human desires on what her God wished to see happen is often all too clear. The episode in which the notorious "Valencian nuns" were doomed to destruction by Domenge's celestial spouse is telling. God responded to Domenge's repeated pleas that he not kill these women, saying: "Why do you plead with me on behalf of the Valencian nuns, since they neither wish to do my holy will nor respond to my holy inspirations nor give you any credit nor initiate the practice of holy prayer, for everything the Prioress said last night in chapter was her own idea and they want to deceive you. . . . You shall tell your confessor and your daughters that I wanted to punish the Prioress [and would have] if not for your pleas" (78r–v).[38] He later went even further, giving her a mixed message: "Do not plead with me on behalf of these nuns, for I wish to punish them. The Prioress with the injured arm and the Superior who fainted today shall die were it not for what you have beseeched me" (79r).[39]

The interchange culminates with Domenge's rather infantile Christ begging Domenge to let him have his way with her enemies, an act over which she is represented as having some control: "Let me punish them, my spouse" [Déjamelas castigar, esposa mía] (78v-79v). The illnesses and misfortunes that befell the prioress and superior, including the broken arm and fainting spells, are described as the minor chastisement that God managed to get through the restraining order placed on his wrath by Domenge's incessant prayers for those who despised her. Although this rendition left God debased, it satisfied Domenge's need to show herself as humble, forgiving, and selfless, while also demonstrating her calming power over God and implying that her enemies owed her their very lives. Such an incident, however, recalls Ludwig Feuerbach's 1957 reading of religious belief, according to which God "is the result of the projection of human wishes, attributes, and desires."[40]

Overall, Domenge's visions give the impression of a baroque fugue gone wild, in which confusion and desire blend into a benevolent chaos, a pastiche of present, past, and future. Reporting how she witnessed the

Annunciation, she related that the Virgin was visited by Gabriel and then immediately by Saint John the Evangelist, who consoled Mary for the pain she felt at the Passion and told her not to worry, that by Lent (which did not exist at the time of the Passion) she would see her son risen to glory (48r–v). Similarly, on the Tuesday of Holy Week, Christ appeared to her to deliver an interesting message: "I have to go suffer. You keep my precious mother company, for she is distraught in the midst of so much anguish and pain, and on Easter morning, after I have appeared to my precious mother and the Marys, I shall appear to you" (17v).[41] Passages such as this suggest that Domenge believed the events celebrated in the liturgical calendar actually happened again and again in divine time and space and that Christ had to hasten off to play his part every year.

The last experience recorded in the manuscript is true to Domenge's solid faith. Her confessor brought her a reliquary holding "a tear of Christ" from France, and one of her companions doubted its authenticity. Domenge was driven to her knees that night in prayer for the soul of her sister who dared to doubt and for herself, who could not help but request confirmation. God appeased her anxiety with a story that assures us that Domenge's orthodoxy, based on her great disposition to believe, could survive continued testing: "From among the five tears, this is the first and it is my will that that drop which fell from my precious eyes be in this convent, for I am its founder and you, my spouse, are the instrument as my spouse. My precious tear was in Rome and a Cardinal took it to Brulle and left it there, and I have made the religious woman who had it pass away because they venerated it little there." (167r–v)[42] The manuscript's final, fitting words are: "All this my spouse Jesus told me" [Todo esto me dijo mi esposo Jesús] (167v).

This remarkable document represents a woman recalling the most stressful event in her life through the haze of a verdict of innocent; had she been proven guilty, Domenge would have not been ordered to dictate her prison visions or any others, and she would never have been permitted to declare that Christ and his heavenly retinue were with her. Ana Domenge affords us a delightful glimpse of a holy woman, illiterate, determined, and anxious to support the ecclesiastical hierarchy, whose inquisitorial encounter ended happily and who turned the entire procedure of her seven-month examination into an apology for the Inquisition it-self. In her extrainquisitorial record, we see what a trial itself does not offer: a true daughter of the Inquisition. Without any of the violent and vexing implications of other women's cases, in which the accused was tortured, repressed, exiled, censored, or killed, Domenge's dossier offers straightforward evidence of the loyal gratitude that the vindicated could proffer on the Inquisition's behalf, serving to perpetuate and justify the institution. The Inquisition's stamp of approval on Domenge's exuberant piety made possible the continued documentation of her visions, and thus Ana Domenge's life began for posterity when she was summoned by what she called "this holy tribunal where gold is purified" [este santo tri-bunal donde se apura el oro] (10r).

CHAPTER EIGHT

María de Jesús de Agreda

The Sweetheart of the Holy Office

CLARK COLAHAN

I have become extremely fond of the Holy Tribunal and of the purity with which it proceeds [he quedado aficionadísima al Santo Tribunal y a su pureza de proceder].
— SOR MARÍA to King Philip IV, February 18, 1650

María Coronel y Arana, known to the world as María de Jesús de Agreda ever since her mother decided the house was to be converted into a convent and her bedroom remodeled with a grill for speaking through the wall, was the sort of woman whose date with the Inquisition, though it turned out to have been made in Heaven (as those things went), was as inevitable as a congressional investigation of a first lady with a life of her own. When not yet twenty she made a name for herself as a mystic, or rather the publicity efforts of her sisters and confessors at her Conceptionist (Franciscan) convent in Soria made it for her, when after taking communion she often fell into trances, was seen to levitate, and reported that she had been carried by angels to New Mexico and preached the gospel in support of Franciscan missionaries there.

Ten years later the custos of the order for the northern frontier of New Spain, Alonso de Benavides, reported in a *Memorial* to the king, and later the pope, that the Indians had confirmed her frequent presence among them preaching and urging them to seek out the Franciscans. The legend of the miraculous bilocation of the Lady in Blue spread throughout both Spain and Spanish North America, subsequently inspiring Fray Junípero

Serra and his missionaries in California and going on to remain very much alive in the southwestern United States in this century.

King Felipe IV knew of her reputation, and while looking for spiritual guidance in a time of personal isolation following the downfall of his favorite, the count-duke of Olivares, he stopped on his way to the battlefront with France to visit her in the out-of-the-way hometown she never left—at least not by conventional means. Despite her geographical isolation, troubled monarch and mystic abbess developed a close friendship through an exchange of letters which lasted until they both died in 1665, more than twenty years later. As royal confidante, informal confessor, and link for communication with heavenly personages, she wielded an influence that those with hidden political agendas sought to utilize. And to add an ideological dimension to her potential social impact, she wrote and shared with the king an eight-volume manuscript of the life of the Virgin Mary, with emphasis on revelations from the protagonist herself which made clear the very nearly equal standing of God's bride/Christ's mother with her divine husband and son.

Sor María was not, then, a low-profile figure in a century in which the Inquisition, guardian of the Counter Reformation, strove determinedly to curb the tendency toward a larger role for women in the church, and for the mysticism through which they increasingly found expression, a role that had been encouraged in the early sixteenth century under Cardinal Cisneros[1] and reached its culmination a century later in the canonization of Teresa of Avila. In addition to the two-week interrogation to which the Inquisition subjected her personally, and the Holy Office's repeated examinations on paper of her character and fame, her writings were several times singled out, both during and after her life, for examination of their orthodoxy. In 1648 a team of theologians met, at the king's orders, to consider her writings, as did a group of canons immediately following her death. Queen Mariana of Austria, Felipe IV's widow, set up a team of examiners for the same purpose, and the Franciscan order organized one of its own to study the biography and decide whether or not it should be published. When the decision was affirmative and the biography appeared in 1670 under the title *La mística ciudad de Dios: Vida de la Virgen* (*The Mystical City of God: A Life of the Virgin*), it provoked a polemic that placed it for some years on the Inquisition's Index of Forbidden Books and made it the subject, in 1696, of a congress at the Sorbonne.[2]

Still, despite all this inquisitorial presence in her life, Pérez Villanueva has correctly stressed that, contrary to what earlier investigators asserted, Sor María was never *procesada* (formally tried).[3] The questions, fact finding, and analysis—the information gathered for the grand jury, in a manner of speaking—never led to the formulation of charges or to her detention. Her intelligence and command of language served her well in finding a balance between the comforts of following her inner direction and the gracious acceptance of a secondary role within a masculine church hierarchy. The fruits of her life, in her assertion of the feminine aspect of the Divine and her efforts to influence public policy in favor of peace and compassion for the poor through her friendship with Felipe IV, necessarily subjected her well-known public example to official scrutiny. But her words, whether spoken or written, sounded in the inquisitors' ears with the ring of humility, good sense, and piety.

The first official investigation took place in 1631, conducted shortly after the publication of the report to the king on the Franciscan missionary efforts in New Mexico. In addition to advocating that the Crown continue to be the funding source for the New World missions of the order, the account contained another important political dimension in that it featured Sor María's missionary bilocation as evidence of divine approval of the order's work. Franciscans had been engaged with members of other orders, including reformers like Bartolomé de las Casas, in a polemic about the extent of religious instruction which should be given to the indigenous peoples of the Americas prior to complying with their requests for baptism. The Franciscan approach allowed baptism in large numbers, in "squadrons" as de las Casas scornfully put it, after a minimum of instruction, as a concession to the large numbers of souls in need and the scarcity of ministers. Further teaching would come later, it was hoped, as part of the ongoing mission work. But it was not, the other orders argued, the correct way to encourage a serious conversion to a new life. And there was, too, a less openly expressed resentment of the unfair advantage it gave the Franciscans in the interorder competition for missionary prestige and financial support. There is little doubt that the Inquisition saw the political importance of finding a definitive interpretation of the bilocation which would set the matter at rest.[4]

Ostensibly with that purpose in mind, three prelates went to Agreda in May 1631: Sebastián Marcilla, head of the Franciscan province of Burgos; Francisco Andrés de la Torre, Sor María's confessor; and Alonso de Benavides, the New Mexican custos who had returned to bring personally his report to the king and seek advancement.[5] The repeatedly published epistolary account of the interview penned by Benavides ("Tanto que se sacó de una carta . . . "), to which was appended a letter in her own hand from Sor María to the missionaries in New Mexico, became the most important vehicle for her growing fame and remains the most puzzling of her encounters with the Inquisition.[6] As we shall see, an investigation later in her life absolved her of responsibility for the extravagant statements made by her as well as by Benavides, who by then was dead, and attributed her cooperation to the timidity of a young subordinate in the presence of "graves padres."

Later researchers, including her friend, confessor, and first biographer, José Ximénez Samaniego, as well as late-twentieth-century historians, including Pérez Villanueva, have also preferred this more flattering view of her involvement. John Kessell, professor of history at the University of New Mexico, has been the scholar most willing to leave the complex question open: "Was fray Alonso leading the witness, or did the youthful abbess go along willingly? His story, after all, lent priestly validation to her earlier experiences, and the publicity was good for fundraising. María may even have read Benavides's *Memorial* before he arrived" (127).

The chief argument advanced for the position that Sor María was a passive victim of unscrupulous publicity agents has been that in later letters and interrogations Sor María invariably maintained that the bilocations had lasted only three years, from 1620 to 1623, after which God granted Sor María's fervent wish that such special favors stop. In marked contrast, the pair of letters from Benavides and Sor María specify that they were still taking place in 1631 and adds that Sor María, when asked by Benavides to allow herself to be seen by the missionaries as well as the Indians, replied that there had been no need for that so far but that she would ask God about it. Many other extravagant details suggest, although still not without leaving a reasonable doubt, that, counter to what she appears to have come to believe about herself later in life, the encouragement (or pressure) received from her three visitors did lead her to take her visions seriously and present them in a less guarded manner than usual to her fascinated audience.

The style and preoccupations of her letter sound authentically like those of her early writings, and one cannot help but wonder whether three high church officials would have dared to repeat on any authority except hers claims such as that Saint Francis, at her intercession, had sent two non-Spanish friars to the region who converted a native king and many of his people before being martyred by them, though their bones were saved in a silver box in a church there. Sor María herself lists in her own letter the names of Indian peoples that she believed, on the basis of revealed knowledge (erroneous, as it turned out), would be soon discovered. On balance, Sor María appears to have demonstrated the ability to adjust her perspective to the needs of the situation, an ability that characterizes all her contacts with church authorities. Observed in other Hispanic women of the period by Ruth Anthony El-Saffar as a typically feminine survival skill, it allowed her tactical retreats, both in outward expression and in inner belief, which preserved her sanity under pressure, her freedom, her voice, and ultimately the chance to influence others.[7]

Four years later, as the fame of Sor María spread throughout the region, the case was reopened as part of the Inquisition's campaign against "*lo maravilloso,*" which it understood as sensational or speciously miraculous forms of religious experience which were best censured as witchcraft or diabolic possession. The supreme court in Madrid ordered the branch in Logroño to ascertain whether or not "the nun at Agreda, who is called María de Jesús, goes into trances in public, whether she hands out crosses and beads, and what sort of divine grace she says they confer" [si la Monja de Agreda, que se llama María de Jesús, se arroba en público, y si reparte cruces y quentas, y qué gracia dize que tienen].[8] The Inquisition's commitment to stopping individuals who publicly displayed trances, speaking in tongues, and other spectacular forms of behavior remained strong over the centuries of its existence, since it was the danger of the spread of heterodox behavior, more than isolated acts of unmediated contact with the Divine or the demonic, which was principally feared.

Statements were taken from four people, including an Inquisition *cal-*

ificador (examiner), who was also Sor María's confessor: Francisco Andrés de la Torre. Though she lived in a community of women, Sor María received constant reminders of what was expected of her and what the acceptable limits were to the life of her spirit and her imagination. However, as the protégée, so to speak, of a member of the investigating committee, she can be assumed to have been protected from the dangers of particularly harsh treatment. The tribunal was told that the friars and nuns who some years earlier had unadvisedly allowed the public to watch while Sor María turned pale after taking communion, seemingly levitating while her spirit traveled to the New World, had discontinued the practice some years before.

The inquisitors at Logroño, clearly on Sor María's side, did what they could to play down to Madrid the famous bilocation, declining to pass any judgment on it themselves: "Here we have no examiners qualified to address it" [Aquí no tenemos calificadores tan a propósito].[9] They argued that the idea had been given to Sor María by a Franciscan friar, Francisco de la Fuente, who claimed to have done the same—his place supposedly having been taken in Spain by an angel while he miraculously traveled to the Indies—and who in 1632 had been found guilty by the Inquisition. He was also the person, they maintained, who had fooled the director of Sor María's Franciscan province into taking the possibility seriously. As always when investigating the nun at Agreda, the Supreme Tribunal found nothing to charge her with, and the witnesses' statements were merely filed away.

True to the Inquisition's spirit of religion in the service of politics, it was a political threat that finally led to a prolonged, systematic interrogation of Sor María. The record of the Inquisition's activity never lets one forget that it reflected a theory of governing which a century and a half earlier had moved the Catholic kings to establish the institution as part of their vision of an Iberia united through the imposition of monolithic religion and autocratic rule. In the middle years of Sor María's friendship with Felipe IV, the duke of Híjar had more than once written to her seeking her support in a plot against the king, and although she offered no support, she committed the indiscretion of writing back to him. The Supreme Tribunal, in Madrid, ordered in September 1649 that her case be reopened and completed with new questioning of the nun, which was specifically to include her statements on the letters exchanged with the duke of Híjar.

Prior to this decision, however, some months earlier in the year, a group of four calificadores had already taken statements from other examiners and from witnesses, who were asked for their views on the papers that had been presented on January 8, 1649, by Andrés de la Torre regarding Sor María's life and writings. A review of the documents generated years before in the case, including depositions given by the nun herself, had led the examiners to request the original copies of the paperwork, including Sor María's writings, and to affirm that "they found it very difficult to convince themselves that it was God's doing and not a passive or active illusion, or both together, and a little credulity on the part of those who have governed her" [Hallaban muchas dificultades a persuadirse a que sea obra de Dios y no ilusión pasiva o activa, o todo junto, y una ligera credulidad de los que la han gobernado].[10] For these reasons they had recommended that she be examined in person, and specifically by a learned and experienced person, since the case contained "many improbable things" [muchas inverosímiles].[11]

After the original documents and writings had been obtained, opinions on them had been requested from three other examiners. The first report had been issued by Lucas Grandín, who felt that there was insufficient evidence to make a final decision about whether Sor María's spirit was good or evil, and that he was sure only that there was cause for suspicion and concern. He questioned the sanctity of her trances, as well as that of the "Litany of the Virgin Mary" that she had written. He criticized the expressive adjectives and forms of address she often used in describing or speaking to God, recommending that she limit herself to conventional ones. He concluded that she suffered from many diabolic delusions, though reserving judgment on the extent of her guilt in the matter. But the Franciscan order, with which her Conceptionist convent was closely tied, also came in for adverse criticism and reprimands: the examiner who would be chosen to interrogate her should be of another order, the Inquisition should not allow her own order to select her confessor but appoint him itself, her order should not publicize the mystical "favors" its nuns might receive from above, and the latter "should live convinced that no one in the world is ever going to recall their existence" [ellas vivan persuadidas a que no ha de haber en el mundo quien se acuerde de ellas].¹² A more thoroughgoing attack on women's importance, sources of validation, and voice would be hard to imagine.

The second examiner, Alonso de Herrera, had been more restrained, reserving judgment until seeing the results of further questioning of Sor María. Still, he mentioned the possibility that everything that had been brought forward might be attributed to an overwrought imagination or demonic arts. Perhaps the devil had entered her body and blocked the use of her senses, turning her into a passive victim of delusion. Anticipating Sor María's own statement to the Inquisition the following year, he also suggested that the vehemence of her desire to be a missionary might be at the root of her believing that she had been taken to New Mexico. The third examiner, Tomás de Herrera, had taken a similar position, finding Sor María's visions to be definitely not from God, probably the result of passive diabolic delusion and the operation of her own imagination.

In response, then, to the recommendations of these several experts, the inquisitor general ordered a learned examiner to be sent from the Inquisition of Logroño, along with a notary of the Holy Office, to Agreda, where they arrived on January 18, 1650. On asking to see Sor María they were told that she was sick in bed and had been bled. It was true, but unknown to the inquisitor, she had burned her copy of *The Mystical City of God* a few months before in anticipation of just such an official visit arising out of the panic surrounding the duke of Híjar's plot. Her questioner was apparently also unaware that Felipe IV had a copy of the manuscript, which he was commenting on in letters to her at the time. After the interrogation was done, in a letter to the king on February 26, 1650, she wrote: "They didn't say anything about the history of the Queen of Heaven; they must not know about it. Until this storm passes, it's best to keep it hidden."¹³ Although the king did not intervene in the Inquisition's deliberations, it is clear that Sor María went into the examination with nerves steadied by royal support, even a degree of complicity.

When the nun learned of the arrival at the convent of the inquisitor, she presented herself in the locutory, took the oath to tell the truth, and began answering the prepared list of eighty questions, a process that required morning and afternoon sessions for ten days. Although the record of the questions and her responses has now disappeared, it was studied in the late nineteenth and early twentieth centuries by two scholars, Francisco Silvela and Eduardo Royo; the latter published a substantial extract in 1914 as part of a multivolume biography of Sor María and demonstration of the authenticity of her authorship of *The Mystical City of God.*

The abbess's attitude toward the Inquisition's representative was appropriately respectful but assertive of her innocence. She declared that she had always tried to tell the truth and been concerned to avoid all censure as serious as that of the Holy Office. With a single affirmation she cleanly discarded the whole subject of demonic influence, nebulous and dangerously susceptible to manipulation by her enemies, insisting that she had always detested the devil. A similar adroitness in redirecting the thrust of the questioning is apparent in her responses to questions about her having seen God and her contact with New Mexican Indians and with angels.[14] She focused not on such "improbable" companions but on the three types of visions she had experienced, which had been described in analytic detail by Teresa of Avila.

The wording of her response demonstrates her ability to make use of what has often been characterized as masculine discourse—logical, abstract, and with the ring of learned authority. The first dictionary of the Royal Academy of the Language includes her as one of the authoritative writers who set the standard for correct usage, citing her particularly to support intellectual neologisms with a Latinate base. Despite her self-protective statements that she had only a sufficient grasp of Latin to understand prayers in church, the geographical and cosmological facts included in her works, such as her description of an astral journey around the world and up into the heavens, demonstrate that she read the language reasonably well.[15]

Theological formulations, not surprisingly, then, such as the one used here in responding to the Inquisition, were frequently presented by Sor María. They provide the dominant linguistic medium in her book-long displacement of self-affirming behavior as a woman onto parallel but theologically differentiated actions by the Virgin, as we encounter it in *The Mystical City of God.* Essentially philosophical language is employed to define the differences that separate the author, who is a woman, from her subject, who is divine, yet at the same time the matrix of ideas points indirectly to the parallels that unite the two women. Sor María commonly uses such distinctions in the interests of a societally required downplaying—at least at the level of a literal reading—of her own importance while still affirming that she has had remarkable experiences.

An equally important result of this strategy, which is a constant in her work whether it was consciously deployed or not, is that those experiences will now be interpreted as blameless, related to but not the same as the unacceptably elevated ones attributed to her by others: "God does not reveal himself in his true nature, but as it is communicated to the understanding by the mediation of a presence within the intellect, a sort of intuitive vision. This does not reveal the true presence, although it does contain it, so it can easily happen that one of God's creatures, and her spiritual director, to whom this vision is communicated may fall into deception, thinking that this is seeing the divinity, when, in fact, that can happen only to the blessed."[16]

Another of her explications of this quintessentially mystical experience shows the same reliance on abstract vocabulary, both to translate into conventional language as closely as possible the fundamentally ineffable character of the God-woman encounter that she has known and to insist that it is God, not the anonymity-seeking woman, who has taken the initiative: "Although through that veil, only partially, the veil that prevents us from seeing him completely, immediately or instinctively, without a veil, for this glasslike medium that I have mentioned . . . is a mirror, but a voluntary one, and reflects only when it is God's will" [Aunque con aquel velo, medio, que impide el verle del todo, inmediata o instintivamente, y sin velo, que este como cristal que he dicho . . . según es la voluntad divina mostrarlo, porque ese espejo es espejo voluntario].[17]

Contrary to the impression that might be left by her letter of February 26 to the king, her biography of the Virgin was an issue raised by the Inquisition with her. She stressed that it had been written at the recommendation of her confessors and other holy men, who had assured her it was a commendable undertaking. She was careful to explain, though, that because of the anxiety of being the author of such a book she had burned it. Some time later she had been ordered by a confessor to rewrite it and had begun to do so. However, with the onset of the problems generated by the letters that she had written to the duke of Híjar, she had stopped writing and burned what she had done. She had recently started again and turned those few pages over to the inquisitor. As noted above, she made no mention of the king's copy. The inquisitor had every reason to believe that she had been caught between conflicting pressures within the church hierarchy, that she had no plans to write further unless so directed by the Holy Office, and that he personally could find satisfaction in reporting having taken possession of the few pages still in existence.

Questioned about the unusual adjectives she had applied to Mary in her litany in honor of the Virgin, she replied first, to diminish the level of presumption and authorial threat that she might represent to the ecclesiastical organization, that she had written it only for the use of the other nuns and that it had been published in Zaragosa against her will. She appealed directly to heavenly sources to justify the inclusion of her newly coined advocations of the Virgin, explaining that she had come to know them by means of *inteligencia,* a term that probably refers to the familiar concept of mystical acquisition of information through "infused knowing" and familiarity with the Bible. She went on to clarify the sense and implications of each term used, logical exposition again coming to the defense of nonstandard, feminine theology.

Sor María, with her perennial gift for winning over her potential enemies by warm expressions of sisterly love, concluded the last day's interrogation with professions of humility and appreciation of the instruction she had received. She pointed out, by way of apology, that her memory might well have failed her, since the events in question had happened so long before. She affirmed her desire to obey the Inquisition, hastening to add that she respected and venerated it to the utmost. She even appealed to the inquisitor's self-image as a fountain of paternal benevolence, thanking him for coming to her spiritual assistance at a time when the death of her confessors had left her very much alone.

The response to such manifestations of a willing and grateful obedience was, as Sor María must have felt fairly confident it would be, entirely positive. The team of examiners declared themselves "admirados y satisfechos" (amazed and satisfied) and asked to be given crosses and other souvenirs of the nun they had found so charming.[18] Their official verdict entirely freed her from suspicion of being a misguided, self-promoting woman of learning, stressing that her great knowledge of the Scriptures came more from continuous inner communication with God than from study. The authors of the *Memorial* of 1631 were censured for having heavily supplemented what Sor María herself had said about the bilocation and attributed her signing the document to "una indiscreta obediencia"[19] that was the result of her tender age at the time. After the inquisitor general had confirmed with his signature the opinion of the examiners and notified Felipe IV, the king wrote to Sor María congratulating her.

In relating the experience of the interrogation to him in her next letter (February 18, 1650) she made it clear that she had been able to see its positive side and that she had approached it almost gladly in that it enabled her to set her conscience at rest from worries about the inaccurate, sensational stories told to each other by her confessors and picked up from the other nuns in the convent. Not even in the intimacy of her relationship with Felipe IV ("I will hold no secrets back from Your Majesty, whom I speak to and esteem and share my confidences with more than with any other human being" [No he de tener secreto reservado para Vuestra Majestad, por lo que le hablo y estimo y por la confianza que de Vuestra Majestad tengo más que de criatura humana])[20] did she reveal any bitterness. She praised the inquisitor's conduct as characterized by "great piety and secrecy" [gran piedad y secreto] and even declared a strong affection for the Holy Tribunal.

Nonetheless, the tone may be partially attributable to euphoria at having so recently escaped from danger. When she wrote to Felipe again on March 11, her choice of words revealed much less enthusiasm. She lamented that she had been so alone and with no one to advise her when the official visit arrived, while describing the sessions of interrogation as long and remarking that they had taken place in the bitter cold of January. The gap separating ambivalent feelings of self-confidence and self-distrust typical of many mystics, including most Old Testament prophets, is clear in the anxiety she expressed about being an ignorant woman with nothing but moments of divine inspiration on which to rely.

Feminist criticism of such women writers has sometimes taken the position that their self-esteem was solid and their self-deprecation a useful ruse to gain a voice. But the tone of passages like the following one suggests that Sor María, though capable of self-bolstering by imaginative displacement to the mythos of the Virgin, had internalized at least a portion of society's evaluation of women's capacities: "It is only through the goodness of God that I find my conscience and will clear in spiritual questions, though I am not without dread of having gone astray because I am an ignorant woman" [Por sola bondad de Dios, me hallo libre la conciencia y voluntad en las materias espirituales, aunque no sin temor de si he errado como mujer ignorante].[21] And while we know now that the self-affirmation expressed by the *The Mystical City of God* would continue in the coming decade, in 1650 she was careful to stress that the cause of the scrutiny she had just undergone—the sensational *exteriori-dades*, outward manifestations of spirituality, of the youthful years of the bilocation—was a thing of the distant past in her life, the bitter fruit of a troubled time.

However, Sor María's written commentary on the interrogation was not limited to her correspondence with the king. She also was instructed to report to Pedro Manero, general director of the Franciscan order in Spain, and did so at length. It is a skillfully composed self-portrait that first sets the encounter in the framework of her childhood and youth and then addresses one by one the most sensational items in the 1631 letters.[22]

She began disarmingly with the words "I confess," though, curiously, she specified that the fault for which she admitted deserving a reprimand was her reticence at times in the past when she was asked to comment on the events in New Mexico, and the excuse she offered was her wish that no memory of herself might survive. Again, as when answering the inquisitor's questions, she stressed that the intervening years might render her memory unreliable, a defense that seems not only prudent but truly reflective of the tendency of the imagination, very powerful in her case, to reshape how we recall the way we were.[23]

She described the events of the bilocation as a continuation of an inner illumination that had been with her since the earliest years she could remember. That it was both God the Father and her own parents who had placed her on the path that led to those controversial experiences was stressed. From an early age, she recounted, in a home atmosphere that would eventually lead to both her parents and all her siblings becoming members of religious orders, she had enjoyed, in alternation with feelings of unworthiness and vulnerability, feelings of God's supporting presence in her life. When the apparent bilocation took place, her reason and judgment were not yet strong enough for her to see it as something different from those earlier favors from God. An implied acceptance of the view that women needed to recognize and struggle against their inherent emotionalism was thereby brought in to her credit.

She explained, however, that when she reached an age to be more rational, the dominant concern with which God illumined her mind was the extent of the tragedy that there should be peoples who did not know him and whose souls, on that account, would be lost—hence her burning desire to be a missionary, strengthened even further when God showed her the New Mexicans and told her that they, more than any others, were in need of conversion. Again, the combination of an adroit defense with a psychological truth. She implied justification by a desire more praiseworthy than censurable, while at the same time remaining true to the reality of many mystics—and intensely religious persons in general—who often feel a keen fear of the Lord's power to inflict suffering on them for wrong behavior.

The intensity of her feelings, she explained, reached the point where she went into trances, but it was her imprudent confessor and sister nuns, not she herself, who publicized the development. She was not even aware, she pointed out in defense of her humility, that people were allowed into the convent to watch her until told of it by a mentally ill patient being cared for there. So bitter was the shock that she made a vow never to take communion unless she had first shut herself with a padlock in the lower choir, where she thought, mistakenly, that she could not be seen. When the key was taken away from her, she drank syrup before breakfast so that she could not be forced to take communion and consequently fall into a trance. What better proof of her pure intentions, her valiant resolve to resist the improper actions of her companions, could the general minister wish? Had she been apprehended in a serious crime and then forced by the civil authorities to parade through the streets of the town on a donkey, she added, she would not have felt as humiliated as she did when she was observed in moments of spiritual elevation.

The interviews of 1631 were forthrightly labeled as inaccurate, and the errors were attributed to the investigators relying on statements made by nuns and friars at Agreda, especially her overly enthusiastic mother, a procedure they adopted not out of any irresponsibility—something unthinkable in such good men—but in response to her keeping everything related to the subject in the rigorous secrecy of the confessional. The consequences had turned out to be unfortunate, and she more than anyone had suffered as a result, but how could she be faulted?

In addressing the specifics contained in Benavides's letter she suggested that God may have allowed her to believe that she was working as a missionary in order to relieve her anguish at the thought of those poor, damned souls. Saint Paul, too, took part of the blame, for he also, despite his much better grasp of God's secrets, had related that he had been carried up into the third heaven but could not tell whether it was in body or soul. In her apparent bewilderment, she even fell back on Francisco de la Fuente's explanation, which had a long and prominent history in medieval Spanish folklore and religion, the belief that cloistered nuns were sometimes impersonated by the Virgin or by angels so that the woman could leave the convent to satisfy some intense longing, marriage, for example. Conversely, the possibility that an angel was impersonating her in New Mexico instead of Spain, while God let her look through her double's eyes there, was also raised. To give Manero the sense of being in control of the discussion, she declined to give a definitive explanation and, instead, organized her arguments into two groups, those in favor of a bodily journey and those against. Once again, rational analysis was used to defuse the threat of irrational feminine mysticism.

The interrogating priests' mistakes were dissected and underlined with logical precision, and their detailed exposure lent credibility to her position. Benavides reported, for example, that she had sometimes been in New Mexico for three days at a time, when in fact it was a question of passing through such bad periods of illness that she was unable to speak for three days. The veil that Benavides claimed she had given him, telling him that it was her husband's, that is, Christ's, was one she rarely used, did not give him, and was probably taken from the wardrobe by her mother. Benavides misunderstood the figure of speech used in the statement that Saint Michael and Saint Francis had carried her to New Mexico, among Franciscan nuns a common metaphor for the intervention with God of those two saints on a sister's behalf. Benavides asserted that she claimed to have several guardian angels, when in fact, although they did watch over her, those angels had not been with her continuously and so could not be classified as guardian angels, for she would never think of herself as worthy of having more guardian angels than anyone else. And as to the nuns' tale that Sor María had had contact of some sort with angels, she scornfully expressed amazement that any educated person could think that an angel, a bodiless, spiritual creature, could have physical contact with a human being.

Further, Sor María objected strenuously to the priests' assertion that they took it all down from her mouth, and she insisted that she was so terrified that she did not know what she was signing, leaving everything in the hands of the supposedly cautious friars. Only the question of her letter exhorting the New Mexican missionaries resisted satisfactory explanation. She dispatched it in a single sentence with an excuse that, for once, was rather lame: that she gave it to Benavides privately, thinking that not a creature would see it.

Never again was Sor María interrogated by the Inquisition, even though her life of the Virgin would provoke so much controversy after her death. There is no reason to doubt the sincerity of her expressions of extreme humility and pious obedience to the church hierarchy. But the abject self-image that made them possible and necessary coexisted—with some psychic friction, perhaps reflected in her constant illnesses, but less than one would imagine—within her personality with another, astonishingly more confident one that asserted itself in her visionary life and gave her the courage to advise her king and outsmart her Inquisition. That part of her knew that she was exceptionally intelligent and articulate, capable of defending herself so as to be able to carry out the transcendent missions entrusted to her by God in return for her awed acceptance of his will. Hers was the gift of making peace between the demands of a narrow world that never let her go beyond the walls of the cloister and those of a strong personality that felt itself called to heroism on the frontiers of the faith.

CHAPTER NINE

Contested Identities

The Morisca Visionary,
Beatriz de Robles

MARY ELIZABETH PERRY

God came to her in rapturous visions, Beatriz de Robles told neighbors
in her Andalusian village, and paid her "a thousand tender compliments"
[mill requiebros y ternuros], letting her know that she was "very beloved
and favored" [muy querida y favorecida de Dios].[1] She experienced these
visions privately "in her house and in its corners and from her window "
[en su cassa y en sus rincones i desde su ventana], as well as in church,
where she went into trances following communion. And, in the words of
the inquisitor reporting on her case, she had made her visions "public and
had boasted" of them [publicado de si y alavadose].

Beatriz de Robles's stories may have amused or impressed her neighbors, but they alarmed inquisitors, who called her before the tribunal of
the Holy Office in the nearby city of Seville. After months of testimony
and interrogation, they led Beatriz de Robles and forty-nine other penitents to the Plaza de San Francisco on the last day of November 1624 to
participate in a public auto-da-fé. At this traditional ritual in which onlookers reaffirmed their faith and listened to the transgressions and sentences read aloud for each of the prisoners, inquisitors condemned Beatriz de Robles for *alumbradismo,* or Illuminist heresies.

Except for her prosecution as an *alumbrada* by the Inquisition, Beatriz
de Robles seemed to have an ordinary life. The Inquisition's report of her
case described her as "wife of Juan de Baestra, resident of the village of
Fuentes" [mujer de Juan de Baestra vecina de la villa de Fuentes], a very

small town not far from Seville, where inquisitors worked in a permanent tribunal of the Holy Office which had first come to Seville in 1480. At the time of the report, Beatriz was forty-eight years old. Her life, as those of so many women, centered on her religious faith. She frequented the village church, and there she told others about her religious experiences and visions.

Inquisitors had concluded that Beatriz's religious experiences resembled too closely illuminist enthusiasms, which had troubled the church for more than a century. Illuminists took communion very often, and they emphasized mental prayer rather than observing the formalities of liturgy. They believed that they could better find God by turning inward than by listening to the sermons of priests, for they saw themselves as temples for the Trinity whereas the clergy were mere mortals whom they were not obligated to obey. To illuminists, no object could symbolize the love of God; even the crucifix appeared to be simply a piece of wood. Their "doctrine of pure love" seemed to inquisitors to be too close to the centuries-old heresy of the Free Spirit, which taught that individuals could attain a state of perfection which placed them above all human authority.[2]

In the early seventeenth century Illuminism had taken on new energy in Andalusia, where social, economic, and political changes bred a special vulnerability to Illuminist appeals among the poor and the powerless, a group that increased in number and visibility during the early modern period. Here towns and cities felt the social dislocations of urban growth that brought far more people into their protective walls than local housing, economy, and charity could support. As trade developed with the New World, Seville became the official port for all ships participating in this trade. The ensuing "price revolution" of this period struck Seville and its environs most directly, bringing higher prices that quickly outran increasing wages. Tensions between the old paternalistic system of landed nobility and a newly developing commercial capitalism also impelled many people to seek a religious faith that could provide consolation and an alternative to customary hierarchies of authority. The tribunal of the Holy Office in Seville made a special effort to obliterate Illuminism at the same time that Beatriz de Robles was telling her neighbors about her visions. Its edict of faith which defined the heretical beliefs of alumbrados elicited so many self-denunciations that in 1624, the year that she was penanced as an alumbrada, inquisitors issued more than four thousand pardons for alumbrado heresies in the archbishopric of Seville.[3]

Not surprisingly, witnesses and inquisitors identified Beatriz de Robles as an alumbrada, for this heresy had become primarily a female transgression associated with women who reported visionary experiences. With her at the auto of 1624 appeared six other women accused of Illuminist heresies but only three men so identified, plus the remains of a fourth man who had died in prison. These accused alumbrados may have responded, in particular, to the appeal of Illuminist beliefs that challenged the authority of the church and recognized the power of the individual to make direct contact with God independent of clergy, liturgy, or saints. For women, the least empowered in the social hierarchy, visions held a special appeal.

In condemning her as an alumbrada, inquisitors also noted one factor that distinguished Beatriz de Robles from the other accused alumbrados: she was a Morisca, that is, a Muslim or descendant of Muslims who had converted to Catholicism from Islam. After the Crown ordered the expulsion of Moriscos in 1609, the Inquisition continued to prosecute some Moriscos who had received permission to remain in Spain, but Beatriz de Robles appears to be the only Morisca prosecuted as an alumbrada. Although available historical sources tell us little of how she identified herself, Inquisition documents assert that she belonged to two very different groups: one associated with the devious apostasy of former Muslims and their descendants, and the other with Christian visionaries whose heretical enthusiasms had been condemned by the church. Her identity as both Morisca and alumbrada presents a paradox that is almost a contradiction in terms, providing a window into early modern Spain, where lines of identity often blurred and different interests met and clashed and somehow mixed together.[4]

As both an exemplar of Illuminism and the exception because she was also a Morisca, Beatriz de Robles represents far more than a single atypical case. Her case, in fact, acts as a prism that illuminates the complexities of an entire landscape of overlapping boundaries, cultural conflicts, and contested identities. Although inquisitors concluded that this woman simply engaged in the delusion of false visions, she actually represents a multiplicity of meanings that reveal the power of ordinary people even against the Inquisition.[5] As a woman in a male-dominated society, Beatriz de Robles signified both the same and the other, a person to protect and also to control, particularly dangerous in asserting visionary experience. As a Morisca increasingly oppressed by a Christian ruling class, she had to accept the identity imposed on her by the Inquisition; yet beneath this label she, as most colonized people, hid both an assimilation with the potential to subvert the dominant culture and a determination to survive.

Dangers of Delusion

At first glance, Beatriz de Robles's religious experiences hardly appeared dangerous. In fact, inquisitors seemed to treat her as simply a victim of her own unbridled imagination feeding upon the delusions of other women. Indeed, this case, except for her Morisca identity, sounds very much like those of countless other women prosecuted for "false visions" and mysticism. True to this pattern, Beatriz de Robles would take communion often, and then she would swoon and go into a trance. "After taking communion, she gave many fearsome roars and sometimes she was propped up at the wall and remained as though unconscious and gave sighs."[6] Superficially, such behavior could be a nuisance to those attempting to maintain the decorum of formal religion, but in itself it did not seem threatening.

Visionary experiences, however, did embolden women to violate gender prescriptions that narrowly limited behavior and speech considered appropriate for them. "Visions," as Elizabeth Petroff has observed, "were a socially sanctioned activity that freed a woman from conventional female roles by identifying her as a genuine religious figure."[7] Although Counter Reformation Spain provided women with "only an internal or psychological space in which to express themselves," people wanted to hear about the visions of Beatriz and other women; hungering for more immediate experiences of the Divine, they urged the women to speak and, even more important, listened to them.[8] Visionary experiences justified the public speech of women, who learned not only to speak out but to use this power as a means to influence others.[9]

In fact, ecclesiastical authorities especially worried about the charismatic power of such women, who, they realized, could infect others with their beliefs and enthusiasms. Beatriz de Robles, after all, had spoken about her visions with a group of *beatas*. Inquisitors regarded these women with suspicion because they usually lived free of any convent or religious rule and often spoke of visions and the messages they received directly from God, free of any clerical intercession or control.[10] When Beatriz had lost consciousness after communion, "other beatas gathering her in their skirts made air for her and asking them what was wrong with her they responded that she was filled with the love of God and was consumed in it."[11] God's favor thus excused behavior that would otherwise be seen as inappropriate for these women. And, significantly, these women undermined clerical authority by answering their own questions and providing their own interpretations of religious experiences. Thus, they learned to define what they considered to be reality and to trust their own experience.

Beatriz's behavior became even more dangerous, for she had made the mistake of speaking out publicly to tell others that God had come to her personally, singling her out as one he favored and loved. God showered her with compliments, as a lover treats his beloved, and she heard them in her house, in its corners, and from her window. Her enthusiasms did not stay in church to erupt only after communion, nor did she curb her sense of God's favor with the humility used by individuals who successfully defended themselves against accusations before the Inquisition. Teresa of Avila, for example, had expressed self-doubt, calling herself a "dunghill," and had written of fear that her visions were the product of "womanish imagination."[12] In contrast, Beatriz de Robles had continued to go into trances and to utter sighs so that, according to the Inquisition, she could convince others of her "saintliness" [para ganar opinion de sancta].

The Inquisition had reason to fear the influence of Beatriz, for it had seen for more than a century how visionary women became charismatic leaders revered not only by common people but by kings and soldiers who believed in their gifts of prophecy. Earlier in the sixteenth century, María of Santo Domingo, for example, had become famous and very influential as the "beata de Piedrahita."[13] In the 1580s, many political leaders venerated Sor María de la Visitación, who blessed the ships of Philip II's Invincible Armada but also supported his opponent for the Portuguese throne.[14] And in 1622, just two years before the auto-da-fé of Beatriz de Robles, the Inquisition had imprisoned Madre Catalina de Jesús, the leader of an alumbrado sect of nearly seven hundred people in Seville and nearby villages. According to inquisitorial records, her followers obeyed her directives, knelt to kiss her hand when they met her on the street, spread stories of her miracles, and venerated pieces of her hair and clothing as relics.[15] Not only did such visionary women invert the gender order by developing their own positions of authority without deferring to male clerics, but many beatas even assumed the role of director to clerics, who became their "spiritual sons."[16]

Although Beatriz de Robles did not seem to have any spiritual sons, the potential power that she could develop from her visions troubled inquisitors. To preserve the authority of the church, which was so deeply rooted in the gender order, inquisitors had to redefine her visions and make certain that male clerics—and not beatas—interpreted them. Inquisitors declared her visions to be false and reported that in these trances "her body trembled in order to win opinion of sanctity and so it would be said as it was said that that proceeded from the love of God."[17] They ordered for her the customary punishment for deluded hysterical women: appearance in a public auto-da-fé to swear her loyalty to the church (*abjure de levi*) to demonstrate her submission to the authority of the church. To correct her delusions further with some lessons in humility, the Inquisition sentenced her to live for two years in reclusion in a women's hospital, where she would work as a servant to earn her food.

During the two years of reclusion, a "knowledgeable and prudent" [dicto y prudente] confessor was to be assigned to her who would direct her "in what [was] appropriate for the salvation of her soul" [en lo que conbiene para la salvación de su alma]. Presumably, he would forbid her to have anything to do with beatas, limit the times she would take communion, and lead her to doubt the visions in which she believed that God whispered tender endearments, wooing her as his most beloved. Emphasizing the marginality of her position, the confessor could seek to control this woman who, as most women in male-dominated societies, represented to authorities a necessary but dangerous frontier between same and different, order and chaos.[18] Confession would become a ritual of ventriloquism in which the confessor's carefully directed questions would elicit from Beatriz the answers believed appropriate and acceptable to the church, rather than provide an opportunity for her to express her own interpretation of her experiences.[19]

In this way, the church could restrain the power ready to burst from the desire that Beatriz's visions seemed to celebrate. When she described herself as wooed by God, Beatriz asserted her own desirability and expressed, at least implicitly, her own desires. It is true that, in what may be termed a politics of desire, she avoided overtly erotic descriptions and clothed her assertions in a discourse of piety which could make them more acceptable to those with power over her. She did not say explicitly how God wooed her or what tender endearments he told her. Nor did she, as other visionaries, describe God in her visions as a handsome youth with whom she experienced physical touching.[20] She did not even report that he had kissed her. Rather, Beatriz left her description of the visions in very general terms, and she presented them as a regular occurrence in her own home. Moreover, she disguised her rapture in God's embrace by avoiding any direct explanation of her visions. Beatas, she had declared, were the ones who explained her rapture following communion as evidence that God had so filled her with his love that it was consuming her.

Yet inquisitors doubted her sincerity, regarding her visions as transgressions against a gender order that prohibited women from even acknowledging their erotic desire except in the confessional, where it would be defined and made safe in the terms of the male confessor's questions. In contrast to conventional literature that portrayed the body as an adversary of the soul, Beatriz's visions seemed to fuse her body and soul in a single self adored by God.[21] Her visions depended upon her body as the agency through which she could express her wonder and ecstasy. In these experiences, Beatriz learned not to deny her desires but to reach out and direct them toward union with God. Such an act subverted the gendered assumption that women needed men's direction in knowing and controlling their desires, and it challenged a widespread denial of the spirituality of sexuality.[22]

In naming her an alumbrada, inquisitors carried out an act of power, imposing their interpretation of her visions upon her understanding of them.[23] Official identification as deluded woman covered over, and thus publicly canceled out, the identity she gave herself as most favored by God. In this naming, inquisitors attempted to confine her in a structure of knowledge in which they could "regulate and organize reality according to well-defined categories."[24] Against such power, Beatriz had to acquiesce.

In defining her, confining her, and assigning her to the strict supervision of a confessor, inquisitors not only checked the potential power of Beatriz's desire, but they also reinforced the authority of the church, which continued to play a significant role during this period when fledgling states attempted to extend and consolidate their powers. The church legitimized rulers, provided a divine rationale for secular government, and also symbolized a common identity that masked regional and class differences.[25] During the period of the Counter Reformation, the church acted in particular to set and maintain boundaries—not so much the geographical limits often associated with territorial states but cultural markers of identification which differentiated Catholics of the Spanish kingdoms from others such as Turks and Protestants.[26] Within Spain, the church and its close associate, the Inquisition, worked vigorously to define both a set of beliefs that all the faithful must share and a corpus of deviant beliefs and behaviors that would not be tolerated.

Visionaries threatened the very foundation of this complex religious institution that buttressed the infant Spanish state. By claiming to enjoy a direct line of communication with God, visionaries undercut the position of the clergy, especially when they conveyed understandings given by God which contradicted church teachings. Their personal experiences with God encouraged them to defy the authority of the church, and their visionary enthusiasms erupted into strange, sometimes ridiculous, and powerful behavior that threatened to overturn all of society. Beatriz de Robles, after all, claimed to be especially favored and beloved by God, she who was but a lowly forty-eight-year-old housewife from a small village near Seville. Just as beatas had inflamed her, so her delusions, if not corrected, would infect other simple people and subvert not only a political system and a gender order but assimilation itself.

Subversion and Assimilation

Already suspect by reason of her identity as a visionary woman, Beatriz de Robles gave authorities further cause for concern by her Muslim ancestry, an identity that most clerics viewed with suspicion.[27] After 1492, when Christian forces defeated the last Muslim stronghold in Spain, Muslims became increasingly subject to pressure to convert, with the result that many Muslims accepted baptism without understanding its significance while thousands of others were forcibly baptized.[28] Long suspected of being false Christians who hid their continuing allegiance to Islam, Moriscos were forbidden to observe any of the cultural and religious practices of their tradition. Yet many Moriscos followed a Muslim tradition of *taqiyya,* that is, outward conformity to an oppressive religion while maintaining Islam internally and continuing these prohibited practices in secret.[29] Clerics believed that women were the most "obstinate" in refusing to abandon their Muslim traditions and assimilate into the Christian culture.[30] Usually inquisitors prosecuted Moriscas for teaching the Arabic language and Muslim prayers to their children, for washing and praying according to Islamic law, and for everyday cultural practices such as cooking with oil rather than lard.

Hostility toward Moriscos sharpened with the dispersion of Granadan Moriscos throughout Castile following their abortive rebellion of 1568–70. The Crown ordered the relocation of some 50,000 Moriscos living in Granada to various places in Castile, where inhabitants regarded them with suspicion. In Seville, which had been directed to receive 4,000 Moriscos from Granada, ecclesiastical leaders ordered stricter surveillance of all people of Muslim ancestry, even those who had lived there for generations.[31] Parish priests took a census of all Morisco inhabitants of Seville in 1589, which indicated a total of 6,655, and carefully noted where each one lived and with whom.[32] Finally, after considerable debate, Philip III ordered the expulsion of Moriscos from the kingdoms of Spain beginning in 1609, declaring that conscience bound him to excise "the things that cause scandal and damage to good subjects, and danger to the State, and especially offense and disservice to God our Lord."[33]

Expulsion decrees exempted a small percentage of Moriscos, including slaves, certain protected groups, and about 6 percent of the Moriscos who worked as vassals for Christian nobles.[34] Marriage probably saved Beatriz de Robles from expulsion, for under the terms of expulsion Moriscas who married Old Christian men could stay in Spain if they were living as "good Christians."[35] Since Inquisition documents do not specifically identify Beatriz's husband, Juan Baestra, as either a Morisco or a *converso*, it is reasonable to assume that he was an Old Christian. Another possible reason why Beatriz was allowed to remain in Spain is that Moriscas were exempt from expulsion if they were professed nuns or beatas. But it seems more likely that at the time of the expulsion in 1609, she was already married, since by then she would have been thirty-three years old and the average age at first marriage for Moriscas was seventeen or eighteen.[36]

The fact that inquisitors found Beatriz to be an alumbrada fifteen years later raises significant questions about assimilation and the means by which the converted populace sought to prove or to mask their assimilation. Perhaps anxiety to be perceived as a good Christian prompted Beatriz to regard frequent communion as persuasive evidence that she was indeed a "good Christian." Perhaps, too, the example of beatas encouraged her to seek further proof in inner religious experience that could be verified by external behavior such as rapture and vision. Moreover, to embrace a new religion with emotional enthusiasm must have relieved the uncomfortable ambiguity of people, such as Moriscos, who had been under pressure to change religious beliefs and practices. Since the Inquisition continued to prosecute Moriscos accused of apostasy, it seems likely that Beatriz sought the protective religious armor of enthusiastic Christian piety, perhaps deliberately attempting to obscure her identity in representing herself as a Christian visionary.

However, in accepting the multivalent identity of alumbrada and Morisca, Beatriz de Robles did not merely conform to an official definition of her; she also resisted the dominant Christians' system of knowledge, which carefully established distinct and separate categories for Christian and Muslim. As both Morisca and alumbrada, Beatriz represented more than one category, thereby demonstrating a mixing of these categories in herself and implying the possibility of syncretism, that is, the fusion of apparently conflicting beliefs. Although most people recognized the differences more than the similarities between Islam and Christianity, some hoped they would gradually combine into a single faith. And even highly placed clerics such as the archbishop of Granada accepted as true the syncretic message of the famous "books of lead" found buried in Sacromonte at the end of the sixteenth century. These books emphasized the similarities between Christianity and Islam and suggested possibilities for a peaceful settlement to enmity between the two religions. Not until 1682 would the papacy declare the leaden books forgeries.[37]

Yet most Christian officials did not accept syncretism as a form of assimilation, for the assimilation they sought required nothing less than complete conformity to a Christian orthodoxy. Christian officials passed laws that forbade Moriscos to honor any beliefs or practices of their Muslim culture, and they scrutinized their daily activity for any small deviance from Christianity. From the middle of the fifteenth century, Christian authorities passed purity-of-blood laws that prevented people of Jewish or Muslim ancestry from entering a university, religious order, or monastery, holding certain offices, or following specific occupations.[38] Even if Beatriz de Robles had hoped simply to hide her identity as a Morisca beneath the official label of visionary and use her excessive piety as proof of her complete assimilation to Christianity, for most authorities her Muslim ancestry threw into question the genuineness of her conversion. Thus, her very blood prevented the assimilation believed acceptable in seventeenth-century Spain; and in accepting for herself a multiplex layering of identities, she subverted conformity even as she appeared to accept it.[39]

Although some historians emphasize the role that Moriscas played in preserving Muslim culture, others note that some of these women became "even fervent" in their Christianity.[40] The possibility remains that Beatriz de Robles was among the Moriscas who became sincere Christians. Her parents and grandparents could have been very well assimilated into Spanish Catholic society even before she was born, and the fact that an Old Christian man married her suggests that Beatriz herself was already assimilated before the expulsion decrees of 1609–11. In prosecuting her as an alumbrada rather than a Morisca, the Inquisition seemingly did not believe—or chose not to believe—that she still clung to Muslim beliefs and practices. Authorities insisted upon regarding Beatriz in terms of a single identity, that is, one that could fit into the dominant structure of knowledge, which assumed that the individual has a unified, integrated identity that conforms to a single category.[41]

Other evidence suggests, however, that Beatriz de Robles does not yield to simple categorization. History shows that Islam and Christianity met and overlapped in messy and confusing mixtures that defied official categories of knowledge. Although leaders of both Christianity and Islam warned against syncretism, ordinary Muslims and Christians did not see so clearly the line that separated their beliefs.[42] As Christian authorities arrested and expelled Muslim leaders, Islam in Spain became mixed with both Judaism and Christianity in a form of popular syncretism.[43] Common people, who had much less education in the tenets of either Islam or Christianity, were more likely to recognize an overlapping area of shared stories from the Bible, beliefs in angels and demons, in heaven and hell, in a Day of Judgment, and the need for prayer and for religious leaders.[44]

Veneration of Mary, the mother of Jesus, also provided a bridge between the two religions, one that especially appealed to women. Both Christian tradition and Morisco legends defended the virginity of Mary, and the leaden books of Sacromonte described Mary as a virgin after giving birth as she was before, and they declared that she had been born free of original sin.[45] As in the Christian tradition, Moriscos had stories in which the angel Gabriel appeared to the maiden Mary with the news that she would bear a son. In the Morisco versions, however, Mary conceived when Gabriel breathed on her body, and as she gave birth to Jesus, he proclaimed on leaving her womb, "There is no God but Allah; I am Jesus, spirit of God and His word."[46]

More specifically relevant to Beatriz de Robles, Moriscos compared Mary to such beloved women as Aixa, cherished wife of Muhammed, and Aminah, Muhammed's mother. Like Mary, Aixa was known as the source of purity, and Aminah as the obedient instrument for a divinely ordained birth.[47] Although Aminah did not conceive and give birth as a virgin, she received many celestial signs and the recognition of holy women: "There is none like you, O Aminah, from whom emanates the perfect friend, the resplendent light, and the supplicant for people in the Day of Judgment."[48] In many ways, God's words to Beatriz in her visions—that she was "very beloved" and "favored"—echo those spoken to

Aminah as she gave birth to Muhammed. Moreover, as in the case of Beatriz and the assurances of beatas, Aminah received important support and legitimation from female figures.

Beatriz de Robles's visions suggest similarities between the Christian alumbrados and the Sufis. Both sects emphasized emotion and personal experience rather than intellectual knowledge and external religious observances, and both Sufis and alumbrados sought union with God through turning inward, away from the world. A Muslim description of Sufism could just as easily apply to alumbrados: "The Sufi approach is based upon constant application to divine worship, complete devotion to God, aversion to the false splendor of the world, abstinence from the pleasure, property, and position to which the great mass aspires, retirement from the world into solitude for divine worship."[49] Both Sufis and alumbrados underwent individual trances and group experiences that sometimes became extravagant expressions of emotion with dancing, weeping, ecstatic shouts, incomprehensible speech, and prophecies.[50]

Not surprisingly, both sects appealed to women, especially those marginalized by poverty and birth. Since women had less worldly power and intellectual learning, they had less to give up in surrendering themselves to the love of God.[51] Mysticism and visionary experience for both alumbrados and Sufis promoted what has been termed a "feminization" of religion which undercut the authority of a male clergy and displaced formal theological learning with individual feeling. Female visionaries became renowned in Christian Spain for their "familiar simplicity" in teaching the love of God, and the Sufi teacher al-Ghazzali urged his followers to "hold to the religion of the old women."[52]

In fact, both Sufis and alumbrados revered some women as saintly leaders and teachers. A beata, Isabel de la Cruz, became known in the sixteenth century as the "true mother and teacher of all the alumbrados," and many other women assumed the title *madre,* although inquisitors subsequently prosecuted them for "spiritual arrogance" and other crimes.[53] Sufis recognized Rabi'a of Basra (died 801) as a saint and great teacher, "the Crown of Men," and "a second spotless Mary."[54] Beatriz de Robles's depiction of herself sounds very similar to a biographer's description of Rabi'a as "on fire with love and longing" and "enamoured of her desire to approach her Lord and be consumed in His glory."[55] The visions that Beatriz de Robles described closely resemble the verses of a prayer by Rabi'a:

> O my Joy and my Desire and my Refuge,
> My Friend and my Sustainer and my Goal,
> Thou art my Intimate, and longing for Thee sustains me. . . .
> Thy love is now my desire and my bliss,
> And has been revealed to the eye of my heart that was athirst,
> I have none beside Thee, Who dost make the desert blossom,
> Thou art my joy, firmly established within me,
> If Thou art satisfied with me, then
> O Desire of my heart, my happiness has appeared.[56]

It is quite possible, of course, that Beatriz de Robles did not know of Rabi'a of Basra, had never heard of Sufism or of the many other Muslim women who had become venerated for their mystical piety, knew nothing of Isabel de la Cruz and the alumbrado heresies. The point here is not a question of causality but a context of contested identities that when examined closely reveal similarities as well as differences. Clearly, Spanish Catholicism differed from Islam; but assimilation rarely means the complete obliteration of a minority by a dominant group. Most often it means adaptation to a dominant group, and usually the group in control lacks the means to enforce complete hegemony. In seventeenth-century Spain, even the awesome Inquisition had limitations. Neither the church nor the Inquisition could eliminate all Moriscos and their culture; in fact, Muslim symbols and ideas continue to influence Christian mystics and visionaries even up to the present.[57]

What the Spanish church and Inquisition could do was to define a boundary between acceptable and unacceptable deviance. In the case of Beatriz de Robles, this boundary referred not to her Muslim background or any alumbrado heresy she had embraced but rather to gender: inquisitors found Beatriz guilty of assimilating so well that they identified her with visionary women whose great crime was to violate gender boundaries. Losing control of the body as they engaged in ecstatic utterances and trances, these visionary women engaged onlookers in a form of "holy theater" which sanctified the female body, undercut clerical authority, and overturned male dominance.[58]

Survival

It is tempting to conclude that Beatriz de Robles, like so many people prosecuted by the Inquisition, was simply a victim, but a closer reading of the evidence shows her as a survivor. While it is true that she had to assimilate as a "good Christian" in order to remain in Spain and that her assimilation into Christianity took such an excessive form that the Inquisition prosecuted her as an alumbrada, the fact remains that fifteen years after successfully escaping expulsion, she received from the Inquisition a lighter sentence for heretical mysticism than did the majority of Moriscos condemned as renegades or apostates. Her punishment of two years of reclusion contrasts sharply with the sentence usually imposed on Moriscos judged to be apostates or renegades: perpetual prison for women, years of galley service for men, and confiscation of goods.

As a Morisca, Beatriz de Robles was particularly vulnerable to official prosecution by the Inquisition and to prejudice from the common people. Survival depended on avoiding statements or behavior that could be construed as evidence of Islamic observance. Not only did she have to avoid any suggestion of ritual bathing or praying while seated on a prayer mat, but she had to be careful not to change into clean clothing on Fridays, sit on the floor as she ate, cook food in oil rather than lard, or sing the songs of her Muslim forebears.[59] Above all, she could not meet or talk with other Moriscos. Intentionally or not, Beatriz de Robles avoided all these pitfalls so successfully that apostasy did not even become an issue at her trial.

Even in terms of the charges of heresy brought against her, Beatriz emerged a survivor, for she received a lighter sentence than other alumbrados penanced by the Inquisition. Her residency in the village of Fuentes undoubtedly affected this lighter sentence because she lived at some distance from the city of Seville and belonged to no alumbrado group. Among the alumbrados penanced with her, only Beatriz was from Fuentes. Inquisitors did not implicate her in any meetings with alumbrados, except for their reference to the beatas who had "made air for her" [hacían aire] when she entered a trance and then explained that she "was full of the love of God" [lleno de amor de Dios]. Nor did inquisitors implicate her in any meetings of the loathsome alumbrados who congregated in Seville's cathedral in the chapel of Our Lady of the Pomegranate. In 1625 inquisitors condemned this large group of alumbrados, which they called the "congregation of the pomegranate" [la congregación de la granada], as a "monstrous machine" [machina monstruosa] whose "poison" [ponçona] had infected 695 people already condemned and had "contaminated thirty cities and villages" [contaminadas treinta ciudades y villas].[60]

Beatriz also survived the heresy prosecution because she limited the description of her visions. She presented them as simply personal experiences in which God wooed her with "a thousand tender compliments" [mill requiebros y ternuros] and made her feel "very beloved and favored by God" [muy querida y favorecida de Dios]. In this respect she appeared more prudent and less dangerous than alumbrados and visionaries who were accused of saying they had seen who would be punished and who would be saved in the next world or, on an even more serious note, of relaying to political leaders information they claimed to have received from God.[61] According to the testimony, Beatriz did not attempt to interpret Scripture or dogma as other accused visionaries did, and no one accused her of engaging in inappropriate behavior with men.[62]

In rendering a lighter sentence for Beatriz, inquisitors may have acted on what they believed would best serve their own power. Possibly they regarded her as a simple beginner in visionary practices who had to be corrected before she attracted a following. Two years of reclusion under the direction of a confessor would be enough to rein in her extravagant tendencies, whereas a more stringent punishment would imply that she had dangerous powers that frightened authorities. In a sense, inquisitors seemed to follow the practice in witch trials when they usually reduced charges to blasphemy or sorcery and thereby defused the power that accrues to any person accused of a serious crime.[63]

The inquisitors' dismissal of Beatriz de Robles's visions as mere personal delusions cannot obscure the fact, however, that these visions empowered a woman who appeared to be otherwise powerless. Through her visions, Beatriz was able to break the prohibitions against acknowledging and expressing her desires. She used the visions to fuse together her body and spirit in defiance of the conventional split between the two, and the trembling of her body as she experienced a trance signified its sanctification as the medium through which God touched her. Although she carefully said nothing about sexuality in describing her visions, she implied a highly political eroticism that challenged all existing hierarchies when she spoke of God pursuing her as his most beloved.[64] In addition, she transformed her desires into a strategy for rising—as God's beloved—far above her marginal position as a rural, middle-aged Morisca in seventeenth-century Spain.

Visions further empowered Beatriz de Robles through providing an interior space for resistance. The evidence about her inner life in the brief official version of her visions offers grounds to speculate on how she might have carried out an inner resistance. Within her own psyche she could define herself and nourish a psychic mobility that would enable her to draw and redraw the boundaries of herself, accommodating to external power conditions.[65] If, for example, the confessor assigned to her made her participate in a ritual of ventriloquism similar to that of inquisitors who asked questions that carried with them the acceptable responses, she could parrot the responses while retaining within herself assurance that she did not have to accept the single and unchanging identity those answers bespoke.

Furthermore, within herself she could take the more radical step of seeking to merge her identity with God in her visions and to dissolve any sense of herself in a vast Oneness of nondifference.[66] No longer separate, no longer different, she could find bliss through melting into union with the Divine. Such drowning of the self meant painful and frightening self-annihilation to some people, but to many others the sense of self-loss brought indescribable pleasure.[67] In the case of Beatriz de Robles, who was supposed to internalize the Inquisition's definition of her self as deluded woman, such self-loss would be no loss at all, for choosing to dissolve herself in Oneness would be for her an act of defiance, making it all but impossible for an institution to locate and differentiate her, to fit her into a category of officially approved identification.[68]

Yet inquisitors did come to the small village where Beatriz lived, and there they located and arrested her; but so intently did they focus on fitting her into the single category of alumbrada that they overlooked another danger implicit in her visions. Perhaps if they had recognized that Islam and Christianity overlapped in Beatriz de Robles, they might have seen that her visions also could reveal a subversive assimilation marked by the persistent influence of three Muslim traditions: outer conformity masking internal faith, Sufi mysticism, and the revered saintly woman. The Inquisition seemed to have the last word in this case, as inquisitors sentenced Beatriz de Robles to work as a servant in a hospital for women under the direction of an assigned confessor. Yet as a Morisca and an alumbrada, Beatriz represented many of the beliefs and traditions that had developed over centuries on the Iberian Peninsula and which continued to persist despite opposition of a ruling class.

Historical records give us no further information about Beatriz de Robles. Evidently she did not run afoul of the Inquisition again, for she appears in no more inquisitorial documents. We can read the silences as well as the contradictions in these records for the political insights they provide not simply for her life but for the society in which she lived. They tell us of contested identities and overlapping categories, of blurred boundaries between Islam and Catholicism, of religious orthodoxy that could not be strictly enforced. They tell us, also, that women cannot be dismissed as mere victims in the past, floating about on the margins of society, for many acted as primary agents who developed strategies for survival even as they quietly subverted an official order. Combining, sorting, and adapting identities, they defined and redefined themselves, living out their lives with intelligence and passion.

CHAPTER TEN

When Bigamy Is the Charge

Gallegan Women and the
Holy Office

ALLYSON M. POSKA

In 1590, Margarida López, a Gallegan peasant woman, decided to get on with her life after having been abandoned by her first husband more than twenty years before. Margarida had heard rumors of his death, and in response she accepted the proposal of a local man and remarried. A few years later, young Caterina de Villaloa, the victim of an abduction, had her marriage to her captor annulled and settled down with her new spouse. In 1601, in order to follow her heart, Catalina Fernández conspired with her lover to falsify documents to prove that she had not been legitimately married to her first husband. Within a decade, all three women had been denounced as bigamists. No doubt poor and illiterate, Margarida, Caterina, and Catalina then came face to face with the most powerful and frightening institution in the land, the Inquisition.

When it comes to the minor crimes that fell under the jurisdiction of the Inquisition, women appear most frequently in bigamy trials. Their visibility is due, in part, to the nature of the crime, for unlike other heretical crimes, bigamy involves at least three people. As a result, the records of those trials offer a fascinating look into the marital lives of Spanish peasants, a view that historians are rarely afforded. In particular, the bigamy cases brought before the tribunal of the Holy Office in Santiago de Compostela between 1560 and 1700 reveal two important aspects of Spanish peasant women's lives: how they became involved in bigamous relationships, especially as the protagonists, and how peasant women dealt with the new Catholic Reformation regulations on marriage and remarriage.[1] While at first glance it would seem that the tremendous power differential between themselves—poor, illiterate women—and the inquisitorial apparatus—wealthy, literate men—would have rendered even the most assertive peasant women incapable of negotiating its bureaucracy, the historical record reveals a much more complex interaction. In fact, the records of the Inquisition trials indicate that, despite the tremendous obstacles placed before them, many women successfully defended themselves against the charge of bigamy.

The Charge

The charge of bigamy evolved from the Catholic notion that marriage created a permanent union meant to satisfy lust and allow for controlled procreation of the species. However, even though the Catholic Church had declared marriage to be permanent and indissoluble, the European populace did not necessarily act accordingly. When late medieval marriages failed, parishioners often took matters into their own hands. Some couples agreed to split up. Others simply abandoned their unhappy lives and moved to other places, where they created new personae and new families. Sympathetic to the plight of unhappily married couples, communities were often complicit in hiding bigamous relationships. In this context, bigamy probably came to light only when the new relationship offended the bigamist's legitimate spouse or disturbed the community.[2] For the most part, people were content to go their own way and to let others do the same without the intervention of the Catholic Church.

As the sacrament of marriage came under increased attack from Protestant reformers during the sixteenth century, the Catholic Church at the Council of Trent (1547–63) formulated more restrictive regulations concerning marriage which, among other things, facilitated the location and prosecution of those people whose actions desecrated the sacrament, that is, bigamists. According to the decrees of the Council of Trent, betrothals were to be announced in public and banns posted for three weeks to ensure that no other spouse existed nor any other impediments to the marriage. Parishioners were to be married in their own parish by a licensed priest in public with witnesses. Under most circumstances, the nuptial blessing would be conferred immediately so that there would be no doubt as to the complete administration of the sacrament. Finally, the names of the contractants and the witnesses would be entered into the parish marriage register. Such documentation was intended to delineate parishioners' spiritual and physical ties in an effort to prevent consanguineous or affilial marriages and bigamy. Moreover, as the church increased its vigilance over the sacrament of marriage, it reasserted the circumstances in which a widow or widower might obtain the dispensation to remarry. The death of a spouse had to be proven to the bishop's provisor before a second marriage could be undertaken. Neither the long absences of spouses, adultery, nor quarrelsome or troublesome spouses were acceptable grounds for terminating marriages. Without previous ecclesiastical intervention, any person who contracted a second marriage could be accused of bigamy.

In terms of legal jurisdiction, people accused of bigamy could be tried in either secular or episcopal courts. Jurists decreed that by marrying twice the bigamist not only contravened canon law but also offended civil society. During the sixteenth century, the Spanish Inquisition, which was mandated to deal only with issues of heresy, further complicated the jurisdictional conflict over bigamy trials. In order to adjudicate those cases, the Inquisition expanded the definition of bigamy to include the presumption of heretical ideas. In the eyes of the Inquisition, failure to uphold the sanctity of the sacrament of marriage created the suspicion of heresy, since Protestant reformers, including both Luther and Calvin, denied the sacramentary nature of marriage. Moreover, less clearly articulated suspicions linked the idea of remarriage to Jewish and Muslim traditions.[3] In truth, from a bureaucratic standpoint, the Inquisition was the institution best able to repress bigamy in early modern Spain because its structure, based on regional tribunals, facilitated the pursuit of bigamists who migrated from one region to another.[4] Thus, despite the protests of the local secular and ecclesiastical courts, the Inquisition gradually appropriated jurisdiction over bigamy.[5]

The crime of bigamy was more frequently prosecuted by the tribunal of the Holy Office in Santiago de Compostela in Galicia than by any of the sixteen other tribunals whose jurisdiction stretched from Peru to Sicily.[6] Galicia, in the northwest corner of the peninsula, had been part of the kingdom of Castile for centuries, but its rough topography left it relatively isolated from the rest of the kingdom. Unlike the wide-open Castilian *meseta* or the sunny Mediterranean coast, Galicia is a labyrinth of mountains, valleys, and hidden, rocky coves. During the religious controversies of the late sixteenth century, the region's ability to hide heresy loomed large. Philip II saw Galicia's Atlantic ports as replete with Anglicans and Huguenots, sieves for the entry of heretical ideas into the rest of Spain. At the same time, the Catholic Church expressed grave concerns about the poor, illiterate populace of the mountains.[7] One sixteenth-century inquisitor noted,

> If any part of these kingdoms needs an Inquisition, it is Galicia, a land prepared to take up any novelty, as it does not have the religion that there is in Old Castile, having no priests, no literate persons nor sumptuous churches nor people interested in hearing mass or sermons nor things befitting a divine state and [people] full of superstitions and the benefices are so tenuous and poor that there are not sufficient clergy to do the clerical offices nor can one have hope that they might have them.... It seems to me that this is something to fear.... We see them lost and because of this and their lack of spirituality one cannot do more good than to bequeath to them the Inquisition, in order to protect them from falling in errors and heresies.[8]

Royal and ecclesiastical demands eventually prevailed, and after two unsuccessful attempts, the Gallegan tribunal was installed in Santiago de Compostela in 1574, the last of the peninsular tribunals to be established.[9]

Horrified by the populace's apparent lack of religion, the Inquisition in Galicia immediately set about to reclaim the northwest for Christendom. In order to protect Gallegans from "falling into errors and heresies," the Inquisition zealously investigated the local population, uncovering dozens of blasphemers, fornicators, witches, and bigamists. Bigamy was the third most prosecuted crime between 1560 and 1700, constituting 11.3 percent of the total number of cases, exceeded only by prosecutions for heretical propositions (35.5%) and Judaizing (20.5%).[10] The Inquisition took very seriously the biblical injunction that what God had created no man could put asunder.

The Accused

For reasons that historians do not yet understand, men dominated the ranks of people brought before the Inquisition on nearly all charges, bigamy included. In Galicia men outnumbered women more than five to one (86.2% men and only 15.2% women).[11] However, this study focuses only on women charged with bigamy by the Gallegan tribunal. Although few in number, the trials of these women, who for a variety of reasons decided to remarry, offer new perspectives on the marital lives of peasant women. Some of the *relaciones de causas,* the summaries of the trials, reveal no more than the woman's name, the charge, and the sentence. However, twenty-three of the cases (62% of total cases of women charged with bigamy) provide some detail about the testimonies and defense presented before inquisitors, bits and pieces of information from which a picture of female bigamists can be sketched.

The accused were remarkably similar in many ways. Most of them were in their twenties and had been married at a relatively young age. Nine of the accused said that they had been wed to their first husbands before the age of eighteen. Ana Rodríguez seems to have been typical; thirty years old at the time of her appearance before inquisitors, she stated that her first husband had been gone for twelve years, making her no more than eighteen at the time of her first marriage.[12] Curiously, only two of the female bigamists mentioned having any children. The case summaries included the occupations of women much less frequently than they did those of men; however, we know that one of the accused was the daughter of a tailor, and four others listed themselves as peasant farm women (*labradoras*). Although the relaciones do not mention the literacy level of the accused, it is safe to assume that all or most of these women could neither read nor write, as other studies have shown that only 3 percent of Gallegan women were literate.[13]

All these women appeared before the Inquisition because evidence existed that they had been married more than once. The story of Margarida López was the most typical. When Margarida appeared before the Inquisition in Santiago de Compostela in 1594, she declared that at the age of eighteen she had legally married Sebastián López. By her own account, they lived together for the first five years and had a "married life."

However, their seemingly normal marriage suddenly came to an end, when at the end of those five years, Sebastián left the region, never to return. Twenty years later, in 1590, Margarida heard that he was dead, and she decided to remarry. Along with Margarida López, eleven of the women told the inquisitors life stories that involved husbands who had been gone for years or even decades. Sometimes the men never returned. The criminal act of bigamy often occurred when, in the absence of news from their husbands, women chose to believe that their men were dead, and then remarried for emotional or economic reasons. For instance, when she was brought before the Inquisition, thirty-six-year-old Margarida Alonso had been separated from her husband for thirteen or fourteen years. She testified that she had waited patiently for his return until she finally received word that he was dead. The devoted widow saw to it that burial masses were said on his behalf. She then remarried, only to discover a year and a half later that, contrary to the report, her first husband was still alive.[14] Ines Delgado found herself in a similar situation. At fifty years old she confessed to the Inquisition that she remarried after her husband had been gone for more than fourteen years. She just assumed that he was dead. Unfortunately, she was wrong.[15]

These women's decision to remarry was by no means impulsive. Based on the testimonies of the eleven women who reported being abandoned, their first husbands had been gone an average of fifteen years. Three of the women reported that their husbands were gone at least twenty years. Many of these extended absences no doubt began as temporary excursions but became permanent as the spouse set up residence in a distant town. One of the most surprising aspects of these female bigamists' stories is the tremendous distance that often separated husbands and wives. After having been abandoned for thirteen years, Margarida Feyxoa got a letter of dubious origin from Oran in North Africa stating that her first husband was alive.[16] Margarida López later learned that her first husband had died in the monastery of Valparaiso, and the Inquisition's *comisario* (official representative) in Torrejón de Velasco reported that the husband of Catalina Golpa was in the power of a Morisco in Torrejón.[17] Dominga Goncález's husband had been gone for twenty years when she heard that he had died in a hospital in Seville. Ana Martínez's husband met a similar fate.[18] Soon after Margarida da Gando married Juan Martíncz in 1623, he went to Castile. For five or six years, she heard nothing of him and then received word that he was alive and living in Ballecas near Madrid. He died there without ever seeing her again.[19] Eventually, she had to go to Madrid herself to obtain proof that he had indeed died there so that she would be free to marry again.

According to demographic historians, Gallegan men regularly traveled far from their homes and families because of an unfortunate combination of high population densities in the region, an abundance of only marginal land, and traditional inheritance practices. Generally, Galicia was a poor region of small tenant farmers who struggled to provide for their families. Not only was much of the territory difficult to cultivate, but the prevalence of partible inheritance in the region meant that parcels became smaller and smaller with each passing generation.[20] Moreover, matrilineal inheritance in some areas often forced men to work lands that belonged to their in-laws. In this context Castile offered a world of new economic possibilities, especially for men whose families teetered on the edge of poverty. However, the role of economics in bigamy cases should not be overestimated in light of the fact that the majority of Gallegan men who left for Castile and the Americas for economic reasons eventually returned to their native Galicia.

Trial records reveal nothing about the lives of these women once their husbands left; however, demographic and anthropological studies allow us to piece together some important influences on their lives. On the one hand, Gallegan society was well prepared to deal with single women, both with children and without them. During the early modern period the region had particularly high rates of female celibacy and illegitimacy, which were no doubt related to both the high rates of male migration and the fact that the predominance of both matrilineal and partible inheritance ensured that many women could care for their families without the aid of men.[21] On the other hand, their husbands' absences must have been very painful for many of these women. Even before their abandonment, their lives were often out of sync with the rest of their peers. Most of them reported marrying before they celebrated their twentieth birthday in a region where women and men usually waited until they were nearly twenty-six years old before taking marriage vows. Moreover, the relative youth of these brides meant that many were still less than twenty years old when their husbands departed. Thus, they were left married but abandoned at a time when most of their peers were still single. As the years passed, their husbands were absent during their prime childbearing years. As other women in their cohort raised families, these forgotten wives could only watch. They were truly "widows of the living," as many people continue to refer to abandoned women in nearby northern Portugal.[22]

These women's inability to create new relationships was poignantly expressed by María Rodríguez, who had been brought before the Inquisition on the charge of simple fornication (the crime of stating that sex between single persons was not a sin). Tearfully, she confessed to having said that being a concubine would have been better than being unhappily married. She believed this assertion to be true because her husband had left her more than twenty-six years before to go to the Indies and never returned.[23] Abandoned women led a life of sad ambiguity, awkwardly trapped between marriage and widowhood.

When questioned about their marital status, many women, like Caterina de Villaloa, reported that they had been forced into the first marriage by abduction or coercive parents. Eighteen-year-old Caterina had suffered the double trauma of having been kidnapped as a child and then accused of bigamy. She told the Inquisition in 1593 that when she was fourteen years old and living with her parents, one of her father's manservants abducted her. According to Caterina, the couple traveled throughout the kingdom fleeing justice until finally settling down somewhere in the bishopric of Lugo. There her kidnapper arranged for a priest to marry them in front of witnesses, and later they consummated the relationship. After four or six days she left her captor and returned to her parents' home. In the intervening four years, she had gone to the bishop's provisor and received license to marry again, but once her second marriage took place, someone reported her to the authorities as a bigamist.[24] Caterina's case reveals an important aspect of the Spanish view of marriage: lack of consent could be a key defense in bigamy trials, as Spanish Catholicism placed a high priority on the individual's right to choose a spouse without interference. Parents might use persuasion or counsel to influence a child's choice of marriage partner, but under no condition did Spanish society condone the use of coercion.[25] Unfortunately, the more pressing concerns of lust and economics sometimes prevailed.

At least four of the women argued that they had been forced into their first marriages when they were too young to offer their consent reasonably. When brought before inquisitors, Mencia de Rocha confessed that her father and stepmother had arranged a marriage with her stepmother's son when she was eight or nine years old. He left soon after the marriage, never to return. Pressing her innocence before the inquisitors, Mencia provided proof that she had not wanted to marry the man, "although they might kill her."[26] Similarly, when thirty-year-old Juana Pérez appeared before the inquisitors on the charge of bigamy, she proved that she had been no more than nine or ten years old when her first marriage had been celebrated at her parents' insistence.[27]

Contrary to the lore about youthful marriages in the past, the church forbade marriages of children before puberty, which was usually defined as age twelve for girls and age fourteen for boys. With this physical and mental boundary the church hoped to ensure that both parties first could consent freely to the marriage and later consummate it.[28] Clearly in contravention of canon law, these child betrothals become an even more curious phenomenon in the context of the typical demographics of marriage in early modern Galicia. The average age at first marriage in the region was one of the highest in the peninsula.[29] The most reasonable explanation for these child marriages must be that the children were promised to each other by their parents with a vow to marry in the future, with *palabras del futuro.* These arranged marriages might have been sincere attempts by parents to secure viable futures for the children through familial alliances or the acquisition of land. Unfortunately, even assuming the best of intentions, these "marriages" failed to meet the post-Tridentine criteria for sacramentally sound marriages. The children were too young to consent, most of the relationships could not be consummated, the banns had not been posted, and the nuptial blessing had rarely been administered.

The use of coercion was not limited to overpowering men and overzealous parents. Strong-willed women sometimes used threats and intimidation to force their suitors or lovers into unwanted marriages. Ana de la Cruz from Salamanca became the mistress of a young Gallegan man, Diego de Canedo, who boarded in the home of Ana's mother while completing his studies at the university. When the time came for him to return home to Tierra de Quiroga, Ana had him put in jail for three months and threatened to keep him there until he agreed to marry her. Under pressure, Diego finally conceded, and they exchanged vows in the jail. However, after a few days back at Ana's home, he packed his things and left for Galicia. When interrogated by the inquisitors on charges of bigamy, he asserted that he had the marriage nullified based on his lack of consent.[30]

Interestingly enough, none of the women accused of bigamy in the Gallegan tribunal claimed that their husbands had betrayed or maltreated them, a situation that stands in stark contrast to the sad tales of abuse and violence described by women to Mexican inquisitors.[31] Female bigamists in New Spain provided inquisitors with graphic descriptions of the physical violence that prompted them to desert their marriages. For example, in 1788 María Ignacia Cervantes testified that her husband "treated her with the greatest cruelty," as could be seen in the scars from eight wounds he gave her. "Various blows and other abuse caused her to abort six times."[32] It seems unlikely that marital violence was absent from Gallegan women's lives; however, it may have been limited by the presence of family. Although residence patterns varied significantly within the region, many parts of Galicia have a history of uxorilocal residence.[33] Consequently, husbands may have had to control their temper in the home of their father-in-law. Alternatively, Gallegan women may have stayed in these painful relationships more readily as the high rates of male migration in this region made it reasonable to expect that their abusive husbands might eventually leave.

The Second Marriage

In most bigamy cases, the temporary absence of a husband often turned into permanent desertion. Emboldened by their new jobs and with ample opportunity to find other relationships in the home or shop where they worked, many men set up new lives and new families after a time. In fact, the majority of men accused of bigamy engaged in professions like soldiering which required mobility or ones like the artisanal trades which facilitated it.[34] However, just as migration contributed to the high percentage of male bigamists, other social factors kept the numbers of female bigamists low. While their men started new lives in new places, most abandoned women remained in their village under the watchful eyes of friends and relatives (often both his and hers owing to high rates of endogamy), unable to enter into a new relationship without their permission. In order to remarry, three courses of action were available to an abandoned woman: after an extended absence she could decide to remarry without proof of the first husband's death and hope that she was correct in her assumption; she could lie or produce forged documentation that might convince a bishop's provisor to allow the second marriage; or she could pursue the legal means to remarriage by producing legitimate evidence of the absent husband's death or burial.

Some abandoned women never inquired into their husband's supposed death. Although the relacion does not give details, Ysabel, the wife of Jerome López of Feans, married again without being certain of the death of her first husband.[35] Ana Rodríguez met her first husband, Julian Díaz Rancano of Lugo, in Ciudad Rodrigo. He promised to marry her, and they signed a dowry contract. However, when she fell seriously ill, Julian, already having second thoughts, left, promising to return and marry her if she recovered. Ana did recover and sent a sibling to Galicia to find her betrothed. The brother returned empty handed, and Ana waited in vain for ten years for Julian to return until she was finally forced by poverty to marry Alonso López.[36] As it turned out, Julian had changed his mind, lied to the bishop's provisor, and married someone else.[37] Both were eventually accused of bigamy.

Certainly impatience or naïveté motivated some women to commit bigamy, but others were purely deceptive. When María Martínez was thirty years old, she married Sebastián de San Paño, a laborer from Santiago de Compostela. He testified that six or seven years earlier they had been legally married by a now deceased priest, but they had not received the nuptial blessing because María was a widow.[38] Their marriage had produced no children, but witnesses disagreed about how long they had lived together, four or six years. Suddenly, María left. Her travels took her eastward into Castile, where in the late summer of 1599 she encountered a prospective second husband, one Gregorio Castaño from San Antón de Arribajos. Even though she was already married, María told the provisor of Zamora that she was single, and soon afterward she and Gregorio were duly married by the parish priest with plenty of witnesses to the event. The couple lived together until the next Easter, when they came to Galicia. While she waited in the city of Ourense, Gregorio went to Santiago, where he discovered that his wife was still married to Sebastián de San Paño. Struck with fear and shame, Gregorio refused to rejoin María and went immediately to confess to the Holy Office.[39] At the same time, María must have seen the writing on the wall because she voluntarily returned to her life with Sebastián.

María Gómez, alias Maripaz, was even more devious. When brought before the Inquisition in 1604, she confessed to having been married to her first husband, Juan de Rubians. They were so impoverished that for the first year they could neither afford to live together nor receive the nuptial blessing. He had been gone for five years when María decided to remarry. In order to facilitate the procedure, María and her prospective second husband, Marcus Gómez, falsified the documents that reported her first husband's death. Although an eager participant initially, María's new beau soon lost his nerve. When Marcus found out that Juan was headed home to Bayona, he fled.[40]

Similarly, Catalina Fernández, a twenty-four-year-old from La Coruña, persuaded the notary Juan Fernández Vidal to provide false documentation to the bishop's provisor to the effect that she had not been properly married to her first husband. Witnesses testified that the notary, Catalina, and Juan de Soto, her soldier lover, had conspired to compose the false documents. Her intrigue fell apart when Catalina failed to pay witnesses the bribes she had promised them. In her own defense, Catalina testified that she had been married to the soldier for two years and had a son. When questioned about her first marriage, she replied that she had been betrothed to Domingo de Cassanova but that they had never had a married life ("vida maridable") nor had he known her sexually because she had been forced into the first marriage by her father at the tender age of ten. Additionally, she testified that she had run away for fifteen days rather than marry Domingo. Upon her return, her family deceived her and forced her to marry against her will. Despite the evidence that Catalina's story included all the typical circumstances of a forced marriage, the fact that she had concocted the documentation and paid witnesses made her earlier story less credible, and as a result she received the full punishment for a bigamist.[41] In another case, Marina de Castro from Verin left her audience with the Inquisition absolved of the bigamy charges against her, but the inquisitors noted that they suspected some of the information she had provided was false. Consequently, they mandated that Marina not live with either husband until an ecclesiastical judge determined which marriage was the true one.[42]

Other women followed a more discreet course of action, remarrying only after receiving news that their first husbands had died and obtaining dispensation. Before beginning a new life with her second husband, Margarida López confirmed the site of her first husband's burial, went to the bishop's provisor, and obtained a license to remarry.[43] The rumor mill did not serve other women as well. After years of loneliness, many women wittingly or unwittingly believed the false information brought by strangers. Although twenty-eight-year-old Cecilia Pérez believed that she had certified that her first husband was dead, the information she had received was false. Fortunately for her, upon his return she left her second husband and returned to the first, thereby receiving a lighter sentence.[44]

The attempt to determine whether an absent husband was alive could be a difficult, time-consuming process. In 1600, only eight months after Ana Martínez of San Pedro de Celas married Juan Pérez Cortas, he left to go to Castile. Twenty-eight years later Juan Martínez from Paredes returned from Castile with the report that her husband was dead. Finding herself alone, Ana decided to accept Bastian Douteyro's offer of marriage. When they later learned that Juan might still be alive, Bastian said that, although it might be costly, they had to find out whether Juan was alive or dead, and the couple sent a man from Porriño to the Amor de Dios hospital in Seville. Assured that Juan was in fact dead, the messenger fulfilled his duty by getting two notaries to attest to that fact. However, by 1642 it appeared that the information had been false and that Juan Pérez Cortas might still be alive. Faced with conflicting information, the confounded inquisitors finally suspended the case, merely chastising Ana for not certifying Juan's death before remarrying.[45]

The most pressing question about female bigamists remains why they remarried when it might have been as easy or easier to live in concubinage, a situation that was in no way connected with heresy.[46] Moreover, judging by Galicia's high rates of illegitimate births during the early modern period, there was little or no social stigma attached to nonmarital sexual relationships.[47] Local culture seems to have tolerated a form of serial monogamy so long as it did not disrupt parish marriage patterns. In her recent work, Elizabeth Kusnesof suggests that respectability was the main motivation for some women to remarry. They may have wanted to be seen as law abiding and very Christian, unlike their neighbors who lived in concubinage.[48] Perhaps marriage provided a certain status that Gallegan women considered desirable but not necessary.[49] Some women believed incorrectly that the Christian legitimization of their new lives and loves balanced out the issues of heresy and sin which so concerned the church. For others, marriage provided the most desirable way to integrate their new families into the social and religious world of the parish.[50] Finally, the economic and emotional benefits that came with having a husband probably seemed all the more attractive to women who had been left alone for many years.

The Sentence

All women found guilty of bigamy by the Inquisition were forced to abjure their heresy, and most received some combination of public lashing, fines, and exile. At times, the Inquisition lessened the severity of the sentence if the woman chose to return voluntarily to her first husband. By doing so, she indicated to the Inquisition that the crime involved no heretical ideas about the sacrament of marriage. Only two of the women made this difficult choice. When twenty-nine-year-old Ines Pérez confessed to having married twice, arranged her affairs, and returned to her first husband, she received a lighter sentence as a result of her spontaneous contrition.[51] For women who did not voluntarily return to their first husbands, their cases were remitted to an ordinary of the ecclesiastical court, who decided which marriage was legal.

Half (six of eleven) of those women found guilty were flogged publicly, which demonstrates that the Inquisition saw no need to relax the severity of physical punishment for women; both men and women typically received either one hundred or two hundred lashes. No doubt the public shame was sharper for women than men, as the penitent typically was stripped to the waist.[52]

The most serious penalty faced by female bigamists was temporary exile, usually from both Santiago de Compostela and their native parish, and when applicable the parish in which the second marriage took place. Exile must have been a painful experience for these women; banishments ranged from three to five years and specified as three to five leagues the distance that the penitent must keep from the designated sites. It is hard to imagine how these women, separated from husbands (both of them) as well as family and friends, survived. Possibly friends and relatives aided the guilty women by providing them with places to live or helping them find work. Whatever the case, shame followed these women everywhere. Even after completing their exile, these women suffered the permanent social stigma of having been prosecuted by the Inquisition.

The most striking aspect of these trials is that, unlike their male counterparts, many more women accused of bigamy returned home to their second husbands and resumed their married lives. Of the twenty-three women examined here, only half were found guilty. Based on Jaime Contreras's analysis of all the bigamy trials brought before the Gallegan tribunal, nearly all the accused men were found guilty. At least 85 percent of male bigamists were sentenced to the galleys, and an additional number were found guilty but not sent to the galleys because of their age, social status, or other concerns.[53] Women may have been found guilty less often because inquisitors either sympathized with their plights or excused their behavior based on traditional ecclesiastical notions of the inferiority of women. In 1567 Catalina Hernández was fined and publicly shamed, but the inquisitor stopped short of ordering a lashing as "the absence of her first husband had been very long and she was a good confessant."[54] However, unlike cases of simple fornication, in which inquisitors frequently excused both men and women because they were old, "rustic" or "ignorant," only the deceitful María Gómez received a lightened sentence because she was "a rustic woman." The trial records, however, point to a fundamental difference in the way women undertook their second marriages and presented their cases. Nearly half of the women (eleven of twenty-three) reported obtaining or attempting to obtain a license to remarry. Despite their inability to read or write, these women demonstrated a remarkable ability both to perceive the importance of written proof to the ecclesiastical hierarchy and to negotiate the channels necessary to obtain the documentation.[55] Moreover, their trials clearly emphasized the women's attempts to obtain dispensations, while most of the men either presented no defense or regaled the inquisitors with long, convoluted tales of deception.[56]

For contrast I analyzed the cases of sixty-five men in which the relaciones de causas provided similar information on their cases. Only nine men (14% of those sixty-five cases) testified to pursuing legal documentation to end their first marriages, and all but one were still found guilty. Moreover, the Inquisition proved unwilling to accept documentation from men, which not only held men responsible for their promiscuity but made it possible for the Inquisition to fulfill its obligations to the royal galleys.[57] In contrast, even though some women based their petitions on false or at least untrustworthy information, their attempt to use written proof clearly influenced the outcome of their cases. For instance, when the daughter of a tailor from Ourense was brought before inquisitors, she proved that she had already had her first marriage to Juan Precado annulled by the bishop's provisor before she married Antón Precado. At the time, she had provided the bishop's provisor with evidence that both she and Juan were underage at the time of the marriage.[58] The inquisitors absolved her of the charges.

The attempt to use legal recourse before remarrying was clearly the determining factor in the successful resolution of a woman's trial. After presenting the inquisitors with necessary documentation that she had confirmed her husband's burial site before remarrying, Margarida López went free. The cases of Caterina de Villaloa and Ysavel González are telling examples of the importance of documentation in determining a verdict. The abducted child Caterina had gone immediately to the bishop's provisor to get her forced marriage annulled, and as a consequence of her action she was absolved of any charges against her, whereas the twenty-six-year-old Ysavel González did not fare as well in similar circumstances. Because she had not obtained a dispensation to remarry, the Inquisition did not sympathize with her plight when she claimed that her first marriage was not legal because she was too young and her parents had forced her to marry. Had she sought episcopal intervention before remarrying, she might not have paid the penalty for bigamy.[59]

Written documentation played such an important role that generally those women who both committed bigamy and falsified documentation suffered the most severe punishments. Catalina Fernández was one of the women who provided forged papers to the Inquisition and paid a high price for her deceit; she was sentenced to the humiliating punishment of one hundred lashes as she was ridden through the streets of Santiago and was exiled from Santiago, Coruña, and her native parish for four years. Similarly, Lorenca Manuela (alias de Ribas), a forty-year-old from Morayme, received the full punishment due to a bigamist even though she testified that she had gone to the provisor for permission to remarry. The inquisitors determined that she had knowingly provided them with false information.[60]

It is difficult to know why women regularly sought the necessary documentation to remarry whereas most men did not. If respectability was the main motivation for women who agreed to marry a second time, they may have hoped that the proper dispensation would help to dispel any community sentiment against their decision. On the theological level, the Catholic Reformation Church continued to discourage the remarriage of widows, and on the personal level an improperly conducted match might result in manifestations of community disapproval like charivaris.[61] Moreover, marginalized by the political and judicial system, women might have felt more pressure than men to conform to the requirements of the ecclesiastical bureaucracy.

Abandoned by their husbands and accused of heresy, these women bigamists could easily become objects of our pity. Their legacy, however, is much richer. Through their testimonies, they have bequeathed to us a valuable source for accessing the history of women and marriage in early modern Spain. Out of the shadows of history, Spanish peasant women become active players in the crucial decisions about their lives and loves. Even when faced with the seemingly repressive and frightening institution of the Inquisition, they do not seem cowed. These cases demonstrate how a number of illiterate women with few economic means managed to negotiate a successful resolution to their encounter with the Holy Office. Poor, illiterate, and inexperienced, they bravely stood before inquisitors, presented their defenses, and waited for their sentences. Then, having stood up to their accusers, women like Margarida López and Caterina de Villaloa went home.

.

PART III

The Inquisition
in the New
World

"More Sins than the Queen of England"

*Marina de San Miguel before the
Mexican Inquisition*

JACQUELINE HOLLER

At the close of the sixteenth century, Mexico City dominated the vast viceroyalty of New Spain as its capital and by far its largest city. Built upon (and with) the rubble of the great Aztec capital Tenochtitlán, the new Spanish city rose triumphant. The city's heart was the *plaza mayor,* with its cathedral, municipal hall, viceregal palace, university, and the great market where a kaleidoscope of humanity peddled goods familiar and exotic. A continuous flow of Spanish immigrants drawn by the promise of wealth rubbed shoulders with African slaves, Amerindians, and their mixed-race progeny. From the great plaza, the city spread outward in a regular grid pattern, still punctuated by Aztec canals. The Spanish population huddled around the plaza, their neighborhoods overflowing with the wealth channeled through the city from the silver mines of the north.

A few blocks from the plaza stood the building occupied by the Holy Office of the Inquisition of New Spain. Inside this building, on the afternoon of October 11, 1599, a Dominican *beata* was making her final confession. She told the inquisitor Don Alonso de Peralta that she had nothing more to say, "even though she might have more sins than the queen of England."[1] With this curious allusion to the arch-heretic Elizabeth I, fifty-four-year-old Marina de San Miguel closed her confession and bowed her head before the justice of the Holy Office of the Inquisition of New Spain.

Accused of the *alumbrado* heresy, Marina had been imprisoned since the previous November and had begun a long series of confessions shortly thereafter.[2] But denunciations of Marina did not speak exclusively to *alumbradismo;* rather, they corresponded to three aspects of her life. She was first a neighborhood holy woman in the community surrounding the Santo Domingo convent. Largely in response to her arrest, her neighbors came to denounce her for the visions and raptures that made her famous. Marina also had a life beyond the neighborhood, as a member or associate of an alleged alumbrado cell stretching from Puebla to Mexico City. Other members of the group, now prisoners in the Inquisition's secret prisons, denounced her role as a prophet and mystic. But there was a third aspect to Marina's life hidden within the walls of her household, which emerged only from her own testimony. The tale Marina told on herself introduced yet another element to her case: that of sexual misconduct. As she put it, she had suffered from a "sensual temptation of the flesh" for fifteen years.[3] To the inquisitor's horror, she had indulged this temptation repeatedly, "putting in execution things so abominable and lewd that even the devil himself would be offended by them."[4]

In a sense, then, Marina's trial was almost like three trials. At the neighborhood level, she was at most a faker of revelations, an indulger of superstition, one of those female pseudosaints disciplined by Inquisitions in Europe and America.[5] In the context of the alumbrado group, she was accused of a crime deserving of "relaxation to the secular arm": death. And in the privacy of her own home, she indulged in forbidden sexual activity in a period when the Inquisition was moving to enforce Tridentine sexual mores. These three "tendencies"—and the three loci of Marina's life in her house, her neighborhood, and a religious network that extended beyond Mexico City—should not, however, be understood as discrete. From the inquisitorial point of view, Marina's crimes presented a seamless case. Raptures like Marina's, whether feigned or actual, were associated with alumbradismo, as was sexual license. Don Alonso de Peralta undoubtedly saw in Marina's case the venerable linkage of heresy and general disorder, and, perhaps, the special dangers inherent in an improperly supervised religious life for women.[6]

For the modern biographer, less likely than the sixteenth-century inquisitor to condemn unorthodox behavior, these three streams of Marina's life converge and complement one another. They illustrate the complex potential of the life of a sixteenth-century beata, the delicate space that existed between prescription and prohibition. Marina enjoyed importance in neighborhood life, participated and held authority in relations with fellow religious, and even for years gave rein to her sensual impulses. Yet her freedom was an illusion; she was to find herself in the Inquisition's dock, her reputation destroyed, her goods sequestered, her sins seemingly greater than those of the queen of England.

"Against heretical depravity and apostasy":
New Spain's Inquisition

After the collapse of the Aztec empire and the establishment of Spanish control over New Spain in 1521, inquisitorial powers were exercised by a monastic inquisition operating under the authority granted in papal bulls of 1521 and 1522. During the 1520s, monks used their quasi-episcopal powers to control blasphemy and heresy among the conquerors and, more controversially, to enforce conversion of the native population.[7] Mexico's first auto-da-fé was held in 1528 and saw the death of two Judaizers. Perhaps in response to the excesses of this ad hoc Dominican inquisition, Fray Juan de Zumárraga was appointed bishop in 1527, and inquisitorial activity came under his episcopal purview. Zumárraga's Inquisition disciplined Amerindian sorcerers, bigamists, and heretics, culminating in the infamous 1539 execution of the Texcocan nobleman Don Carlos Chichimecatecuhtli.[8] Outrage at such harsh punishment of those so new to the faith—and at the execution of a nobleman—led to the removal of Zumárraga's inquisitorial title. After the 1540s, the Inquisition concentrated increasingly upon regulating the non-Amerindian population, becoming itself more regularized until it was replaced by a firmly constituted tribunal.

The tribunal of the Holy Office of the Inquisition of New Spain, founded in 1571, was given jurisdiction over a massive geographical area comprising present-day Mexico, Central America, the American Southwest, and the Philippines.[9] The Mexican Inquisition thus attempted to exercise control over an area larger than that policed by all the peninsular tribunals together.[10] The population inhabiting this region included peninsular and American-born (criollo) Spaniards and Portuguese; other Europeans; Africans; persons of mixed European, African, and Amerindian blood (*castas*); and, of course, a dense and massive population of Amerindians. The last, however, were expressly excluded from the jurisdiction of the Holy Office because of their recent conversion to the faith—a decision reflecting the outrage that had greeted the execution of Don Carlos.[11] Solange Alberro estimates that from 75 to 80 percent of New Spain's population was thus exempt from inquisitorial jurisdiction.[12]

The Mexican tribunal, then, policed an essentially unpoliceable territory containing, in large part, an untouchable Amerindian population in which mixed-race and other people could hide with relative ease. Alberro emphasizes that while the Mexican Inquisition was comparable to peninsular tribunals in its severity,[13] a certain sloppiness marked its workings. Many cases were left hanging, for example, and the tribunal sometimes exhibited a rather cavalier attitude toward elements of procedure. Alberro describes personnel problems such as "inertia, contingent incompetence and corruption" as an outgrowth of the impossibility of adequately policing New Spain.[14]

In addition to the limitations and frustrations bred by geography and demography, the character of the permanent tribunal of New Spain was determined by the historical moment of its establishment. Founded after the closure of the Council of Trent, the tribunal was devoted as much to the enforcement of Tridentine religio-social norms as to the eradication of crypto-Jews and other serious heretics.[15] To be sure, the Mexican Holy Office was active in suppressing Judaism and rooting out those of Jewish origin. Such prosecutions peaked first in the 1590s—with the infamous case of the Carvajal family, nine of whose members were executed in the auto-da-fé of 1596—and again in 1640–50, when the most prominent Jews in the colony were executed.[16] Trials and punishments for heresy, including Judaism, were the most dramatic, the most severe, and the most remembered by the citizens who gathered to watch an auto-da-fé.[17] Nonetheless, though officially dedicated to acting "against heretical depravity and apostasy" [contra la herética pravedad y apostasía], the Mexican tribunal found itself policing less dramatic crimes. Heresy prosecutions in Mexico constitute only some 11 percent of the total number of *procesos;* comparable figures from peninsular tribunals suggest a proportion of 40 percent.[18] At least in terms of statistics, then, major heresy investigations were far less frequent in Mexico than in Spain. Trials such as Marina's, as well as the trials of unfortunate *conversos,* were less common than investigations and trials for bigamy, blasphemy, superstition, and witchcraft.[19] In 1598, however, the Holy Office would have its first encounter with an organized clandestine heretic cell. Almost seventy-five years after the uprooting of alumbradismo in Toledo, the Holy Office found evidence of its germination in New Spain. Thus we know the story of Marina de San Miguel.

"Through her work and industry":
 The Discourse of Marina's Life

Marina was born in 1544 or 1545 in Córdoba, Spain, into a family she identified as Old Christians, apparently of a middling social status.[20] Marina said that one of her uncles had been an ensign in Italy and was now married with children, "and they were rich farming folk." Among her uncles she also counted a field marshal, a medical doctor, and a merchant. Marina told the inquisitor that she had one brother, Juan Abril, an unmarried blacksmith "who died in Peru," and one sister, Luisa de los Angeles, a maiden who had died in Mexico in Marina's house. Thus in 1598, Marina had no family left in Mexico; nor had she any connection with her extended family in Castile.

Marina's biography was in some ways typical of sixteenth-century immigrants to New Spain. Her father obviously looked to the Indies with the expectation—realistic in the sixteenth century—of upward mobility.[21] When Marina was only three years old, her father moved the family from Córdoba to Mexico City, where they took up residence in the Calle de San Agustín. There the family remained until Marina was twelve. At that point, in the mid-1550s, the Abrils returned to Córdoba, "having earned something to live on" [aviendo ganado de comer].[22] Back in Spain, like the stereotypical emigrant returnee, Marina's father quickly dissipated his American earnings. According to Marina he spent lavishly in such a fashion that he became impoverished ("el dicho su padre gasto muy largo de manera que vino a empobrecer").

Marina, however, was already interested in more spiritual matters. As she recalled in a later confession, "since her childhood she had had an exercise of interior prayer in which she always [felt] great gifts from Our Lord."[23] At sixteen, Marina confirmed her commitment to the spiritual life, taking a vow of chastity in the convent of La Merced in Seville.[24] For Marina, whose spendthrift father would probably never amass the means for a convent dowry, the life of a beata must have been appealing. The path was essentially self-defined; the extent of one's vows, for example, varied tremendously. Living conditions also varied; a beata might live in a *beaterio*, almost like a nun in a convent, or in her own home. Like a nun, she might live a life of intense spiritual engagement. Unlike the nun, however, the beata enjoyed freedom of movement and might determine the nature of her own work. From this dubious liberty flowed the special dangers of the beata's life. Free from the close control of convent life, with its rule, its routine, its supervision, a beata might go seriously astray. One wonders whether Marina heard of—or perhaps even observed—the execution of the beata Marina de Boborques for Lutheranism at Seville in 1559, only a year or two before Marina made her own vow.[25]

Marina might have become a Sevillian beata of the type so ably described by Mary Elizabeth Perry had Marina's father been less profligate in his spending. As it was, however, he brought his family to economic ruin, forcing a return to Mexico, where Marina's mother soon died. Marina's father placed her in the Colegio de las Niñas to facilitate his remarriage.[26] Marina's possibility of entering a convent was even smaller in New Spain than in Spain. In the early 1560s, Mexico City had only one true convent for women: La Concepción, which required a substantial dowry.[27] Like Seville, however, Mexico City offered the option of life as a beata. Beatas had been present in Mexico since the earliest days of the colony, at least since the late 1520s, when they assisted in the conversion of the Indian population. By the 1560s beatas were an established presence in the city and included women of varying vows, ethnic groups, and social status working in a variety of informal occupations. Some, like Marina, lived in their own homes, others in private homes belonging to patrons. Marina's friend María de los Angeles, a black (*negra*) beata, served the nuns of Santa Clara.[28] Clearly, becoming a beata was an option accessible and attractive to a heterogeneous group of women.

Marina remained in the Colegio de las Niñas for four years after her father's marriage. Already a grown woman, she might have continued there indefinitely had her father's life not taken another picaresque turn. Returning home to find his wife with another man, he reacted violently, killing the man and wounding his wife—who, according to Marina, recovered from her wounds—before fleeing to Peru. As a result, Marina left the Colegio de las Niñas and went to live with María de Acosta, the wife of a tanner, in whose home she lived for two years, until, now presumably in her early twenties, she and her sister, Luisa de los Angeles, took a house in the Calle de San Agustín. For the next seven to ten years Marina and Luisa lived on their earnings from sewing and from teaching girls.[29]

Marina and Luisa moved once more, this time to the house of Juan Núñez de León, accountant of the royal treasury, a wealthy man who would become important in Marina's life as a patron and a "spiritual brother".[30] After living in Núñez's house for ten months, Marina purchased the house opposite his, in a wealthy area near the friary of Santo Domingo, using her inheritance from her now deceased father along with her own earnings. Marina's total outlay of five hundred pesos for the purchase and renovation of the home was a considerable sum, indicating some modicum of prosperity. The house contained several rooms and was large enough to contain Marina, lodgers, and at least one servant. In this home, Marina said, she had lived for the past thirteen years, "associating all this time with honorable, clean-living people, both religious and secular" [ha tratado en todo este tiempo con gente muy honrada de buena vida assi religiosos como seculares].

The proceso reveals that Marina was a well-educated woman and, as befitted a beata, an observant Catholic. She told the inquisitor that she had been confirmed in Mexico City by the Dominican Fray Diego de San Francisco and that she confessed and took communion at all the required times; her most recent communion had been eight days earlier in Santo Domingo. She crossed herself and recited the Our Father, Hail Mary, Creed, Salve Regina, Ten Commandments, and the Fourteen Articles of Faith "very well in Castilian" [bien dichos en romance]. In addition, her brother had taught her the alphabet and to join letters and had given her a primer from which she learned to read and write "without more teaching, through her work and industry" [sin mas ensenança por su trabajo y industria]. Marina was also proud of her financial independence, perhaps because she was a woman alone, or perhaps because her solvency contrasted with her father's inability to support his family adequately.

If Marina's recounting of her biography provides insight into her development, the testimony of witnesses during the course of her trial is also of use in reconstructing her daily life. Marina's dossier runs to a substantial 125 folio pages, ostensibly dedicated to her alleged crimes, of course, but brimming with information about her daily activities in her community. Marina gave no description of the thirteen years preceding her trial, but her neighbors related details dating back as far as eight years before 1598. Before moving to the elements of her case which invited inquisitorial censure in 1598, then, we might well attempt a reconstruction of Marina's life as an established beata of Mexico City.

"A woman of great devotion": Marina as Neighborhood Holy Woman

Judging from the testimony of her neighbors, Marina seems to have enjoyed respect in the community centered on the monastery of Santo Domingo. Part of her respect and fame came from her function as a kind of spiritual social worker. For example, Ysabel Gutiérrez, the forty-year-old wife of the silk worker Luis de Valverde, reported that being very afflicted ("estando muy aflixida") with the death of her mother seven years earlier, she had received a consolatory visit from Marina.[31] She was also consulted in cases we might describe as medical or psychiatric. García Hernández de Corona, a forty-four-year-old tailor, testified that he had met Marina some years earlier when he had been "very melancholy and ill" [muy melancolico y enfermo] suffering from a "despair" [desesperacion] that he judged to be of diabolical origin, as it was accompanied by visions of demons. Marina's spiritual abilities also led people to ask her to ascertain their standing with God. Ynés de Montesdoca, a thirty-year-old maiden, reported having consulted Marina for this reason.[32] Clearly, Marina's neighbors considered her possessed of special gifts.

In fact, the intensity of Marina's spiritual life seems to have aroused admiration rather than skepticism in most of her neighbors. Marina was frequently visited by spells of shaking, by trances in which she was "transported" and "left her senses." Marina and her neighbors also described her many illnesses, all of them apparently related to gifts from God.[33] Virtually all those who testified described Marina's illnesses, trances, and encounters with various saints and even Christ himself. Yet if their testimony is to be believed, few regarded Marina with a jaundiced eye. Her visions and trances seemed rather to boost her credibility as a holy woman. María de Cárdenas, for example, said that after she and her depressed husband saw Marina in one of her trances, the couple "asked with more determination that she commend them to God" [le pedian esta y el dicho su marido con mas ahynco].[34]

As well as providing such services to her neighbors, Marina also functioned as a spiritual adviser to devoted laymen. Beatriz Gutiérrez remembered that Fulano de Vargas, a "spiritual married youth" [hombre tambien spiritual moço casado], had told her that he had been discussing matters of God and the spirit with Marina.[35] Alonso Gutiérrez de Castro, who lived with Marina, described his relationship to her as a virtual apprenticeship in the spiritual life.[36] Marina herself detailed how Alonso would address her, saying, "Mother, I love you very much in the Lord" [madre mia mucho la amo en el señor]. She would reply, "God make you holy and pure of heart" [dios te hago sancto y limpio de coraçon].[37] Alonso's use of "Mother" and the formal second-person address suggest a teacher-disciple relationship.[38]

Marina's spiritual authority extended beyond laymen such as Alonso and Fulano to at least some members of the clergy. Juana Ruiz described how she went to see Marina and found Fray Diego de Aragón, Marina's confessor, already in the house. Marina went into a trance that lasted for about an hour. Fray Diego remained at her side, and when she came to her senses, he asked her what had happened. Marina described for him (and for Juana, who had not left) her vision, in which she had been given milk and honey to drink.[39] Other friars were similarly interested in Marina's spiritual gifts. According to Juana Ruiz, Marina claimed that Christ would take her to him on the Day of the Incarnation, meaning that she would die. Alerted, Juana went to Marina's house on the day in question to watch the proceedings. Others had gathered at Marina's bedside: not only a group of neighborhood women but two Dominican friars and Don Francisco de Bocanegra, "who brought wax for the funeral" [el qual llevo cera para el entierro]. Clearly, these men were expecting a miraculous occurrence, at least a vicarious experience of direct contact with the Divine.

Indeed, male interest in and support of female mystics was common in early modern Europe and contemporary Spanish America.[40] Holy women and their male patrons enjoyed a kind of "dyadic cooperation."[41] The women received guidance, support, and sometimes even protection from their male patrons. As well, such patrons sometimes publicized holy women's gifts and recorded their biographies. In exchange, the men received access to an exciting realm of direct revelation and, often, ostensibly divine support of their own endeavors and beliefs. During her confessions, Marina herself attempted to gain legitimacy through claiming that she had communicated with—and had been approved by—religious men. She told Inquisitor Peralta of a vision in which she went to purgatory and was given power to remit the sentences of the souls therein, who in gratitude addressed her as "Our Redemptress." Aware of the presumptuous sound of the title and the vision itself, she claimed that she had described her vision to Fray Andrés de la Cruz, a discalced Franciscan "who went to China" and who, according to Marina, expressed approval of the vision. Marina also said that she had discussed "devotion to the love of God and his union" with "religious men of all orders except La Merced."[42] Here she was, to be sure, attempting to gain authority from the approval of the friars. Yet one can infer that such friars themselves saw Marina as a conduit to a spiritual realm of direct revelation.

So too did Marina's neighbors, who when asked to describe her character were nearly unanimous. Ysabel Gutiérrez said that she considered Marina a good Christian and that "for such she was taken by the whole neighborhood, and as a woman of great devotion" [por tal la an thenido en todo el barrio y por muger de grande rrecogimito].[43] García Hernández de Corona said that he had "taken her for a saint, for the things she said as well as for the good advice she gave him."[44] García's wife, María de Cárdenas, also emphasized that she had a high opinion of Marina because of her good advice and saintly reputation.[45]

Yet to the modern reader at least, the testimony does not suggest a stereotypically saintly woman: no penances, fasts, or charitable works like feeding the poor or tending the sick. Indeed, some of Marina's "social work" activities seem to have been motivated not by charity but by a desire for material gain. María de Cárdenas remembered that when she and her husband, García Hernández de Corona, were consulting Marina about his mental illness, María "took her delicate bread and fruit five hundred times" [esta la llebo al quinientos vezes pan rregalado y fruta].[46] Marina, María claimed, told her that "God had promised to remember and give health to people who might give her things, which seemed to her a peculiar and petty thing."[47] This is not what one might expect from a woman described by so many as saintly and casts a shadow, however faint, upon Marina's neighborhood reputation. Juana Ruiz said that she had once thought of Marina as a saint, but now "takes her for a fake, and everything she says is a lie" [la tiene por embustera y que son mentiras todas las que dize].[48] Testimony given after Marina's imprisonment cannot, of course, provide an accurate picture of her status before. With hindsight, neighbors may have seen much that they had earlier overlooked. Yet there is evidence that Marina was beginning to arouse suspicion well before 1598. In fact, two years before Marina was imprisoned for suspicion of alumbradismo, one of her neighbors had felt it necessary to denounce her.

In 1596, Beatriz Gutiérrez, a thirty-eight-year-old widow, appeared before Inquisitor Loboguerrero. She testified that Marina de San Miguel had claimed that her tremors and shakes were indications of God's love,[49] and recounted an episode two years earlier, when she had met Marina in church. Seizing Beatriz's hand, Marina pressed it to her breast, crying, "Look, daughter, what I'm feeling!" Beatriz felt Marina's heart pounding heavily and quickly.[50] Beatriz noted that every time she had seen Marina take communion, the beata had failed to adore the Host or even to see it when it was elevated, because she was always looking at the ground, "as though she was enraptured and carried away" [como arrebatada y robada].[51] However, when asked what she thought of Marina in relation to her Christianity and her raptures, and what kind of a woman Marina was, Beatriz answered that she took Marina for "a good Christian, humble, and not haughty or arrogant" [buena xpiana humilde y no sobervia ni arrogante].[52] Apparently Loboguerrero accepted Beatriz's opinion, or perhaps he was simply uninterested in pursuing Marina, because Beatriz's denunciation was not followed up for more than two years and would probably have languished unnoticed forever had Marina's name not come up in a more serious context in 1598.

"She said the Antichrist was already born":
Marina as Alumbrada Heretic

In 1598 New Spain's ecclesiastical establishments were rocked by the discovery of a cell of alleged alumbrado heretics operating in Mexico City and Puebla.[53] The Mexican tribunal had in the past acted against Jews and Lutherans, but this would be its first encounter with alumbradismo. In Spain, alumbradismo was by this time associated less with a coherent belief akin to Lutheranism than with pseudomysticism.[54] By the seventeenth century, the terms *alumbradismo* and *iluminismo* would both be bandied about to describe the female pseudosanctity more properly called *ilusionismo*.[55] The Mexican trials of 1598 provide a rather brief appearance of alumbradismo in New Spain before the term became meaningless. The 1598 group contained men and women in apparently equal numbers and adhered to illuminist principles first identified with the sect active around Toledo in the early sixteenth century.[56] Many of the alumbrados of New Spain were immigrants from Córdoba and Seville,[57] where illuminism had been uncovered earlier in the century. They may have brought their beliefs with them on their transatlantic journey, perhaps foolishly hoping to escape the possibility of persecution.

The first to be tried was Juan Plata, the chaplain of the convent of Santa Catalina de Sena in Puebla. He was accused of a typically alumbrado combination of sexual license and heretical teachings. Plata had solicited the nuns in his pastoral care and claimed direct revelations from God. In true alumbrado fashion, he told the nuns of his convent that they need not use the sacraments of penitence and communion and expressed contempt for the "external things" of religion.[58] The prioress of Santa Catalina, Mariana de Jesús, had also surprised him and Sor Agustina de Santa Clara in the course of "indecent touchings."[59] During the course of his confessions Plata revealed his participation in a heretical group and named the rest of its members, including Marina de San Miguel. The group Plata described was apparently led by Marina's friend

Juan Núñez and based itself on the teachings of Gregorio López, a holy hermit and mystic. López, a Madrileño who arrived in New Spain in 1562, had lived outside Mexico City and died in the hermitage of Santa Fé in 1593.[60] Though suspected of heresy—he did not use the sacraments, nor did he keep any holy image—López was never prosecuted by the Inquisition.[61] Clearly, however, he was important to the alumbrado group, as all those accused mentioned him and his teachings.

Plata related how López believed that the world would soon end and that a small group of perfect people would be saved from the destruction and would inhabit the New Jerusalem, soon to be founded on earth.[62] Here, Marina de San Miguel entered Plata's story. Plata did not clarify how or when López had made contact with Marina but reported that López had asked her to prophesy the date of the end of the world.[63] Within the alumbrado group, as within her neighborhood, Marina was presumed to have privileged access to the Divine, and her prophecies were given credence.

In a later interview, Plata also mentioned an episode in which Marina's direct link with God extended beyond prophecy to the ability to dispense God's favor. Like Marina's neighbor Ynés de Montesdoca, Plata took advantage of Marina's direct link to God: "He said that he asked that he be made humble, and the said Marina de San Miguel searched inwardly to respond to him and said that His Majesty said that he would give him more humility."[64] Like Ynés de Montesdoca, Juan Plata trusted Marina enough to ask her how he stood with God. Plata also asked Marina for other spiritual advice, notably about eating. Marina recommended that Plata eat meat and fish.[65] Marina's advice was astounding: she denied the effectiveness of fasting, a counsel that smacked of heresy. She herself later admitted that she had eaten chickens for nine years on fasting days, having received a special permission for one year on the basis of her ill health.[66] This cavalier attitude toward religious regulation was also borne out in Juan Plata's testimony. Plata said that Marina had informed him that God had granted him a plenary indulgence.[67] He also asked her whether he was obliged to comply with certain vows of religion he had made (probably those concerning chastity), explaining that doctors had told him that he would die if he entered religion. Marina, he claimed, responded that "His Majesty says that when [Plata] made the vows, He didn't accept them, and [Plata] believes she told him he need not observe them."[68] Here Marina obviously far exceeded the role of a spiritual adviser; granting indulgences and canceling vows, she virtually denied the validity of the church as necessary mediator between the individual and God.

Other alumbrado witnesses confirmed Marina's dangerous spiritual path and described her apocalyptic prophecies. Luis de Zárate reported that "among other things that [Marina] said to him, she said that the Antichrist was already born" [entre las cossas que dijo a este le dixo que habia nacido ya el antixpo].[69] Zárate, however, seems to have been less credulous than Plata; when Marina "said to him that the Holy Spirit had been incarnated in her and other nonsense which made him leave her," he marveled "that the said Gregorio López would have sent him to such a woman to ask God about the New Jerusalem."[70] Thus, though Marina functioned as a prophet within the Mexico-Puebla group, she did not enjoy the respect of all its members. Still, with Gregorio López and Juan Núñez on her side, she was undoubtedly a key figure.

By the time Marina began her confessions, Inquisitor Peralta had information on both her neighborhood activities and her function within the Mexico-Puebla group. Yet Marina was extremely cautious in confessing and admitted virtually nothing. During her third confession, a week after her imprisonment, she admitted her custom of interior prayer and described the "gifts" she received during her trances. After so doing, she went into a trance, astonishing Inquisitor Peralta, who ordered the notary to be very quiet and to continue transcribing whatever occurred.[71] After awakening from her trance, Marina continued to detail the visions she had experienced both before and after imprisonment: she had been to purgatory and seen the souls there being refreshed by the masses said for them on earth; she had seen Christ in the form of a youth, dressed either in purple or in white; and in her very prison cell she had been comforted by circles of angels and saints as well as by Christ himself.[72] Perhaps Marina was hoping that Inquisitor Peralta, like so many other religious men she had known, would be thus convinced of her sanctity, but Peralta grew impatient. At the end of November, after five interviews, he had achieved virtually no progress, as Marina admitted nothing. No further interviews with Marina appear in the dossier for two months. Then, on January 25, 1599, after two months alone in her cell, Marina requested an audience.

"Many filthy and lascivious things":
Marina as Sexual Criminal

Marina was brought before Inquisitor Peralta and asked what she had to say. She reported yet another spiritual experience: this time, however, an experience that offered no comfort. In fact, she had heard a voice say that she was condemned to hell for her sins. Still shaken, Marina told Peralta that for fifteen years, she had suffered from a

> sensual temptation of the flesh which forced her to dishonest acts with her own hands in her shameful parts. She came to pollution saying dishonest words, provoking to lewdness, calling by their own and dishonest names many filthy and lascivious things, to which she was inclined by the devil, who appeared to her internally as an angel of light . . . and the said devil appeared to her in the form of Christ . . . and asked her to uncover her breasts and to have intercourse with him, and thus for the said fifteen years she has had the said carnal intercourse . . . and seeing that she scorned the married life, highly estimating virginity, the said devil, in the form of Christ as when they paint him resurrected, in the same obscene act, told her: this is the law of matrimony, and it is also pleasing to me, and thou should not scorn it.[73]

This testimony should not have surprised Inquisitor Peralta. Women had been presumed prone to demonic seduction at least since the publication of the *Malleus Malificarum* in the fifteenth century, and contemporary cases abounded. In 1546, for example, the Spanish nun Magdalena de la Cruz was pronounced a false visionary, having seen the devil as an angel of light and in the shape of Christ and receiving "carnal delights" from these visions.[74] Some Sevillian beatas saw the devil in the form of a handsome youth exposing his genitals.[75] And while she denied sex with the devil, the Italian nun Benedetta Carlini took on the form of an angel of light to have sex with another nun.[76] Demonically inspired sexual activity by women, however serious and suggestive of a pact with the devil, would not have surprised a sixteenth-century inquisitor.

[223]

Nor would Peralta have been very surprised by Marina's next admission: that for twenty years she had had a relationship with Juan Núñez, "as with a spiritual brother," "and he talked to her about things of God and about His love and resignation to His will, and talking like this he kissed and hugged her and put his tongue in her mouth and with his hand touched her breasts and her shameful parts, saying 'all of this is earth.' And once she remembers he put his finger in her shameful parts."[77] Marina's confessions now became more detailed. Juan Núñez, her spiritual brother, had engaged with her in a long-term sexual relationship. Though she denied actual sexual intercourse, she freely spoke of the other "dishonesties" they had enjoyed: Juan Núñez showed Marina his private parts and made her touch them; he made her show him her private parts; on a regular basis he kissed her, put his tongue in her mouth, and touched her breasts; and immediately after engaging in such acts, the two would sit down and talk about God. Marina added further incriminating details in later confessions. In the course of one of their sessions, Juan Núñez had said, "Unless you become as children you will not enter into the Kingdom of Heaven" [sino os volvieredes como niños no entrareis en el rreyno de los cielos], and "To the clean all things are clean" [al limpio todas las cossas le son limpias], blasphemously legitimizing their actions.[78] These statements reeked of alumbradismo in their denial of the mortal sin inherent in such acts.

Marina also admitted touching the thirty-three-year-old Alonso Gutiérrez, who lived with her. But she said that when she kissed Alonso, it was "with purity of conscience as if two children would kiss" [con la pureza de conciencia que si se bessaran dos niños].[79] Later, however, Marina admitted that sometimes when she kissed Alonso, she was filled with the desire that he should touch her breasts ("le dio a esta apetito de que le metiesse los dedos en los pechos"), though she insisted that nothing of this sort had ever occurred.[80] Marina had, however, engaged in sexual acts with someone other than Juan Núñez. She reported "a friendship" with a beata, now dead; when they saw each other, "ordinarily they kissed and hugged, and [Marina] put her hands on her breasts, and . . . she came to pollution ten or twelve times, twice in the church."[81]

Not content with showing her private parts to Juan Núñez, Marina confessed that she had taken a mirror to look at herself, which she had done eight or ten times, "with interior touchings of her shameful parts, and two times she had pollution."[82] Not only had she concealed these actions from her confessors, thus receiving communion in a state of mortal sin, but she refused to admit that she had known she was sinning. She claimed that "she had no intent of doing [these things] to delight in them, but only because she was melancholy, she did them with good love and clean intention, because as St. Augustine says the sin is in the bad intention and will."[83] In fact, Marina testified, when she had taken the mirror to look at her private parts, she had not done it to offend God but rather to give thanks for the way "He put things in order for the increase of His creatures" [puestolas en horden para el augmento de las criaturas].[84]

If Marina did not know she was sinning and believed her actions blameless, why did she confess them? Why, after two months alone in her cell, did she make the decision to tell Peralta about her relationship with Núñez? One is tempted to see her confession as a stratagem. She would engage Peralta with lurid details of her lascivious excesses and draw attention away from the heretical beliefs and activities she had been careful to avoid describing. This theory, however, fails miserably for two reasons. First, such a stratagem would work only if Marina played the woman tricked, the passive victim of Núñez's desires. She did not; indeed, she admitted her own concupiscence. In her desire for Alonso and her activities with her beata friend, *she* was the sexual aggressor. Moreover, her refusal to admit that what she had done had been mortal sin would clearly suggest the very heresy in which she was implicated. It seems rather that in those two bleak months in her cell, Marina experienced doubts as well as the visions of hell she described. Indeed, one of Marina's co-accused lost his sanity in the dungeons of the Inquisition.[85] Marina probably followed Peralta's stern admonition to search her memory, and what she found there caused her grave doubts. More important, her visions of hell must have terrified her. Where she had once enjoyed Christ's gallant attentions and comforts, she now experienced the horrors of true demonic visitation. She told Peralta that for fifteen days she had known that her relationship with Christ had actually been a diabolical trick, because now the devil showed himself in his demonic figure and she saw with her bodily eyes both him and many demons with snouts and ugly bodies . . . sticking out their tongues and spitting fire (though in small quantity) and lifting her and her bed three or four times a day . . . and she asked the bailiff that they give her a confessor because the demons were taking her, and she heard, having been abducted by bad spirits, a proclamation that said, this is the justice that was ordered for Marina de San Miguel, beata.[86]

After fifteen days of such visions, Marina was no longer the confident woman of November.

And yet she refused to admit that all along she had known what she was doing. This was, for Inquisitor Peralta, the most unsettling element of Marina's confession. He needed, of course, to bring her to true penitence so that she could be reconciled to the church. Over the course of her final six confessions, Marina and Peralta engaged in a debate highlighting the issue of Marina's consent in the sinful acts she had described. Certainly, Marina's obduracy in this matter of consent to sin was an indication of alumbradismo, as indeed were all the revelations about her sexual activities. Juan Núñez clearly believed, as did the *solicitante* Juan Plata, that "for the pure all things are pure." Whether or not this alumbrado doctrine sanctioned sexual license—the inquisitors believed it did—it clearly gave free rein to laymen of predatory sexual appetite such as Núñez, as well as to confessors like Juan Plata.[87] But Marina was no victim of Núñez, who was after all not her only sexual contact. So while Peralta was careful to find out what doctrines Núñez might have taught her, he was most concerned to conquer her stubbornness.

Repeatedly, in a frustrated tone that fairly leaps off the page, he asked her "how she could believe that she didn't sin in doing the said things when she said she was incited to them by the devil, *by the devil*."[88] Marina was strong willed, but she could not for long withstand the psychological pressure brought to bear on her "contradictions." Though she insisted to the end that she "had always based herself on the interior will" [se a fundado siempre en la voluntad interior],[89] Peralta finally convinced her by asking "if she went to bed with a man and had with him carnal intercourse, if she would sin mortally, even though she did not consent with her interior will."[90] Marina agreed, and Peralta pressed home his point. What difference was there between this situation and Marina's, even if Marina's actions were worse "for being against nature" [por ser contra natura]?[91] Perhaps the scales fell from Marina's eyes, as Peralta no doubt hoped; perhaps she simply realized that language could carry her no further. Whatever the case, she surrendered, saying that she finally understood "what a blind woman she had been" [quan ciega ha estado].[92] Satisfied, Peralta proceeded with the formal accusation. Marina admitted nearly all its fifty-three charges, denying only that she had faked her visions. She preferred the term "imagination." And then there was nothing more to say, "even though she might have more sins than the queen of England."

On March 25, 1601, Marina was paraded through the streets of Mexico City, naked to the waist upon a saddle mount, with a halter and gag. A crier preceded her, describing her crimes. Surely her neighbors must have been among the crowd as the procession wended its way through the Santo Domingo neighborhood. If so, they must have marveled at how little they had known of Marina's life. After abjuring her errors *de vehementi*, Marina received one hundred lashes. She was fined one hundred pesos and transported to the Hospital de las Bubas, where she was to serve the sick for ten years. Among those alumbrados disciplined in the same auto-da-fé, Marina received arguably the harshest penalties of all the accused, probably because of her long resistance to full confession.

Soon after her participation in the auto-da-fé, Marina was summoned to the Holy Office to ratify her testimony against Juan Núñez so that proceedings against him might begin.[93] There was a special urgency, apparently, as Marina was "very ill and at risk of dying" [muy enferma y con riesgo de morirse].[94] On April 13, Marina appeared before Peralta and ratified her testimony. She did so again on July 3. Then she disappears from the annals of the Inquisition.

Marina de San Miguel was a woman cast upon her own resources at an early age. Her mother dead, her father an irresponsible outlaw, her extended family distant, she had used her faith and considerable energy to survive and prosper. Virtually alone, she taught herself reading and writing, purchased a home, and for thirty years defied the Hispanic belief that women belonged in marriage or the convent. Marina forged her own way in colonial society using her talents as a seamstress and her gifts as a holy woman. She was a success, prosperous enough to indulge her need to eat chicken even on fast days. But like her father, Marina was profligate with her capital. Her reputation was everything; and yet in demanding gifts for her services, she went too far. The very excesses of her trances were similarly dangerous. We cannot know, of course, whether the doubts expressed by some of her neighbors would with time have become general in Marina's neighborhood, for her trial intervened, humiliating her and forcing her to renounce all her sources of power and identity. Her spiritual gifts, once so renowned, were now to be known as fakery. Her carefully garnered knowledge and theology were a sham, a delusion. Her relationship with Christ, once so satisfying, was a trick of the devil. Her spiritual friend Juan Núñez was a debaucher of women, their special spiritual friendship the lowest depravity. And now she was to serve in a hospital for ten years, deprived of her very identity, her white beata's habit. Though the rest of her life remains in the shadows, it is possible that Marina served her time and was released. Perhaps she even found a new patron within the hospital. She was, after all, a survivor.

CHAPTER TWELVE

Blasphemy as Resistance

An African Slave Woman before
the Mexican Inquisition

KATHRYN JOY MCKNIGHT

On February 26, 1610, in Mexico City, a black woman who identified herself as María Blanca of Congolese origin, the slave of Don Antonio de Saavedra, was found guilty of blasphemy by the Holy Office of the Inquisition.[1] On March 6, the inquisitors Gutierre Bernardo de Quirós and Dr. Martos de Bohorques, together with the senior canon Alonso López de Cárdenas, sentenced María Blanca to hear mass in the chapel of the Holy Office, marked by the symbols of the blasphemer: gagged, a candle in her hands, a rope about her neck. In addition, being under suspicion of heresy, she was to make the *abjuration de levi*. Lastly, she was to be carried on a pack animal through the city streets, naked from the waist up, still wearing rope and gag, while a town crier proclaimed her offense and her body was scourged by two hundred lashes. The sentence, carried out immediately following its proclamation, was sufficiently harsh to evoke criticism from the Supreme Council of the Inquisition in Madrid.[2]

The crime against the faith which María Blanca had committed was by far the most common cause that brought slaves before the Mexican Inquisition at the turn of the seventeenth century. The index to Mexico's Archivo General de la Nación identifies 101 slaves who were denounced or accused of blasphemy between 1590 and 1620, representing about 80 percent of the slaves whose prosecutions are recorded for those years.[3] The circumstances under which María Blanca blasphemed were identical to those of many slaves: while being whipped for running away from

[229]

her owners, she renounced God and all his saints. Not all denunciations of slaves for blasphemy in colonial Mexico resulted in such harsh punishment. The *querella,* or complaint, entered on July 15, 1609, against a mulatta slave named Gerónima, living in Tulançingo, was dropped after four witnesses, including three members of the slave owner's family, testified not only to the offense but also to the slave's remorse.[4] A few colonial slaves were even successful in using blasphemy as a means to negotiate a lesser punishment. Obtaining the intervention of the Inquisition, they used the arena of the trial to invoke Spanish laws decreeing humane treatment of slaves, thus showing their masters as cruel and winning a simple reprimand as punishment for their own transgression. Such was not the case of either María Blanca or Gerónima.[5]

The Question of Gender

Considering the cases of blaspheming bondswomen in a critical anthology dedicated to the experiences of women before the Inquisition proves both necessary and problematic. Blasphemy was neither a particularly male nor female offense among slaves; of the blasphemy cases brought before the Mexican tribunal in the colonial period, roughly 20 percent dealt with women, while in the first decade of the seventeenth century, women accounted for one-third of these cases.[6] To the extent that this anthology focuses on constructions of gender as they shaped the conflicts between women and the Inquisition, the cases of María Blanca and Gerónima figure to a small degree in the discussion, whereas the rebellious acts that brought witches, *ilusas,* nuns, and other female visionaries to trial were generally steeped in definitions of the feminine and provoked by limitations imposed on women's activities. In the case of female slaves accused of blasphemy, race, ethnicity—especially African religious practices—and, most of all, the institution of slavery determined their treatment, while gender played a secondary role. This difference between the cases of slaves and free women itself makes important their juxtaposition in this volume. Making this comparison provides a reminder that the category of womanhood is not universal. It also begins to address the ways in which racial and class differences constructed gender differently in the Spanish colonies.

If the trials for blasphemy were intended to pacify rebellious voices and bodies, they also became stages on which Afro-Mexican slaves struggled to protect themselves from further punishment, criticize the oppression they suffered, and define themselves in opposition to the words of their oppressors. In a society in which slaves did not leave a written legacy expressive of their visions of themselves and their world, legal documents such as those of the Inquisition trials become a valuable source of self-representation. These documents provide only a mediated voice, however, as everything said by the slaves had to be recorded by a scribe. Nevertheless, the quality of the narratives suggests a strong attempt to record faithfully the slaves' stories, particular expressions they used, and their perspective on events.

Documents relating to blasphemy by slaves have been examined within broader studies of slavery, control, and resistance. This historiography sees blasphemy as an act of resistance to cultural domination, rebellion against physical abuse, and manipulation of an imposed ideological system, all of which were attempts by slaves to gain a measure of protection from abuse.[7] More research needs to be done to open up these documents as sources of slave voices, especially in the case of women, whom these studies do not specifically address. These trial documents allow Afro-Mexican slave women to speak as agents, to exercise power over their own lives—in ways that, in the twentieth century, we have heard even more rarely than we have the voices of male slaves. A fuller study of these individual voices in comparison with those of men might lead to a better understanding of female agency and voice among Afro-Mexican slaves.

The blasphemy trials record a verbal power struggle to define both the accused slave and the relationships among the slave, the slaveholders, and the church and the state, as represented by the Inquisition. In her trial, María Blanca repeatedly asserted the power to name herself and her acts and even to criticize her mistress, but she was ultimately required by inquisitors to mouth the words of Catholic orthodoxy. Corporal punishment reinforced her verbal submission, asserting the control of the Inquisition and that of her owner over her body. The mulatta Gerónima, on the other hand, avoided punishment by the Inquisition, thanks perhaps to her more ready submission and less threatening racial identity, or to the latitude slavery permitted individual owners to make life more or less harsh for their slaves. Together, the two documents open a window onto the lives and voices of women slaves as they walked the narrow line between rebelling against the ideology and institutions of Spanish society, which sought to control their bodies and coerce their minds, and choosing a degree of social integration which would allow them to survive.

Blasphemy: A Definition and a Historical Context

Using the colonial Inquisition, church and state tried unsuccessfully for centuries to purge their subjects of blasphemy, which church officials considered dangerously close to heresy. In fact, during the sixteenth century in Mexico, "lengthy and tedious investigations of bigamy and blasphemy" constituted most of the work of Inquisition officials.[8] Blasphemy crossed racial, class, and gender lines, bringing to trial inhabitants of New Spain from all walks of life, though Spanish laws generally ensured less severe punishment for those of higher social standing.[9]

Conflicts in defining the offense allowed the colonial Inquisition flexibility to use the charge to govern the slave population more harshly. In the sixteenth century, the celebrated Aragonese inquisitor Eymerich considered any curse that reviled or expressed ingratitude to God or the Virgin to be simple blasphemy and, as such, an act that did not concern the Inquisition unless accompanied by a denial of some article of the faith. Eymerich believed that the widespread use of expressions such as "I renounce God!" [reniego a Dios], "Despite God!" [pese a Dios], and "I do not believe in God!" [no creo en Dios], which constituted the bulk of slave offenses, did not by themselves warrant prosecution by an institution founded to preserve the purity of the faith. Fifteenth- and sixteenth-century Spain, however, witnessed constant debates over the distinction between simple and heretical blasphemy and the jurisdiction for their prosecution. These debates led to a consensus in the seventeenth century that the expressions listed above constituted heresy in and of themselves.[10]

In colonial trials, inquisitors and slaves disputed the exact words uttered, the circumstances of their utterance, and whether or not the words were repeated, since repetition signaled the offender's obstinacy. The parties to these conflicts negotiated the power to classify the blasphemy and thus determine the appropriateness and character of its punishment. If the tribunal could stamp the deed with the label of heresy, it could claim jurisdiction to prosecute the crime. If slaves succeeded in establishing that their words were not heretical, they won a lighter punishment and might prove the cruelty of their masters. Over and against the slaves' remorseful insistence that they had only blasphemed once, prosecutors sought avidly to prove heresy, revealing their desire to restrain with the Inquisition what was as much a social as a spiritual rebelliousness. In this way a transplanted Spanish institution responded to the particular realities of colonial society.[11]

Although blasphemy was by no means unique to slaves, the prosecutions that resulted from the oaths of slaves took on a widely divergent significance from those involving free men and women. Spaniards and Portuguese both at home and in the colonies blasphemed frequently in the excitement of gambling and the explosiveness of interpersonal quarrels.[12] Examples also exist on the part of these European subjects of grave rejections of Catholic beliefs more elaborate than those most commonly expressed by slaves. When slaves blasphemed, they usually did so while being flogged or threatened with punishment so that their blasphemy revealed the very nature of the slave system, constituting as it did the slaves' instinctive reaction to an unbearable situation of physical punishment.[13]

Blasphemy on the part of some slaves might also have involved a kind of resistance which emerged from within a syncretic or folk Catholicism; the words uttered resemble an Ashanti oath intended to restrain the punisher and call for arbitration from a central authority. Slaves may have projected the responsibilities they understood a human master to have onto the figure of the Christian God, and when this God did not intervene to halt their punishment, they felt justified in renouncing him for not "playing the role ascribed to him."[14] Blasphemy could also function as a symbolic separation from the uniformly Christian society that Spanish church and state sought to consolidate, "a global rejection of the dominant group's ideology that determines all aspects of the imposed European culture, the conception of the hereafter, the temporal order, the social and familial structure, morality and daily life; blasphemy becomes a symbolic summary of all of this" [un rechazo global de la ideología del grupo dominante que determina todos los aspectos de la cultura europea impuesta, la concepción del más allá, el orden temporal, la estructura social y familiar, la moral y la vida diaria; la blasfemia viene a ser un resumen simbólico de ello].[15]

In some cases, blasphemy indicated the degree to which certain slaves understood the Spanish social system and ideology, as they turned the imposed language and beliefs against their masters to end corporal punishment and perhaps secure the intervention of the Inquisition on their behalf. The tribunal of the Holy Office did sometimes act in defense of slaves when the punishment that provoked the offense was judged unacceptably severe.[16] The Archivo General de la Nación provides evidence that the Inquisition was at least marginally concerned about such cruelty.[17] José Toribio Medina claims that the slaves in Cartagena, Nuevo Reino de Granada, were so effective in manipulating the jurisdiction of the Inquisition over blasphemy—so that a simple reprimand from the tribunal replaced a flogging at the hands of the master—that inquisitors were moved to register their complaint.[18] The inquisitors' prosecution of blasphemy by slaves, then, did not constitute a monolithic exercise of power on their part but rather created a theater in which the interests of the church, state, landowners, and slaves were contested. If the slaves generally lost these battles, they nonetheless left the legacy of a few successes, and many voices of protest.

Fear of Rebellion

The church, the state, and the slave owners shared a desire to constrain slaves in a social situation that caused them great anxiety. One reason for their fear was the fact that Europeans were outnumbered by black slaves three to one.[19] Spaniards were caught between their dependence on slave labor and fear of their slaves' resistance, watching anxiously as the number of Afro-Mexicans increased. In 1537 Viceroy Mendoza wrote to the king requesting that the importation of slaves to Mexico be curtailed, and in 1613 the high court of Mexico City asked that it be halted temporarily.[20]

Church, state, and slave owners tried a myriad of tactics in their efforts to subdue slaves. Early on, the church naively believed that conversion to Christianity would pacify slaves. Similarly motivated, the state's encouragement of limited manumission proved equally ineffective.[21] Legislators attempted to restrict the movement of slaves, free blacks, and mulattoes and to prevent them from carrying arms.[22] Colonial governments discouraged intermarriage and even contact between blacks and Indians, fearing rebellious alliances between these groups.[23] When these measures failed, Spanish officials and slave owners alike resorted to violence: severe floggings, executions, and organized military campaigns.[24]

Spanish fears were well founded. Slaves did resist, their opposition to bondage and ill-treatment running the gamut from individual work slowdowns to escape, blasphemy, suicide, abortion, infanticide, conspiracy, and violent rebellion.[25] In New Spain, blacks rebelled or planned revolts in 1537, 1546, 1570, 1608, 1609, 1611, 1612, and 1670.[26] In 1537, in Mexico City, where the largest concentration of slaves lived, conspirators plotted to join with the Indians of that city and Tlatelolco and murder all Spaniards; the uprising was aborted when a conspirator revealed the plans to the viceroy.[27] A more serious threat was presented by the large *palenques,* or colonies of runaway slaves known as *cimarrones.* Gonzalo Aguirre Beltrán estimates that in 1570 there were about two thousand *cimarrones* in New Spain, more than 10 percent of the total slave population.[28] During the late sixteenth and early seventeenth centuries, one particular *palenque* was organized and led by a reputedly Congolese chief named Yanga (Nanga or Ñanga) in the countryside near Orizaba. The group of some eighty men, twenty-four black and Indian women, and a number of children preyed on travelers on the road from Veracruz to Mexico City and raided towns and haciendas.[29] After several failed military attacks, the Spaniards were finally successful in forcing a truce with the *palenque* early in 1609.[30] The *cimarrones* negotiated free status for their town, San Lorenzo de los Negros, with the concession that they would return any runaway slaves who subsequently came to them.[31]

By this time Mexico City had seen the specter of renewed slave rebellion. In 1608, a Christmas Eve conspiracy in the home of a free mulatto confirmed Spanish fears of the collaboration between free blacks and mulattoes and slaves. Women participated in this and similar rebellions; two female slaves and five free women joined sixteen male slaves and eight free men, all of whom were rounded up and arrested when, once again, a conspirator betrayed the group, this time to an employer. In 1611, fifteen hundred blacks marched through the streets of Mexico City to protest the mistreatment and subsequent death of a female slave. The next year another rebellion foundered in the capital city, this time because conspirators carelessly spoke about the plot within earshot of some Portuguese slave traders. Thirty-five were hanged and quartered.[32] It is not surprising, then, that slave owners feared more than a loss of property when their slaves ran away. It is precisely during these first years of the seventeenth century that the highest numbers of slaves, both men and women, were tried for blasphemy resulting from their flight and punishment.

As an arm of religious control bolstered by the state, the Holy Office of the Inquisition participated in the wider Spanish efforts to coopt and suppress slaves, employing in its trials the instruments of ideological persuasion, flogging, imprisonment, forced labor, execution, and exemplary punishment through public spectacle. The purpose of all measures was to strike sufficient awe into the hearts of both the offender and the public as to compel self-control.[33] Such were the mechanisms that propelled the trial of María Blanca in Mexico City, beginning within a month of the Spanish truce with King Yanga's *palenque* and taking place between the uprisings of 1608 and 1611 which struck fear into the hearts of the slave-owning class.

Race, slavery, and to some extent gender combined to shape the relationship of Afro-Mexican slave women with the Inquisition,[34] though slave women appear to have used blasphemy in asserting themselves against their oppressors to the same degree as their male companions.[35] The Inquisition's preoccupation with blaspheming slave women was especially strong at the turn of the seventeenth century. The inquisitors' concern was not strictly a matter of either race or morality but rather was entangled in the conditions created by slavery, as suggested by the comparatively low incidence of blasphemy cases among free black and mulatta women.[36] Timing was not insignificant; most of the trials occurred during a period of intense slave rebellion.

The prosecution of slaves for blasphemy suggests that other instruments of coercion had already been used and had failed. The case of María Blanca is typical in that her flight and subsequent flogging did not intimidate her into submission but rather provoked her to use the language and beliefs of her oppressors to reject their actions. The fact that she ran away in the first place indicates on one level the owner's failure and in the larger context the general inability of society to convince her that as a presumably inferior creature bondage was her necessary lot.

The Blasphemy of María Blanca and Gerónima

María Blanca's case opened on Wednesday, April 8, 1609, with the testimony of two witnesses. Isabel de Balça, a free mulatta women, thirty-three years old and a servant in the same household as María, made the first denunciation. She claimed to speak out of her own free will with the desire to clear her conscience. María Magdalena, a nineteen-year-old mestiza servant who also worked for María's mistress, Doña Catalina de Villafañe, being the only other witness to testify, cited the same motivation. Isabel de Balça identified María's race and ethnicity as being between *bozal* and *ladina,* the first a term that named a slave recently arrived from Africa, the second, one who had been in bondage more than a year or who had become Europeanized. According to Balça, María had committed the offense four days before, on a Saturday, at about noon, having been brought back to the house after an attempted escape. Although María Blanca is consistently referred to in the documents as the slave of Don Antonio de Saavedra, of Mexico City, it is Doña Catalina, Saavedra's wife, whom Balça identifies as the person who ordered and supervised the punishment:

> And having tied her up to punish her, by order of the said Doña Catalina de Villafañe her mistress, at the first ten or twelve lashes that this witness [Isabel de Balça] gave her with a leather thong with which they whip the girls who perform menial labor, this black woman María said that she renounced the milk she suckled, the bread she ate, the water she drank *and God and all his saints, all of which she said twice, and her mistress* hit her with a shoe for it, and ordered her whipped again and dripped with some tallow candles, and this was done. And when she [María] spoke these words, this witness and María Magdalena, the Spanish portress, and the said Doña Catalina de Villafañe were present, and nothing else happened.[37]

Key parts of the testimony have been underlined and annotated in the margins of the document, showing the inquisitors' specific interest in the fact that María "renounced God and all his saints two times." Their criteria for defining heretical blasphemy emerge both here and in their further questioning of the witness: "Asked if this black woman, María, was sober when she made these renunciations, and what she [Isabel de Balça] presumes about her regarding her Christianity, she stated that this black woman, María, was sober when she spoke these renunciations, because she never got drunk and that she is reputed to be a good Christian because she fasts and wears the scapular of Our Lady."[38]

The second witness testified on the same day as Isabel de Balça. "A woman who said she was called María Magdalena, a mestiza in the service of Doña Catalina de Villafañe . . . who said she was nineteen years old, promised to tell the truth."[39] María Magdalena's version of the story differed somewhat from Isabel's. On the one hand she added the comments that María Blanca had been brought home from the jail where she had been held after her escape and that after six or seven lashes María renounced the mother who gave birth to her. On the other, she omitted details such as the identity of the person who administered the punishment. Her testimony corresponds with that of the other witness in naming the persons present as Balça, Doña Catalina, and herself and in assessing María Blanca's sobriety and faithfulness: "*She said that [María Blanca] was sober and not drunk, because* she is not in the habit of getting drunk. And that she regards her as a good Christian, because she sees her fasting on Saturdays and advents. And that this is the truth under the oath that she has made, and she does not say it out of hatred."[40]

Two different perspectives emerge from the testimony, that of the slave owners and inquisitors and the more enigmatic attitude of the witnesses. Master and mistress did not speak at the trial, but their actions as registered in the document imply their point of view. In ordering that María Blanca be flogged for having escaped, master or mistress (or both) reasserted "rightful" ownership and reestablished a broken social order. (There appears to be controversy over which of the two presided. When María Blanca related her flogging at the hands of her "amo," or master, she may have made either a grammatical error or a strategic move in her own defense. She may also have been telling a truth denied by the witnesses' testimony.) The blows given by master or mistress with a shoe show their characterization of María Blanca as rebellious not only against the slave-master relationship endorsed by the state but also against the Catholic faith.

Although the Inquisition sometimes criticized extremely cruel punishments meted out by slave owners, this particular case reveals that the Inquisition perceived María in the same light as did Don Antonio and Doña Catalina. It would seem from the documentation that this trial was initiated by the testimony of two fellow servants, rather than that of the owners or the slave herself—both of which did occur in other cases. Nevertheless, a primary interest served by the Inquisition here was that of the slave owners, whose efforts to keep "their *castas*" in line were bolstered by the trial.

Any personal opinion on the part of the servants is difficult to discern. While the mistress's use of the shoe to beat María Blanca in the face suggests rage, indignation, or fear, no identifiable passion is recorded on the part of the witnesses. Both women clearly reported the contradiction between María's usual character as a good Christian and the blasphemy they witnessed; they did not, however, convey a negative judgment of her actions. They did provide key material for the case the prosecutor was constructing when they attested to the blasphemy without mentioning any remorse on the part of María Blanca. Furthermore, in naming a small number of blows preceding the outburst, they jeopardized María Blanca's attempt to excuse her offense. When the prosecutor reshaped the witnesses' testimony in a discourse that argued for guilt, he cited the lower number of blows mentioned and emphasized the connection between the flogging and the "original" offense: he stated in his *querella* that María Blanca had blasphemed after "having been given only six or eight lashes, compassionately and without any cruelty and because she should be punished" [abiéndole dado solos seis o ocho açotes piadossam[en]te y sin crueldad alg[un]a y porque debe ser castigada] (fol. 2r). The documents do not reveal whether the servants' lack of solidarity with María Blanca indicates success by the slave-owning class in using ideological persuasion to separate free women from slave, mulatta and mestiza from black—all members of the plebeian class—or whether the servants betrayed María Blanca under duress.[41] The question is worthy of examination over a broader spectrum of cases and could enrich our understanding of the interracial relations among the female servant and slave classes.

The servants' assertions that the mistress rather than the master whipped María and the fact that the case against María was built from the testimony of two members of the plebeian class clearly establish an absence of solidarity among women in this case: womanhood was not a universal category in the colonial world. Indeed, given the documents available, the dynamics of the case suggest that race and class defined subjectivity, here, almost to the exclusion of gender. Ownership and antagonism differentiated the femaleness of the slave from that of her mistress. As a woman and slave, María Blanca served in the household of her mistress, who, as the woman of the slave-owning family, exercised her authority over the household slaves and servants, their work, their needs, and their discipline. The free status of the mulatta and mestiza servants as well as their greater appropriation of Spanish cultural attitudes and behaviors would have led them to receive more rewards within the household than did the African slave, provided they maintained their distance from her.

Yet another dynamic of oppression may lurk behind the discourses of the tribunal in María Blanca's case. Addressing slavery in the United States, bell hooks discusses the interactions between women of different races, which have left us even today with a painful and problematic legacy. Here, master-slave sexual relationships played a key role in the tensions between the slave and her mistress:

> In a white supremacist patriarchy, that relationship which most threat-
> ened to disrupt, challenge, and dismantle white power [and] its con-
> comitant social order was the legalized union between a white man
> and a black woman. Slave testimony, as well as the diaries of southern
> white women, record incidents of jealousy, rivalry, and sexual competi-
> tion between white mistresses and enslaved black women. Court rec-
> ords document that individual white men did try to gain public rec-
> ognition of their bonds with black women either through attempts to
> marry or through efforts to leave property and money in wills. Most
> of these cases were contested by white family members. Importantly,

white females were protecting their fragile social positions and power within patriarchal culture by asserting their superiority over black women.[42]

Although slave systems in British and Spanish America differed in many respects, sexual relationships between male slave owners and female slaves, whether forced or willing, were a reality in all American colonial societies. The documents in María Blanca's case give no explicit reason to suspect a sexual relationship, but such would always have been a possible motivation for the flight of a female slave and for a special desire on the part of the mistress to inflict pain on her and exact submission. Rather than blaming the master, white colonists sexualized black and mulatta women, portraying them as morally inferior whores. Whether or not such interaction existed between Don Antonio and María Blanca, the general social attitude was likely a part of Doña Catalina's estimation of her slave's worth and would have further justified in her mind her antagonism and the rigors of her punishment.

A full nine months elapsed before María Blanca was able to tell her own version of the events, even though Dr. Martos de Bohorques had requested that María be arrested when filing his initial complaint.[43] On Thursday, April 9, 1609, after receiving the two testimonies, the inquisitors Don Alonso de Peralta and Gutierre Bernardo de Quirós decided that the case should be tried and María be brought to the tribunal chambers. On January 30, 1610, María Blanca was finally brought from her master's house and officially sworn to tell the truth during the entire proceedings. The denounced slave identified herself as "María Blanca, Congolese, slave of Don Antonio de Saavedra, propertied resident of this city" [María Blanca, de nación conga, esclava de Don Antonio de Saavedra, vezino desta çiudad] (fol. 8r). With the irony of coincidence, the woman who up to this point had been called "the black slave María" [María negra esclava] told the inquisitors that her name was "Mary White." Thus she began her testimony by contradicting the official story, a kind of resistance which she sustained throughout five appearances. In the end, she would be silenced, her courageous self-naming replaced by the official discourse of submission in the abjuration de levi, and her identity reduced to the general category of repentant sinner.

As the trial proceeded, this African woman revealed that although she did not know the personal fact of her own age, she could establish her colonized identity as a Christian. Her knowledge of Catholic doctrine was important to the inquisitors, as only a Christian would be able to commit heretical blasphemy by rejecting it:

> She did not know her age and by her appearance she seems to be thirty, and [she said] that her office is to serve her master.
>
> Asked if she has been imprisoned or punished before by the Holy Office of the Inquisition, she said, "no."
>
> Asked if she is baptized and confirmed as a Christian, and if she hears mass, confesses and takes communion when the holy mother church requires it, she said that she is a baptized Christian, and that, in the city of Seville, being the slave of Marqués de Jarifa, a bishop confirmed her, whose name she does not know, and that she attends mass, confesses and takes communion when the holy mother church requires it, and that during Lent just passed she confessed in the convent of Saint Francis in this city with a monk whose name she does not remember and there she took communion.
>
> She made the sign of the cross in Romance and recited the Lord's Prayer, Hail Mary, Credo and Hail Holy Queen in Romance, uttering a few wrong words, and the Ten Commandments she only knew partially.[44]

María Blanca's knowledge of doctrine and her self-representation as a faithful Christian demonstrated that she had internalized Spanish culture to a degree, but when she later questioned the impositions of this dominant culture on other grounds, she revealed that the internalization was anything but complete.

Asked if she knew why she had been brought before the inquisitors, she gave the following explanation:

> She said that she suspects she has been sent for because one day, during Holy Week of Lent past, while two Tapisque Indians, a mestiza and a mulatta were whipping her with great cruelty by order of her master, because she had escaped, using a leather whip, she said twice that for the love of God they leave her alone, and seeing that they did not leave her, with that pain, she said *twice more that she renounced God*

and all of his saints, for which they hit her in the face with a shoe which could have damaged her eyes, and they whipped her until all four were tired, and she does not know for what other reason she may have been brought, and that having blasphemed grieves her greatly because she is very devoted to Our Lady.[45]

When María Blanca was questioned as to whether she knew why she had been brought before the Inquisition, in effect she was being asked to confess her crime. She did not respond with such a confession but instead built her own defense by portraying in a very different light the acts recounted by the witnesses. She had not heard their testimonies and theoretically did not even know who had denounced her. Because the effectiveness of the Inquisition depended on secrecy, each participant was sworn not to reveal any of the proceedings outside the chambers. María Blanca, of course, was well aware of who was present at the beating and heard the blasphemy that resulted in the trial.

María's first words to the inquisitors marked her sense of self as different from the representation that had been made of her. Not only did she give her full name, María *Blanca,* which others had ignored, but unlike those who had called her "black" and vaguely placed her between the categories of *bozal* and *ladina,* she gave herself the specific cultural-national identity of Congolese. She also detailed her punishment quite differently than how the witnesses related it. María Blanca insisted that there were four people involved in her beating and that they beat her until all were tired; thus she emphasized the violence of the punishment and explicitly characterized it as "cruel." Rather than a leather thong, she remembered a whip, and such were the blows to her face that she feared her eyes would be injured. Her words convey not the rightful restitution of a paternalistic system by a slave mistress but the unrestrained violence of an irresponsible master and his servants.

In describing events, María shifted blame to her owners: their cruelty was the true cause of her blasphemy. In coloring her master as the real perpetrator, she effectively questioned the validity of the entire proceedings and the institutions that those proceedings protected. If her owners had rightful control over her, Spanish laws demanded that they care for her and treat her well, provide adequate food and clothing, and refrain from using cruelty in punishing her.[46] The key question for María Blanca and the prosecutor was how to define "cruelty" and whether the term applied in her case.

As for María Blanca's own character and her role in the master-slave relationship, she asserted that the first words to have escaped her mouth during the flogging were not rebellious blasphemy but an appeal to the goodness of her owners and a demonstration of her Catholic piety: before her involuntary blasphemy, she had pleaded in the name of God for mercy. In her story, the continued punishment demonstrated a lack of sensitivity on the part of her punishers to the compassionate character of the Divinity whom they and the Catholic slave society had brought into her life. María Blanca emphasized her own devotion and the remorse she felt as a good Christian for having been provoked to sin by the physical distress inflicted upon her. Her narrative stresses that her acts of flight and blasphemy were not rebellion against two rightful systems but rather indicated the failure of her own master and mistress to live up to their responsibilities as slave owners and, more important, as Catholics. When pressed in a second audience with the inquisitors to give a full and true confession, she added that "her mistress requires her to say these things and that she does not want to be with her and that the order be given that she sell her" [su ama la obliga a dezir estas cossas y que no quiere estar con ella q[ue] se dé orden la venda].[47] María Blanca did not overtly criticize the institution of slavery, but she did justify her dissatisfaction with her own mistress and attempted to negotiate a change. Such negotiation by slaves was not uncommon, but the slaves were rarely successful.[48]

María Blanca failed to persuade the inquisitors to have her sold. Neither did she succeed in making her version of her offense and its circumstances prevail, even though she held persistently to her story throughout the trial. It was an ordeal designed to intimidate her and persuade her of the rightness and benevolence of the institution that held her on trial. On the five separate days when she was brought before the inquisitors and questioned—January 30, February 10, 12, 16, and 20—she was admonished a total of three times to examine her memory of the offense and to make a full confession; four times she was asked whether she remembered any more of the event. Her confession was clearly unsatisfactory to an institution that, according to the inquisitors, did not arrest any person without sufficient evidence that an offense against the faith had been committed. Frequently the warnings and interrogations were accompanied by assurances that greater mercy would be granted those who showed themselves to be truly repentant. Finally, they assigned María Blanca a defense lawyer, but his function was only to echo the inquisitors, advise her to confess fully and, if found guilty, to request a merciful penance.[49] In these ways, the inquisitors constructed a benevolent and righteous façade for the tribunal.

María Blanca responded to each warning and interrogation with a defiant negative:

> Therefore and out of reverence to our Lord God and his blessed and glorious mother, our lady the virgin Mary, she is warned and charged to examine her memory and to state and confess entirely the truth concerning the guilt she feels or what she might know of others who are guilty, without covering up any of this about herself or them, nor giving false testimony against herself or another. Because by doing thus she will unburden her conscience as a Catholic Christian and she will save her soul. And her case will be dispatched with the brevity and mercy allowed and she will not be tried. And having given her to understand this admonition
>
> She stated that she had no more to say. . . .
>
> And being present, she was asked if she had remembered anything more in her situation and that she state it and the truth under the oath that she has taken.
>
> She said she does not remember more. . . .
>
> She said no. . . .
>
> She said no sir. . . .
>
> She said, "I have nothing more to say."[50]

The effects of María Blanca's appearances before the tribunal day after day and the repeated admonitions and interrogation mounted as the inquisitors presented, one after another, the signs of her approaching condemnation and punishment. Clearly, the purpose was to wear her down to the point of a submission and confession. At her second appearance, she was warned that the prosecutor planned to present an accusation (fol. 10r). She had so far been denied knowledge of her exact predicament, unaware of the charges against her before she confessed. She may have well believed that she had made a full confession, in which case her fears would have been exacerbated by confusion as to why her confession was deemed insufficient. She may, on the other hand, have expected such manipulation, as it is likely that she had heard the stories of trials told by other slaves.

Prosecutor Pedro de Fonseca presented his formal accusation constructed from the witnesses' testimony and framed in such a way as to make the offense appear as serious as possible. First, he affirmed that as a Christian who enjoyed the full benefits of the faith, María, the black slave of Don Antonio de Saavedra, had blasphemed against God and his saints (fol. 11r). Next, he explained the specific circumstances to show that heretical blasphemy had occurred:

> After Doña Catalina de Villafañe, her mistress, had ordered that she be punished because she had escaped, and being tied up, at the first ten or twelve lashes that they gave her with an ordinary thong with which they whip the female laborers, mercifully and without cruelty, the prisoner said that she renounced the milk that she suckled and the bread that she ate and the water that she drank and God and all his saints, all of which she said twice causing scandal to the people who were present, it being a woman who was punishing her, and only so that she correct herself, and because the prisoner was sober and of sound understanding.[51]

In an accusation common to blasphemy cases, Fonseca further stated that María had committed other offenses, which he would bring up in the prosecution; this did not happen. Finally, he accused her of perjury. In his statement, the prosecutor sustained the master and mistress's perspective of María as a slave who had rebelled against rightful ownership and had offended both the church and God. He further emphasized the danger of her crime by suggesting the power it had to corrupt the weakness of the other women present. Faced with the full accusation, María Blanca stood firm in her response to each charge:

> C1 To the first chapter [of the accusation]
> She said that, as she has confessed, she is a Christian, baptized and confirmed, and that she has done nothing more than she has declared.

C2 To the second chapter
She said that there is nothing more than what she has confessed.
C3 To the third and final chapter of this accusation
She said that she has told no lie here and that she has done nothing else, and that this is the truth under the oath that she has taken.[52]

On her third appearance before the inquisitors, María Blanca adopted some of the submissive posture that the tribunal desired, reiterating remorse for the blasphemy and requesting a merciful punishment. She continued to insist, however, that she had told the full truth: "She said that she has confessed the truth, and she does not remember anything more. And that having blasphemed grieves her. And the cause was that she was out of her mind with the pain of the punishment. And she requests a merciful penance."[53] Intimidation escalated during her fourth appearance as the two anonymous testimonies against her were read aloud. María Blanca cracked a little more: "She said that she remits to what she has declared, and that it might be that she said thusly that she renounced the mother who bore her, but not the rest."[54]

The tribunal seems to have placed prime importance on slight discrepancies between the two stories: whether or not María Blanca renounced milk, bread, and water and who was involved in her physical punishment. If these were the key points on which the prosecutor based his charge of perjury and the reason the inquisitors demanded a more complete confession, the matter turned more on the degree of submission desired from the slave than on the substantive issue of heretical blasphemy. In similar prosecutions, a key issue was whether the accused had blasphemed once, which could be an involuntary exclamation brought on by pain, or twice, indicating a reaffirmation or a will to blaspheme.[55] María Blanca, however, admitted in her initial testimony that she had exclaimed twice, arguing that both exclamations were involuntary. The prosecutor made no argument to the contrary.

The case was heard on February 26 by the inquisitors Gutierre Bernardo de Quirós and Dr. Martos de Bohorques, joined by senior canon Alonso López de Cárdenas, the high court judges Pedro Suárez de Longoria and Don Marcos Guerrero as consultants, and the magistrate Antonio de Morga.[56] In the publication of the conviction and sentencing, the tribunal laid a benevolent façade over the cruel punishment it pre-scribed. Invoking the name of Christ, the inquisitors declared that if they were to follow the full rigor of the law, they could impose a greater pen-alty, but that they chose rather to act with "kindness and mercy" [benig-nidad y misericordia] in sentencing María Blanca; they finally used the name she had given herself. They sentenced her to the penitential mass, the abjuration de levi, and the public flogging previously described. Though her sentence did not provide the great spectacle of the autos-da-fé of 1596, 1601, and 1605, in which dozens of slaves were punished for blasphemy, it did share with the autos a public reaffirmation of the Cath-olic faith and the church's power to control, coerce, or persuade the bodies and minds of the populace, especially those of rebellious slaves.[57] Though María Blanca insisted to the end on a different version of the events, the condemnation of her crime which was spoken for her on the streets of Mexico City as she was carried, gagged and half naked, on a beast of burden and the words that she herself was compelled to utter painted for the public the picture of a formerly rebellious black slave woman now subdued by the legitimate and benevolent Inquisition:

> I, María Blanca, black slave of Don Antonio de Saavedra, property-owning resident of this Mexico City, being present before your Lord-ships as inquisitors that you are against the heretical gravity and apos-tasy in this city and its region, by apostolic and ordinary authority, and placed before me this sign of the cross and the holy gospels that I touch bodily with my hands, and knowing and recognizing the true catholic and apostolic faith, abjure, detest and anathematize all classes of heresy that arise against the holy Catholic faith and evangelical law of our redeemer and savior Jesus Christ and against the Holy Apos-tolic See of the Roman Church, especially that of which I, before your Lordships have been accused and am lightly suspect. And I swear and promise to always hold and keep the holy Catholic faith that the holy mother church holds, keeps and teaches, and I will be ever obedient to our lord the Pope. . . . And I confess that all of those who rise against this holy faith are worthy of condemnation and I promise never to join them, and to the extent that I am able, I will persecute them and the heresies that I know from them, I will reveal and notify to any inquis-itor. . . . I swear and promise that I will receive humbly and with pa-

tience the punishment that has been or is ever imposed on me. . . . And I beg the present secretary to take this as my testimony and those present as witnesses.[58]

The outcome of María Blanca's trial contrasts sharply with the decision not to pursue a similar case against the mulatta slave Gerónima, whom Dr. Martos de Bohorques brought before the same inquisitors, Don Alonso de Peralta and Gutierre Bernardo de Quirós. The commissioning of a notary to carry out investigations into the incident was made on April 30, 1609, only three weeks after Bohorques filed his complaint against María Blanca.[59] The juxtaposition of the documents poses questions regarding the specific mechanisms by which the tribunal sought to subdue unruly slaves and the decisions slaves made to choose either tactics of survival or resistance in their relationships with both owners and inquisitors. What were the exact reasons that led the tribunal to punish María Blanca with two hundred lashes and not to try Gerónima? Any of several factors may have contributed to these reactions to the two female slaves: differing desires by the slave owners concerning the participation of the Inquisition in the control of their slaves, a possible consideration by the tribunal that the punishment rendered one slave was more cruel than that meted out to the other, the satisfaction the Inquisition took in the more immediate and profoundly submissive posture of Gerónima, or different values attributed to the racial and ethnic identities of the two.

In Gerónima's case, it is unclear who brought the offense to the attention of the Inquisition. No witness came forward of his or her own free will; rather, a religious notary was assigned to travel to the Tulançingo residence to gather information because "news [had] been received that a mulatta slave of Augustín de Çevallos, propertied resident of this town, on being whipped by her master for having run away, renounced God and his saints" [se a tenido notiçia que una mulata esclava de Augustín de Çevallos, vezino de este pueblo, en occassión de estarla açotando su amo por averse huido, renegó de Dios y de sus sanctos] (fol. 5r). Neither is it clear why the case was not pursued after the testimony was gathered and brought before the inquisitors. Possibly the family had no intention of bringing Gerónima before the Inquisition and someone else reported the deed, which could explain why the family members testified in such a way as to discourage prosecution and thus maintain full control over the situation.

On the other hand, the punishment that provoked Gerónima's oath appears more violent than that received by María Blanca, though none of the four witnesses called it cruel. All the witnesses noted that Gerónima was tied naked to a stairway before her master dealt her some sixteen to twenty lashes. Thereupon, according to Çevallos, she renounced the mother who gave birth to her, the father who made her and, after being told to shut up, God, all his saints, and the Virgin Mary. Having untied Gerónima, Çevallos gagged her and began whipping her again as she knelt on the floor. Çevallos's sister-in-law, Doña Catalina de Navarrete, added that when Gerónima blasphemed, Çevallos hit her across the mouth and cheeks, saying, "Don't say that, dog" [no digas eso, perra] (fol. 9r, 13r).

Would the inquisitors have seen the removal of Gerónima's clothing, in itself a symbolic denial of Catholic Spanish culture, as a suitable humiliation for a slave who had demonstrated her unworthiness by running away? Would they have judged the act of stripping the slave to her skin a scandalous immodesty on the part of her master? Perhaps one reason the case was not tried is that the inquisitors immediately saw the blasphemy as involuntary and occurring in extremely harsh circumstances.

In contrast to María Blanca's delayed remorse, the retraction of the oath by Gerónima was immediate. When her gag fell during the second beating and her master demanded to know whom she had renounced, her answer was that she renounced not God but the devil. According to the testimony of Doña Beatriz de Orduña, Çevallos's wife, when Doña Beatriz's sister entered the room where Gerónima was being punished, the slave woman threw herself on the other, begging, for the love of God, that the punishment cease (fol. 11v). Doña Catalina's intervention in her favor suggests a difference of opinion within the slaveholding family over appropriate discipline which may have led to a family decision not to pursue the case.

Both Doña Beatriz and Doña Catalina attested to Gerónima's deep remorse, which they witnessed when they visited her in her room after the beating. Doña Beatriz found the slave crying and very afflicted. When she reprehended Gerónima for the words she had used, the mulatta asked why her mistress had not burned or broken her mouth. Doña Catalina recounted that the mulatta slave had told her, weeping, that the devil had come into her mouth and that she was Christian and believed truly in God. Doña Catalina returned on Easter Sunday night, the day following the punishment, to treat Gerónima's swollen face and again found her deeply remorseful, this time desirous of confession (fols. 12r, 13v, 14r). Doña Catalina consoled her, telling her she could confess the following day and that she should trust in God's mercy. The strongest clues to the dismissal of the case lie in these scenes in which the "rightful" social order is reestablished and the women of the slaveholder family play out the Christian message of compassion in justification of the barbarous treatment that has gone before. Chance may have had a hand in the merciful outcome, since the slave's punishment and remorse coincided with the highest of Catholic holy days.

Race may also have been a factor in differentiating the outcomes of Gerónima's and María Blanca's trials: unlike her mulatta contemporary, María was an African. In analyzing slave resistance, Colin A. Palmer notes that slaves recently imported from Africa resisted more frequently than did Creole slaves, "who had been socialized into the slave systems and had known no other type of existence."[60] Moreover, slaves of certain African nationalities were considered more threatening than others; the high court in Mexico City, for example, requested in 1613 that importations from Angola be entirely halted because of the rebelliousness of Angolan slaves.[61] María Blanca hailed from the Congo, the same nation as did King Yanga of the insurgent *palenque*. Despite instances of black-mulatto collaboration in resistance, the mulatta Gerónima was likely perceived as less threatening than María Blanca.

Conclusions

In 1609, Mexico found itself in a period of intense unrest among Afro-Mexican slaves. The large numbers of *cimarrones* provoked Spaniards to acute anxiety. Individual owners and the institutions of Spanish colonial society sought to use corporal punishment to repress slave resistance, and verbal and symbolic discourse to persuade or terrorize slaves. Exasperated owners brought their slaves before the Inquisition when beatings not only failed to repress them but also provoked the verbal rejection named blasphemy. In the chambers of the Inquisition, the church sought ideological control over these rebellious "children," rooting out and punishing heretical blasphemy. But inquisitors did not merely attempt to extirpate heresy; they were also reinforcing the individual efforts of slave owners to repress their slaves for the "good" of all Spanish society. The Inquisition could hardly have processed all those whose rebellion involved the renunciation of the Catholic God; the trials were meant to pacify not by means of large-scale corporal punishment but rather by the exemplary and awe-filled character of their spectacle.[62] The Spanish Crown shared this need for an inquisitorial spectacle of benevolent but effective power to frighten slaves into acquiescence and thereby enable colonial economies to flourish, though at times it found such punishment as well as the actions of the slave owners to exceed prudent governance: "As the king frankly stated on more than one occasion, slaves in Mexico and the Spanish Indies in general were subject to 'scandalous abuses,' and mistreated 'to such an extreme that some die without confession.'"[63]

Slaves did not quietly acquiesce to the Inquisition. Rather, they contested their oppression before the tribunal with sporadic success, naming their suffering and condemning the use of cruelty that bolstered slavery, if not the system itself. Testimony about owners' harsh treatment reveals slaves crying out against the ideological foundation on which the entire system rested. "Reniego a Dios!" "I renounce the God who would allow you such cruelty over my body; you do not control my mind or my tongue." Not only did the slave owners' actions betray the benevolence of a religious justification, but they also contradicted the model of the responsible patriarch which undergirded monarchical society.

Documents of these trials show Africans and Creoles, blacks and mulattoes, men and women grasping for a modicum of power to determine their own lives under slavery. To understand the role played by gender in the stories of oppression of María Blanca and Gerónima, to see how gender affected the procedures and outcomes of the trials, or to comprehend how their cases demonstrate the construction of womanhood during colonial times is challenging. Dozens of documents await more extensive scrutiny. The two cases examined emphasize the lack of a shared experience of womanhood between mistress and slave as well as among slave women and free servants of oppressed racial groups. The cases also provide evidence for a picture of womanhood which is not unified even within the Spanish elite, showing that slave-owning women played out roles of maternal compassion as well as of violent antagonism. Most important, the present study begins to open a channel whereby we might hear the voices of the many Afro-Mexican women who chose active resistance to slavery and its conceptions of them and who persevered when their attempts at escaping the system had failed, acting on hope to better their daily lives.

These trial documents record the actions of the mulatta Gerónima, who, having failed to escape slavery, chose survival over continued resistance, expressing a remorseful and submissive attitude that kept her from the jaws of the Inquisition. They also show the futile attempts of the Congolese slave woman María Blanca to use the same survival tactic of remorse to avoid the Inquisition's brutal punishment. María Blanca may have been less able or willing to work with the system than her mulatta counterpart; her remorse came too late, her insistence on her own story proved too threatening. Her voice, filled with pride and justice throughout the trial, was finally silenced by a faceless recitation of a dogma of obedience, her body punished more cruelly by the church than by her owners. Perhaps as a strong-willed woman, an African, and a slave, María Blanca's fate was sealed.

CHAPTER THIRTEEN

Rosa de Escalante's Private Party

Popular Female Religiosity in
Colonial Mexico City

LINDA A. CURCIO-NAGY

During the spring of 1691, two sisters, Rosa de Escalante and Margarita de Narana, organized a number of ceremonies in which Rosa reverentially placed a statue of Saint Anthony on an altar especially constructed for the event.[1] Immediately after placing the saint on the altar, she "se arrodillaba" [knelt before] a young man, Juan de Galdo, a page to the viceroy, the count of Galve,[2] and "le echaba un escapulario" [placed upon him a scapular] of Saint Anthony and then danced with the young man. After some time passed, she removed the scapular. Then everyone danced, "y continuaba la música hasta las ocho de la noche" [and the music continued until eight at night]. Afterward, "tomaban dulces y chocolate" [they had sweets and hot chocolate].[3] The event lasted five hours, beginning at three in the afternoon, and took place in the home of silversmith Joseph de Piñeda, whose wife, Lolita, was the cousin of Rosa and Margarita. In attendance were some twenty individuals, "otros criados de su Excelencia" [mostly employees of the viceroy].[4] The husbands of Margarita and Lolita were not present at the ceremony. Subsequent *oratorio* rituals, always occurring on Sunday, featured performers, "unos mozos bailarines, hijos del maestro Reina" [the teenage sons of a dance master, one Señor Reina], who were contracted specifically for the ceremony. Special invitations were extended to other women to witness what some participants referred to as "la fiesta de Rosa" [Rosa's party].[5]

Much of the research of the last fifteen years regarding female piety in colonial Mexico has centered on the lives and spirituality of nuns, notable among them Sor Juana Inés de la Cruz and Madre María de San José. The writings of these women religious are an invaluable repository of details about conventual life, difficulties with male confessors and the patriarchal Catholic Church, and the women's personal spiritual journeys.[6] Other studies present the lives of *beatas,* those laywomen renowned for their piety and charity who, although they had no affiliation with female religious orders and were highly suspect in the eyes of some male ecclesiastical authorities, lived celibate and semicloistered lives of religious contemplation.[7] Yet these official and unofficial "daughters of Christ" represented a small and, in many cases, elite fraction of the female inhabitants of New Spain.

The story of Rosa de Escalante, who appeared before the Holy Office of the Inquisition in Mexico City in 1691, is particularly significant because it sheds light not on the usual subject—nun or beata—but rather on the average woman of the viceregal capital. Rosa was a young single woman of seventeen who lived with her sister, Margarita, and her brother-in-law, Joseph de Urrutia, a tax collector for the Real Hacienda. As a family, they represented Spaniards of some means, ostensibly reputable, devout Catholics, holding to traditional Iberian views of women as pious, loyal, and obedient.[8] Paradoxically, the women's piety manifested itself in a manner anathema to those views and, more important, to the concept of orthodoxy espoused by the church and the Inquisition, for Rosa and Margarita were the principal organizers of private rituals that the inquisitors had identified as oratorios and which the Holy Office found reason to prohibit.

The brief and limited number of examples of the oratorio tradition might lead scholars to believe that these ceremonies were isolated events connected to this particular household, that, in short, Rosa's case was an anomaly rather than a manifestation of popular religious belief. But the promulgation of edicts against the oratorios which began as early as 1626 and continued with actions in 1643, 1684, and 1704, with little effect it might be noted, suggest that Rosa's "party" was not an exceptional case but representative of a widespread devotional practice. Although it is unclear why the Inquisition decided to attack the oratorio tradition during these particular years, the historical context of the time may provide reason for speculation about the actions of the inquisitors. The economic woes incurred by the decline in silver production were compounded by dramatic changes in demography as the native population, which always constituted the largest percentage of the Novohispanic population, decreased in numbers. At the same time, the colony became home to a more diverse population because of the importation of African slaves and miscegenation.[9] Perceiving a certain precariousness to the established order, Spanish colonists and authorities expressed feelings of unease, which proved to be well founded as riots and rebellions shattered illusions of peace and prosperity in seventeenth-century Mexico.[10] Most important, this emergent multiethnic society meant a mixing of cultures which affected religious mores and practices, forcing the inquisitors to a keener scrutiny of popular religious forms. In this atmosphere of fear and mistrust by authorities of church and state, the timing of the edicts against the oratorios is noteworthy: the dates of publication of the edicts correspond to a documented increase in denunciations and investigations of *hechicería* (magic or enchantment), to be discussed later in the chapter.[11]

In light of these developments, the fact that the oratorio phenomenon was not exclusive to Spanish or criolla (Spaniard born in the New World) is important. Years earlier, on July 6, 1647, Petrona, "una mestiza casada con un indio" [a mestiza married to an Indian] and a servant of Juan de Suárez, a street paver, hosted an oratorio ritual in the living room of her employer's home, where she wanted to "tañer y baylar" [play music and dance]. At the service, in which "muchos mulatos, negros, y mestizos bailaban" [many mulattoes, blacks, and mestizos danced], including "una mulata Las Rarritas, una mujer paña, [y otra que] se llama Gerónimca la Listonera . . . la madrina" [a mulatto called the Strange one, a washer woman, and a ribbon maker named Gerónima, who was also the godmother of Petrona], Saint Anthony was venerated along with other saints and the crucifix on the altar. As in the story of Rosa, attendees danced for hours, ate, and drank, in this case wine. Although no mention of a scapular appears in this all too briefly described case, the informant did discuss how before the fiesta the statue of Anthony was taken to mass at the cathedral and afterward to mass at the Church of the Colegio de las Niñas.[12]

The Inquisition denunciations of oratorios as being unorthodox reflect its general concern with the misuse of official Catholic symbols and devotions connected to crosses, scapulars, and the statues of saints. The edicts attacked "gente comun y ordinara" [common and ordinary people][13] who "made private oratories in their homes, to particular (saintly) devotions, putting on those altars a certain superstitious number of candles and the paintings of persons who had died and who they considered to be virtuous (holy)."[14] Additionally, the edicts questioned the use of scapulars in the context of dancing and feasting, suggesting that oratory participants went too far and the ceremonies served as locations where "hombres y mujeres, [iban] á comer y beber demasiadamente, a jugar, cantar, y baylar con grande deshonestidad" [women and men went to eat and drink in excess, to play games, sing and dance with great lewdness], resulting in "muchos malos abusos" [much abuse].[15] The church was also suspicious because many people hosted and participated in the rituals and "[ofrecían] dinero [para] hacerlas de fuerte q[ue] causaba emulación diabólica la ofrenda" [spent money to make the festivals great, causing the emulation of these diabolical offerings] and "gran escándalo y la admiración a todas las personas timoratas" [a great scandal and the admiration of timorous people].[16] These ceremonies were tantamount to superstition in the eyes of the inquisitors, who lamented that they lacked sufficient manpower to suppress such widespread practices.[17]

Working with such documents as these edicts, historians are increasingly aware of the role of the religious festival and processions in the lives of Novohispanic people.[18] Admittedly, some effort and a good helping of educated speculation are required, and much future research is in order. These rituals reinforced community identity and served as integrative elements, a catharsis, and a means by which individuals defined their relationship to the Divine. In some cases, the rituals were desperate attempts to influence and make sense of such mysterious and uncontrollable forces as drought or plague. Account books and the minutes of organizations such as religious confraternities and published contemporary festival descriptions are sources of information about these rituals;[19] in them the reader catches an occasional glimpse of an individual, though the average woman and her beliefs are rarely discernible. Such sources are limited, as are Inquisition oratorio documents, though the latter not only clarify what religious considered to be unorthodox but also provide evidence of female religious piety, albeit filtered through the sometimes questionable lens of the inquisitorial scribe.

The oratorio ceremonies were part of a larger altar tradition that was an integral part of Novohispanic Catholicism. Permanent altars in the home were a common feature for well-off members of society. For example, many eighteenth-century wealthy criollos in Mexico requested permission to build or create private chapels or altars in their homes,[20] which would serve as domestic sanctuaries for prayer, contemplation of the Scriptures, and meditation on the life of Christ. Many altars were attached to libraries that held volumes depicting the lives of saints or other men and women whom the church held up as models for the devout.[21] Native American household compounds included the *santopan*, the saint's house, which was a small building with an altar which contained the statues of saints.[22] Another feature of daily religious life for many people was the *retablo*, a small portable structure made of wood (similar to a cabinet) with doors in which the devout placed images of saints, the Virgin Mary, or Jesus. Thus, almost every household displayed religious images as part of the widespread devotion to the saints which grew rapidly in the viceroyalty.

Large ephemeral or temporary altars were mostly constructed for public devotional celebrations, like those erected by confraternities during feast days of patron saints, processions seeking the intervention of the Virgin of Remedies, and the annual Corpus Christi celebration.[23] The ephemeral private altar was probably connected to the oratorio phenomenon and to Todos Santos (All Saints' Day) as celebrated by the indigenous community in the capital, especially at the Royal Hospital for Natives.[24] Although no exact description of the oratorio altars was included in the Inquisition documents, these Todos Santos altars could serve as their prototype. The devout placed a table against the central wall in the largest room of the house, usually the sala, where all other furniture had been removed. The table was then decorated with fine cloth or lace (depending upon a family's financial condition), a set number of candles, food, flowers, and special gifts for deceased family members. Statues of saints were sometimes placed to the back of the table near the wall, and depictions of saints, the Virgin Mary, and Jesus were hung on the wall above the table in a manner that imitated the large *retablo* decorations of chapels and main altars in Catholic churches of the period.[25]

The importance of both public and private worship centering on devotion to the saints which emerges from the documents is traceable to a similar tradition in folk Catholicism throughout Europe. Individuals, confraternities, and entire communities made vows to saints and Mary in return for relief from such adversities as drought, shipwreck, and illness, which vows often led the devout to participate in *romerías* (large-scale organized pilgrimages to a particular shrine for community welfare), pilgrimages, processions, and novenas. The church came to regard many aspects of these pervasive folk practices as unorthodox, and the Inquisition was given the task of reeducating misguided believers and creating a popular religiosity under church control.[26] However, the devotion to the saints in Europe, and especially in Spain, had a long tradition of localism and autonomy.[27] Pierre Sanchis points out that the very religious forms sanctioned by the church and which included processions and novenas ironically afforded individuals the opportunity to establish a direct relationship with their saint which by definition was not mediated by the church. In fact, Sanchis believes that such practices represented "resistance to the clergy's religious monopoly and a demand for autonomy so far as relations with the sacred [were] concerned." This same historian points out that in the Portuguese *romaria*, the clergy had nothing whatsoever to do with its organization, nor were they consulted.[28]

Devotion to the saints which allowed for autonomy at the individual level created networks of solidarity among believers, which in turn had ramifications in the larger community. Even if only one or two people organized an oratorio, their guests benefited from the private location in which to express their devotion to Saint Anthony or some other saint. Organized without the consultation, approval, or participation of the clergy and officiated by laywomen who brought together the devotees, these rituals challenged the authority of the church to prescribe and ordain religious events. The oratorio ritual, then, demonstrates an autonomous popular interpretation of Catholic ritual and belief which speaks to the "independent creativity of popular tradition."[29]

Additionally, Rosa and Petrona organized and officiated at ceremonies that stood well outside the bounds of standard practices accepted

[259]

by the Inquisition. Much like Todos Santos altars, the oratorios were popularly and independently conceived, and, because they were private, they were extremely difficult to detect and root out from an institutional perspective. Additionally, Rosa and Petrona and their guests could cloak whatever was taking place behind the church's promotion and acceptance of the devotion to the saints. That is, Rosa and Petrona constructed the ritual so as to marshal the spiritual force inherent in such orthodox symbols and ceremonies as petitions to saints and the sacrament of the mass.

Among the symbols that Rosa adapted for her private ceremonies was that of the scapular, a tradition that originated before the thirteenth century. Scapulars were long pieces of cloth that fitted over the head and hung down the front and back of the wearer; they were tied in place with shorter pieces of cloth which crossed horizontally across the chest and back, forming the sign of the cross. Regular clergy bestowed scapulars on devout laity who identified with the lifestyle of their order.[30] At the beginning of the sixteenth century, the popularity of scapulars increased substantially with the introduction of small scapulars that fit over the head of the wearer somewhat like a necklace and frequently were embroidered with the image of the Virgin or a saint in whose honor they were worn. Although scapulars were intended to be worn as a badge of honor and devotion to the Virgin or saint, they came to be regarded as possessing magical powers and functioned as a kind of talisman. Some clergy even believed that simply wearing the scapular assured immediate entry into heaven upon death.[31] Consistent with much of the folk Catholic tradition, the scapular was utilized for purposes that the church neither intended nor approved.[32]

In terms of such issues as intimacy, autonomous interpretation, the appropriation of the sanctity from orthodox symbols and rituals, and the development of a scapular usage that was of suspect orthodoxy, the oratorios are akin to the practice and belief known as *hechicería*, which was of popular origin and also of concern to the Holy Office. Under the rubric of *hechicería* were such practices as fortunetelling, using potions, powders, effigies, and talismans to affect the lives of individuals in a positive or negative way, and, most important, for our discussion, love magic. Individuals, usually female, resorted to magic in an effort to secure a man and, on some occasions, to dominate, tame, or eliminate a spouse. The connection between oratorios and *hechicería* in the case of Rosa and Petrona may not be merely coincidental as we consider the role of saints in popular belief, especially the place that Saint Anthony of Padua held in popular devotion.

Saint Anthony of Padua (1195–1231), a father of the church, revered as a Wondermaker, was a Franciscan renowned for his holiness, energy, and dynamic preaching style that attracted large crowds and won over the hearts of many lapsed Christians and heretics. He denounced usury and was considered an advocate of the poor and also was the patron of miners. Anthony was and still is evoked in the search for lost objects. However, his efficacy as an advocate and miracle worker was also connected to relief from diabolic obsessions, fevers, and even animal diseases.

Most important, for our analysis, Anthony's help was consistently invoked for affairs of the heart in his role as patron saint of lovers, marriage, and childless (barren) women.[33] According to Portuguese tradition, where the devotion to Lisbon-born Anthony was particularly strong, the saint enjoyed homage from pretty girls seeking a husband. Some festivals included overtly sexual rituals as part of requests to the saint.[34] In her discussion of love magic in Venice, Ruth Martin duplicates a chant to Saint Anthony utilized by an *hechicera* (a practitioner of *hechicería*) to ensure the love of a particular man for her female client.[35] In colonial Brazil, Saint Anthony was never invoked for lovers (unlawful unions), but only for those who wished to marry. A popular prayer to Saint Anthony went as follows: "Father Saint Anthony of the captives, you who are a sure fastener, tie, through your love, he who would flee me; attach him to your habit or with your sainted cord, like strong and hard bars, so that so-and-so who wants to run from me, will be impeded and make it, my good-fortuned Saint Anthony, so that he marries me without delay."[36] In the Luso-Brazilian world, then, Saint Anthony clearly was linked to some sort of binding ritual, which, as the above prayer demonstrates, had quasi-magical attributes similar to those of love magic. Many *hechicería* chants, for example, sought to bind and hold individuals for love purposes, and even Saint Anthony's statue could be bound and placed in a coffee jar, tied to the foot of the bed, and finally thrown across the room in an effort to secure a spouse. Additionally, women placed the name of a potential spouse on a piece of paper, which was then folded three times and placed underneath the statue of the saint so that Anthony would read the name and cause that person to ask for the writer's hand in marriage.[37] Women also invoked his help in situations in which they were abused by their husbands or mistreated by their mothers-in-law. The saint's feast day on June 13 was a special occasion when an egg white was placed in a glass of water and the patterns formed were read in order to foretell the future.[38]

The emphasis on the Luso-Brazilian devotion to Saint Anthony as binder of hearts is particularly intriguing in light of the fact that seventeenth-century Mexico saw a marked increase in Portuguese immigration to the Spanish colony, as a result of the union of the Spanish and Portuguese Crowns from 1580 to 1640. More than four hundred Portuguese males applied for residency status between 1619 and 1625, each one representing a larger extended family. Although the exact number of Portuguese in the colony is unknown, in part because not all Portuguese elected to register legally with the Spanish state, they were the largest group of resident foreigners and were particularly active in both legal and illegal commerce. Spanish authorities regarded the Portuguese as suspect on two accounts: religious orthodoxy and potential subversion. The suspicions with respect to the second matter were not misplaced given the fact that Portuguese immigrants were active in the 1624 rebellion that brought down the viceroy, the marquis of Gelves.[39] In addition to the large number of Portuguese immigrants, the majority of Spaniards who made their way to colonial Mexico came from Andalusia and Extremadura, the latter area more closely linked culturally to Portugal.[40] We can only speculate regarding the impact of this large Portuguese contingent on the devotion to Saint Anthony in the viceregal capital; but it is possible that many of the Luso-Brazilian traditions surrounding the saint had Mexican counterparts during the seventeenth century, when a majority of oratorios to Saint Anthony appear to have occurred.

Given the Portuguese and Brazilian examples of binding rituals involving Saint Anthony, no clear separation apparently existed between recourse to saints and recourse to magic. A hierarchy of saints existed in folk Catholicism in which each saint served as a source of possible alleviation from problems that plagued everyday existence. Supplicants channeled their rogations accordingly and entered into a contractual relationship with a particular saint. During this period, the miraculous and the remarkable, ranging from apparitions to enraptured mystical visions, were believed to be common to the course of human events. The devout regularly sought divine intervention in the firm belief that their petitions would bear fruit. Even within the sacrament of the mass, the church glorified "magical" transformation. In this context, the conjuration of saints for love magic merely sought the saint's power to obtain a suitor, revenge upon a suitor, or the righting of domestic abuse such as a husband's infidelity. This use of the devotion to the saints—or as the Inquisition saw matters, this abuse—was also evident in Catalonia, Valencia, Andalusia, and Castile during the same time period, when Anthony as heavenly intercessor in romantic matters shared company with Saints Marta, Elena, Silvestre, and Onofrio.[41]

Love magic (*hechicería* in general) accounts for between 7.2 percent and 8.3 percent of all cases investigated or processed by the Holy Office in Mexico between 1571 and 1700.[42] The cases are replete with efforts by men and women to attract members of the opposite sex in which they utilize a variety of methods to procure and sustain romantic liaisons, both licit and illicit.[43] Some scholars view extensive female participation in *hechicería* as an empowering means by which women sought to remedy issues central to their own economic and physical well-being. The issue of empowerment assumes particular importance in the patriarchal society that was colonial Mexico and where the two approved venues for female development were wife-mother and nun. Since women were legally subject to male authorities, either a husband or a priest in both circumstances,[44] the procurement of a materially generous and kind spouse or lover took on new meaning. Female love magic generally sought to control, dominate, and certainly manipulate the designated male, who did not suspect that rituals, potions, and chants were being exercised to influence his behavior with respect to a woman.[45] In some cases, love magic was a woman's only defense against an abusive spouse in a society in which men had the legal right to discipline their wives. Not only were men objects of love magic, but they themselves turned to its use when they wanted quick and easy wealth, as in finding gold. In this regard, men could invoke Saint Anthony, as he was the patron of miners. It is noteworthy that men also sought supernatural help when they desired physical prowess (strength) or the romantic skills to conquer many women.[46]

Thus, some aspects of the devotion to the saints overlapped with the goals of love magic. Returning to the case of Rosa, we can get a clearer sense of the relationship between love magic and the devotion to the saints. No potions, powders, or scissors, typically associated with *hechicería*, were evident, nor did anyone testify that chants were recited at Rosa's oratorio. Nevertheless, her actions and the particulars of the ceremony may still shed light on the significance of the festival. Rosa was unmarried and seventeen years old, the proper age to seek a spouse, and, as her options were limited, she had to marry and marry well. Juan de Galdo was eighteen and single and seemingly well placed as a page of the viceroy. Thus Rosa, a criolla, elected to make a young man from Spain with important connections the centerpiece of a ritual that invoked the intercession of Saint Anthony. At the beginning of the ceremony, she personally stepped forward, knelt down before Galdo, and placed the scapular over his head, as though she were selecting or anointing him. In her testimony, she stated that "hubo fiesta para que le echara a Juan el escapulario" [the celebration occurred so that Juan would wear the scapular].[47] These gestures indicate that the relationship between Rosa and Juan ought to be central to our discussion; yet we are frustrated by the fact that neither of the parties involved nor the inquisitors sought to comment or ask about that relationship.

The presence of the other participants who danced and feasted with Rosa and Juan may assist us further in our discussion. The fact that many people attended the event is significant because it differentiates the oratorio phenomenon from conventional love magic, where witnesses were not usually or necessarily required or desired for the magic to take effect. In Rosa's fiesta, the guests were co-workers of Juan and appear to have served as witnesses, or, at least, their presence lends an air of official approval by the community to the young couple's "dance." Ritually speaking, this ceremony had much in common with a marriage ceremony: first, a sacred interchange took place between the couple; second, the couple sealed that act with a dance; and third, all the guests joined in the dance and subsequent celebration. It is possible that Rosa's oratorio event was her attempt to gain Galdo's affection for the purpose of an eventual marriage. In this regard, the testimony of Francisca Paz de Bustillo is illuminating; she stated that "always on Sundays, there was a party where a page of the viceroy put on the scapular of Saint Anthony."[48] Perhaps Rosa's festivals represented a sequence of rituals leading to formal betrothal and marriage. Formal betrothal was as an official promise of marriage which could have long-lasting legal repercussions if one of the parties had a change of heart. The seriousness of betrothal was evident when parents and the clergy were involved, but even without a priest and parental consent, such promises were still considered legal and binding as oral contracts, especially when performed before an audience.[49]

One final element must be added to our analysis of Rosa and Juan's situation: the prominent males in Rosa's family were not in attendance, nor did the events take place at her house, leading us to suspect that Rosa's brother-in-law, Joseph de Urrutia, who was probably her legal guardian, did not know about the rituals. Perhaps Urrutia did not approve of eighteen-year-old Juan, who was too young and not sufficiently financially established to qualify as a fine suitor in the Novohispanic context. Rosa and her female relatives and friends resorted to popular religious traditions to seek some sort of remedy, either to change Urrutia's mind or to tie Juan to a promise of future marriage. They probably believed that if Juan wore the scapular of Saint Anthony, the marrying saint, he would simply have to become Rosa's spouse some day. Accordingly, the fact that Francisca claimed that the celebration was "la fiesta de Rosa" merits note,[50] as it implies that perhaps Rosa was not only the hostess but also the hopeful recipient of whatever benefits might come from the ceremony. Francisca did not call the event a gathering to honor Saint Anthony or to show devotion to the saints. Galdo denounced Rosa because he feared excommunication for having participated in a prohibited ritual.[51] Apparently, Rosa and Galdo had severed ties by that time, suggesting that Rosa's recourse to religious magic had failed.

Regardless of Rosa's bad fortune with Galdo, love magic and offerings to the saints generally were associated with the resolution of immediate problems that afflicted daily existence. Even when love magic included the saints, its use did not extend to matters of marriage but rather emphasized eroticism and sexual union.[52] Rosa's oratorio celebration probably represented the ritual path to seek marriage partners as opposed to a sexual liaison. Depending upon their particular needs and circumstances, the lovelorn appeared to enjoy a variety of options, of which the devotion to the saints was but one. Individuals resorted to love potions and incantations without any references to religious symbols provided by an *hechicera*; they presented individual requests to the saints through the chants of an *hechicera*; or they orchestrated a group ritual to seek a potential marriage partner. The devotion to the saints may not have been viewed as separate from love magic; both could have been part of an efficacious system of recourse for individuals, especially women. Perhaps, in the popular mind, any barrier between magic and religion would have been artificial,[53] resulting in a single syncretic system and a magic-religious world.

The case of Petrona appears to represent a similar ritual approach to Saint Anthony, although the ceremony probably did not relate to betrothal or marriage, since Petrona was already married. Much less is known about her case because a third party denounced Petrona and neither she nor any of the other women named in the case were ever called before the inquisitors.[54] She may have been invoking Saint Anthony's help in becoming pregnant or receiving kinder treatment from her spouse. We may never know her intention. Interestingly, however, priests became unwitting participants in this oratorio because the ritual began and ended with the statue of Saint Anthony attending mass. What is unique about Petrona's case is the heterogeneous makeup of those in attendance, indicating that at some point in popular culture the oratorio rituals had become codified to the extent that mestizas, *mulatas*, and Afro-Mexicans turned to the altar tradition for remedy.[55]

The phenomenon of private altar fiestas raises fundamental questions about popular piety in colonial Mexico City with respect to individual interpretation and control of otherwise official church symbols—for example, the saints and the crucifix, and rituals like novenas and the mass. Apparently participants defined the sacred in their own terms as they sacralized the private and profane by hosting in their private living quarters ceremonies that included dancing. The nature of the ceremony shows that the real issue was not the existence of private altars for prayer and reflection but rather how the altar was used in an atmosphere that was clearly festive. Neither the party atmosphere nor the intention of the ritual accorded with the thinking of the church about the devotion to the saints. To the inquisitors the oratorios of Petrona and Rosa not only stood outside official control, but they represented a basic misunderstanding on the part of the women as to what constituted proper devotion to Saint Anthony.

In understanding the attitude of the church and the Inquisition toward the oratorios, we need to factor in considerations of gender as well as the issue of orthodoxy concerning the ceremonies themselves. Rosa and Petrona were not mere spectators but organizers and interpreters of this popular religious form. As such, they challenged the standard view of female religious piety in which women's spirituality was controlled, regulated, or mitigated by male superiors. In this case, women like Rosa officiated at sacred ceremonies and led other people, particularly young men, in the worship of saints. Clearly they did not behave like the wards of confessors, fathers, husbands, and brothers they were supposed to be. Equally significant in terms of gender and authority is the fact that the rituals took place in the home, the so-called domestic sphere, which tradition and theory identify as the center of female authority. In hosting these ceremonies in their sphere of authority, women utilized the accepted Catholic tradition of the home altar and the devotion to the saints as a cloak for their own religious purposes, which in the case of Rosa probably included garnering a husband, for Petrona, perhaps a child. Although popular Catholicism was sufficiently flexible to allow these women considerable control and independence in their piety, Rosa and Petrona were relatively circumspect in choosing oratorio rituals over *hechicería*: of the two rituals that were efficacious in matters of love, marriage, and mothering, the oratorio ritual would be less vulnerable to disapproval by the Inquisition. Ironically, the challenge to authority which the oratorio rituals implied turned out to be anything but threatening to the societal order because, in seeking aid to secure a husband or have a child, the women were validating conventional and proper roles for women in colonial Mexico.

In organizing their oratorios within a network of female relatives and friends, Rosa and Petrona created a loosely defined organization that may have complemented the male-dominated confraternity system. Like confraternity brothers, these women expended large sums of money to host rituals, some of which included professional dancers. Thus, the oratorio tradition may have reflected a form of empowerment and prestige for women in which they controlled a type of knowledge and a ritual system that were considered efficacious, effective, and legitimate by the general (female) population of the capital even though they were heterodox according to the Fathers of the Church.

Although the oratorio tradition appears to have had links to an overall system of belief which included *hechicería*, the Mexican Inquisition took a totally different approach to the oratorio rituals. The Inquisition regarded both popular traditions as superstitious folk practices that could be remedied through education, guidance, and, as a last resort, punishment. Despite their seemingly lenient attitude, the inquisitors did investigate egregious cases of *hechicería* and condemn individuals before the general public.[56] However, the Inquisition did not investigate oratorios, nor did the Holy Office punish or even verbally chastise those who participated in the rituals. Aside from the publication of edicts, the Inquisition did not publicly challenge the private altar tradition. One reason why the inquisitors did not take action against the participants in private altar rituals is that they already were overwhelmed by the magnitude of a charge that included jurisdiction over the Caribbean, Mexico, the Philippines, and Central America. Inundated by the sheer number of denunciations, the inquisitors selected only cases of egregious unorthodoxy for investigation and trial. Thus, only approximately 6 percent of all cases were actually processed from 1571 to 1700.[57] However, this situation alone cannot explain their attitude regarding the oratorios. The question of inquisitorial effectiveness in this area may be answered by the pervasive role of the devotion to the saints within the church. The Inquisition was severely limited in its approach to the oratorios because it could never prohibit the devotion to the saints or private altars. The inquisitors banned those aspects of the devotion to the saints which it considered heretical or misguided, such as the misuse of scapulars and drinking and dancing at the ceremonies. However, they could not effectively eliminate the oratorio tradition without opposing private group supplication to the saints. In effect, the oratorio tradition represented a particular popular twist to the cult of the saints which could not be easily controlled or stopped.

Studies of love magic elsewhere show that individuals generally came to realize the error of their ways.[58] In the cases under discussion here, the devotees stated they were aware of the edicts and even came to express remorse for their actions. Francisca had been paid the hefty sum of four pesos to remain quiet about the fiestas, but fear for her immortal soul sent her to the Holy Office. She and Juan both admitted that what they had done was wrong, and their repentance sounds genuine.[59] Even Rosa denounced herself, although her protestations of regret for her actions ring insincere in light of the fact that, after her appearance before the Inquisition, she hosted even more rituals with Galdo.[60] Perhaps she denounced herself to the Inquisition to thwart action against her by other people. Perhaps she continued the rituals because her need to remedy her civil status or her devotion to Saint Anthony overrode prudence and fear. Whatever the motivations, Rosa and her female relatives found in the oratorio tradition a relatively safe area from which to exercise a more independent kind of religiosity. That power the women were unwilling to relinquish, even in the face of possible inquisitorial action.

CHAPTER FOURTEEN

Testimony for Canonization or Proof of Blasphemy?

The New Spanish Inquisition and the
Hagiographic Biography of
Catarina de San Juan

KATHLEEN MYERS

New Spain is a period in which a nun's spiritual flight, a terminally-ill person's miraculous cure, a sinner's repentance, or a holy woman's vaticinations [prophecies] are more important news than the rise in prices in business or the imposition of a sales tax; a period in which a spiritual journey to the interior of the soul is more momentous than the expeditions to California and the Philippines. . . . The historian who ignores this hierarchy of period values, might offer us an exhaustive and well-documented narrative of the historical events, but he will never penetrate the secret interior of the most significant events.

—EDMUNDO O'GORMAN, as quoted in Francisco de la Maza

On January 5, 1688, people living in New Spain's second largest city, Puebla de los Angeles, heard the death bells toll for a visionary woman from Delhi, India, who had lived in their midst for nearly seventy years. Hoping to catch a glimpse of her and to participate to some degree in her holiness, crowds descended on the house where Catarina de San Juan's body was displayed. Over the next two days, the line of people waiting to enter the house grew to be four blocks long. Although first brought to the New World as a slave by Portuguese pirates and sold to a couple in Puebla, Catarina had been free from masters for nearly half a century and had become a popular, if reclusive, visionary. The widespread recognition of her holiness earned Catarina the sort of farewell usually reserved for the highest elite: most of the city's ranking ecclesiastical and civil officials attended an elaborate funeral mass, and she was buried in the Jesuit Church of the Colegio del Espíritu Santo. The laudatory biographical sermon delivered at her funeral and two hagiographic biographies about Catarina were published within four years of her death. In addition, several portraits of Catarina went into circulation, and the *aposentilla* (little room) where she had spent much of her time praying was converted into an altar dedicated to her memory.

The outpouring of popular devotion to Catarina de San Juan and the initial ecclesiastical support for it exemplify the rise of spontaneous religious devotions in seventeenth-century New Spain, and in Puebla in particular. Equally illustrative of the interplay between individual lives, society, and the role of the church is the denouement of Catarina's story as a local religious hero. Within three years of her death, the New Spanish Inquisition had prohibited the display of her portrait; by 1692, the Spanish Inquisition had banned one of the biographies on the grounds that it was blasphemous; and by 1696, eight years after Catarina's death, the Mexican Holy Office had followed suit, demanding that the biography be confiscated throughout the viceroyalty and ordering the altar dedicated to her to be boarded up. What caused the sudden campaign against devotion to Catarina de San Juan? What definitions and guidelines did church leaders use to determine sanctity and blasphemy, orthodoxy and heterodoxy?

Earlier in this volume authors study records that reveal the lives and fates of a variety of early modern Spanish and Spanish American women brought before the Inquisition. Because we have only recently begun to cull such documents for women's stories, we are just beginning to note differences in the types of women examined and to study the breadth of what the Inquisition controlled.[1] Catarina de San Juan's story illustrates the Inquisition's scrutiny and control of books, specifically official church texts such as vitas (*vidas*), sermons, and religious chronicles about holy people which, if approved, set forth life models for Catholics to emulate and, if censured, were silenced and often soon forgotten.

By 1600 the Holy Office was firmly rooted in American soil, where, like its peninsular counterpart, it fought daily to maintain the religious and social status quo by controlling people, books, and ideas. Although it was first run by monks and later by bishops, in 1571 the king of Spain himself took control of the Inquisition, in response to perceived abuses and ineffective administration on the part of local ecclesiastics. Striving to decrease mistreatment of the Spanish and Indian populations (the latter, in fact, became exempt from the Inquisition's control) as well as conflicts between regular and secular clergy, the 1571 edict put into place a new bureaucracy that included expert prosecutors and *calificadores* (officials who assessed evidence) who were to examine and prepare reports about both people and printed matter of questionable orthodoxy.

As Richard Greenleaf notes, the majority of studies about the Mexican Inquisition have focused on heretics processed by the Holy Office rather than on how heresy itself was repressed. Yet the restriction of reading materials and of the circulation of ideas among New Spanish inhabitants occupied a major portion of the Inquisition's efforts—indeed, it is in this area that the Holy Office was most successful until the eighteenth century.[2] American colonists were seen by the Counter Reformation church as Christians living among a horde of neophyte Indians who were more vulnerable than those of European extraction to heretical ideas and to the poor examples set by fiction; as a consequence, the colonists in theory were only allowed to read books that had passed the inspection of the Inquisition. The 1571 edict made it a crime to read prohibited books, and another ordered that all such books be turned in to the Holy Office. Two years later, the Inquisition distributed the official Index of Prohibited Books to the population and created an infrastructure to search ships arriving in New Spain and to monitor book dealers and publishers in major cities. Although many books slipped through the cracks of this system, it is telling of the ideological hegemony the church tried to impose.[3]

The vicissitudes of the biographical portraits of Catarina de San Juan illustrate the often complex dynamics involved in determining the orthodoxy of texts and the representation of holy women in New Spain. Surprisingly, the 1689 publication of the first volume of the Jesuit Alonso Ramos's biography of Catarina, *Primera Parte de los Prodigios de la Omnipotencia. Y milagros de la Gracia En la vida de la Venerable Sierva de Dios Catharina de S. Joan* . . . (First part of the Almighty's wonders and miracles that graced the life of the venerable servant of God Catharina de S. Joan)—the volume that would later be banned by the Inquisition—was approved by many of New Spain's highest-ranking ecclesiastical officials, even including a calificador. Published within a year of the first part, the second volume also met with success. But soon the tide turned, and in the same year the final volume was published (1692), the first had been put on the Index of Prohibited Books in Spain. In a strikingly slow response, New Spain followed suit four years later. And yet the same year Ramos's first volume was censored in the peninsula, a much shorter version of Catarina's life story, *Compendio de la vida y virtudes de la venerable Catarina de San Juan* (Compendium of the life and virtues of the venerable Catarina de San Juan), was allowed to be published in Puebla by the cleric José Castillo de Graxeda. Why would a woman who was never brought before the Inquisition during her lifetime for questioning about her visions and prophecies have one of her biographies first approved and then prohibited by the Holy Office? What did Alonso Ramos's version contain or possibly omit that condemned it while the second biography was allowed to stand? If not aimed at the circumstances of Catarina's life, what was the Inquisition's concern about the written representation of her life?

As we will see below, new rules established by the Counter Reformation requiring historical documentation for the canonization process have as much to do with Ramos's failure and Graxeda's success as the Inquisition's rules for determining blasphemous books. Combating criticism of Catholicism's emphasis on affective spirituality and its cult of the saints and heavily influenced by Renaissance humanist theories about historical truth, the Council of Trent revamped the guidelines for sainthood. With extravagant exclamations from people about the candidate's holiness, Ramos's hagiographic biography followed the older style, however, and as such clashed with the new hagiographic requirements. Graxeda's text, on the other hand, attempted to balance the exotic appeal of Catarina's story while attending to the historical rigor demanded by the church.

Catarina de San Juan: Fact and Fiction

History confirms few facts with regard to Catarina de San Juan, but her biographers concur on the general chronology and significant events of her life. All accounts plot a compelling story that echoes elements from the most popular forms of baroque narrative, including captives' tales, picaresque novels, and, of course, hagiographic biography. A composite account follows: born of pagan royal parents in the Mogul empire of India, Catarina (born Mirra) was singled out at birth for special favors by the Virgin Mary. Among other incidents, she was miraculously saved as a toddler after having fallen into a river more than three days before. Within a decade of her birth, however, local wars forced Catarina and her family to flee to the coast, where the child was kidnapped by Portuguese slave traders.

Catarina was taken first to Cochín and then to Manila, where she came into contact with Jesuit missionaries for the first time and converted to Christianity. In 1619, she was designated to be one of the house slaves for the viceroy of New Spain, and the Portuguese took the adolescent girl to Acapulco. Here a change in fortune resulted in her becoming a servant in Puebla for a childless couple, Margarita Chávez and Miguel Sosa. Upon Miguel's death less than ten years later and her mistress's subsequent decision to enter the convent, Catarina was taken in by a cleric, who forced her to marry his Chinese slave. Catarina had already taken a vow of chastity and had prayed (successfully, according to the accounts) to look old and ugly in order to ward off men's advances; she now fought heroically to maintain a chaste marriage with an abusive husband.

By the 1640s both husband and master had died, and Catarina at last was free to devote her life to Christ as a lay holy woman. She took no formal religious vows but lived a life of reclusion, prayer, and penance in a small room that a wealthy neighbor had given her across from Catarina's favorite church, run by the Jesuits. Within these confines, she prayed for the larger Christian community, experienced visions of a host of heavenly figures, and made prophecies about Jesuit souls, important political and ecclesiastical figures, and occurrences in the Spanish empire, such as the arrival of ships from Spain and battles in Europe. She lived the last four decades of her life under the protection of the Jesuits, following this contemplative, visionary path. Nearly blind and half paralyzed by a stroke, Catarina de San Juan died in 1688. Upon her death, commoners and high-ranking officials alike declared that the octogenarian *china poblana*—all peoples from Asia were called *chinos,* and *poblana* refers to people living in Puebla—had died in the "odor of sanctity." As mentioned earlier, crowds fought to see her one last time before her burial; many reportedly tried to tear off a bit of her tunic in order to have a personal relic that might provide a powerful link to this charismatic woman.

As these highly charged scenes of popular devotion suggest, Catarina de San Juan lived in a deeply religious society that believed in the importance and efficacy of local holy people bringing special divine favor to their community. The biographies written about Catarina participate in this broader religious and spiritual phenomenon occurring in Puebla; the city tops the list of colonial Spanish cities devoted to publishing the life stories of its holy people. Like the other mostly feminine subjects of these hagiographic *vidas*, Catarina is lauded for continuing the spiritual conquest of America begun more than a century before by the conquistadors: through creating a veritable paradise of Christian virtue in America, she served as a valuable example to both the New World and the Old.[4]

In addition to being the subject of *vidas* herself, Catarina had a powerful link to two of New Spain's most important religious women (likewise subjects of *vidas*) and to most of the clergy who promoted the production of these works. The founder of the Carmelite convent in Puebla, Isabel de la Encarnación, and the Conceptionist María Jesús Tomellín had been informal spiritual teachers for Catarina; she had talked with both women, particularly with the latter, through their convents' grilles as well as by supernatural communication.[5] Of the host of notable seventeenth-century clerics involved in creating these live and literary exemplars of holiness, four men became especially involved in Catarina de San Juan's spiritual path. Juan Palafox y Mendoza, the controversial bishop of Puebla from 1640 to 1649, was himself entered into the canonization process. His successor, Manuel Fernández de Santa Cruz, is well known in our century for his role as the real addressee of Sor Juana Inés de la Cruz's *Respuesta* but was famed in his own epoch for founding many religious institutions. The Jesuit Antonio Núñez de Miranda had been Sor Juana's antagonistic confessor as well as a noted theologian and calificador. Miguel Godínez was the influential Jesuit author of several manuals on mysticism. Although Spanish law prohibited the nonwhite Catarina from being a nun, a prestigious status that required full Spanish ancestry and often a hefty dowry, race did not keep her from intimate contact with prominent religious figures.

With all the attention Catarina received from male and female spiritual leaders, it is not surprising that she was an important figure in society and the subject of no fewer than three biographies. What is surprising, however, is that she is the only nonwhite layperson in New Spain to have been accorded the literary treatment reserved for the elite, who were thought to be particularly prone to possible holiness. Even a late-eighteenth-century compilation of life stories of Native American noblewomen who took the veil at the first convent for Indians (established in 1724) does not offer a close parallel to Catarina's situation; the text, *Indias caciques*, was not published during the colonial period, and it is a collective history of women in an established religious order.[6] Perhaps Catarina's uniqueness as a subject explains in part the Inquisition's stance about the biographies of her life. In fact, Ramos's biography of Catarina de San Juan is the only published *vida* of a holy person to be censored during the colonial period.[7]

Although our discussion focuses on the portraits of Catarina de San Juan in Ramos's and Graxeda's full-length biographies, the Jesuit Francisco de Aguilera's hagiographic *Sermon en que se da noticia de la vida . . . de la Venerable Señora Chatharima de San Joan* (Sermon reporting the life . . . of the venerable Senora Chatharima de San Joan; 1688) deserves mention as the founding narrative for her story; he sketches themes that will show up full-blown in Ramos's biography. First delivered shortly after her death to an emotionally charged group of *poblanos* attending her funeral, the sermon introduces the *china poblana* as an exotic woman with prolific miraculous powers. Relying on baroque literary paradoxes and antitheses in order to inspire wonder and emulation in the listener/reader, Aguilera provides paradigmatic incidents as clear evidence of her chosen status. Catarina's rescue from the river parallels Moses' beginnings, her kidnapping reads like a Byzantine novel, and her undying desire for chastity persuades God to grant Catarina her wish to turn her beautiful white (!) face into that of an ugly, old dark woman. As far as available records demonstrate, this funerary biography was banned by the Inquisition only when republished with Ramos's third volume.[8]

In contrast to Aguilera's brief biographical sketch, Alonso Ramos's three-volume *Prodigios* weighs in as the largest, most voluminous work published in New Spain, a physical testimony to his efforts to prove beyond a shadow of a doubt the case for his spiritual daughter's sanctity. An influential figure within the powerful Jesuit order, Ramos occupied for a period of time the position of rector of the order in Puebla. This position helps to explain how he could publish a triple-decker comprising more than five hundred folio-sized pages, that is, one thousand pages printed on high-quality paper, a fact that graphically illustrates the expense the Jesuits were willing to incur in order to promote the woman who had made their order and Puebla famous. Obviously not meant for private consumption, the *Prodigios* functions as an epic story of New Spain's identity. Unfortunately, the epic goes overboard even by baroque standards, which celebrated exuberantly awe-inspiring stories that juxtapose the spirit and the flesh, vice and virtue, licentiousness and virginity, the exotic and the familiar.

Depicted in an affective, florid style, Catarina de San Juan becomes an anagram of a marvelous, exotic, deeply holy ascetic in Ramos's biography. In particular, he reveals a fascination with her virginal body and the heroic tests of her virtue it had to endure on both the human and supernatural planes. Upon her kidnap by pirates, for example, the prepubescent Catarina becomes the target of men's lust, barely surviving with chastity intact a series of assaults by men who either want to own her or marry her. In one of the first scenes, Ramos describes how Catarina's Portuguese kidnappers begin a brawl that injures her. Ramos draws a scriptural parallel with the spilling of Christ's blood:

> The disagreements and disputes among the pirates grew to such a pitch that, dividing into factions, they fell to swordplay and spear-throwing; until one of the soldiers, seeing the quarrel turn so bloody, said (speaking to his comrades), It is better for one person to die, rather than that all of us perish: similar counsel was spoken by Caiaphas the High Priest to the Jews in the council that their malice had formed against Christ; but this soldier, speaking and acting without advice, hurled a pike or lance toward that innocent young girl with the intention of ending her life, so that the life of an innocent ewe lamb would become a rainbow of peace among so many criminals. But the thoughtless and cruel pirate did not succeed in his design, for either because the girl dodged, or because a hand from above lessened the thrust of the lance, it pierced only her thigh; and the blood that flowed

from the wound was enough that, saddened and compassionate, they dropped their anger and their dispute; and that, leaving all their weapons, they went to dress her wound; and thus her innocent blood so spilled became a bond of harmony and concord. They then returned to the *Bageles*, and one of the principal captains, having won her, kept her, with the obligation to heal her and to treat her as a daughter and not as a slave.[9]

Saved by a bloodied leg, the young girl moves from one bad situation to another. An Asian Indian merchant falls in love with her beauty, buys her, and shelters her in a woman's house, planning to marry the girl when she becomes of age. These plans collapse when the insanely jealous woman beats Catarina in order to make her ugly and thus have the merchant to herself in marriage. When this ploy fails, the woman attempts to drown Catarina. Ramos depicts with flourish the abuse the young girl endures:

This jealous woman decided to vent her anger on the beauty that she judged to be the cause or the occasion of her own rejection; undertaking to rob her of her natural loveliness, she mistreated her in word and in deed, often seeking to wear her down to nothing, disheveling her bit by bit, dragging her by the hair, flogging her, cudgeling her, and disfiguring her cheeks with the blood flowing from her wounds. She saw to it that hunger withered away the color and the pleasing qualities of her face: and finally she became the drudge of a vindictive, excessively jealous woman, for no other crime but that of being the beautiful and beloved Myrrha, and with no other prospect than that of being the object of an invidious loathing. This last grew to such a height that, unable to sufficiently avenge her anger and appease her wrath with the blood of an innocent ewe lamb, she tried time and again to take her life. Her anger prepared knives, with the resolution of killing her; but her fear lest the blood so spilled should cry out, like that of Abel, which clamored against invidious fratricide, curbed her and held her back. It seemed to her that killing her bloodlessly and out of sight would hide her wickedness; and thus she resolved on another, more treacherous deed, which was to fling her into the sea weighted down by a stone, so that the studied cunning of her rage might be taken for a possible mishap. In a fury she carried out this perfidy, but by Myrrha's good fortune, an anchor had already been set by Divine Providence at the place where she had fallen, so that raising herself by the cable she was able to pull her head out of the water and cry out for help, succor, and Baptism, which was her principal and only concern; she was rescued by a Portuguese nobleman who was near the seaside, like a foreordained instrument of Divine Omnipotence, to liberate her from the shipwreck and preserve her life as in other dangers. Through this lucky mishap this young girl was settled in another house, where, when her Mogul suitor saw her loveliness and beauty emaciated and disfigured, his love passed over to the Mogul lady who had so anxiously sought him.[10]

After Catarina is deserted by the Mogul merchant, yet another man enamored of her beauty goes mad when he cannot have Catarina, until, once again, she is rescued, this time to sail to New Spain, where she is sold as a house slave. Even en route to New Spain, however, Ramos paints the titillating scene of a sailor who desires her, even though (or, perhaps, because) she is now disguised as a *mancebo* (young man) as a ruse to elude the viceroy's messenger, who awaits her at the port in Acapulco to take her to Mexico City. The disguise a success, Catarina makes her way to Puebla, where with her new masters/parents she enjoys a few years of relative peace from men's sexual advances until her owner dies and she is forced by her new master, a cleric, to marry his Chinese slave, Domingo. Frustrated and jealous because Catarina insists on remaining faithful to her Divine Spouse, Domingo subjects her to years of physical abuse. Later he takes a mistress, with whom he has a child, and at his death Catarina is left not only with his debts but also the child (bk. 1, chaps. 27–28).

If Ramos's version of Catarina's relationships with men is melodramatic, the treatment of her prophetic nature and supernatural encounters is perhaps even more theatrical and daring. Although more than a third of Catarina's visionary life is retold in the last volume (which I have been unable to consult),[11] the first two volumes provide abundant evidence to judge Ramos's depiction of the role of the supernatural in Catarina's life. The title itself, *Prodigios,* points to the wonder and abundance of Catarina's visions, prophecies, and revelations dealing with people and events throughout the Spanish empire. She intercedes on Spain's behalf in its European conflicts and commerce, comes to the aid of a troubled monarchy, and at times even bilocates to aid the Jesuit missionary project in the Mexican borderlands and in the Philippines. Ramos's flair for descriptive symbolism and scriptural parallels, for example, comes through in an account of Catarina's vision of Carlos II's royal wedding in 1680 and her subsequent prophecy about royal succession. Catarina sees a monstrous creature ("A monstrous fish, whose ugliness and ferocity caused her horror, and which she was unable to describe, calling it now a shark, now an alligator, now a sea monster; for it had a peculiar and abominable shape, with scales so spotted and mottled as to make it horrible to see")[12] circle around the queen and threaten to deform the child she was to carry. With the aid of Catarina's fervent supplications to God, he grants her wish that the queen give birth to a healthy child. Catarina emerges as having a divine connection—one powerful enough to play a role in the Crown's destiny. Ramos concludes the passage with a scriptural parallel to authorize his tale:

> Reader, to see that this vision was worthy of the most profound and lengthy explications, compare it with what St. John the Evangelist has left us written in the twelfth chapter of his Apocalypse, and you will discover how uniformly God speaks and communicates his secrets in all ages to his servants and chosen ones; you will also see that everything could not but be verified that he showed to his Chosen Benjamin about his sacred lastborn, the Catholic Church, always persecuted and always victorious in the shape of a prodigious woman.[13]

In situations dealing with Catarina's ability to intercede and the outcome of historically documentable incidents Ramos occasionally interjects a short statement about his methodology, even citing secondary sources or including letters from other clergy which confirm his own account (for example, bk. 1, chap. 28). But once he moves outside the realm of historical events, Ramos often includes rather shocking tales of encounters with the Divine and adds little authorial reflection on the veracity of the content. In recounting these scenes, Ramos often discusses hearing Catarina talk of these incidents in the confessional and, at times even quoting her, in language that sounds more like set speeches transferred into simple language than real conversations.[14]

In one recurring case, he takes the mystical commonplace of the bride-husband relationship to such an extreme that several critics view it as the basis for the censorship of the entire book. In a typically exaggerated baroque style, the biographer describes how Catarina endured a series of amorous struggles ("luchas amorosas") with Christ, engaging for years in debates with a nearly naked Son of God, who reveals himself to his beloved:

On one occasion, the Lord showed himself to her in that same form of a child, but almost naked, much as we are accustomed to dress his images on the feast of his Resurrection, or of his Nativity in the manger: in the latter season Catharina was always most solicitous to clothe Christ, naked in his most holy birth, and with the above-mentioned apparition it appears that the Lord responded to her wishes, saying to her, like someone longing to throw himself into her lap and her chaste embrace: "Catharina, will you dress me?" The charity and love of this, his beloved and dear Spouse, grew with this vision, almost to the point of causing a rapture, and rendering violent her impulse to clasp the Child God in her arms, to no longer be held back by the shackles of her virginal reserve, being frightened by the nakedness of her only and divine Lover: and thus she said to him, or asked him, "Why haven't you come dressed? Did you lack angels, and your Mother, to cover with precious cloths the loveliness and beauty that the heavenly courts gaze on and enjoy?" He answered her that he wanted it to be she who dressed and adorned him. Catharina replied that she had nothing to clothe him with, nor hands to touch him with, nor even eyes to see him naked, and, succeeding in turning aside her gaze from that God of Purity, her Divine Lover, she would have wished to hide, and sink deep into the center of the earth. . . .

But when she was more off her guard, she found herself one day with the same sight, and with manifestations and with the most affectionate expressions of yearning to receive the clothing he had requested from the hands of his beloved. Even though Catharina responded with new, greater, and more ample refusals of his loving purity, that he should leave her alone, go away, disappear; for this nakedness of his humanized divinity frightened and unnerved her, and she could not find the strength to embrace him; seeing him so naked caused her no less embarrassment than divine horror, until such time as she might see him decently clothed to human eyes. This loving dispute between the Divine Love and his beloved spouse went on for more than two years.[15]

A tantalizing image of a woman of such modesty that she refused even to let anyone shake her vile, unworthy hand is eroticized when Catarina is pursued by a God made-man and refuses to bow to her beloved's supplications. These gripping tales of aggression and submission, sexual desire and chastity embellish the few documented facts of Catarina's life.

Whereas Ramos's work is the coffee-table showpiece, the third biographical narrative, the secular cleric José Castillo de Graxeda's *Compendio* (1692), represents the portable paperback, consisting of fewer than 150 quarto-sized pages (that is, a page a fourth the size of Ramos's folios). In a striking contrast to Ramos's work, Graxeda recounts Catarina's life before arriving in Puebla in only two chapters, each one consisting of no more than a handful of pages. We are simply told that Catarina endured many abuses ("maltratos") because Domingo had married her without fully understanding her vow to God. The detailed descriptions of Catarina as first and foremost a sexual being who is subject to bloody, abusive, death-threatening encounters with her husband disappear from this new portrait of the *china poblana*:

> And he [Domingo], since up to then he did not understand her, tried to avail himself now of endearments, now of threats, now of harsh treatment, but she only availed herself of the truth with which she admonished him and availed herself of the cries she raised to her divine Spouse, and availed herself of many and devout anxieties with which she called out to the Virgin Mary. If, at this resistance from Catarina, annoyance, irascibility, and ill-usage grew in him, in her there grew all the more the steadfastness of her pledge and vow.[16]

In addition, Graxeda never mentions Domingo's mistress and child but rather focuses on how effectively Catarina wards off her husband's advances with a strategically placed cross between their two beds.

Although Ramos creates a fictional character who overcomes traumatic experiences, Graxeda glosses over the particularities of the suffering and paints a portrait of model behavior, using an understated, condensed narrative style to depict with singularity of purpose an exotic yet ideal holy

woman. Catarina as a conventional model comes forth at particularly crucial points in the narrative. When talking of one of the miracles attributed
to her (the case of a cross that sweated blood), Graxeda turns first to a
simple, reasoned portrait of her virtuous equanimity: "This venerable and
devout woman was always circumspect in her deeds, moderate in her
words, sensible in her answers, discreet in her works, prudent without pas-
sions, courteous without showiness, quiet without insolence."[17] Catarina
emerges as a credible source of divine favor and helps inspire readers to
model their own lives on these same behavioral codes.

In addition, Graxeda's narrative terseness when dealing with the supernatural is diametrically opposed to Ramos's extravagance. Graxeda
briefly lists a series of revelations Catarina received about Jesuits and the
affairs of the Spanish empire, but they are treated matter-of-factly, and
the narrative highlights Catarina's visions and discernment of souls
closer to home, focusing primarily on New Spain and Puebla. When
treating Catarina's colloquies with heavenly figures, Graxeda selects several scenes to describe in more detail, but he opens or closes the passages
with a discussion of his sources and method for recording such supernatural occurrences.

> Before continuing, I would like to anticipate with the reader's leave a
> question which may recur insistently to anyone, to wit, the question of
> why I report the virtues that Catarina exercised in that youthful period
> of her life? And how can I give information in such detail about what
> I never saw at the time? And about more than that, if I never saw it?
> Later when I communicated with her, she reported her virtues to me
> with the reluctance of a good spirit that only speaks of her faults and
> not her virtues, leaving those to the understanding of the person who
> directs her.[18]

Moreover, he cautiously leaves room for his superiors to judge the nature
of certain visions. For instance, in the case of Catarina's vision of Saint
Anne (in which the young Indian girl promised to live a chaste life),
Graxeda claims that he cannot determine the category of the vision (cor-
poreal, intellectual, etc.): "I cannot ascertain the manner in which she
received this favor, whether she was transported out of her senses and
faculties or whether it was an imaginary vision [i.e., seen with the imagi-

nation] or whether she saw it visibly [i.e., with her normal physical eye-sight], for as I wished to know about the category of thing that happened to her, she was in the habit of telling me."[19] And, as one might have anticipated, no mention is made of a nearly nude Christ.

The Inquisition, Hagiography, and Counter Reformation Literature

In fact, Graxeda's narrative method responds point by point to the charges the Inquisition made against Ramos's text. The 1692 Spanish edict declared the *Prodigios* to be indecent, unbelievable, and nearly blasphemous. Although we only have an excerpt of the edict, it is clear that the Holy Office viewed the text as falling into grave error regarding doctrinal content and narrative credibility: "Because it contains revelations, visions, and apparitions that are useless and improbable and full of contradictions and improper, indecent, and dangerous comparisons—*que sapiunt blasphemias* [that are almost blasphemous]—that abuse the highest and ineffable Mystery of the Incarnation of the Son of God, and in other places, Holy Scripture and because it contains dangerous doctrines that contradict the understandings of the Doctors and practices of the Universal Catholic Church on no more grounds than the author's vain beliefs."[20] The charge reflects the dual line of inquiry which the Inquisition used for judging texts: did they contradict or undermine either the holy faith ("la santa fe") or good taste ("las buenas costumbres")? In other words, narrative content and style had to uphold Counter Reformation doctrine *and* follow acceptable societal and literary norms. Interestingly, the edict also points to Ramos's "vain credulity," a criticism that reflects the church's wish to establish a reputation for its historical rigor in determining evidence of the work of God.

Although we have little information surrounding the discussion that led to the Inquisition's decision, the prefatory material to books published in New Spain provides valuable information regarding a book's approbation by secular and sacred institutions. Whereas Graxeda's biography opens with the standard licenses from a calificador and another from the bishop's office, Ramos's introductory material is overwhelmingly long and complex. His first volume opens with the largest amount of prefatory material I have seen in any period text published in New Spain. More than seventy pages of licenses, approvals, and letters from the highest-ranking ecclesiastics and government leaders inundate the reader and arouse curiosity about the need for such extensive documentation.[21] Is the biography already on trial, and does the ambiguity of the case require extra witnesses? While all the highest authorities over Ramos—the viceroy, bishop, and Jesuit superior—write formulaic statements, the calificadores and theologians address in detail the text's ability to pass the Inquisition's test that books contain no material "contra la fe y las buenas costumbres." Likewise, the four extra "pareceres" [opinions] requested by Bishop Santa Cruz second this opinion, as they also emphasize the significant role Catarina de San Juan plays in Puebla history.

Key to understanding the tenor and purpose of this outpouring of support is the personal letter that the calificador and onetime spiritual director of Catarina de San Juan, Antonio Núñez de Miranda, writes to his Jesuit brother Ramos. Strategically placed after the prologue and before the massive narrative, this nonstandard letter from one of New Spain's most highly regarded theologians serves an unusual purpose.[22] Elsewhere in the prefatory pages, Núñez grants an official Inquisition license for publication of Ramos's first volume, but the ten-page personal letter reflects a certain anxiety about the text. His license details seeds of doubt in two areas. First, the "vast ocean" of examples of God's handiwork seen in Catarina's visions, revelations, and prophecies might well make the reader seasick ("marear") and forget that God's will alone can render one holy. Núñez warns that cases of self-willed visions will bring people into the hands of the Inquisition, as indeed had happened in the case of Sor María de la Visitación. Second, Núñez advises the reader to avoid the temptation to skip ahead to passages about awe-inspiring, supernatural occurrences and instead to focus on (and imitate) the narrative examples of humility and obedience exemplified by Catarina. With these caveats Núñez, both as calificador and as a Jesuit personally involved with Catarina's story, anticipates the charges that will be made later against the biography. Yet he holds them at bay for a time with his defense, even extending as an example of hope for Ramos the case of Saint Teresa's autobiographical *Vida*, which first was withheld from publication by the Inquisition and later approved.

In striking contrast, Ramos's second volume contains far fewer licenses, and the Inquisition's approval is absent. The other licenses are from the most powerful figures in New Spain, the archbishop and the viceroy.[23] Ramos apparently either bypassed the Inquisition or did not need permission for a continuation of a *vida*. Though the absence of a license from the Inquisition might be explained by Ramos's move to Mexico City after the publication of volume 1, it may also be indicative of trouble already brewing, as Núñez himself foresaw a year earlier.[24]

Although Graxeda never reveals any knowledge of the 1692 Spanish edict, the metadiscourse he employs about his narrative method points precisely to the problems Ramos's text will have, or was having. Diplomatically worded, Graxeda's prologue discusses the merits of both Ramos's biography and his own "compendium" of Catarina's life story. Although the compendium ostensibly aims to make the wonders of Catarina's life available to a wider public, Graxeda does mention several motives for writing which revolve around concepts of truth and narrative authority. The first motive is that he, too, had served as a spiritual director for the holy woman; for eleven years he heard, up to three times a day, her confession in a stammering pronunciation ("su balbuciente pronunción") that he came to understand as angelic or mystic language. Graxeda reports that in one such rapture Catarina revealed that God wished Graxeda to serve as her confessor, which he then interpreted as divine authorization for his relationship with her and the source of his ability to bear witness to her life. A second motive is implicit in the fact that even as Graxeda writes, death is knocking at his door. No doubt aware of the attempts to beatify her, Graxeda confesses a sense of urgency to leave a permanent record of Catarina's story. A third, unspoken motive was almost certainly the desire to undo the damage done to the process of Catarina's beatification—not to mention the credibility of her supporters—by Ramos's uncritical and extravagant approach to biography. From the outset Graxeda signals that he takes very seriously his duty to keep to the verifiable facts. Echoing the humanist historians who had influenced the documentary quality of hagiographic-inspired biography by the turn of the seventeenth century, Graxeda declares: "Let it be known that everything that I report here, I saw, experienced, and verified, proving that all of the material was truthful and reliable. Placing my hand on my heart and making the sign of the cross, *Iuro in verbo Sacerdoitis* to tell the truth in everything."[25] Although he assures his readers that he writes with Ramos's blessing, a rivalry or tension with the *Prodigios* emerges between the lines, as well as a sense that the cause of Catarina's beatification might be in danger because of Ramos's lack of historical rigor. Like his colleagues, Graxeda no doubt felt that Puebla could not afford to lose such a good candidate for sainthood.

Graxeda comments on his historical method throughout the book until he comes to the last two chapters, where he resorts to hagiographic models by reserving the penultimate chapter to recount Catarina's burial and the last one for identifying miracles that had been wrought through her intercession after death. Although the formulae for evidence of sanctity included the working of miracles, along with the demonstration of heroic virtue, the new seventeenth-century norms established for canonization advised clerics to tread carefully in an area that by that time had been reserved for papal interpretation. Graxeda is here caught in the bind of needing to provide evidence in order to promote his case and yet not wanting to overstep boundaries regarding the determination of the sacred. Graxeda falls back on his methodological metadiscourse, promising to produce a succinct, truthful narrative based on eyewitness testimony of Catarina's virtue:

> The one miracle that I will here report suffices to substantiate all the rest because it was widely known to many people who witnessed it and who can verify it. I will leave aside the other miracles because there are issues in them that are very difficult to ascertain and are best left to the understanding of those people in the Church whose official ministry is in this area. I do not wish stories of other miracles to be an obstacle to seeing the good reputation and virtues in this servant of God, nor do I wish to prolong this story which is intended only to awaken and incite devotion in the faithful.[26]

In a single paragraph when he cites an example of Catarina's portrait (before it was banned, of course) aiding in the cure of a sick man, he warns the reader not to interpret the healing as the holy woman's own work but rather as God working through her (200).

In the "Conclusión del Autor," Graxeda describes yet another dilemma he has had to negotiate: to write a complete history of Catarina's life, he must depend on other eyewitness testimony, which he carefully weighs for reliability before including it in his account (201-2). In discussing the trustworthiness of his sources and the authority of his narrative, Graxeda echoes the prologue and at the same time confuses the narrative voice as he reveals in the process that an anonymous woman wrote the last chapters using his own notes. Although the twentieth-century reader may interpret this assertion as calling into question Graxeda's narrative authority, his contemporaries, and in particular church officials, must have read these statements as support for the account's reliability.[27]

Besides painstakingly elucidating his methodology, Graxeda develops a series of stratagems to highlight his unrelenting commitment to historical truth. Like Ramos, he had privileged access to the semicloistered woman in his role as her confessor. But he also shows how as a learned man he understood the importance of accurately recording the language and dialect of people's testimony. Curiously, Graxeda never mentions the fact that he was a professor of the Totoneca language, but he employs his expertise as a linguist to decipher and interpret before the reader's eyes Catarina's halting Spanish. He transcribes it—grammatical errors and all—for the reader to "hear." He then "translates" her words into a Spanish that is grammatical but highly rhetorical and often sermonic:

> [Catarina] In truth my angel, y'worships tell the truth, and so beg God no lose me.
> [Graxeda] Which is to say: In truth, your worships tell the truth and sense what I am, that I am a liar and yet for that reason I ask that for the love of God you pray for me, that my soul may not be lost; indeed I recognize that I am a Chinese [Asian] woman, indeed I see that I am rubbish, that I am a piece of filth and a bitch dog, but for this same circumstance, because of both what you believe and what you say, for this very reason I implore you to make a special entreaty that I end well. (This was Catarina's reply to occasional passersby who called her *esta perra china embustera*—"that lying Chinese bitch.")[28]

A notable graphic characteristic of the first edition of the *Compendio* is that the italics used for both the transcription and translation of Catarina's speech dominate nearly a third of the text. Graxeda thus creates a sense of historical truth—if only as narrative and graphic verisimilitude—that piques the reader's curiosity in the exotic nature of the protagonist, and simultaneously indoctrinates by rendering an "Inquisition-safe" conventional Counter Reformation model of female holiness.

. . .

Graxeda's text, in fact, reflects church attempts to establish control in several areas. Besides tightening the definition of heresy, the Council of Trent had also stiffened the requirements for sainthood in the spirit of rigor advocated by humanist historians, which among other things dictated the need for reliable witnesses and stylistic decorum befitting historical truth. Urban VIII further centralized and formalized the process by mandating a fifty-year rule that required a fifty-year lapse between a candidate's death and her canonization. A process first begun by Gregory IX in the thirteenth century which attempted to define with legalistic precision both saints through a strict canonization process and heretics with the establishment of the first Inquisition, canonization now required witnesses, trials, judges, prosecutors, and defenders—all orchestrated from Rome. As a result of the ever increasing need to define, grade, and limit sainthood, there were only six formal canonizations in the sixteenth century, with a sixty-five-year hiatus between 1523 and 1588, and in the period from 1629 to 1658 there were no canonizations whatsoever.[29]

Even as official sanctity was on the wane, the popular imitation of it was on the rise, especially in Spain and Spanish America. The example of Teresa of Avila's canonization in 1622 lit a fire under Catholics for the next century and a half; hundreds of women emulated her life, while dozens of clergy wrote *vidas* about religious women who were following in Teresa's footsteps. Because these *vidas* were often written as supporting evidence sent to Rome to attempt to initiate the process for beatification, the narratives respond to the requirements established for canonization. Both Ramos's and Graxeda's texts participate in this trend and were meant to help beatify Catarina de San Juan, but Graxeda circumscribes his material according to the Vatican's rules, well aware that any definitive claims of miracles or evidence of unapproved cults would count against Catarina's candidacy for sainthood. He uses notions of decorum proper to the times, employing a "natural" style befitting Catarina's pidgin Spanish.[30] Moreover, he has recourse to only reliable witnesses, explicitly defers to papal authority, and always reins in the baroque tales of marvel he includes before they begin to lose credibility. Perhaps more than any other *vida* produced in New Spain to initiate the beatification procedure, Graxeda's successfully embodies the new historical discourse required by Rome.

A third factor comes into play when examining Graxeda's narrative strategies. Given the restrictions placed on fiction in Spanish America, colonial authors frequently may have employed the rhetoric of historiography, but they created texts that were a hybrid of literary and historical genres with almost novelesque qualities. Graxeda's text, like that of his contemporary Carlos de Sigüenza y Góngora's popular historical chronicle of a shipwrecked man (*Los Infortunios de Alonso Ramírez*), is a series of rapid narrative sequences that read almost like an early novel, except that they are framed by a painstaking exposition of how the author came to find the historical record of the adventures and how each adventure illustrates the exemplarity of Catarina's life. This structure clearly reflects Counter Reformation guidelines for literary production.

Authors were to observe rules set by the Council of Trent which governed almost every aspect of practice of the Catholic faith, highlighting in particular the importance of the spiritual world, salvation as the meaning of existence, and the church's role as mediator between God and his earthly subjects. This ideology was transmitted to the faithful through preaching, frequent confession, insistence on complete obedience to church hierarchy, and control of religious practices, which included new rules for religious orders and oratorical style as well as guidelines for art and literature. The goals underlying this program were to achieve religious homogeneity and to maintain the political, economic, social, and religious status quo in a period of increasingly rapid change.

Specific to understanding the tenets that would have informed works by learned men like Ramos and Graxeda were guidelines for doctrinal and devotional literature which emphasized that moral instruction should teach (*enseñar*) and entertain through aesthetic appeal (*deleitar*) in order to persuade by moving (*mover*) the reader or listener to salutary change. To effect change, literature depended on appeal to the emotions—rather than the intellect. Gwendolyn Barnes-Karol explains how one of the most important theologians of Counter Reformation Spain, Fray Luis de Granada, details this approach in his *Ecclesiasticae rhetoricae* (1567).[31] Techniques like creating visual images in the mind's eye of the reader, dramatizing events, employing rhetorical devices to astound and provoke awe, and placing a premium on linguistic novelty rather than substance worked to effect a suspense of the ordinary state of understanding (*suspenso*) and thus a state of mind in which the reader or listener might be more easily persuaded to absorb the doctrines being preached. Granada warns, however, that theatricality had to be tempered with "naturalness" or verisimilitude in order to be believable and, therefore, emulated. These guidelines for literary practice and indoctrination clearly shape both Graxeda's and Ramos's authorial intentions, narrative style, and content. Both biographies draw on highly charged, exotic material to strike awe in readers and act as springboards for preaching. Graxeda's creation of narrative strategies to underline his adherence to the criteria of brevity and eyewitness testimony, however, saves his text from the hands of the Holy Office, while Ramos's abundant flourishes and theatricality—lack of verisimilitude—eventually wiped his works from bookshelves in both the Old World and the New.

Not surprisingly, the literary practices advocated by the Council of Trent are echoed in the Inquisition's rules regarding books. Within a decade of the close of Trent the first official tribunal of the Holy Office was established on American soil and, as mentioned earlier, pronounced edicts regarding the ownership of books. By the mid-seventeenth century the majority of autos-da-fé had already been staged, and the censorship of books was now one of the most vital roles played by the Inquisition. A set of fourteen rules, "Reglas, Mandatos y Advertencias generales del novissimus Librorum et expurgandorum," drafted at the turn of the eighteenth century, illustrates the determining factors in a book's fate when examined by the Inquisition.[32] Depending on a book's perceived danger to the faith, it could be placed in one of the three categories of censorship: complete prohibition, ownership by designated people such as priests, or censorship of offending passages. Although not condemned on the gravest charge as being heretical or containing witchcraft, Ramos's text received the toughest sentence possible for a book: complete prohibition from being owned or read. The type of censorship depended not only on the gravity of the errors found in the material but also on the frequency with which they appeared in the book.[33]

Assertions about Catarina's holiness and visionary powers were so abundant and extensive in Ramos's three-volume work that the Holy Office could not merely censor certain passages. As judged by the second round of calificadores, who lived in Spain and had not known Catarina, *Prodigios* commits errors outlined in several rules, as in Rule 6, books that contain "things against holy doctrine" [cosas contra la buena y santa doctrina], and Rule 7, works that "endanger the good practices of the Holy Catholic Church" [dañosas a las buenas costumbres de la Iglesia Christiana], citing love stories and the like.

Rule 8, which bans all types of portraits, medals, rings, and crosses that bear a person's image,[34] also clarifies why in 1691 the New Spanish Inquisition brought forth an edict prohibiting portraits of Catarina de San Juan. The edict elaborates that any images in which Catarina de San Juan appears alone or next to Bishop Palafox y Mendoza be limited to private use, and it banned the lighting of candles around them, thus reflecting Pope Urban VIII's restriction of such practices to beatified or canonized holy people.[35] The 1696 New Spanish edict ordering the closure of the oratory dedicated to Catarina de San Juan further demonstrates the church's desire to control popular devotion. While Ramos's record of frequent supernatural occurrences and continual recourse to *suspenso* may have led to the Inquisition's verdict that the text lacked verisimilitude and was nearly blasphemous, the fact that a cult was forming around the holy woman was surely a major factor that could have tipped the judgment against Ramos.

Sanctity, Cults, and Church Politics

Why, however, did New Spain lag behind the Spanish censorship of Ramos's biography, only prohibiting it four years later, in the same year that the oratory was closed? In theory, the New Spanish Holy Office had to observe all edicts pronounced in Spain about censored books, and communication between metropolis and colony tended to be efficient. Although our documentation is limited about the debate that surely would have surrounded the 1696 edict,[36] a letter written by Mexico's inquisitor general three years after the Spanish censorship of Ramos's work asked the Spanish office about the status of the text: many people had claimed that it had been prohibited, but he had not been officially informed of its censorship.[37] Certainly the head of the Inquisition could not have been so completely in the dark about the verdict in Spain—there must have been strong forces behind the delay. Quite probably, the simultaneous prohibition of the oratory and biography came only under great pressure. Perhaps the fact that the first prohibition came from Spain, even as portraits of Catarina were being confiscated in Puebla, points to the possibility that the case was too hot to handle in New Spain. Although the church had to regulate popular cults in order to maintain its authority, local ecclesiastics may have been reluctant to censor the circulation of a book that they themselves had approved earlier and one about a local hero who was the spiritual daughter of the locally powerful Jesuits.

Loath to lose a good candidate for sainthood, Jesuits undoubtedly would have been reluctant to give up on making a case for Catarina de San Juan. Having a saint associated with their order would have enhanced its power and prestige, and as one of the more powerful orders in New Spain by the turn of the eighteenth century, the Jesuits may have lobbied successfully for a time and warded off censorship. Not only locally powerful, the Jesuits also championed the criollo cause, enhancing a strong, independent identity for colonists under Spanish rule—a posture that would lead to the whole order being expelled from Spanish America nearly a century later. The Inquisition's prohibition of the two Jesuit-written biographies (Aguilera and Ramos) and the approval of the non-Jesuit Graxeda's text may also indicate a backlash against the order.

Jesuit records about Ramos's sorry finale, in fact, reveal how the order clearly attempted to protect its image. Ramos was recalled to Puebla to resume his position as rector of the order in 1693 after his move to Mexico City three years earlier, and by 1694 records report a discussion about possibly removing him from office because of his "lack of moderation and excessive drinking" [destemplanza y exceso de beber]. By 1695, however, another entry details a change in tactic: because news had arrived that the prohibition of Ramos's text was in the works, the father general approved a decision to keep Ramos on as rector for the time being in order to avoid fueling the fire of the scandal that was sure to erupt upon the news of the censorship. Soon after, however, Ramos was confined to a cell, where he languished for years, escaping once in 1698 with a knife and nearly stabbing to death the man who replaced him as rector.[38]

Repeated assertions of Catarina's popularity among townspeople and the censorship of her portraits and oratory suggest that devotion to her was hard to stamp out.[39] Perhaps even more intriguing is the broader question of why the Jesuits and Puebla itself would fervently promote a nonwhite, lay holy woman when she deviated so vividly from the model female saint promoted by the Counter Reformation church? From what we have seen, Catarina may have had a strong local appeal not only because she satisfied the popular taste for heroes who embodied the paradoxes of the baroque age but also because she exemplified the racial and cultural mixture that characterized New Spain. The edict may have served as a warning to keep nonwhite populations in their place.[40]

In fact, Catarina de San Juan's life story was a far cry from the typical biography of a Counter Reformation saint. As Peter Burke notes, the typology of a saint canonized between 1588 and 1767 reflected a collective representation of people well born, of white upper-class parents, living in powerful countries (Italy and Spain dominate), and professed in important religious orders, primarily the Franciscans, Dominicans, and Jesuits.[41] Most saints were founders of religious orders or missionaries, and a significant number were ecclesiastic pastors, mystics, or people devoted to charitable works. The centralization and control of sanctity demanded that candidates conform to Rome's definition of holiness as judged by its examiners, which discouraged individualization and local cults. In the prefatory pages to Ramos's first volume, several licenses discuss how local opinion of a person's sanctity had been considered essential as a reliable collective witness for a case, but unlike earlier cases, such local support was now insufficient for establishing sainthood. The backlash against Ramos's biography could have come from all these forces: the role of the Jesuits in New Spain, Catarina's race, and Counter Reformation rules for literature and sainthood.

· · ·

Not a simple case of how one life or book was deemed heterodox, the story of the representation of Catarina de San Juan's life showcases the issues involved when studying colonial Mexico, the church, and women. Race, social status, religious status, and the role of male patrons and life stories as mediated by male biographers need to be taken into consideration when studying women's history and literary works from this period. As we have seen in Catarina's case, she was construed as the essence of holiness, an important symbol of religious identity for New Spanish citizens and ecclesiastics. It is her male biographers' works that are targeted by the Inquisition. Her story helps broaden our view of the range of activities a religious woman could engage in and supplements as well recent portraits that scholars have sketched of such well-known Spanish American contemporaries of Catarina as the star poet Sor Juana Inés de la Cruz, the mystic nun from Puebla Madre María de San José, and the theological author Madre María Ana Agueda de San Ignacio. But perhaps more significant, Catarina de San Juan's case demonstrates how the lives of holy women became important to the definition of New Spanish society and, accordingly, were targets of mediation and control by church hierarchy.

Catarina as a person gets lost in the shuffle of church politics and didactic ends. Historical facts about religious women and writings by them often faded as official discourse took over to paint an ideal portrait—albeit, in this case, a hotly contested one—which might serve the institutional church.[42] The true face and voice of an Asian Indian woman who ended her final days surrounded by revering townspeople and clergy are impossible to recover completely; the facts are eclipsed first by an out-of-control confessor's account that completely fictionalizes and eroticizes Catarina's life story, and then by a biographer who follows rules so closely that he turns her story into a paradigm of sanctity. Catarina's opportunity for sainthood was lost in the crossfire of rules about holiness, hagiography, and blasphemy. And yet, as blasphemy and inspirational prose, heresy and sanctity, the role of the elite and the lower classes in the church, popular devotion and institutional religion, historical truth and literary verisimilitude are discussed in letters, Inquisition edicts, and hagiographic biographies about Catarina de San Juan, we begin to glimpse more fully the complexity of issues and concerns found in mid-colonial Mexican society and literature.

Notes

1. Representative of recent work on the Inquisition is the international symposium held in New York in 1983, whose proceedings were edited by Angel Alcalá in a volume entitled *Inquisición española y mentalidad inquisitorial* (Barcelona: Editorial Ariel, S.A., 1984).

2. For a lucid introduction to the history of the Spanish Inquisition and theories about its origins, see especially Henry Kamen, *The Inquisition and Society in Spain in the Sixteenth and Seventeenth Centuries* (Bloomington: Indiana University Press, 1985). The social conflicts of the fifteenth century contributed to popular support for the Inquisition. As increasing numbers of conversos entered the mainstream of Spanish society, to their economic and political advantage, envy and resentment mounted among the Old Christians, who constituted the majority of the population and who prided themselves on a lineage untainted by Jewish or Moorish blood. Jealousy festered into hate, hate into fanaticism until demands were made for the elimination of the converso population. In *Conversos, Inquisition, and the Expulsion of the Jews from Spain* (Madison: University of Wisconsin Press, 1995), Norman Roth explains how a justification for the expulsion of the Jews and extirpation of the conversos was found: since canon law and church theology forbade Christians to discriminate against other Christians, Old Christians justified their hatred in racial terms with "the insidiously clever doctrine that it was not the *religion* of the convert which really was objectionable" but "the tainted 'Jewish blood' which somehow created a *racial* inferiority" (230). Familiar to twentieth-century readers as anti-Semitism, racial hatred had given rise early in the fifteenth century to the notion of *limpieza de sangre,* or purity of blood, which was legalized in a long series of actions, beginning when the Colegio de San Bartolomé in Salamanca secured papal permission (1414 and 1418) to deny admission to any person of Jewish origin (Roth, *Conversos,* 230) and gradually but inexorably throughout the sixteenth century closing to conversos

entry into all manner of religious and secular institutions.

3. This theory informs the studies of some eminent nineteenth-century historians, including José Amador de los Ríos with his *Historia social, política y religiosa de los judíos de España y Portugal*, 3 vols. (Madrid: Fortanet, 1875–76).

4. From 1391, when Jews were the victims of pogroms and forced conversions, until their expulsion in 1492, Spain had both a converso and a Jewish community; the latter continued to observe Jewish law and custom while the members of the former supposedly were Christian in belief and practice. The fact that Jews suffered violence at the hands of Christians and that fear and despair drove many Jews to baptism makes plausible Henry Kamen's statement that "many if not most" of the conversos "continued to practise the Jewish rites both secretly and openly, so that the authorities were faced with a large minority of pseudo-Christians who had neither respect nor love for their new faith" (*Inquisition and Society*, 26). Conversos who practiced Judaism secretly are known as crypto-Jews; their religion, crypto-Judaism. The Inquisition tried conversos as heretics for practicing crypto-Judaism.

5. In *The Marranos of Spain: From the Late Fourteenth to the Early Sixteenth Century According to the Hebrew Sources* (New York: American Academy for Jewish Research, 1966) and more recently in *The Origins of the Inquisition in Fifteenth Century Spain* (New York: Random House, 1995), Benzion Netanyahu explains the origins of the Inquisition in terms of anti-Semitism rather than crypto-Judaism, which he concludes was only a fiction made up by the Inquisition as propaganda against conversos and justification for their persecution on grounds of heresy. In refuting both the existence of crypto-Judaism and the reliability of the Inquisition documents in matters pertaining to crypto-Judaism, Netanyahu differs from the majority of Jewish historians. Haim Beinart maintains, on the basis of meticulous examination of Inquisition documents (see his monumental work on the conversos of Ciudad Real), that every converso sought to live as a Jew and that crypto-Judaism was a widespread phenomenon. Beinart and other historians discount Netanyahu's theory that the Inquisition created a fiction of crypto-Judaism in order to justify extirpation of the conversos.

To make the case against the existence of crypto-Judaism, Netanyahu turns to *responsa* that rabbis in North African Sephardic centers gave to conversos who had left Spain and in joining diaspora communities sought rabbinic opinion on legal questions pertaining to such issues as inheritance and marriage and divorce. A woman who emigrated to a Sephardic community, for example, and who left behind a husband in Spain would question if she was barred by Jewish law from remarriage. If in the rabbinic *responsa* she was declared to be a non-Jew, that decision did not necessarily mean that she was not a Jew; rather, calling her a non-Jew was the rabbinic way of allowing her to go through a ritual immersion so that she could then marry a Jewish man. Employing rabbinical *responsa* that were intended for diaspora communities to describe the religious attitude of conversos in Spain and to discredit their crypto-Judaism has drawn criticism from scholars like Gerson D. Cohen, who reviewed Netanyahu's first book in *Jewish Social Studies* (July 1967): 178–84.

Netanyahu has also been criticized for dismissing Inquisition documents as no more than a fiction made up by the Holy Office for the purpose of propagandizing against the conversos. Yosef H. Yerushalmi in *From Spanish Court to Italian Ghetto: Isaac Cardoso: A Study in Seventeenth-Century Marranism and Jewish Apologetics* (New York: Columbia University Press, 1971) considers it "manifestly absurd" that the inquisitors "were engaged in a universal conspiracy of fabrication," and to accept that notion, he adds, is to "ignore the mentality of a bygone day, and to flatter them with Machiavellian intentions and capabilities somewhat beyond their reach" (24). Furthermore, he asserts, a thorough and critical approach to Inquisition documents will disclose that the notaries of the Holy Office "did not level the recorded witnesses to conform to one another, nor did they omit or disguise the doubts which even some of the inquisitors themselves entertained as to the guilt of the accused" (24).

6. Kamen, *Inquisition and Society*, 41.

7. Ibid., 42.

8. Ibid., 41.

9. The classic study of this period is Marcel Bataillon's *Erasmo y España*, 2d ed., trans. Antonio Alatorre (Madrid: Fondo de Cultura Económica, 1966).

10. Some beatas lived in or near religious houses, others in their own homes, still others in communities of beatas known as beaterios.

11. Among the many studies on the alumbrados, see especially Antonio Márquez, *Los alumbrados: Orígenes y filosofía (1525–1559)*, 2d ed. (Madrid: Taurus Ediciones, S.A., 1980), and the five-volume study by Alvaro Huerga, *Historia de los alumbrados* (Madrid: Fundación Universitaria Española, 1972–94). For studies of specific charismatic women, see Ronald E. Surtz, *The Guitar of God: Gender, Power, and Authority in the Visionary World of Mother Juana de la Cruz (1481–1534)* (Philadelphia: University of Pennsylvania Press, 1990), and Mary E. Giles, *The Book of Prayer of Sor María of Santo Domingo: A Study and Translation* (Albany: State University of New York Press, 1990). See the Selected Bibliography for further entries on charismatic women.

12. Gillian T. W. Ahlgren examines the effects of the Valdés Index and censorship on spiritual writers, especially Teresa of Avila, in *Teresa of Avila and the Politics of Sanctity* (Ithaca, N.Y.: Cornell University Press, 1996).

13. On the fortunes of visionary women in Counter Reformation Spain, see Ahlgren, *Teresa of Avila*.

14. Richard E. Greenleaf, *The Mexican Inquisition of the Sixteenth Century* (Albuquerque: University of New Mexico Press, 1969), 158.

15. See Electa Arenal and Stacey Schlau, *Untold Sisters: Hispanic Nuns in Their Own Works*, trans. Amanda Powell (Albuquerque: University of New Mexico Press, 1989).

16. See Ahlgren, *Teresa of Avila*, and Alison Weber, *Teresa of Avila and the Rhetoric of Femininity* (Princeton: Princeton University Press, 1990).

17. Cited by Melquíades Andrés in *La teología española en el siglo XVI* (Madrid: La Editorial Católica, S.A., 1977), 2:558: La mujer, por sabia que sea, en los misterios de ls fe y de la Iglesia ponga un candado de silencio a su boca. Pues es cierto lo que dijeron los antiguos, que la joya que más alinda a la hembra es el candado del silencio a las puertas de sus labios para todas pláticas, y particularmente para los misterios de santidad y para no ser maestra de doctrina de Escrituras Santas.

18. Mary Elizabeth Perry, *Gender and Disorder in Early Modern Seville* (Princeton: Princeton University Press, 1990), 137–52.

19. For a brilliant examination of the issue of visionary authority in sixteenth-century Spain, see Ahlgren, *Teresa of Avila*.

20. Perry, *Gender and Disorder*, 118–36.

21. Giles, *Book of Prayer*, 107.

22. Ibid., 108–9:

It is commonly said in religious circles that language about God is only a finger pointing at the moon; so long as it points in the right direction, the finger draws attention to understandings that are true albeit inadequate.

The feminist scholar goes one step further. Not only does she have questions about how accurately the finger points but—and here let us see the moon as metaphor for the literary text—she wonders about the moon itself. She would have us look first of all to another moon—the woman's text—that by previous standards would not have made its way into the canon. Then she would ask us not to sight along our finger with the eye of the intellect but to leap for the moon with our entire body.

It is this kind of leaping that we readers must make in the presence of Sor Maria's ecstatic text. In spite of individual sightings of the inner structure of the contemplations and their indebtedness to the context of literary models, the text remains a distant moon unless we somehow experience it with quickened senses and emotions and unless, like the men and women who were physically present at her drama, we engage the text in the fullness of our bodies and thus engage the woman, who in the fullness of her body, is the text.

For further consideration of the body, see Mary E. Giles, "Holy Theatre/Ecstatic Theatre," in *Vox Mystica: Essays on Medieval Mysticism,* ed. Anne Clarke Bartlett (Cambridge, England: D. S. Brewer, 1995), 117–28, and Mary E. Giles, "The Discourse of Ecstasy: Late Medieval Spanish Women and Their Texts," in *Gender and Text in the Later Middle Ages,* ed. Jane Chance (Gainesville: University Press of Florida, 1996), 306–30.

CHAPTER I · MARI SÁNCHEZ AND INÉS GONZÁLEZ

My thanks to Angelique Bamberg, Sara Terry, and especially Mary Giles, who provided many helpful comments on an earlier draft. The research for this chapter was made possible by a Fulbright-Hays fellowship, an Andrew W. Mellon candidacy fellowship, and several grants from the University of Michigan. Mari Sánchez's Inquisition file is available at the Archivo Histórico Nacional (AHN) in Madrid, Inquisición legajo 183, expediente 20. For more on the Inquisition in Guadalupe and its connection to social and political shifts in Guadalupe and the peninsula, see my unpublished dissertation, "Guadalupe: Political Authority and Religious Identity in Fifteenth-Century Spain," University of Michigan, 1996.

1. The place of conversos in fifteenth-century Spain and the nature of converso religious attitudes remain at the center of highly charged debates among scholars of the period. In *Conversos on Trial: The Inquisition in Ciudad Real* (Jerusalem: Hebrew University, 1981), Haim Beinart analyzes many early Inquisition trials from Ciudad Real and emphasizes the continuing importance of Judaism in the lives of many conversos. Throughout, he is particularly interested in evidence of converso community identity and solidarity. In contrast, Benzion Netanyahu's latest work, *The Origins of the Inquisition in Fifteenth Century Spain* (New York: Random House, 1995), ascribes a racial motive to Old Christian suspicion of New Christians and minimizes the extent of Jewish practices among conversos. He has argued that a common "converso identity" did not exist until the Inquisition began its work. A younger generation of scholars has turned from an analysis of conversos collectively to examine the range of religious practices among conversos; see, for example, Mark Meyerson, "Aragonese and Catalan Jewish Converts at the Time of the Expulsion," *Jewish History* 1–2 (1992): 131–49, and Pilar Huerga Criado, *En la Raya de Portugal: Solidaridad y tensiones en la comunidad judeoconversa* (Salamanca: University of Salamanca Press, 1993).

2. Elsewhere in Castile these officials were elected by the village.

3. Mari Sánchez's husband was also the first cousin of Alonso González de Mesa, a tailor associated with the merchants.

4. AHN, Inquisición legajo 183, expediente 20, 6v.

5. Ibid., 2r: . . . me paresco ante Vuestras Reverencias con muy gran vergüenza

y contrición y arrepentimiento de mis pecados que yo cometí y hice contra nuestro maestro y redentor Jesús Cristo y contra nuestra santa fe católica pesandome mucho y arrepentiendome de ellos con gran [dessian] contrición digo mis culpas demando Señores penitencia.

6. Ibid.: Et digo Señores que todas las otras pascuas y ceremonias de la ley de Moisés que pudiera y las supiera hacer, las hiciera por mi voluntad, pensando que por ellas me había de salvar, por lo cual mucho me arrepiento con gran [dissian] contrición demando a mi Señor Jesús Cristo perdón y a vosotros Señores penitencia.

7. "I say, Sirs, that I ate some cheese tarts in the house of that Jew from Trujillo. For which, Sirs, I ask penitence" [Digo Señores que comí en casa de aquel judío de Trujillo (Mose Arrovas) unas quesadillas. De lo cual, Señores, pido penitencia]. AHN, Inquisición legajo 183, expediente 20, 2r.

8. Ibid.: . . . un judío de Trujillo que se llamaba Mose Arrovas, una vez que fui a Trujillo pasando por la calle me dijo [dad] acá, la de Diego Jiménez, veréis la sinagoga que tenemos acá como yo vea allá vuestra iglesia. Y yo entré con él. De esto, Señores, demando penitencia.

9. Ibid.: Y entraron conmigo la de Lope García y otras cristianas viejas.

10. See AHN, Inquisición legajo 146, expediente 6. Alonso's mother, Marina, was later found guilty of heresy, in part as a result of the testimony of her son. See AHN, Clero expediente 1423, legajos 89 and 93.

11. See AHN, Clero legajo 1423, expediente 89 (unfoliated), 27v–28r, 31r, 41r–v, 57v. It is certain that Mari's husband, Diego, had already been posthumously accused when Mari first appeared before the inquisitors, since her lawyer mentioned his case in the questions posed to defense witnesses. See AHN, Inquisición legajo 183, expediente 20, 4r, a written series of questions by Juan de Tejeda for the defense witnesses, presented on September 16, 1485. " . . . and that the friars demanded that her husband take in [the Jews], as was proved by the statements and depositions of witnesses presented in the trial of the aforementioned Diego Jiménez" [. . . y los frailes se los mandaban acojer a su marido según que está probado por los dichos y deposiciones de los testigos presentados en el proceso del dicho Diego Jiménez].

12. No author specifically described what *adafinas* was, but references in passing suggest that it was a type of stew. In modern-day North Africa, Jewish communities prepare a dish known as *adafinas*, which is cooked over low heat for several hours, often beginning on Friday. In this way Jews can consume a hot dinner on the Sabbath without breaking the Sabbath by preparing food or lighting a fire.

13. AHN, Inquisición legajo 183, expediente 20, 3v: . . . si algunos judíos venían a su casa, era porque eran hacedores de esta casa y monasterio . . . y portazgueros, y los frailes se los mandaban acojer a su marido según que está probado por los dichos y deposiciones de los testigos presentados en el proceso del dicho Diego Jiménez.

14. Ibid., 3v–4r: . . . si en su casa algunas se hubiesen hecho, que niego haberlas, y han hecho los dichos judíos estando a su fuego y aparte.

15. Ibid., 7r.

16. Mari's other daughter, also named Inés, was married to Oro Blásquez and apparently lived in Guadalupe. Mari's son was named Diego. Both Blásquez and his wife were tried by the inquisitors, Inés posthumously.

17. AHN, Inquisición legajo 183, expediente 20, 6v, testimony of Francisco García, scribe from Cañamero: . . . dijo la dicha Inés, "por cierto mi padre buen cristiano es, y yo por tal le tengo; pero mi madre Mari Sánchez no."

18. Ibid., 7v: . . . trajo un crucifixo de Nuestro Señor figurado en un papel. Al cual tomó la dicha Mari Sánchez y lo echó en una necesaria diciendo que no había ella menester de tener aquello en su casa.

19. Ibid.: . . . salvo de tres cosas que son más graves y principales conviene a saber de como había lavado la crisma a Diego su hijo y de como había dado aceite para la sinagoga de Trujillo y de como un crucifixo que compró su padre difunto, marido de la susodicha, ite cual traía a los pies de la cama por el suelo le había echado la dicha Mari Sánchez en una privada.

20. Ibid., 8r: . . . no les quería confesar porque no se las podrían probar.

21. Ibid., 7v–8r: Y al tiempo Doctor de Villaescusa su letrado fue a estar con la dicha su madre y a mostrarle los testigos que deponían contra ella; entonces confesó lo del aceite y lavar de la crisma, pero no lo del crucifixo; y que luego entró en la [cámara?] donde estaba este testigo en la cárcel, muy amarilla y medio muerta, y dijo a este testigo "ahora hoyo muerta por lo que he confesado," y la dicha Inés le dijo, "¿dijistes lo del crucifixo?" y la madre le respondió, "hija, no lo sabe persona si tú no. Por eso dime si lo dijiste," a dar a entender que de otra manera no lo confesaría; y entonces le respondió que sí había dicho por eso, que lo confesase. Y luego la dicha su madre a causa que supo que este testigo lo había dicho, trabajó de estar con el alguacil, y con Albornóz su amado por lo tornar a confesar.

22. Ibid., 12r: . . . de todo ello dandose la dicha mi parte muchos y grandes golpes en los pechos arrepentiendose por haber hecho tan grandes errores y ofensas contra Nuestro Señor le demandó y demanda misericordia y perdón y a Vuestras Reverencias penitencia.

23. See Mari Sánchez's statements in the following AHN Inquisition files: legajo 153, expediente 9 (trial of Beatriz González, wife of Juan Fernández Peñafiel); legajo 183, expediente 21 (trial of Mari Sánchez, wife of Juan González de la Corte); legajo 148, expediente 9 (trial of Mari Flores, mother of Andres González de la República); legajo 165, expediente 4 (Mayor, wife of Juan de Segovia); legajo 147, expediente 8 (Marina Fernández, wife of el físico portugués); legajo 147, expediente 9 (Martín Fernández el gotoso, deceased); and legajo 183, expediente 10

(trial of Catalina Sánchez, wife of Gonzalo Fernández). Fewer than 40 of the 220-odd trials remain, and presumably Mari also testified in some of those other trials.

24. It is unclear what significance this action had. Catalina later described it as one way the family mocked their son. More likely is a connection between this practice and the Genesis narrative of Jacob and Esau. Jacob dressed in the clothing of his larger brother and fooled his blind father into awarding him the birthright rather than his brother Esau. See Genesis, chap. 27.

25. See AHN, Inquisición legajo 183, expediente 10.

26. Ibid., expediente 20, 14r.

27. Ibid., 14r: . . . levada y metida dentro en la dicha casa dijo siendo amonestada "dijiese todo lo que sabía por entero"; la cual sin otro tormento ni cosa alguna ni molestia que por ello recibiese dijo.

CHAPTER 2 · INÉS OF HERRERA DEL DUQUE

1. See Haim Beinart, *Trujillo, a Jewish Community in Extremadura on the Eve of the the Expulsion* (Jerusalem, 1980).

2. See Haim Beinart, "The Spanish Inquisition and a Converso Community in Extremadura," *Medieval Studies* 43 (1981): 445–71.

3. See, for instance, Haim Beinart, "The Conversos of Chillón and Siruela and the Prophetesses Mari Gómez and Inés, the daughter of Juan Esteban" (in Hebrew), *Zion* 48 (1983): 241–72; Haim Beinart, "The Movement around the Prophetess Inés in Puebla de Alcocer and Talarrubias" (in Hebrew), *Tarbiz* 51 (1982): 634–58; Haim Beinart, "The Prophetess Inés in Herrera Her Place of Birth" (in Hebrew), in *I. Tishby Jubilee Volume* (Jerusalem, 1986), 459–506.

4. He was her third husband. The first one was Alonso de Baeza, with whom she lived in Alcázar de Consuegra; the second one was Pedro de Alcaraz, and they lived in a place called Quintanar. Beatriz Ramírez was tried by the Inquisition and condemned to be burned.

5. See trial of Beatriz, a servant girl in the house of Luis de Toledo, Archivo Histórico Nacional (AHN), Inquisición Toledo, leg. 133, no. 7 (102), fol. 2r. Beatriz told the court of the Inquisition on December 7, 1500, of Inés's arrest, which occurred some eight months before, in April 1500. See also Henry Charles Lea, *A History of the Inquisition of Spain,* 4 vols. (New York: Macmillan, 1906–7), 1:186, 4:526; Yitzhak Fritz Baer, "The Messianic Movement in the Period of the Expulsion" (in Hebrew), *Measef Zion* 5 (1933): 61–74; Haim Beinart, "A Messianic Movement in Córdoba in the Years 1499–1500" (in Hebrew), *Zion* 44 (1979): 490–200; Haim Beinart, "Agudo a Converso Community in La Mancha" (in Hebrew), *Tarbiz* 50 (1981): 423–49; Haim Beinart, "Almadén, the Conversos of a Village in La Mancha" (in Hebrew), *Zion* 45 (1981): 17–55.

6. See his trial, AHN, Inquisición Toledo, leg. 184, no. 6 (795), fol. 9r. See as well the trial of Mencía López, inhabitant of Puebla de Alcocer, leg. 163, no. 11 (523), fol. 7v.

7. See also the trial of Beatriz Ramírez, leg. 176, no. 1 (672), fol. 2r.

8. Juan de Segovia abjured and was accepted back into the fold of the church on February 12, 1486. He was arrested again on August 6, 1500, and condemned to be burned. The sentence was carried out on March 30, 1501. In this trial the testimony made by Inés on May 21, 1500, is to be found (see fol. 2r–v).

9. See leg. 140, no. 13 (259), fol. 9r–v. This passage and the next three passages are from the same proceso.

En Herrera, veynte e vn días del mes de mayo de, Vd años, ante los señores ynquisidores en la general ynquisiçion.

Ynes, fija de Juan Esteban, vesyno de la vylla de Herrera, testigo jurado etç., dixo que en el año próximo pasado, tres días después de todos santos, este testigo soño a su madre que es defunta, e la paresçio que verdaderamente que la avia vysto, vesyblemente, e le paresçio en el sueño que la avia dicho: fija, di que hasian bien por la mi anima e que den limosnas e otras cosas, que por su proxilidad no se pusyeron aqui.

Item dixo que dende a çierto tiempo çerca de la navidad, primera que paso, vyno a ella una claridad que antes otras veses dixo avya venido, e este testigo le dixo que era su venida, pués que tantas veses venia, e respondió e dixo que venía a le desir de venir Elias en el año de quinientos, e que para esto cunplir que hisyesen ayunos e diesen limosnas e hisyesen el mas bien que pudiesen. E este testigo le pregunto: ¿quien era esta Elias e a que avia de venir? E dixole que avia de venir por mandamiento de Dios a predicar en el mundo e que avyan de salir los conversos e vyan de yr a unas tierras. E les pregunto esta confesante: ¿En estas tierras que avya? E dixole que avya poblaçiones e mantenimientos de pan e frutas e de las cosas que cumplian. E luego desapareçio. E primero que se fuese le dixo que dixiese esto que le avya dicho.

E despues desto esta confesante lo dixo a Gonçalo Bichancho e a atros muchos conversos, vesynos de la dicha vylla. E al paresçer deste testigo la escuchauan, el pareçer deste testigo lo creyan, porque lo escuchauan con buena gana e voluntad. E dixo que este testigo ovo preguntado a la dicha claridad de que manera le desya que ayvan de ser los dichos ayunos e limosnas, e le desya que los dichos ayunos ayan de ser fechos fasta la noche. E que asymismo le dixo la dicha claridad que guardasen los sabados e se vystyesen ropa linpia en ellos e lo hisyesen por amor de Dios e por que alcançasen aquel bien que esperaban que avya de venir. E que esto mismo dixo esta testigo al dicho Gonçalo Bichancho e a quantos conversos yvan a verla a su casa.

Item dixo que desian en casa [que] este testigo ayuno desde en adelante cada semana un día e dos, o lo que mas podía, que eran lunes e jueues, no comiendo todo el dia hasta la noche salida el estrella, e a la noche çenaba pescado, e guardo los sabados desde el dicho tiempo fasta que fue presa, por obra vystyendose e atavyandose en ellos por la voluntad fasta agora.

Preguntada: ¿con que yntençion e creençia ayuno aquellos ayunos e guardaba los sabados? Dixo, que por alcançar aquel bien que le avyan seydo dicho. E que este mismo le desya que creyese aquella los que dicho ha que venia en aquella claridad.

E que asymismo este testigo desya esto todo, como todo lo otro, al dicho Gonçalo Bichancho e a todos los otros conversos que gelo preguntauan desta vylla. E dixo que vna de las personas a quien dixo lo susodicho e con quien lo partyçipo e comunico en todo lo que dicho ha e creyesen en la ley de Moysen e diesen limosnas, e como avya de venir Elias a lleuarlos a tierras abundosas, e todo lo otro segund dicho tyene, fue Pero Fernandes de Chillon, texedor, e a quanto este testigo pudo conosçer e syntyo del segund Dios le dio a entender, creya lo que este testigo le desya.

10. In the trial of Martín de Alcocer, inhabitant of Alia, leg. 132, no. 3 (23), fol. 22r, the text is different: "e que vendra[n] presto Elias e Enox a los llevar, e que vendra el Mexias tenyendo una bozina . . . [a los llevar] a las tierras buenas e santas que eran las tierras de promisión." See Haim Beinart, "The Conversos of Halia and the Movement of the Prophetess Inés" (in Hebrew), *Zion* 53 (1988): 13–52.

11. See above, note 8: . . . como su madre que hera ya defunta venia a ella y la tomaba la mano y la desya que no temyese porque la voluntad de Dios hera que subiese al çielo que viese los secretos e viese cosas maravillosas. Y asymismo la tomaba de la otra mano otro moço que hera falleçido pocos dias antes, y el Angel que les avia girando, y asy desya que la sobyan al çielo donde veya el purgatorio e las ánimas que en el estaban penando. Y asymismo en otro cabo como estauan en unas sillas de oro, otros en gloria. Y asymismo me dixo que estando ansy ençima de su cabeça en otra estançia mas alta le paresçia que avia mucho mormollo, y que pregunto al Angel: ¿que que hera aquello que ally sonava ençima? Y el angel le dixo: Amiga de Dios, aquellos que suenan alli arriba son los que han quemado aca en la tierra que estan alli en gloria. Y asymismo que via angeles de tres maneras y otras cosas que me dixo que no tengo en la memoria.

12. See the trial of Elvira González, wife of Gonzalo Palomino, inhabitant of Agudo, leg. 153, no. 18 (342), fols. 3r–4v. According to her Inés "veya los angeles e

los muertos e los quemados por hereges en syllas de oro e a Elias predicar, e que auia de venir en una nuve a predicar en la tierra a los conversos."

13. Herrera was a well-known center of leather tanners and shoemakers.

14. See the trial of Juan de Segovia, fol. 4r: ". . . y pregunte a la dicha moça que me contase que es lo que aconteçia y como subía al çielo. Y ella se embaraço un poco, y el dicho su padre Juan Estevan la dixo: Fija, di la toda la verdad como pasa. Y entonçes la dicha moça me dixo como su madre, que hera defunta, venia a ella y le tomaua la mano y le desya que no temyese porque la voluntad de Dios hera que subiese al çielo que viese los secretos y viese cosas maravillosas."

15. Luis Guantero (the glove maker) told this to Juan de Segovia (fol. 4v): ". . . Y entre las otras cosas que la susodicha moça me dixo que avia pedido al Angel que la diese una señal por donde fuese creyda lo que dixiese, que el Angel le respondió que el trayeria una letra del Señor. Y como yo estava encredulo y non con chica turbaçion dixele al dicho Juan Esteuan que me fisyese saber quando aquella carta truxesen a la dicha su fija o a qualquier otra cosa que de nueuo se ofreçiese. . . . En çiertos dias vino a esta çibdad Luis Guantero, vesino de la dicha villa de Herrera que quien avia conprado çierto cordouan, que me sy auya traydo alguna señal del çielo, el me dixo: tres; la una hera una espiga tan grande y la otra una aseytuna y la otra una cartyca."

16. It is worth noting that one María González sewed for herself a special shirt or shift for that occasion. We may presume this to have become a special way among converso women to get ready for the great event. See trial of María González, wife of Men Gutiérrez, inhabitant of Almadén, leg. 154, no. 35 (382), fol. 15r.

17. Ibid. "Porque en aquella tierra de Herrera todas lo fasyan asy fasta las criaturas de syete o de ocho años las fasyan ayunos y que no curauan nadie de fasyenda porque lo tenian por muy çierto que ansy lo que temian dauan a los que no tenyan con aquel esperança de ser llevados [a] aquellas tierras de promisyon. Y como Dios tenya fecha una çibdad en el çielo muy exçelente que avia de ser transladada a la tierra donde todos los conversos auian de morar y beuir en grande abundançia syn neçesydad ninguna."

18. See leg. 169, no. 6 (804), fol. 2r–v: ". . . que avia visto una çibdad muy riquisima y con mesas puestas y pan cosido aparejado para que comiesen los conversos que avian de yr todos a aquella çibdad."

19. See the trial of Elvira González, inhabitant of Agudo, leg. 153, no. 18 (342), fol. 6v: ". . . que la noche pasada avia estado desnuda en camisa por los corrales, esperando que desque avia de venir una nuve por nosotros, que nos avia de levar a tierra de promisión donde no avemos de haser otra cosa syno poner un plato sobre otro, e sy quisiesemos perdiz-perdis [sic] e sy gallina-gallina."

20. See the trial of Mencia López, inhabitant of Puebla de Alcocer, in the tes-

timony of Juan del Castillo from Almadén, leg. 163, no. 11 (523), fol. 6r–v. See Beinart, "Almadén," and Beinart, "Conversos of Chillón."

21. See Beinart, "Conversos of Chillón," esp. leg. 139, no. 16 (150), fols. 6r and 5s. Mari Gómez was the wife of Juan López, a cloth shearer.

22. "Que veia en el çielo a los angeles e Elias predicar y que andava Elias y la nieta de Jacob mano a mano y que veya alla a la hija de Juan Estevan y a otra de Cordoba, e que veya en las Tierras de Promision las mesas puestas e el pan cocido e muerto el pez leuiatan para que comiesen los conversos que avyan de yr alla, que los avia de llevar Elias." See Beinart, "Conversos of Chillón."

23. See *Alpha Beta d'Ben Sira*, ed. J. Steinschneider (Berlin, 1858), 4; M. Kasher, *Torah Shelema* (New York, 1946), 1663; Y. Heinemann, *Agaddot ve Toldotheyhen* (Jerusalem, 1974), 60–63.

24. II Kings 2:11.

25. See the testimony of Francisco Pizarro in the trial of Juan de Córdoba, leg. 158, no. 19 (448), fol. 2r. Fernando de Belalcázar was tried in 1500–1501, leg. 137, no. 11 (106), fol. 2r: ". . . como la hija Juan Esteban avya traydo de las tierras de promisyon unas clavelinas e un manojo de alcaçar." Alcaçar (or alcaçel or alcaur) is the green part of the rye used as food for the herds in Extremadura. See also Fritz Baer, ed., *Die Juden im christlichen Spanien* (Berlin, 1936), 2:532.

26. See the trial of Rodrigo Cordón, inhabitant of Siruela, leg. 139, no. 15 (149), fol. 6v.

27. Ibid. ". . . que a ocho dias del mes de março avya de venir un Angel a cada puerta de cada un converso e avya de poner alli unas Letras a que dixese: judio apareaos: E que avya de estar despues desto en su casa cada uno aquel dia. E otro dya de mañana no auya de amaneçer ninguno dellos." In his confession before the court of the Inquisition he used a different wording. Ibid.: ". . . avia de venir un anjel [*sic*] a señarles las partes de un nombre que dixese judio y despues otro dia avian de amanesçer todos ydos."

28. See Daniel, chap. 14. This belief was common among the Chuetas of Majorca. See Angela Selke, *Los Chuetas y la Inquisición* (Madrid, 1972), 226. See the words said by Inés to María Alvarez, leg. 134, no. 7 (6a), fol. 6v: ". . . que venia un Angel a ella e que primero avia venido su madre que era muerta e que le paresçia que llevaua el Angel al purgatorio e que veia alli muchos muertos e las penas que padeçian, e que asymismo veya sillas, e que en este año de quinientos avia de venir Elias y el Antichristo." See also Baer, *Die Juden*, 2:53a.

29. "Que aya de aver grandes perdones por este linaje de conversos e avyan de ser perdonado este pueblo de conversos e que avyan de ser lleuado este pueblo a Tierra de Promisyon." See trial of Pero Fernández, inhabitant of Chillón, leg. 147, no. 13 (259), fol. 3r. The use of the term "este pueblo" for the conversos had a special significance for them.

30. Trial of Rodrigo Cordón, fol. 6v: " Que aquella moça dezia que los conversos avian de yr a Tierra de Promisyon, que los avia de llevar Dios, y que todos los conversos avian de yr alla que quisiesen o no, y que les avia de predicar una boz del çielo un lunes que se avian de yr luego el jueves a delante." And further on: "Que avia oydo que auemos de pasar un ryo y que alli aviamos de dexar todas las joyas que llevasemos, y que aviamos de pasar en camysas blancas" (ibid., fol. 7r, addition to Cordón's confession). The confusion here may perhaps allude to the legend of the River Sambation. For a later period, see Haim Beinart, "The Jews in the Canary Islands: A Reevaluation," *Transaction of the Jewish Historical Society of England* 25 (1977): 53. In the trial of Isabel Rodríguez of Agudo, the prophetess predicted that those will not go: "se quedauan en el puerto perdidos comiendo coscosa." leg. 178, no. 15 (719), fol. 3r–v.

31. Trial of Rodrigo Cordón, fol. 6v. E se avian de quedar aca las hasiendas e que entre los Christianos viejos avian de aver mucha question e se avian de matar.

Another tried converso (Diego García, leg. 150, no. 6 [280], fol. 5v) expressed his wish not to pay his debt of seven thousand maravedi. Every converso had his personal desires and hopes.

32. Diego García testified in Toledo on May 2, 1500, leg. 158, no. 19 (448), fol. 2r–v. He was a smith. The verdict of this trial is unknown.

33. "Sabed que uiene un Angel en casa de Diego, ollero, vuestro vesyino, muy relumbrante unio de oro y se pone sobre la cama dellos e no dise nada ni habla." Trial of Rodrigo Cordón, fol. 6v.

34. Ibid.

35. See the trial of Diego García of Puebla de Alcocer, leg. 150, no. 6 (280), fol. 5r and following folios.

36. Our main concern here is the Messianic movement founded by Inés of Herrera del Duque.

37. The court's notaries nicknamed her Inesica. Her trial, leg. 158, no. 2 (431), contains three folio pages of her sentence.

38. See leg. 176, no. 12 (683), fol. 4r. The file lacks the sentence passed by the court.

39. López Sánchez was a shoemaker. His wife's file is not extant.

40. See leg. 158, no. 17 (446), fol. 5r. The case lacks many details of the trial.

41. See Haim Beinart, *Conversos on Trial* (Jerusalem, 1981).

42. See the trial of Rodrigo, son of the smith Fernando Sánchez and María García, his wife, leg. 176, no. 13 (684), fol. 3r. "Me tope con otros moços que andavan auiendo plaser con vihuelas y otras cosas, y yo tenia cuerno y me fue con ellos tanyendola por aver plaser, pero no porque yo por otra cosa ninguna los hisyese, salvo por plaser que dello avia."

43. Both of them were conversos. See the trial of María González, wife of Rodrigo Foronda, leg. 154, no. 31 (378), fol. 12r–2v.

44. See leg. 137, no. 7 (102), fol. 2r. This proceso has only four folio pages. It lacks the arraignment, the consulta de fe, and the sentence.

45. See her proceso, leg. 158, no. 6 (435), fol. 3v. The file lacks the sentence, but according to the decision reached by the consulta de fe, she was admitted back into the church.

46. See leg. 137, no. 8 (103), fol. 4r. The file lacks the sentence. According to the decision reached by the consulta de fe, she was admitted back into the church.

47. See leg. 158, no. 7 (436), fol. 3r. The file lacks the sentence, but on the first folio page the notary remarked that she was to do penance according to the decisions of the court.

48. Leg. 137, no. 9 (104), fol. 74. Sentenced to life imprisonment.

49. "Y asimismo entrando una mañana en el palaçio de mi casa pareçiome que vi claridades, e dixele a mi madre, y Elvira Gonsales nos dixo que era Abraham que estaba aposentado en nuestra casa" (fol. 3r). On the case of Abraham visiting their home we may comment that Abraham is one of the Amphitrions (Ushpizin) who visit the Succah. It is a unique testimony of this tradition among the conversos.

50. See his trial, leg. 158, no. 17 (446), fol. 2r.

CHAPTER 3 · MARÍA LÓPEZ

1. Cogolludo is about 33 kilometers north of Guadalajara; at this time, there were approximately 350–400 inhabitants in this village in eastern Castile. See Francisco Cantera Burgos and Carlos Carrete Parrondo, "Las juderías medievales en la provincia de Guadalajara," *Sefarad* 33 (1973): 35–38. For a very brief study of this family and its interactions with other members of the village, see Renée Levine Melammed, "The Conversos of Cogolludo," *Proceedings of the Ninth World Congress of Jewish Studies,* division B, vol. 1 (Jerusalem, 1986): 135–42. A detailed and lengthy study of the trials of the entire family and the effects of one upon another constitutes a chapter in my book *Heretics or Daughters of Israel: The Crypto-Jewish Women of Castile* (New York: Oxford University Press, 1998).

2. For an excellent discussion of the developments in Spain and Portugal as of 1391, see Yosef H. Yerushalmi, *From Spanish Court to Italian Ghetto* (New York: Columbia University Press, 1971), 1–50.

3. For a study of Isabel's trial, see Renée Levine Melammed, "Sixteenth Century Justice in Action: The Case of Isabel López," *Revue des Études Juives* 145, nos. 1–2 (1986): 51–73.

4. On this day, the court determined what was to be confiscated from both María's and her husband's property.

5. The accusation appears in legajo 163, número 8 (1516–21), fol. 2r–v. This *le-*

gajo, or file, can be found in the Archivo Histórico Nacional (AHN) in Madrid. Henceforth the abbreviations "leg." (*legajo*) and "no." (*número*) will be used.

6. "En el dicho tiempo vio que los dichos sus amos no comyan toçino ni lo echavan en la olla." Ibid., fol. 6v.

7. Ibid., fol. 7r.

8. Ibid., fol. 6v.

9. Ibid., fol. 7r.

10. Ibid., fol. 8r. It is interesting that three other children of María are mentioned more than once in these testimonies, yet the prosecution chose to focus on her oldest daughter, Isabel.

11. Vio este testigo como la dicha Marya Lopez lavava mucho la carne que trayan de la carnesçeria para la echar en la olla mas que la suelen lavar los christianos viejos. Ibid., fol. 10r. The term used here is *criadas* rather than *mozas*, implying a lower class of servants.

12. Ibid., fol. 6r.

13. Ibid., fol. 7r.

14. Ibid., fol. 10r.

15. Ibid.

16. Ibid., fol. 7r.

17. Ibid., fol. 8r.

18. Aberrations in conforming with restrictions were often attributed to health problems; the prosecutor was making the point clear that this was not an issue here.

19. Leg. 163, no. 8, fol. 7r. Often the servants returned to find the fat or the nerve of the leg of meat to have disappeared.

20. Both the fifth and sixth testimonies were presented much later in the course of the trial, in 1518. This gap in time probably accounts for the fact that Pedro was accused of observing the Sabbath while his wife, with whom he had observed, was not. The testimony mentioned lighting a lamp on Friday afternoons and letting it burn out on its own; reference was also made to a cave where the defendant, her husband, and others supposedly secluded themselves for several hours on Friday evenings. There was ample discussion of this cave in Pedro's trial. In addition, the family was said to have dressed up in honor of the Sabbath, and María had her lamps cleaned on Fridays for the same reason. See ibid., fol. 9r–v.

21. It is a bit difficult to date the time of this first response; there are a number of torn pages in the beginning of the record. The accusation seems to have been presented on January 29, 1517. Although María's response was recorded by a different notary, it did follow directly and gives the impression that she responded immediately, most likely on the same day.

22. Leg. 163, no. 8, fol. 3r–v.

23. While most ritual slaughtering was carried out by men, there were situations or locales in which competent men were not available; consequently, women would take over these roles. See, for example, the discussion by Howard Adelman, "Rabbis and Reality: Public Activities of Jewish Women in Italy during the Renaissance and Catholic Restoration," *Jewish History* 5 (Spring 1991): 32–34.

24. Leg. 163, no. 8, fols. 4v–5r.

25. Ibid., fols. 12r–v, 13v. The first four testimonies were read to her, and she responded; when the last two were added, she responded again. Needless to say, the identity of each of these witnesses was withheld from the defense.

26. Ibid., fols. 14r–15r. A list of witnesses who could testify to the good Christian life led by the defendant constituted the abonos. Because the list of prosecution witnesses was not revealed to the defense, the only way to attempt to invalidate the prosecution's evidence was to guess who might have testified; this process will become clear in the discussion of tacha lists which follows.

27. Nunca dios quiera que en mi casa oviese lanpara los viernes ny sabados ny otros dias algunos. Ibid., fol. 16r.

28. Nunca dios quiera que yo ençendiese ni mandase ençender los que dize candiles con mechas nuevas ny menos echaria lo que dizen masa en el fuego y lavar mucho la carne no es ricto ni çerimonya judayca antes linpieza y buena diligençia. Ibid., fol. 16r.

29. Ibid., fol. 16v.

30. Yten sy saben etç que la dicha Maria Lopez hera muger que dava buena dotrinas e consejos a sus criados e criadas e procurava que fuesen ynstruydos en las cosas tocantes a Nuestra Santa Fee Catolica. Ibid., fol. 18v.

31. Ibid., fols. 18r–19r.

32. The witnesses that were rejected and not allowed to testify were all New Christians. A rather untenable situation occurred here once the same individual was named by both sides to testify. This happened because the names of the prosecution witnesses were withheld from the defense; otherwise, Ropero never would have been considered as a trustworthy witness for the defense.

33. Le dixo si la avian llamado los Inquisidores que si la llamavan que les rogava que dixese lo que sabia e que no le dixo mas. Ibid., fol. 22v.

34. These testimonies appear in ibid., fols. 21r–23r.

35. The questions and the list appear in ibid., fol. 24r–v.

36. Una vez luego como començio a entra[r] en su casa que la vio a la dicha Maria Lopez e a Ysabel su hija muger de Françisco de Murçia abrir una pierna de vaca por medio para echar en coçina e que no vio quitarle cosa ninguna de en medio. Ibid., fol. 27v.

37. See ibid., fol. 27r–v.

38. Hera muger muy escasa que no se confiava de nadie. Ibid., fol. 30v.

39. He was questioned twice on the same day; see ibid, fols. 25r, 30v.

40. See ibid., fols. 30v–31v.

41. See ibid., fols. 29r, 34v, 40r.

42. The skirts appear in two references to Ana, the daughter of Pedro del Pozo, in ibid., fols. 34v, 52v, and in two references to María, the daughter of Pelingres, in ibid., fols. 36v, 52v; a blouse is discussed in the claim regarding Maria de la Pena, ibid., fol. 38r.

43. See ibid., fol. 35r; this woman was one of the prosecution witnesses.

44. Catalina, the wife of Nablero, is listed in ibid., fol. 35r.

45. Juana fija de Juan Yague vesino de Jocar criada que fue de la dicha Mari Lopes fera y es su enemyga de la dicha Mari Lopes a cabsa que la hiera e castigava porque fuese buena muger y no se ensuziase en la cama y por esto se le fue de la casa. Ibid., fol. 41v.

46. Three tachas mention this servant; see ibid., fols. 40v, 47v, 52r.

47. Her name appears a number of times; see ibid., fols. 35r, 41v, 51v.

48. La hazi castigar y aun la dicha my hija porque serase buena muger e no feses mala de su cuerpo ny ladrona como lo es y a esta cavsa lo le hazia dar hartas vezes. See ibid., fol. 51v.

49. Criada que fue de la dicha Mari Lopes a sido y es testimoniera y enemyga de la dicha Mari Lopes porque la hiera y castigava muchas vezes porque fuese buena muger.

María, the niece of Matiz's wife, was cited in ibid., fol. 35r.

50. Criada que fue de la dicha Mari Lopes le a tenydo y tiene odio y enemystad porque la hiera y castigava y dava de palos porque fuese buena muger y la llamava de puta golosa que andava con los moços de Señor Don Alonso pidiendoles golosinas.

Juana, the niece of Mateo de Medranda's wife of Membrillera, is described in ibid., fol. 35r.

51. See ibid., fol. 41v.

52. This servant is simply called María, a *loca* (crazy woman); see ibid., fol. 47r.

53. These two were among those presented by Pedro of Villarreal Jr. in his father's name; they both appear in ibid., fol. 51r.

54. See ibid., fol. 41v.

55. See ibid., fol. 38r.

56. See ibid., fol. 45r.

57. The husband involved in the deal was Antón Zamarillo; see ibid., fol. 47v.

58. Juan Carpintero and his family were angry with the defendant and her family; various members appear in two different tachas. See ibid., fol. 37r.

59. See ibid., fol. 52r.

60. Both tailors appear in ibid., fol. 37v.

61. Reñyan con el muchas veses porque seyendo su molinero se yva del molino y lo dexava a mal recabdo.

This was Juan Estevan; see ibid., fol. 38r.

62. See ibid., fol. 37v.

63. This multilayered contention appears in ibid., fol. 36v.

64. For this list of men and women, see ibid., fol. 29r.

65. See ibid., fol. 36r.

66. See ibid., fol. 47r.

67. See ibid., fol. 37r.

68. See ibid., fol. 56r; this was probably a fight with knives as well as fists.

69. Me devie dineros e me tyene malquerençia porque se los pedia y andava diziendo que le pedi lo que no me devie y porque le vendieron unas casas por vnos los dineros me tyene malquerençia el y su myger Catalina e Pedro su hyjo. See ibid., fols. 46r, 51r; María's statement appeared on the former page.

70. A *botero* is a maker or vendor of leather bags and bottles of wine. See ibid., fol. 35v, regarding both Burgos and Catalina.

71. Catalina muger de Fernando de Cavallero a sydo y es mala de su cuerpo con Pedro de Brihuega y a tenydo y tiene odio y enemystad con la dicha Mari Lopes y su marido a cabsa que seyendo su vezina no le enprestavan lo que ella pedio ny le quisyeron a alquylar una casa que tenyan. Ibid., fol. 40r.

72. In all likelihood, an element of desperation emerged here as well; for months, more and more names were suggested while repetitions of people already listed became more common. As has been demonstrated, success for the defense nonetheless remained elusive.

73. This is a reference to the Black Madonna of Montserrat, a medieval image of the virgin kept in the shrine on the mountain of Montserrat, near Barcelona. Pilgrimages were made to the Black Madonna, and, as can be seen here, knowledge of the existence of this image was not limited to Catalonia. My thanks to Mary Elizabeth Perry for this information.

74. E luego los dichos señores ynquisydores mandaron llevar a la dicha Marya Lopes a la camara del tormento e desnudala e ponerla en la escalera del tormento e atar con vnos cordeles de cañamo la qual fue desnuda e puesta en la dicha escalera e atada con los dichos cordeles e fue requerida e amonestada por los dichos señores inquisidores que diga verdad quyenes son los personas a quien vio fazer los delitos de heregia de que es acusada porque la intençion de sus merçedes no es syno saber enteramente la verdad e que sy moriere en el tormento o reçebiere lision de myenbro alguno que sea a su culpa e no a la de sus Merçedes. La susodicha dixo, "O vea santa Marya de Monserrate valme señor Ihesu Christo que

buena christiana a seydo O señora vca santa Marya porque consentio tal cosa señores Vuestras Reverençias me encomiendo." Fuele mandado hechar agua con
un jarro que cave fasta media açumbre e algo mas sobre la cara en çima de una
toca de seda que tenya sobre la cara. Fuele mandado apretar los cordeles con un
garrote e fueron le apretado con dos garrotes.

This is all that is recorded in leg. 163, no. 8, fol. 59r; the following page is blank
page (fol. 59v). This water torture consisted of tying the defendant down on a
scaffold with one's head lower than one's body and covering the face with a head-
piece. The victim experienced a sense of suffocation; pressure was simultaneously
being applied as the various ropes were tightened.

75. This decision seems extreme in the light of the fact that there was no confession. In a similar case where no confession emerged, even after torture, the tribunal demanded that the defendant, in this case Marina González, provide the
names of eight compurgatory witnesses. See Haim Beinart, *Records of the Trials of
the Spanish Inquisition in Ciudad Real* (Jerusalem: Israel Academy of Sciences
and Humanities, 1977), 2:33–34. However, this trial was held in 1494 in Ciudad
Real, and the degree of severity displayed by one court at a given time often varied from the next (court or time period).

76. The final description of the Judaizing activities differed from the prosecution's list at the beginning. Because one testimony was not brought forth until
later in the trial, the prosecutor could not possibly have included these charges at
the outset. At the end, however, mention was clearly made of three Sabbath observances: wearing good clothes, lighting candles and letting them burn out by themselves, and removing a piece of dough from the *hallah.* Leg. 163, no. 8, fol. 60r.

77. Dada e pronunçiada fue esta sentençya por los Reverendos Señores Inquisidores los liçençiados Sancho Velez e Juan de Mendoça en la Çiudad de
Toledo a treynta dias de Noviembre de IVdXVIIIº años estando en la plaça de
Coçadover en un cadalso donde se hizo el auto de la fe. Presentes los Muy Reverendos y manyficos Señores Don Diego de Ribera obispo de Segovia e Don
Françisco Ruyz obispo de Avila e el Liçençiado Alonso de Mariana e Pedro Fernandes de Yepes canonygos de Toledo e Pedro Lopez de Padilla su hijo e otras
muchas personas vesinos de Toledo e de otras partes. Ibid., fol. 61r.

78. This occurred in other trials, even within the family. See Melammed, "Sixteenth Century Justice."

79. See leg. 188, no. 9 (1518–21), fols. 16v–17v.

CHAPTER 4 · FRANCISCA HERNÁNDEZ AND THE
SEXUALITY OF RELIGIOUS DISSENT

1. Major sources of biographical information about Francisca Hernández are
Alastair Hamilton, *Heresy and Mysticism in Sixteenth-Century Spain: The Alum-*

brados (Toronto: University of Toronto Press, 1992); Angela Selke, *El Santo Oficio de la Inquisición: Proceso de Fr. Francisco Ortiz (1529–1532)* (Madrid: Ediciones Guadarrama, 1968); Ralph J. Tapia, *The Alumbrados of Toledo: A Study in Sixteenth Century Spanish Spirituality* (Park Falls, Wis.: Weber and Sons, 1974).

2. The Spanish text of the Edict of Toledo is reproduced in the appendix of the following study by Antonio Márquez: *Los alumbrados: Orígenes y filosofía (1525–1559)*, 2d ed. (Madrid: Taurus Ediciones, S.A., 1980).

3. See Mary E. Giles, *The Book of Prayer of Sor María of Santo Domingo: A Study and Translation* (Albany: State University of New York Press, 1990), and Ronald E. Surtz, *The Guitar of God: Gender, Power, and Authority in the Visionary World of Mother Juana de la Cruz (1481–1534)* (Philadelphia: University of Pennsylvania Press, 1990).

4. Tapia, *Alumbrados of Toledo*, 89.

5. Fue preguntado si dixo que Fca. H. no hablava cosa, en que pudiese errar, porque era persona alumbrada. Dixo que no dixo este declarante que no podía errar, sino que la veía hablar tales palabras, que creía que no errava en ellas (276). This excerpt and others from Medrano's trial (Archivo Histórico Nacional (AHN), Madrid, legajo 104, no. 15) appear in Bernardino Llorca, *La Inquisición española y los alumbrados (1509–1667): Según las actas originales de Madrid y de otros archivos* (Salamanca: Universidad Pontificia, 1980).

6. Fue preguntado si ha leído todo lo que dize Sant Pablo, que se contiene en la Sagrada Escritura. . . . Dixo que ha leído las epístolas e que no ha dexado de leer cosa alguna de las epístolas, y las ha leído muchas y muchas vezes. Fue preguntado qué cosas son las que ha visto en Fca. H., que no ha visto en Sant Pablo. Dixo que no se acuerda aver dicho de Sant Pablo ninguna cosa; pero que, si alguna cosa dixo fue, que veía en Fca. H. una humildad muy grandísima e que veía tener acatamiento a su madre, que nunca tal acatamiento vio tener a nadie, y que vio en ella una simplicidad e una niñez quel nunca a nadie; y que de muchos que vio comunicar con ella, que de malos se trocaron muy siervos de Dios, y que vio en ella un saber muy maravillosisimo, lo qual vio muchas vezes experimentar delante grandes Teólogos y deste declarante, que es theólogo y canonista, e otras muchas cosas, que veía este declarante en ella (277).

7. E hincóse de rodillas e puestas las manos juntas, dixo: "O Dios mío, tú sabes que mi intención ha sido de buscarte y servirte en mis obras. . . . Que dexé las letras e pompas y me recogí en aquel benefiçuelo, a donde consolava a los desconsolados y aconsejava y esforçava a los afligidos y remediava a las necesitades." E dixo otras palabras semejantes, y alçado, dixo: que se haga lo que quisieren; que él perdona a todos los que le ofendieron, y que se cumpla la voluntad de Dios (279).

8. Fue puesto en la escalera del dicho tormento e siempre fue amonestado que dixese verdad. Dixo que nunca se llegó a aquella muger, sino por servicio de Dios

y empezó a decir: "In manus tuas, Domine, commendo spiritum meum." Y empezó a confesar a Dios. Fuéronle empeçadas a ligar las piernas, desde los muslos hasta los tovillos con otros cordeles y fue amonestado que diga la verdad, e dixo muchas vezes: "¿Cómo, entre christianos, se hace tal cosa? Ave piedad de mí, Señor" (280).

9. "Quiten, quiten, que yo diré." Cesó el agua e siendo preguntado, dixo que, si quieren que fuera mala su intención, que sea, e pidió que le quitasen la toca. Fuele quitada y fue amonestado que diga la verdad. Dixo que, si agora tornara a comunicar a Fca. H., que la comunicaría de otra manera. Preguntado que de qué otra manera. Dixo que más prudentemente (281).

10. Fuele tornado a continuar el agua de dicho tercer jarro, e dixo: "ay, que me matan" muchas veces. Acabóse el agua de dicho tercer jarro e dixo: "que me quiten la toca." E siéndole quitada, dixo: "ay, Señor, que quieres que confiese." E dixo más: que todo es verdad cuanto decía, y que tuve mala intención; pues lo dezís, y que a los mártires no davan tan crueles tormentos (281–82).

11. M. Serrano y Sanz, "Francisca Hernández y el Bachiller Antonio de Medrano: Sus procesos por la Inquisición (1519–1532)," *Boletín de la Real Academia de la Historia* 41 (1902): 107.

12. Llorca, *Inquisición española*, 77.

13. Román de la Inmaculada, "El fenómeno de los alumbrados y su interpretación," *Ephemerides Carmelíticas* 9 (1958): 49–80.

14. Angela Selke, "El caso del Bachiller Antonio de Medrano: Iluminado epicúreo del siglo XVI," *Bulletin Hispanique* 58 (1956): 393–420.

15. In *Prison of Women* (Albany: State University of New York Press, 1998), an anthology of women's oral testimonies about life in prison during the period from 1939 to 1975, compiled by Tomasa Cuevas and translated into English and edited by Mary E. Giles, one woman makes the statement that perhaps she and other women prisoners had been too harsh on a former communist colleague who had betrayed them to the Francoist police after the war; perhaps, she adds, their former friend simply could endure the pain of prison and torture no longer.

16. Tapia, *Alumbrados of Toledo*, 56.

17. Ibid.

18. Among the fifty propositions that Ortiz had to abjure at the end of his trial was number 28: "Iten da a entender que sanó a fluxu seminis con el cordón de Francisca Hernández, como sanó la mujer a fluxu sanguinis tactu fimbrie Christi." Propositions 21–50 are included in the appendix in Llorca, *Inquisición española*, 284–88.

19. This excerpt and others from Ortiz's trial appear in Selke, *Santo Oficio*: . . . y digo que quasi por quatro años padescí una tentación penosíssima y vergonçosa, que es que contra toda mi voluntad (aunque diese grandes bozes a Dios y

me diese muchos açotes y pellizcos), y mísero miserable, caya en pollución estando despierto. Y aunque sé muy bien que estava mi voluntad ajena de culpa . . . pero yo triste e infelice que por la misericordia de Dios me sentía ajeno de culpa tal, por mi gran miseria estava lleno de pena y tristeza muy grande por tan trabajosa y quasi continua guerra como dentro de me veya (42).

20. . . . que estando esta santa . . . corporalmente absente de mí, su indigno hijo, donde por vía humana no me era posible alcançar a ver su deseable presencia, la vi a su merced con estos ojos pecadores y corporales . . . estando yo velando. Vila, digo alçada de tierra y muy cerquita de mí con hermosura maravillosa que me estava mirando con muy lindos y benigníssimos ojos, como quien sobre mí velava, la qual cosa juntamente causó en mi ánima una admiración grande que me tornó como estúpido, no dexándome libertad para que fuese o me menease para ir a su merced, y un gozo bienaventurado al ver una tan nueva novedad (60).

21. "Así en su manera puso Dios para mi alma en esta su sierva un no sé qué, y sí sé qué (que sé lo sentir y no lo sé hablar), con que en su bendita memoria es mi coraçón despertado a divino amor, de arte que me es su memoria como aguja del norte por do se rigen los mareantes" (61).

22. Ibid., 249–50.

23. Ibid., 280–87.

24. Tapia, *Alumbrados of Toledo*, 56.

25. Hamilton, *Heresy and Mysticism*, 84.

26. M. Serrano y Sanz, "Juan de Vergara y la Inquisición de Toledo," *Revista de Archivos, Bibliotecas y Museos* 5 (1901): 897.

27. Selke, *Santo Oficio*, 251.

28. Ibid., 296.

29. Llorca, *Inquisición española*, 290. The excerpts quoted in notes 30 and 31 are from this source.

30. Preguntada si es verdad que alguna persona se acostava en la cama desta declarante algunas noches, dixo que algunas vezes, estando mala, esta declarante, ivan a donde estava echada esta declarante Tovar y M. Cabrera y Villareal, y que algunas vezes se echava en la cama a donde estava esta declarante, encima de la ropa el dicho M. a dormir un rato (290).

31. . . . vino una mañana a donde estava esta declarante en su mesma casa, estando en Salamanca, y esta declarante estava en la cama, y le fue a besar la mano a esta declarante y esta declarante le fue a besar la mano a él, y entonces el dicho Cabrera apretó las manos muy bellacamente, y como esta declarante sintió su mala intención, le respondió rreciamente, y él la dixo que daría el alma al diablo por tener un hijo desta declarante y procuró de la tentar las tetas e besarla, y que esta declarante le resistió y le echó de sí (292).

32. Ibid., 295.

33. M. Serrano y Sanz, "Juan de Vergara y la Inquisición de Toledo," *Revista de Archivos, Bibliotecas y Museos* 6 (1902): 40.

34. For information on Alcaraz and the relationship with Francisca Hernández, see especially M. Serrano y Sanz, "Pedro Ruiz del Alcaraz, iluminado alcarreño del siglo XVI," *Revista de Archivos, Bibliotecas y Museos* 8 (1903): 1–16, 126–39.

35. Milagros Ortega Costa, *Proceso de la Inquisición contra María de Cazalla* (Madrid: Fundación Universitaria Española, 1978).

36. Ibid., 549.

37. Ibid., 552.

38. Llorca asserts in *Inquisición española* (78) that Boehmer considered Francisca the personification of the new reforming spirit.

39. Serrano y Sanz, "Juan de Vergara," *Revista de Archivos* 5 (1901): 897.

40. Llorca, *Inquisición española*, 78.

41. Serrano y Sanz cites Vergara's testimony in an appendix to his article "Juan de Vergara," *Revista de Archivos* 6 (1902): 477.

42. Cited by Serrano y Sanz, "Juan de Vergara," *Revista de Archivos* 5 (1901): 897.

CHAPTER 5 · MARÍA DE CAZALLA

1. For studies about the influence of Cardinal Cisneros on the religious climate of Spain, see especially J. Martínez de Bujanda's introduction to his edition of Juan de Cazalla, *Lumbre del alma* (Madrid: Universidad Pontificia de Salamanca–Fundación Universitaria Española, 1974); Tarsicio de Azcona, *Isabel la Católica: Estudio crítico de su vida y su reinado* (Madrid: Biblioteca de Autores Cristianos, 1964); and Pedro Sainz Rodríguez, *La siembra mística del cardenal Cisneros y las Reformas en la Iglesia* (Madrid: Fundación Universitaria Española, 1979).

2. Roland H. Bainton, *Women of the Reformation: From Spain to Scandinavia* (Minneapolis: Augsburg Publishing House, 1977), 15.

3. The classic study on alumbradismo and Erasmus is Marcel Bataillon's *Erasmo y España: Estudios sobre la historia espiritual del siglo xvi,* 2d ed., trans. Antonio Alatorre (Mexico City: Fondo de Cultura Económica, 1966). The case that the alumbrados were mystics was made strongly by Antonio Márquez in his review of José C. Nieto's work on Juan de Valdés in *Bibliothèque d'Humanisme et Renaissance* 35 (1977): 374–81. However, Márquez confuses their real doctrine with some of the masks they strategically adopted, including the Erasmian mask. Angela Selke is judicious in her appraisal of alumbradismo in light of Lutheranism in the article "Algunos datos nuevos sobre los primeros alumbrados: El edicto de 1525 y su relación con el proceso de Alcaraz," *Bulletin Hispanique* 54 (1952): 125–52. Her intuition seems to have been confirmed by Nieto in such

works as "En torno al problema de los alumbrados de Toledo," *Revista Española de Teología* 35 (1975): 77–93, and "The Non-Mystical Nature of the Sixteenth Century Alumbrados of Toledo," in *The Spanish Inquisition and the Inquisitorial Mind*, ed. Angel Alcalá (Boulder, Colo.: Atlantic Research and Publications, 1987), 431–56.

4. Nieto calls the letters "the most authentic and personal documents we have"; "Non-Mystical Nature," 452.

5. It is difficult to understand why the Inquisition did not act expeditiously after receiving the accusations. Cardinal Adrian, the bishop of Tortosa and emissary of King Charles, had followed Cisneros as inquisitor general on March 14, 1518. The position was left empty for more than one year after his departure for Rome when he was elected pope, on August 4, 1522. For him and for the Spanish officials it must have taken time to become aware of a possible similarity, and even connection, between Castilian alumbradismo, Luther's doctrines, and the wars of the communities in Castile and Aragon. When they realized the similarity, the reaction was quick and ominous.

6. Spanish translations of the original texts in Latin are included in Antonio Márquez, *Los alumbrados: Orígines y filosofía (1525–1559)*, 2d ed. (Madrid: Taurus Ediciones, S.A., 1980), 244–93.

7. Milagros Ortega-Costa, *Proceso de la Inquisición contra María de Cazalla* (Madrid: Fundación Universitaria Española, 1978), 272. All citations from the trial are from this edition.

8. ". . . que hera cosa muy abominable que predicase una muger y ylla a oyr" (47).

9. Juan, a Franciscan, had been an aide, secretary, and close advocate for Cisneros in all his cultural, spiritual, and even military enterprises (he accompanied him on the Orán campaign) almost until his death or until his promotion to auxiliary bishop of Avila in 1517. As the author of *Lumbre del alma*, he is not too original, since this little text is simply an abbreviation of some chapters of the French Carthusian Pierre Dorland's *Viola animae*, which in turn condenses Raymond Sabunde's *Liber creaturarum*. We know from Juan de Vergara's proceso that the Inquisition started a trial against the bishop, but perhaps it was interrupted at his death early in 1530.

10. No se aman syno por los dineros y por la hermosura. No veo onbre christiano a quién dé mi hija, que me parece que no es más casarlas agora que ponerlas a la putería. . . . que antes fuesen putas que monjas (quoted by Diego Hernández, 81).

11. De hazerme el Obispo, su her[man]o, perder los temorçillos, entiendo que me diere libertad para andar con quien quiera, con osadía y alegre, que éste era su ofiçio exentar cristianos de servidunbre y darles libertad evangélica (85).

12. . . . yo no sé más destos herrores que ponen a estos que llaman alumbrados (101).

13. For ease of reading I have omitted translation of "esta declar[ant]e," meaning the one who makes the declaration, throughout passages in English.

Dixo que no se acuerda esta declar[ant]e aver dicho que no reçibiría el sacramento ni confesaría ni oyría misa syno por conplir con el mundo, mas que se acuerda algunas vezes aver dicho esta declar[ant]e que buscásemos a Dios en los tenplos bivos mas no negava esta declar[ant]e que no estava Dios en los tenplos, en sus sacramentos, e que se avia de yr a buscar a los tenplos materiales.(106)

. . . si tanta diligençia pusiésemos en alinpiar las conçiencias e quitar las malas costumbres, que se agradaría Dios mucho dello. (107)

. . . podría ser que dixese esta declar[ant]e que hera cosa rezia ésta que Dios nos avía obligado a dezir n[uest]ras faltas a otro onbre, mas no por eso lo negava syno que lo tenía por muy bueno. (107)

Preg[unta]da sy a dicho esta declar[ant]e que quando su marido le pagaba la debda marital estava toda divina e que estando con él en el abto carnal estava más allegada a Dios que quando estava en la más alta oraçión del mundo, dixo que nunca tal dixo. (113)

Preguntada sy dezía esta declar[ant]e que conçebía a sus fijos syn delectaçión carnal e que no los quería como a sus fijos syno como a fijos de sus vezinos, dixo que muchas vezes preguntó esta declar[ant]e a sus confesores sy hera posible conçebir a sus fijos syn deletaçión carnal esta declar[ant]e porque le paresçía a esta declar[ant]e que no sentía aquellos regozijos que solía en la deletaçión carnal. . . . Preguntada qué es la causa porque hazía diferençia esta declar[ant]e . . . dixo que la causa hera porquesta declar[ant]e se ocupava en obras de penitençia e en guardar e refrenar sus sentidos lo mejor que podía. (113–14)

. . . como esta declarante ha sido muy flaca y tentada de la carne . . . se hazía mucha fuerça y con muy gran pena pagava la deuda y por no caer en desorden y delectaçión se ponía en pensar un paso de la Pasión o en el juizio universal. (119)

Preguntada sy enseñó esta declar[ant]e a algunas personas diziendo que no se arrimasen a los açidentes de las obras e abtos esteriores de la adoraçión e oraçión e humiliaçión, dixo que lo que dezía esta decla[ant]e muchas vezes hera que las obras esteriores las avían de tomar por medio para yr a las ynteriores. (117)

14. Digo que no sé de personas sospechosas más de lo que tengo dicho (141).

15. Juan Antonio Llorente, *Historia crítica de la Inquisición de España,* 4 vols.

(Madrid: Ediciones Hiperión, 1980), 1:26; trans. of *Histoire critique de l'Inquisition d'Espagne,* 4 vols. (Paris, 1817).

16.

. . . seríe posible . . . cuando se ofreçe sy tenía unas oras en la mano, dezir un verso o dos y no en modo de dar dotrina en público ni alegando autoridad[e]s como él dize. . . no dize el dicho testigo herror alguno que yo dixese. (199)

Mas sy por leer una Epístola en romançe se oviese de ynputar a delito o se oviese de dezir que predicavan, pocas mugeres avríe devotas o que supiesen leer no fuesen notadas desto, mayormente que lo que los dichos t[estig]os dizen que dezía, "que amásemos a Dios" más son en mi favor . . . más es de favoresçer a quien da buenos consejos que de oprimillos pues no faltan en el mundo quién los dé malos. (200–201)

. . . digo que posible seríe que yo dixese que era más alta cosa contenplar en la divinidad que no en la humanidad de Christo nuestro Redentor . . . no es cosa dubdosa pues dize la Santa Escriptura. (205)

. . . he murmurado de alg[un]os pedricadores que pedricavan fríamente y no con tanta dotrina como yo quisiera para el provecho de mi ánima e de los otros fieles christianos. (206)

. . . lo que yo quiçá dixe, seríe que en el amor que toviésemos a nuestros hijos avía destar fundado en caridad e no en carnalidad . . . porque dezir que yo meresçía más en el estado del matrimonio no se sygue que por eso menospreçie el estado virginal. Posyble es que merezca más una buena casada delante de Dios en los travajos y cargas del matrimonio que no algunas vírgines en el cuerpo e disolutas y corrutas en el ánima como se prueva en la parábola del Evangelio de las vírgines locas. (211)

. . . aunque a las mugeres les está proybido el predicar, no les está proybido aprender y leer y hablar en cosas de Dios. (228)

17. Henry Charles Lea, *A History of the Inquisition of Spain* (New York: Macmillan, 1906–7), 3:54.

18. ". . . pareçió presente la dicha María de Caçalla que pidió audi[ençi]a y, salida, dixo que ya sus Mds. saben como ella tiene concluido muchos días ha para definitiva, que suplicava e suplicó a sus Mds. mandasen con toda brevedad despachar su causa o sy no se pudiese despachar en breve la mandasen dar en fiado para que tuviese esta çibdad por cárçel y que esto pide se haga de pareçer de su marido" (424).

19. Dixo que no se acuerda e que sy algo le escrivió, sería dezir lo que esta declar[ant]e avía confesado o negado, confesando la verdad e negando lo contrario (488).

20. . . . pues el proçeso de esta muger está concluso . . . que se deve luego ver y voctar en forma (434).

21. "Señores, esto meresco yo por aver tornado por la honrra de Jesuchristo, que si no fuera por mí estuviera medio reyno dañado y agora quiérenme dar este pago" (454).

22. "Señor, lo que tengo dicho en Toledo y en Torrijos y en Guadalajara aquello es la verdad . . . que aquellos que son Pedro de Alcaraz e Ysabel de la Cruz e María de Caçalla son herejes y más la María de Caçalla porque este t[estig]o sintió en ella mayor çeguedad que no en los otros porque hera mucho su enbeveçimi[ent]o que tenía con los alunbrados" (455).

23. Dixo que dize lo que dicho tiene (469).

24. "¡O, Rey del çielo y atado tú a la colugna!" (470).

25. "Redentor del mundo, Jesús, adorado seas tú en la cruz y adórote. En el pesebre naçiste por mí no más, pues soy flaca. ¡Noramala tengáys, tanta fuerça contra los flacos," e dio algunos gritos e dixo "ansí que por los falsarios los ynoçentes" e syendo atada los dichos braços fue tornada a amonestar dixese le verdad. Dixo, "dicho la tengo." Fue mandada poner en el escalera del dicho tormente y estando en ella, dixo: "ay, señores, por qué creéys a mentirosos," e dixo, "Señor, suple tú, que sueles suplir en las neçesidades. Yo te confieso y adoro e dame esfuerço en la turbaçión. No lo hize, señores, e sy tomáys sobre v[uest]ras conçiençias" (470).

26. "No pequé, Señor mío, tú lo sabes, señor Santistevan, señor sant Lorenço, señor sant Simón e Judas a quien yo me tengo prometida . . . y esto a los ynoçentes . . . y que ynoçente no confesará lo que no ha fecho . . . enoramala, Gaspar Martínez, mucha fuerça tenéys . . . queréys que mienta" e dixo "a los ganapanes con tanta fuerça e no a los flacos. Que me ahogo, que soy enferma" (471).

27. . . . sea absuelta *ab instançia judicii* y le sea inpuesta peni[tençi]a pecuniaria hasta en çinquenta ducados y que sea aperçibida con graves penas que no se junte a comunicar con aquellas personas de quien tiene dicho que eran alunbrados ni con otras personas sospechosas en este caso e que haga una peni[tençi]a pública en su perrochia de Guadalajara . . . por las otras culpas que . . . resultaban de la comunicaçión que tuvo en la cárçel con los presos e otras personas . . . que se le ynponga en peni[tençi]a a otros çinquenta ducados (472).

28. Es de suponer que, en efecto, el marido que no parece haber participado en absoluto en las inquietudes religiosas de su mujer (383).

CHAPTER 6 · FRANCISCA DE LOS APÓSTOLES

1. See Gillian T. W. Ahlgren, *Teresa of Avila and the Politics of Sanctity* (Ithaca, N.Y.: Cornell University Press, 1996), 53–61.

2. See Alison Weber, *Teresa of Avila and the Rhetoric of Femininity* (Princeton: Princeton University Press, 1990), esp. 162–64.

3. Archivo Histórico Nacional (AHN), Madrid, Inq., leg. 113, no. 5, *Resumen*, fol. 1r. For modern commentary, see, for example, Alvaro Huerga, *Historia de los Alumbrados* (Madrid: Fundación Universitaria Española, 1975–95), 1:232–33: "El episodio toledano . . . se redujo a una mezcla de neurosis profética. . . . La Inquisición acabó pronto con aquel hervidero." See also Juan Blázquez Miguel, *Sueños y procesos de Lucrecia de León* (Madrid: Tecnos, 1987), 65–66. Comparing her with Lucrecia de León, Blázquez concludes: "Estos eran personajes concretos, con nombres y rostros, pero, al margen de ellos, las lenguas desatadas, las imaginaciones ávidas de sucesos sobrenaturales y la superstición imperante rodeaban la atmósfera de una aire irreal de presagios macabros y de hechos extraordinarios que se decía que acaecían en todos los lugares del reino" (66). Much of Blázquez's information about Francisca is erroneous. For example, he says that Francisca went to Rome when it was her sister, Isabel Bautista, who made the pilgrimage. He also says that the sisters rented the beaterio in June 1577, although at that point Francisca had been imprisoned for more than a year. He dates Francisca's trial to 1587, when it actually concluded in 1578. See also Blázquez Miguel, *La Inquisición en Castilla–La Mancha* (Madrid: Universidad de Córdoba, 1986), 114–15, where he says essentially the same thing.

4. Beatas constituted a form of religious life of significant influence in sixteenth-century Spain. For a description of the social and religious functions of beatas, see Mary Elizabeth Perry, *Gender and Disorder in Early Modern Seville* (Princeton: Princeton University Press, 1990), 97–104. See also Francisco Avallá Cháfer, "Beatas y beaterios en Sevilla," *Archivo Hispalense* 65 (1982): 99–132.

5. AHN, Inq., leg. 113, no. 5, fol. 171r: tenia entendido el camino por donde se perdian muchas donzellas y mugeres que andavan perdidas se enpleava en rrecoger algunas y enseñarles labor que savia.

6. AHN, Inq., leg. 113, no. 5, fol. 110r.

7. Ibid., fols. 152v–153r: Es grande la multitud de gente q a tenido a casa dende q ella se fue a fama q fue con una señora q queria hacer un monesterio para pobres y a esta cosa son muchas las necesidades q entendio y la gran ocasion q tiene gran numero de doncellas y biudas de ofender a dios por necesidad . . . [153r] si no tubiese la fe q tengo en dios q le a de traer para rremediar todo esto no se q consuelo me bastaria porq ya ban las cosas tan en las heces q no parece sino q a todos los eclesiasticos les a mandado dios q gasten sus rrentas en holgarse y dejen perecer los pobres y perder las tristes doncellas.

8. Linda Martz, *Poverty and Welfare in Habsburg Spain: The Example of Toledo* (Cambridge: Cambridge University Press, 1983), 139.

9. AHN, Inq., leg. 113, no. 5, fol. 204r: Luego vio venir a s[an]t pedro diçiendo

delante de aquella magestad padre eterno duro castigo sea sobre los saçerdotes q[ue] tan malos [h]an seguido porque yo desnudo segui al desnudo y ellos van cargados de rrentas y vicios.

10. Ibid., fol. 153r: y a esta causa se an puesto muchos onestas contalle de otra jente q a venido a mi a la misma fama q se espantava personas muy rricas ansi doncellas como biudas y de tan gran santidad q me espantan tanto q todas me quentan q an deseado toda su bida meterse en rreligion y por ber el destraumiento q ay en los monesterios tienen por bien estarse en su casa y q an entendido q a de ser esta rreligion de gran santidad y pidenme q las tenga por rrecebidas a las quales rrespondo q yo no puedo nada mas q lo encomienden a dios . . . y la q menos tiene son tres mil ducados q si enpezasemos seria grande el llamamiento de las jentes q se entraria con sus haciendas.

11. See ibid., fols. 178v–179v. Church officials and ordinary Toledans were divided in their opinions about the authenticity of the women's visions, which were the subject of gossip. Francisca's sister Isabel's need for repeated exorcisms only increased doubt. For some, the women's pursuit of religious reform without official approval appeared scandalous.

12. Resistance to new religious houses was not uncommon. Teresa of Avila experienced more than six months of legal opposition to her first foundation, that of San José. In her analysis of this period, Jodi Bilinkoff has suggested that Teresa's reform ideals stirred controversy because, by being founded in poverty, they rejected the elaborate patronage system that served the interests of the nobility at least as much as those of the religious women. See Bilinkoff, *The Avila of Saint Teresa: Religious Reform in a Sixteenth-Century City* (Ithaca, N.Y.: Cornell University Press, 1989), 137–51. Opposition to Francisca's reforms might have been connected to similar issues: whether or not the endowment was sufficient, the perceived viability of the convents, the fact that women of varied social classes would be mixing, the perceived undesirability of some of the poorest women, and the rumors flying about that many of the women were controlled by the devil. (See AHN, Inq., leg. 113, no. 5, fol. 182r–v.)

13. Ibid., fol. 180r.

14. See ibid., fol. 4r.

15. See ibid., fol. 5r: Dixo apostoles q . . . su h[erman]a . . . es mas santa q muchos del cielo.

16. Ibid., fols. 6v–7r. The testimony of Catalina de Jesús elicited little that was controversial.

17. AHN, Inq., leg. 3072, no. 35: Carta al Consejo 1 septiembre 1575: Y lo q en ello pasa es q en esta çiudad residen tres hermanas beatas, las quales han estado spiritadas y an tractado de p[ersonas] muy xnas y loarse dello, y a otras beatas contava revela[cio]nes y cosas que veyan: y tratavan de hazer un mon[aste]rio en

esta çiudad: y porq son pobres y no tienen hazienda, la una dellas acordo de yr a Roma sobre ello ha mas de año y m[edi]o y despues de yda se tuvo noti[ci]a en este s[an]to offi[ci]o y por estar en oppinion q aun no estava fuera de tener [e]sp[irit]us y por la infor[maci]on flaca no hezimos dilig[enci]a en ello.

Pedro Chacón, a cleric who enjoyed a good reputation in Toledo, was one of those who spoke in favor of the women. See AHN, Inq., leg. 113, no. 5, fol. 110r.

18. AHN, Inq., leg. 113, no. 5, fol. 4r: "Dixo q ha muchos dias q esta q declara hablo al padre sebastian her[nand]ez de la compañia de jesus para q diesse noti[ci]a a los s[eñore]s inqui[sido]res de alg[un]as cosas q sabe de una fran [cis]ca de los ap[osto]les y de bapt[ist]a su her[man]a beatas vezinas desta çiudad y al doctor velazquez can[onig]o en la s[an]ta igl[es]ia q vino por man[da]do del s[eñ]or gover[na]dor pa[ra] se informar."

Busto de Villegas was apparently not unsympathetic to the plight of the poor in Toledo; in December 1573 he drew up a list of instructions for all who distributed alms in the parishes, urging that "young marriageable women or orphan girls 'who [were] in danger of being lost,' virtuous journeymen and small retailers who lacked means, and any person who was sick, be given special consideration in the distribution." Martz, *Poverty and Welfare*, 202.

19. AHN, Inq., leg. 113, no. 5, fol. 166v: Creer con gran facilidad lo q interiormente se le ofreçe entendiendo que es enseñami[en]to de n[uest]ro señor y creer en sueños es eregia de alunbrados.

See also fol. 166r: ". . . en quanto diga que le fue enseñado en espiritu es lenguaje de alunbrados."

20. See Ahlgren, *Teresa of Avila*, 42–45.

21. AHN, Inq., leg. 113, no. 5, fol. 186r.

22. Ibid., fol. 188r: "No es bastante seguridad lo que [h]a d[ic]ho y declarado en dezir que porque le [h]a acaezido en acabando de comulgar porque en ese tiempo y antes y en la mesma comunion y en todos tiempos el demonio anda buscando como engañar a las personas q[ue] diga si [h]ay otra rraçon alguna."

23. Ibid., fol. 188r–v: Echava de ver q[ue] hera cosa de dios y no del demonio lo primero porq[ue] se le ba arrobando el espiritu con gran suavidad q[ue] en ese tiempo los sentidos no sienten cosa corporal ni q[ue] perturbe al alma sino todo una grande suavidad y da en estando el alma grandisima luz y gran conozimiento de su baxeza y de que a pasado lo que se behe y la persona torna en si halla en si gran humildad y gran sujezion para todo lo que toca al servic[i]o de nuestro s[eño]r para con gran façilidad obrar todas las cosas de virtud y que da con gran aborreçimiento de todo lo que [e]s culpa y abraça con grande eficazia todas las cosas q[ue] son de pena y fatiga por amor de nuestro señor y en esta seguridad que q[ue]dava en su alma po[d]ria entender si hera bueno y si hera de parte de nuestro s[eño]r. . . . Y no fiandose de si mesma esta confesante lo tratava con miguel

Ruiz para satisfacerse mas y el dho miguel Ruiz le decia q[ue] ynprimian en su alma seguir con Rectitud los caminos de nuestro s[eño]r y guardan los mandamientos q[ue] podia estar segura no ser de parte del demonio y q[ue] se metiese la confesante en su baxeza porq[ue] ella hera obligada aborreçer lo q[ue] fuese ofensa de nuestro s[eño]r y amar las cosas de travajos por amor de nuestro s[eño]r.

24. Ibid., fol. 190r: "Fuele dicho que buelva sobre si y mire en lo que dize y lo que trata porq[ue] estas cossas de dios son de tanto pesso y de tanta importancia que no las avia de ossar tratar tan palpablemente aunq[ue] fuera verdad lo q[ue] a dho quanto mas que no lleva semejança de verdad."

25. Ibid., fol. 193r.

26. Ibid., fol. 194r: "Dixo que porq[ue] dexa al alma en una paz y humildad profunda."

27. Ibid., fol. 194v: "Si el demonio entrara con rrigor çierto es que se entenderia quien hera y se huyria del y por eso biene con blandura."

28. Ibid., fol. 183(a)v: . . . dieron q[uen]ta del modo con que avian echo bibir a las criaturas y ansy esta conf[esant]e en acavando de comulgar hizo una oblig[aci]on de la manera que n[uest]ro s[eñ]or ynspiro en su alma q hera para satisfaçion de los vizios que en aquel pecado pecavan los honbres.

29. Ibid., fol. 147r: bi una gran majestad q rrespondia mucho me pedis hijo q rrenuebe toda la tierra porque son grandes las ofensas q me an hecho.

30. Ibid., fol. 147v: "Pusose nuestra señora de por medio y salio porfiado ofreciendole q se harian dos monesterios en q se habian de dedicar de su mano gentes de grandespiritu q fuesen bastantes a sastisfacer a su majestad las ofensas q todo el mundo le abia hecho y los monesterios eran con la misma Regla q ella llebo escrita y bi como esta majestad se bolbia a mi alma pecadora y me dijo q te parece hija q ofendido me tiene el mu[n]do en especial esta ylesia porq con sus boces me ofenden y con sus misas me crucifican a mi y yo con grande[s] lagrimas no dicia otra cosa sino pedille misericordia y luego bi como tomo el hijo de dios al arzobispo de un braço y le presento a su padre diciendo padre nro bes aqui a bartolome q sera bastante a Reformar todo lo eclesiastico contenta os mucho porq yo muy agradado estoy del y yo salgo por su fiador q perdera la bida por la honrra de buestra majestad y Reformacion de buestra ylesia y el padre eterno le Recibio muy agradado del y despues de abelle abraçado le echo multiplicadas bendiciones."

31. Ibid., fol. 141v: ". . . y que no le dio entera credulidad a la vision por la enfermedad que la dicha fran[cis]ca de los apostoles tiene." See also ibid.: "Pidio al confesante que la hiziesse tan gran plazer que la escriviese de su mano aquella vision porque la queria enbiar a su her[ma]na a Roma para que la viese y el confesante mas por darle esse contento que por el credito que totalmente tenia a la dicha vission se la escrivio."

32. Ibid., fol. 142r: "... Andando en esto un demonio que se dixo llamar luçifer con muchos exerçitos dixo que tenia liçençia de n[uest]ro s[eñ]or de bajar a la christiandad como pareçe por el dicho papel y que n[uestr]o s[eñ]or le mandava a el y a los suyos irse al infierno si este confesante y fran[cis]ca de los apostoles se obligasen con los monesterios que se avian de hazer de bibir en perpetua pobreza en ayunos y oraçion y penitençia y ellos ambos a dos se obligaron a esto como pareçe por los dichos dos papeles y esto es lo q[ue] quieren dezir y dizen los dichos papeles. ... Esto lo dixo a este conf[esant]e el dicho demonio por la boca de la dicha fran[cis]ca de los apostoles despues de aver comulgado."

33. See Raimundo de Capua, *Vida de la bienaventurada sancta Catharina de Sena,* trans. Antonio de la Peña (Medina del Campo: Francisco de Carnto, 1569), fols. 92r–93v. A similar example, this one rooted in Antony's temptation by demons in the desert, is described in the "Suma de los engaños," BRAH ms. 12-26-7.D 185, fol. 19r.

34. For commentary on women mystics and their role in the tradition of redemptive suffering, see Caroline Walker Bynum, *Holy Feast and Holy Fast: The Religious Significance of Food to Medieval Women* (Berkeley: University of California Press, 1987).

35. For a discussion of changing views toward vernacular mysticism and the changing theological orientations of the century, see, for example, Marcel Bataillon, *Erasmo y España: Estudios sobre la historia espiritual del siglo xvi,* trans. Antonio Alatorre (Mexico City: Fondo de Cultura Económica, 1966), 1–71, and Melquíades Andrés, *La teología española en el siglo XVI* (Madrid: Editorial Católica, S.A., 1977), 2:107–294, 507–628. For a discussion of the effects of these trends on Teresa of Avila, see Ahlgren, *Teresa of Avila,* 9–15.

36. AHN, Inq., leg. 113, no. 5, fol. 203r: Yten a dicho dize y confiesa q por los llamamientos q nro s[eñ]or le a hecho en su ynterior avia hecho ziertas obligaçiones de padesçer por la yglesia de dios todos quantos tormentos fuese dios servido de darle a trueque de que su mag[es]t[ad] fuese satisfecho de tantas ofensas como se le hazian y que aquello avian de hazer las q fuesen monjas en el monesterio q ella avia de fundar.

37. Ibid., fol. 207r–v: Le tomo un desmayo y estubo un poco desmayada y bolbio en si llorando y bolbio en si diziendo como no se a de acavar el juycio en estas cosas y dixo q[ue] no estava agora para poder responder a la dha acusacion y pedia al Sr. Inq. lo dexe para otra audiencia.

38. Ibid., fol. 207v: E luego la dha fran[cis]ca de apostoles dixo que ella es muger de muy flaco animo y el señor ynq[uisid]or es una persona de tanto Rigor en sus preguntas y en todas las demas cosas y que ella no tiene animo para esperar sus Redarguiziones tan terribles y pide q todavia se le de letrado en quien sienta tiene un poco de favor.

39. Ibid., fol. 232r: Lo que dize y [h]a d[ic]ho se muestra la falsedad de su neg[oci]o porq claro esta que quando la mage[stad] de dios nuestro s[eño]r determinara de hacer tan grandes Rebelaçiones que avia de ser alguna persona muy avisada en oraçion diziplinas ayunos y en otros actos de virtud.

40. Ibid., fol. 235v: Dixo que ella crehe todo lo q[ue] el señor ynquisidor le dize como persona que terna [*sic*] mas luz de dios para entender esas cosas que no ella y que lo que ella trata es que no a dicho ni pretendido hazer cosas en ofensa de nuestro señor y que si entendiera q lo hera no lo hiziera por el cielo ni por la tierra.

41. Ibid., fol. 243r: Primeramente q la susodicha fingiendo y dando a entender ser sancta diçiendo y publicando tener Rebelaçiones de nro s[eñ]or y que dios se [h]avia desposado con ella y q [h]avia dios embiado a pedir liçençia a su padre para ello y q le [h]avia dicho q havia hallado una anima justa y s[an]ta y que satisfaria por el mundo y por el peccador y q [h]avia pedido las arras del desposorio a dios y q la avia dado las virtudes para ser s[an]ta o rresistir las tentaçiones diçiendo y tratando en publico estas y otras cosas como sancta en las carceles en secreto [h]a tratado y tiene conçertado de se casar con çierta persona y le llama marido y el a ella muger y le procura ver y hablar como en efecto lo ha hecho.

42. Ibid., unnumbered folio: yo no me [he] tenido por santa ni [h]e hecho obras para sello [*sic*: serlo] sino de gran pecadora sino q como mujer ynprudente y de poca espirencia en las cosas de nuestro señor trate con las q tenia por amigas las cosas q tengo declaradas en todas las audiencias q conmigo se [h]an tenido y estas amigas me [h]an puesto todas las cosas contrarias.

43. Ibid.: todas las audencias q conmigo se [h]an tenido [h]a sido dandome a entender q yba engañada por el camino q yo pense yba muy segura en el serbicio de dios. [H]e determinado de cerrar mi entendimiento a todas las cosas q me [h]an pasado y solo creer lo q en este santo oficio se me [h]a enseñado y si un angel me dixere lo contrario no lo creere sino q pensare es el demoño q me quiere engañar y biendo yo en el gran trabaxo q me a puesto este negocio y tiniendo por gran peligro la libertad e determinado de mudar estado y casarme porq quiza me salbare mejor que a lo contrario.

44. See Ahlgren, *Teresa of Avila*; see also Weber, *Teresa of Avila*.

CHAPTER 7 · Y YO DIGE, "SÍ SEÑOR"

1. Ms. 1610, Universitat Central, Barcelona, 2r–v. Here and throughout, I modernize and punctuate the Spanish manuscript text, resolve abbreviations and use brackets to indicate words I have added for comprehension. I translate ungrammatical clauses, such as the final one here, as grammatical, and refer to the Divinity as masculine following seventeenth-century usage. Domenge did indeed need a cloak where she was going, since she spent the winter months in jail,

and the fact that she was without it serves to dramatize further her suffering there: Yo fui a la Santa Inquisición el sábado de la octava del Corpus; me fue a buscar a Santa Catalina el Alcalde de la Inquisición, y me llevó y estuve en casa de dicho alcalde hasta la víspera de la visitación de Santa Isabel y este día a las tres, me llamaron el alcalde y el secretario a una instancia y yo fui muy alegre y dijo "¿Es menester manto?" y me dijeron, "No, que adonde la hemos de llevar no ha menester manto." Y dichas estas palabras me llevaron a una prisión muy apartada y muy oscura y era de tal manera la prisión de mal olor que me parecía era una necesaria y muy húmeda, que cuando estaba sentada los escarabajos y arañas sentía me corrían por lado de mí. Y el hábito que llevé blanco [de] tanta [humedad] que había, se me cubrió que negreaba.

2. Domenge is described as illiterate in the manuscript (31v), and she supposedly dictated what material in the manuscript is hers. I refer to the experiences described in the manuscript as "hers" with reservation, since she did not write any of it, her confessor had a hand in the document's production, and there is no evidence that it was read back to her for confirmation of veracity. The visions, like so many others of their type, are best considered a group production whose main protagonist is Domenge.

3. The sixty-nine *avisos,* short cautionary statements, appear unmodified in the manuscript. They were written by Padre Plaza, and Teresa adapted some of them, perhaps adding some of her own. Widely copied in the seventeenth century, they were then believed to be the work of Teresa herself; see Tomás Alvarez, "Un espurio teresiano: Los 69 avisos," *Monte Carmelo* 91 (1983): 23–101.

4. Esta religiosa de quien este libro habla y que ella misma dictó se llama Soror Anna Domenge, fundadora del Convento de Religiosas Dominicas de Perpignán, la cual, aunque estuvo con la Inquisición, salió calificado su proceder.

It continues: "Thus it is narrated not only in this book but also in the archives of said convent, in the book of antiquities, referred to in the Annals of Catalunya" [Así se narra no solamente en este libro si(no) también en el Archivo de dicho convento, lib. de Antiquitat, referido en los Anales de Cataluña]. Domenge's manuscript originally formed part of the convent archive, which was probably obtained by the university library in the nineteenth century (the manuscript's history is not available at the library); I have not been able to locate the references made here. Although the word *calificar* (to judge) carried connotations of condemnation in the seventeenth century, here it clearly means that Domenge was exonerated. See Sebastián de Covarrubias, *Tesoro de la lengua castellana o española,* ed. Martín de Riquer (1611; 1617; Barcelona: Editorial Alta Fulla, 1987), 269.

5. . . . no quisieron venir a esto, diciendo que no era de su religión horas de oración, que eso eran cosas de descalzos y de franciscanos.

6. Bilocation is the ability to be in two places at the same time and was a prac-

tice traditionally ascribed to the Virgin, whose supernatural powers were often attributed to holy women in the seventeenth century. The famous case of Sor María de Ágreda, who supposedly appeared to natives in New Mexico in 1629 to preach to them and baptize them while also in her convent cell in Spain, is exemplary. Sor María was investigated by the Inquisition in 1635; she was an adviser and favorite of King Philip IV and was never formally tried. For a sensitive and sensible interpretation of these events and their influence on Ágreda's famous book about the Virgin, *The Mystical City of God,* see Kate Risse, "Strategy of a Provincial Nun" (paper presented at the Kentucky Foreign Language Conference, Lexington, April 1996).

7. Antonio Márquez, *Literatura e Inquisición en España, 1478–1834* (Madrid: Taurus Ediciones, S.A., 1980), 45.

8. The tribunal to which Domenge was taken is not specified in the manuscript. She reports being at Santa Catalina, a Dominican convent in Barcelona, when arrested but describes herself as wanting to return to Perpignan, where presumably she was living. The tribunal in Perpignan functioned but sporadically, and Henry Charles Lea finds no evidence that it was extant after 1566. See his *History of the Inquisition of Spain* (New York: Macmillan, 1906–7), 2:552.

9. See ibid., 2:465, 1:461–82. Lea's book is quite out of date yet is the only one to deal specifically with the Catalan tribunals. The history of the Inquisition in Catalonia awaits study; what records are extant are in Simancas. I have been unable to determine whether Domenge's trial documents are there.

10. Lea offers comparative statistics of sentences executed by the various tribunals, largely from the early sixteenth century (ibid., 4:524).

11. See entry for October 20 in *Manual de novells ardits, vulgarment apellat Dietari del Antich Consell Barceloní, 1609–1619* (Barcelona: Ajuntament, 1900).

12. I thank Juan de Déu Domenech, a historian of Barcelona, for this information.

13. Cuando el alcalde y secretario me tuvieron dentro de la prisión, se pusieron a llorar y me dijeron, "Para mujer, muy cruel y muy desierta es esta prisión, mas los señores inquisidores nos han mandado que diésemos esta prisión." Y me consolaron y me decían que el Padre Ignacio había estado dos veces a la Inquisición y San Pedro mártir, que era de mi santa religión, que también había estado y que era buen padre el bendito San Domingo y que él me sacaría. En fin, me hicieron caridad de consolarme con vidas de santos. Y el secretario dijo al alcalde, "Señor, traiga aquí una silla, que lástima es dejar aquí una mujer entre tanta bruticia." Y esto lo decía con lágrimas. Y dichas estas palabras me dejaron en la dicha prisión y me cerraron con dos puertas.

14. Y yo, viéndome así cerrada, alcé los ojos al cielo y dije, "Señor, vos lo queréis, y pues vos lo queréis, yo lo quiero, que más que esto es deseo yo padecer por

vos. No digo yo, Señor, estar en esta prisión entre tanta bruticia sino estar en medio de una rueda de navajas, si es de gusto y contento de vuestra majestad estaré yo por mis pecados." Esto decía yo con muchas lágrimas, que consideraba yo que más que esto merecía yo por mis pecados. Y cuando yo decía estas palabras, Jesús Cristo, mi esposo, me llamó y me dijo estas palabras. "Sor Ana, religiosa del Padre San Domingo, ¿de qué te afliges? ¿No estoy yo en la cárcel con tú?" ("Con tú" is a Catalanism, one of many in the manuscript.)

15. "Di, ¿tú no eres mi esposa? Y yo respondí, 'Si, Señor. Yo esposa soy de Jesús de Nazaret.' Díjome, 'Pues eres mi esposa, ¿por qué te afliges tanto? No me has tú dicho muchas veces que deseabas padecer por mí?' Y yo respondí, 'Sí señor.'"

16. "No me has demandado tú que querrás ser mártir muchas veces?" Y yo respondí, "Sí señor."

17. Domenge identified 1610 as the date of her imprisonment in the first sentence of the manuscript, cited above; the year 1611 cited here, then, probably refers to when she dictated the account: por mandarme mi confesor hago escribir esto, cuando yo fui a la Santa Inquisición, el año de 1611.

18. San Juan de Ávila, *Obras completas,* 6 vols., ed. Luis Sala Balust (Madrid: Editorial Católica, 1970), 3:249, 250.

19. The phrase from Isa. 24:16, "My secret for me," with which Angela of Folignio (d. 1309) and other women of the premodern era were able to keep men from meddling in their spiritual intimacies, was unavailable to women as a protective device by the time of the Spanish Inquisition, as this quote makes evident. See Elizabeth Rhodes, "Women on Their Knees: Pornography and Female Religious Discourse in Early Modern Spain" (lecture at the Women's Studies Seminar, Center for Cultural and Literary Studies, Harvard University, Cambridge, Mass., February 1993).

20. Yo estaba temerosa que no quería escribir las misericordias que el Señor me hacía por ver no era digna de recibirlas y aunque mi confesor me lo había mandado lo hiciese, con todo temía y quería callarlas. Y el Señor me dijo "Esposa mía, no temas. Dirás a tu confesor cuando venga que es mi voluntad que escribas mis misericordias y que los que se aparejaran a servirme y a amarme perfectamente, yo les haré mayores misericordias que a tú."

21. Yo no sé por qué me tienen aquí. [Si es] por lo de la oración que me tienen, los predicadores lo predican.

22. Ha sido mi voluntad que las criaturas te persiguiesen y te murmurasen y así de mi voluntad que vinieses a la Santa Inquisición.

23. . . . porque se declarasen mis secretos y [tesoros)] del cielo en mi santo tribunal, adonde se declaran las verdades y donde [se] representa mi persona. The manuscript says "tresores," a defective Catalanism (*tresors* is "treasures" in Catalan).

24. For example, María Legarda was tried by the Toledo tribunal in 1639–42 as "a false saint, haughty and reckless" [santa fingida, soberbia temeraria] who "tried to be a saint on many occasions and in different homes and has told different people the many mercies which Our Lord shows her . . . and although many people, ecclesiastical as well as secular, reprehended her, telling her to keep quiet . . . she did not do so, rather showed resentment that they would so advise her, all of which is contrary to true virtue" [trató de ser santa, en muchas ocasiones y en diferentes casas y a diferentes personas ha dicho las muchas mercedes que Nuestro Señor le hace . . . y aunque muchas personas, así eclesiásticas como seglares, le reprehendían, diciéndole que callase . . . no lo hizo, antes mostraba sentimiento de que la aconsejasen, siendo todo contrario a verdadera virtud]. The list of complaints brought against her is found in María de la Encarnación [Maseda y Legarda], Caso, Alumbrados y iluminados, Inquisición, Toledo, Archivo Histórico Nacional (AHN), Inq. leg. 104, exp. 2; leg. 102, exp. 2, fols. 160–69. Turned in for the second time by her female neighbors in 1649, Legarda claimed that the women who had reported her were her "capital enemies" [enemigas capitales] (55v). Virgilio Pinto Crespo considers a similar case, technically one of false sanctity, as mere disobedience of the woman's confessor in "La difusión de la literatura espiritual en el Madrid del Siglo XVII: Los textos de María Bautista," *Edad de Oro* 12 (1993): 243–55.

25. Estos santos se desaparecieron, mas se quedó Santo Tomás de Aquino conmigo y se estuvo todo el tiempo que estaba presa, que nunca me desampara, siempre me acompañaba.

26. Raymond of Capua's highly influential *Vida de la bienaventurada santa Caterina de Sena* (Alcalá: Guillén de Brocar, 1511) was among the books Cardinal Ximénez de Cisneros had translated from Latin into Spanish specifically for placement in convents, where women could have access to them. It is hagiography, hardly a historical account, yet many women authors of seventeenth-century Spain represent themselves as imitating Catherine's behavior, particularly her practices of mortification and dietary habits (Catherine starved herself to death).

27. Teresa does mention angels and some saints in her writings, but they are what she calls intellectual, not physical, visions and are insignificant relative to the intimacy she communicates between her soul and Christ. For example, from her spiritual diary, now called her "Cuentas de conciencia": "In the Prioress's chair I saw a great multitude of angels descend with the Mother of God and settle there. . . . They seemed to me to be . . . angels, although not with bodily form, since it was an intellectual vision" [Vi en la silla prioral . . . bajar con gran multitud de ángeles la Madre de Dios y ponerse allí. . . . Parecíanme . . . ángeles, aunque no con forma corporal, que era visión intelectual] (Santa Teresa de Avila,

Obras completas, 8th ed., Biblioteca de Autores Cristianos 12, ed. Efren de la Madre de Dios and Otger Steggink [Madrid: Editorial Católica, 1986], 602).

28. The *Vida maravillosa de la venerable virgen doña Marina de Escobar* (Madrid: Francisco Nieto María, 1665) was written by Escobar's confessor, the Jesuit Luis de la Puente, himself quite a figure, known for ecstasies in which light filled his cell, levitations to great heights in which the entire building he was in would shake, prophecies, and mind reading.

29. There is a later reference to how the priests leading the procession had complained about the heat and their sore feet (38v).

30. Habiendo aquí en Perpignan una grande necesidad de agua, se hacían muchas procesiones, e hicieron una del devoto crucifijo de San Juan, que dicen es uno de los que hizo Nicodemos y dicen nunca habían sacado esta santa figura sin que lloviese luego. Esta procesión la hicieron de noche. No fue servido Nuestro Señor servido de dar agua. A las apariencias parecía iba la procesión muy devota, que iban las religiones y muchos disciplinantes y habían acudido la gente de los lugares. Preguntamos a nuestra madre qué era la causa de que Nuestro Señor no nos hacía misericordia de llover. Nos dijo que la procesión que habían hecho no era como había de ser, que Nuestro Señor la había dicho habían hecho complacencias en ella y que no habían pasado su santa figura por donde la habían de pasar, sino que habían torcido el camino por hacer complacencias y que también la había dicho Nuestro Señor que importaba que los disciplinantes derramasen la sangre hasta la tierra si no se habían confesado y que después de venidos de la procesión, muchos habían ido a ofender a su divina majestad mortalmente. Nos dijo Nuestro Señor, "Esposa mía, no abriré los cielos hasta que vuelvan a hacer una procesión de mi santa figura y que pasen por donde pasan la del santísimo sacramento, y que después haya llovido hagan otra, dándome gracias." Y después de esto la habló Santo Tomás Aquino y la dijo la orden que se había de tener para que Nuestro Señor usase de misericordia con Perpignan.

31. Merry Wiesner describes this process of increased enclosure in the secular and religious environments in *Women and Gender in Early Modern Europe* (Cambridge: Cambridge University Press, 1994).

32. Yo no quería decir [lo] de los sacerdotes, y el Señor me dijo "Esposa mía, no temas. Escríbelo y dirás a tu confesor, 'Padre, Jesu Cristo mi esposo me ha dicho que no temiese sino que lo escribiese,'" y que así como creo en los artículos de la fe y en los mandamientos de la iglesia santa, así ha de creer Vuestra Reverencia que Jesu Cristo mi esposo me ha dicho que escriba esto.

33. R. I. Moore says, "Heresy (unlike Judaism or leprosy) can only arise in the context of the assertion of authority, which the heretic resists, and is therefore by definition a political matter" (*The Formation of a Persecuting Society* [Oxford: Blackwell, 1987], 68–72). By the 1600s, the question was by no means that simple,

as Francisco Peñas's 1578 rendition of Nicholau Eimeric's *Inquisitor's Manual* makes clear (see the section on heretics in *El manual de los Inquisidores,* trans. Francisco Martín, ed. Luis Sala-Molins [Barcelona: Muchnik, 1983], 58–113). Still, the overall leniency of the Spanish Inquisition in cases of witchcraft, which was generally believed to be delusion and evidence of ignorance, suggests that the original definition of heresy still held sway. On the Inquisition's evaluation of female discourse, see Claire Guilhem, "La Inquisición y la devaluación del verbo femenino," in *Inquisition española: Poder política y control social,* ed. Bartolomé Bennassar (1979; Barcelona: Crítica, 1984), 171–207.

34. Yo quise obedecer a los Señores Inquisidores por ver era la voluntad de Nuestro Señor que aquel Santo Tribunal representa la persona de Nuestro Señor.

35. Teresa says, "If I thought there were reason for me to fear the Inquisition, I would turn myself in" [si pensase había para qué (temer la Inquisición), yo me la iría a buscar] (*Obras,* 180).

36. I have punctuated the final sentence to accommodate the abrupt change in point of view, although it likely went unnoticed by Domenge. The game playing here recalls a sermon attributed to the Franciscan tertiary Juana de la Cruz (1481–1534) in which God repeatedly requests to play with the Virgin's breasts; Ronald Surtz rightly suspects child abuse (*Writing Women in Late Medieval and Early Modern Spain* [Philadelphia: University of Pennsylvania Press, 1995], 124–25). Certainly the echo here of an elderly male figure "playing" with a grown woman may suggest the same: El Señor me dijo, "Esposa mía, ¿quieres jugar?" Y yo dije, "Sí señor." "¿No ves cuánto te quiero? ¿No ves cuánto te amo, que vengo a jugar contigo y tú juegas conmigo? Yo te regalo con aquellos juegos celestiales. Y dirás a tu confesor, 'Padre, Jesucristo mi esposo me ha dicho que dijese a Vuestra Reverencia que mi esposo Jesús jugaba conmigo con aquellos juegos celestiales.' Y dirásle que son unos juegos tan suaves y tan dulces y con tanta suavidad que 'mi ánima quedaba muy contenta y muy animosa para más servir y agradar a su divina majestad.'"

37. As the seventeenth century progressed, the role of the confessor became increasingly pronounced, not only in the recording of women's visions but also in their reception, and Christ often delivers messages to women destined for their male supervisors. María Legarda, who describes herself as always being visited by Christ at night, recalls (through her scribe) "that he came another night and he told her who he was and asked her to keep quiet about it and she asked him 'Lord, not even my confessor?' And he responded, "Your confessor yes, and tell him that your Master came at eleven at night" [que otra noche vino y que le dijo quién era y le pidió a ésta que callase y ésta le dijo, "Señor, ¿ni a mi confesor?" Y él le respondió, "A tu confesor sí, y dile que tu Dueño vino a las once de la noche," np].

38. ¿Por qué me ruegas por las monjas valencianas, pues ellas no quieren hacer mi santa voluntad ni responder a mis santas inspiraciones ni darte crédito ni poner la oración santa, que todo lo que anoche dijo en el capítulo la priora eran industrias y os quieren engañar. . . . Dirás a tu confesor y a tus hijas que yo quería castigar a la priora si no [fuera] por tus ruegos.

39. The tenses are confused in both sentences: No me ruegues por estas monjas, que las quiero enviar un castigo. La priora del mal del brazo y la superiora del desmayo que ha tenido hoy quedarán sin vida si no [fuera] por lo que tú me has rogado.

40. Cited by Amy Hollywood, who discusses Feuerbach's theory, in "Beauvoir, Irigaray, and the Mystical," *Hypatia* 9 (1994): 175.

41. Yo me he de ir a padecer. Acompaña tú a mi preciosa madre que está muy afligida en medio de tantas angustias y dolores y la mañana de Pascua, después que yo me habré parecido a mi preciosa madre y a las Marías, ya me aparecerá a ti.

42. De entre las cinco lágrimas, es ésa la una y es mi voluntad que esa gota que salió de mis preciosos ojos esté en este convento, que yo soy el fundador de él y tú, esposa mía, eres el instrumento como esposa mía. Mi preciosa lágrima estaba en Roma y un Cardenal la llevó a Brulla y la dejó allí, y yo he expirado a la religiosa que la tenía porque allí la tenían en poca veneración.

CHAPTER 8 · MARÍA DE JESÚS DE AGREDA

1. Alison Weber has pointed out women's gains in the Spain of the years prior to the Council of Trent and women's strategies for retaining power and voice during the following century. See Weber, *Teresa of Avila and the Rhetoric of Femininity* (Princeton: Princeton University Press, 1990), 35.

2. The most thoroughly documented historical study of Sor María's contact with the Inquisition is that of the late Joaquín Pérez Villanueva, who for several years was president of the Center for Inquisition Studies operated in Madrid by the Consejo de Investigación Científica. See his *Sor María de Agreda y Felipe IV: Un epistolario en su tiempo*, vol. 4 of *Historia de la Iglesia en España*, 5 vols. (Madrid: Biblioteca de Autores Cristianos, 1979), 347, 378–90.

3. Ibid., 384.

4. Pérez Villanueva examines the baptismal controversy in detail in relation to the Inquisition's recurring questioning of Sor María on the subject. See Joaquín Pérez Villanueva, "Algo más sobre la Inquisición y Sor María de Agreda: La prodigiosa evangelización americana," *Hispania Sacra* 37 (1985): 597–602.

5. Benavides promoted the idea of a New Mexican bishopric and himself as the first bishop. The idea did not become a reality during his lifetime. See John L. Kessell, "Miracles or Mystery: María de Agreda's Ministry to the Jumano In-

dians of the Southwest in the 1620s," in *Great Mysteries of the West* (Golden, Colo.: Fulcrum, 1993), 124–27.

6. The paired letters from Benavides and Sor María can be consulted in Alonso Benavides and María de Jesús de Agreda, "Tanto que se sacó de una carta . . . ," Mexico City, 1730, reprinted in Francisco Palou, *Evangelista del Mar Pacífico: Fray Junípero Serra* (Madrid: Aguilar, 1944), 308–17. I also recently republished an English translation; see Clark Colahan, *Writing Knowledge and Power: The Visions of Sor María de Agreda* (Tucson: University of Arizona Press, 1994), 104–15.

7. For a fuller discussion of psychological as well as rhetorical strategies for feminine self-esteem used by Teresa of Avila and Margery Kempe, as well as by Sor María, see my observations, *Writing Knowledge and Power,* 149–50.

8. Cited by Pérez Villanueva, "Algo más sobre la Inquisición," 8.

9. Ibid., 11.

10. Cited in Pérez Villanueva, *Sor María,* 385.

11. Ibid.

12. Ibid.

13. De la historia de la Reina del cielo no han dicho nada: no lo deben saber. Hasta que se aquiete esta tormenta, mejor está oculta. Cited in Pérez Villanueva, *Sor María,* 378.

14. Sor María, who was of Jewish descent, was the author of a short treatise with unmistakable Cabalistic overtones on the six guardian angels who reportedly watched over and conversed with her. See Celia Weller and Clark Colahan, "An Angelic Epilogue," *Studia Mystica* 13 (1990): 50–59.

15. The treatise is entitled *Face of the Earth and Map of the Spheres* (Redondez de la tierra y mapa de los orbes celestes). It has been published only in my English translation, *Writing Knowledge and Power,* 47–91. On Sor María's education, see 39–40.

16. No descubriéndose el Señor en sí mismo, sino mediatamente al entendimiento con presencia intelectual, especie de visión intuitiva. Que no enseña la presencia real, aunque la contiene, y así es fácil que la criatura y el Padre espiritual a quien se comunica esta visión se engañen y se piense que eso es ver la divinidad, cuando eso es propio sólo de los bienaventurados. Cited in Pérez Villanueva, *Sor María,* 387.

17. Cited by Pérez Villanueva, "Algo más sobre la Inquisición," 586.

18. Pérez Villanueva, *Sor María,* 387.

19. Ibid., 388.

20. Ibid., 389.

21. Ibid., 390.

22. Her report has been published only in my English version (*Writing*

Knowledge and Power, 115–27): it is based on manuscripts that I transcribed and compared in the Spanish National Library. To date I have been unable to find a publisher for the work in its original Spanish.

23. Rosa Rossi has stressed these dangers in working with memoirs in her *Teresa de Avila: Biografía de una escritora*, trans. Marieta Gargatagli (Barcelona: Icaria, 1984). For the relevance of these concerns to Sor María's case, see my remarks, *Writing Knowledge and Power*, 17.

CHAPTER 9 · CONTESTED IDENTITIES

1. Archivo Histórico Nacional (hereafter AHN), Inquisición, legajo 2075, número 31, "Relación de causas de fe," contains the report of the fifty people penanced at the 1624 auto-da-fé in Seville, including two from the "sect of Muhammed," thirty-seven Judaizers, and eleven (including Beatriz de Robles) from the "sect of Alumbrados," of whom one had already died in prison. All subsequent references to this case are from this document. All quotations use the spelling and punctuation as they appear in documents, and unless otherwise noted, all translations are by me. See also Antonio Domínguez Ortiz, *Autos de la Inquisición de Sevilla (siglo XVII)* (Seville: Servicio de Publicaciones del Ayuntamiento, 1981), 81. I want to thank Carole Levin and Esther Cope for helpful comments on an earlier version of this chapter, and Mary Giles, Deborah Martinson, and Daniel Feinstein for their lively assistance as I wrote the present version.

2. AHN, Inquisición, libro 1299, contains the Illuminist heresies identified in 1525. For more on the heresy of the Free Spirit, see Norman Cohn, *The Pursuit of the Millennium: Revolutionary Messianism in Medieval and Reformation Europe and Its Bearing on Modern Totalitarian Movements* (New York: Harper Torchbooks, 1961), 170, 186–87.

3. The 1624 report is from Archivo Municipal de Sevilla, *Efemérides*, "Noticias y casos," número 1. Two excellent sources for more information on the alumbrados are Alvaro Huerga, *Predicadores, alumbrados e inquisición* (Madrid: Fundación Universitaria Española, 1973), and Antonio Márquez, *Los alumbrados: Orígenes y filosofía, 1525–1559*, 2d ed. (Madrid: Taurus Ediciones, S.A., 1980). The formal edict pronouncing this a heresy is in AHN, Inquisición, legajo 107, número 10.

4. Boundaries, of course, exist at many different levels. Two stimulating and very different books that discuss some of these levels include Fredrik Barth, ed., *Ethnic Groups and Boundaries* (Boston: Little, Brown and Co., 1969), and Peter Sahlins, *Boundaries: The Making of France and Spain in the Pyrenees* (Berkeley: University of California Press, 1989).

5. Useful here is the discussion of feminist theory in Toril Moi, *Sexual/Textual Politics: Feminist Literary Theory* (London: Methuen, 1985), 12–13, and esp. 158–67.

6. The original text in Spanish reads: despues de aver comulgado daba mu-

chos bramidos temblores y algunas veces se ademava a la pared i se quedava alforta como sin sentido y dava suspiros.

See the accusation of Teresa of Avila as an alumbrada in AHN, Inquisición, legajo 2072, número 43; Claire Guilhem, "L'Inquisition et la dévaluation des discours féminins," in Bartolomé Bennassar et al., *L'Inquisition espagnole, XV–XIX siècles* (Paris: Hachette, 1979), 197–240; Jesús Imirizaldu, *Monjas y beatas embaucadoras* (Madrid: Editorial Nacional, 1977); and Mary Elizabeth Perry, "Beatas and the Inquisition in Early Modern Seville," in *Inquisition and Society in Early Modern Europe,* ed. Stephen Haliczer (London: Croom Helm, 1986), 147–68.

7. Elizabeth Alvida Petroff, ed., *Medieval Women's Visionary Literature* (New York: Oxford University Press, 1986), 6. See also Mary E. Giles, *The Feminist Mystic* (1982; New York: Crossroad, 1987).

8. Paul Julian Smith, *The Body Hispanic: Gender and Sexuality in Spanish and Spanish American Literature* (Oxford: Clarendon Press, 1989), 24.

9. Moi, *Sexual/Textual Politics,* quotes Luce Irigaray in saying that mystical discourse is "the only place in Western history where woman speaks and acts in such a public way" (quoted here 136). Angela Muñoz Fernández, *Acciones e intenciones de mujeres en la vida religiosa de los siglos XV y XVI* (Madrid: Dirección General de la Mujer, 1995), 95–101, discusses the visionary Juana de la Cruz; she is also the subject of the excellent study of Ronald Surtz, *The Guitar of God: Gender, Power, and Authority in the Visionary World of Mother Juana de la Cruz (1481–1534)* (Philadelphia: University of Pennsylvania Press, 1990).

10. Smith, *The Body Hispanic,* points out that mysticism is the discourse "par excellence" of the other or nonpowerful (iii). For more on beatas, see Muñoz Fernández, *Acciones e intenciones,* 105–21, and Perry, "Beatas and the Inquisition," 147–68.

11. AHN, Inquisición, legajo 2075, número 31; the original text reads: y echandola otras beatas en sus faldas le hacian aire y preguntandoles que tenia respondian que estava lleno de amor de Dios y que se estava abrasando de el.

12. *The Life of S. Teresa of Avila, Including the Relations of Her Spiritual State,* trans. David Lewis (Westminster, Md.: Newman Press, 1962), 66, 394. See Alison Weber, *Teresa of Avila and the Rhetoric of Femininity* (Princeton: Princeton University Press, 1990), for an interesting analysis of Teresa's use of language.

13. For more on this religious figure, see Mary E. Giles, *The Book of Prayer of Sor María of Santo Domingo: A Study and Translation* (Albany: State University of New York Press, 1990).

14. Richard L. Kagan, "Politics, Prophecy, and the Inquisition," in *Cultural Encounters: The Impact of the Inquisition in Spain and the New World,* ed. Mary Elizabeth Perry and Anne J. Cruz (Berkeley: University of California Press, 1991), 118–19; Weber, *Teresa of Avila,* 5.

15. AHN, Inquisición, legajo 2962, tomo 1. For more on Catalina de Jesús, see Perry, "Beatas and the Inquisition."

16. Angela Selke, *El Santo Oficio de la Inquisición: Proceso de Fr. Francisco Ortiz (1529–1532)* (Madrid: Ediciones Guadarrama, 1968); see also Mary Elizabeth Perry, *Gender and Disorder in Early Modern Seville* (Princeton: Princeton University Press, 1990), 83–84, and María Helena Sánchez Ortega, "La mujer, el amor y la religión en el antiguo régimen," in *La mujer en la historia de España (siglos XVI–XX)*, ed. María Angeles Durán (Madrid: Universidad Autónoma, 1984), 35–58.

17. AHN, Inquisición, legajo 2075, número 31; the original text reads: estramuva el cuerpo para ganar opinion de sancta i que se dixese como se decia que Aquello le procedia de amor de Dios.

18. Moi, *Sexual/Textual Politics*, 167, makes this point in her discussion of Julia Kristeva's emphasis on positionality rather than essentialism, arguing that from a phallocentric point of view, women "come to represent the necessary frontier between man and chaos; but because of their very marginality they will also always seem to recede into and merge with the chaos of the outside."

19. Leo Bersani, *Homos* (Cambridge: Harvard University Press, 1995), 12. For some of the details that confessors would be most likely to ask visionaries such as Beatriz, see Diego Pérez de Valdivia, *Aviso de gente recogida* (1585), 2d ed. (Madrid: Universidad Pontificia de Salamanca y Fundación Universitaria Española, 1977); for example, priests had special concern that "spiritual arrogance" in these women brought on false visions by making the devil into an "angel of light," often mistaken for God or Jesus (389, 470, 566–70).

20. Perry, "Beatas and the Inquisition," 156–57.

21. Petroff, *Medieval Women's Visionary Literature*, 36–37. For another discussion of the body and ecstatic visions, see Mary E. Giles, "The Discourse of Ecstasy: Late Medieval Spanish Women and Their Texts," in *Gender and Text in the Later Middle Ages*, ed. Jane Chance (University Press of Florida, 1996), 306–30.

22. Margaret Hunt discusses the erotic component of religious devotion of this period in her afterword in *Queering the Renaissance* (Durham: Duke University Press, 1994), 360. For more on women's desires, see Rosalind Coward, *Female Desires: How They Are Sought, Bought, and Packaged* (New York: Grove Press, 1985), who argues that women's desires are socially constructed tools to maintain a status quo. Riane Eisler, *Sacred Pleasure: Sex, Myth, and the Politics of the Body* (New York: HarperCollins, 1995), discusses the split between spirituality and sexuality, as does Abdelwahab Bouhdiga, *Sexuality in Islam*, trans. Alan Sheridan (London: Routledge and Kegan Paul, 1985).

23. Moi, *Sexual/Textual Politics*, 160.

24. Ibid.

25. Antonio Gramsci, *Letters from Prison*, ed., trans., and intro. by Lynne Lawner (New York: Harper and Row, 1973), describes the state as "a balance between political society and civil society," by which he means "the hegemony of one social group over the entire nation, exercised through so-called private organizations like the Church, trade unions, or schools" (204). In his *Selections from the Prison Notebooks*, ed. and trans. Quintin Hoare and Geoffrey Nowell-Smith (New York: International Publishers, 1972), Gramsci uses an analogy to trench warfare to describe the state as simply "an outer ditch" buttressed by civil society, which is a "powerful system of fortresses and earthworks" (238).

26. Manning Nash, *The Cauldron of Ethnicity in the Modern World* (Chicago: University of Chicago Press, 1989), discusses cultural marks of difference and religion as a marker of difference (35 and esp. 38); he describes a "civil-religious hierarchy" that unifies people and maintains their boundaries against outsiders (103).

27. Not all clerics looked unfavorably on Moriscos; some worked patiently with them to make them into good Christians, while others sought to incorporate Muslim traditions into Christian liturgy as a way to facilitate their conversion. See, e.g., Francisco Borja de Medina, S.I., "La Compañía de Jesús y la minoría morisca (1545–1614)," *Archivum Historicum Societatis Iesu* 57 (1988): 3–136.

28. For more information, see Antonio Domínguez Ortiz and Bernard Vincent, *Historia de los moriscos: Vida y tragedia de una minoría* (Madrid: Revista de Occidente, 1978), and Mark Meyerson, *The Muslims of Valencia in the Age of Fernando and Isabel: Between Coexistence and Crusade* (Berkeley: University of California Press, 1991).

29. For more on *taqiyya*, see "Respuesta que hizo el mufti de Oran a ciertas preguntas que le hicieron desde la Andalucía," dated May 3, 1563, reprinted in Mercedes García Arenal, *Los moriscos* (Madrid: Editora Nacional, 1975), 44–45; H. Lammens, *Islam: Beliefs and Institutions*, trans. Sir E. Denison Ross (London: Methuen, 1968), 168; *Shorter Encyclopaedia of Islam*, ed. H. A. R. Gibb and J. H. Kramers (Ithaca, N.Y.: Cornell University Press, 1961), 561–62; and also surah 16:106 of *The Holy Qur-an: Text, Translation, and Commentary*, 2 vols., transl. and comm. by Abdullah Yusuf Ali (Cambridge, Mass.: Hafner Publishing Co., 1946), 1:685.

30. See the "Informe de Madrid a Valencia sobre instrucción de los moriscos," reprinted in Mercedes García-Arenal, *Los moriscos*, 122; Ricardo García Cárcel, *Herejía y sociedad en el siglo XVI: La Inquisición en Valencia, 1530–1609* (Barcelona: Ediciones Penínsulas, 1980), 229; and Bernard Vincent, *Minorías y marginados en la España del siglo XVI* (Granada: Diputación de Granada, 1987), 139. For more information on *taqiyya*, see Lammens, *Islam*, 168–75.

31. *Constituciones del Arçobispado de Sevilla* (Seville: Alonso Rodríguez Gamarra, 1609), 19–20.

32. Archivo General de Simancas (hereafter AGS), Camara de Castilla, legajo 2196.

33. "Traslado de la cédula real que se publicó en la ciudad de Córdova a diez y siete días del mes de Enero," Córdova, 1610, ms. V.E. 36-4 in the Biblioteca Nacional (hereafter BN); this document is also available in the Archivo Municipal de Sevilla, sección 4, tomo 23, no. 35.

34. Don Juan de Mendoça, "Declaración del Bando que se a publicado de la expulsion de los Moriscos," Seville, February 13, 1610, BN ms. V.E. 44-68.

35. Pascual Boronat y Barrachina, *Los moriscos españoles y su expulsión: Estudio histórico-crítico,* 2 vols. (Valencia: Francisco Vives y Mora, 1901), 1:550. The expulsion decrees and the king's explanation for them are in BN, ms. V.E. 195-19, "Cedula Real sobre los moriscos," and BN, ms. V.E. 44-68, "Declaración del Bando que se a publicado de la expulsión de los moriscos." Philip III's letter to prelates is reprinted in Ignacio Bauer Landauer, *Papeles de mi archivo: Relaciones y manuscritos moriscos* (Madrid: Editorial Ibero-Africano-Americana, n.d.), 167.

36. Vincent, *Minorías,* 49. Note that Old Christian women in Spain also married early, usually at the age of eighteen or nineteen. Vincent shows that there is only a twelve- or fourteen-month difference between the two groups.

37. Pedro de Castro y Quiñones, archbishop of Granada, and other clerics believed the books of lead were divine writings, but those who doubted them succeeded in having the dispute submitted to Rome in 1641. For a contemporary view supporting their veracity, see Adam Centurion, *Información para la historia del Sacromonte, llamado de Valparaiso y antiguamente Illipulitano junto a Granada,* parte 1 (1632), ms. 56-3 detrás 13 in the Biblioteca Capitular de Sevilla; for a more recent view, see Américo Castro, *The Spaniards: An Introduction to Their History,* trans. Willard F. King and Selma Margaretten (Berkeley: University of California Press, 1971), 238–40.

38. For laws against Muslim cultural practices, see Domínguez Ortiz and Vincent, *Historia de los moriscos,* and Mary Elizabeth Perry, "Moriscas and the Limits of Assimilation," in *Christians, Muslims, and Jews in Medieval and Early Modern Spain: Interaction and Cultural Change,* ed. Mark D. Meyerson (Notre Dame: University Press of Notre Dame, forthcoming); an interesting list of offending Morisco behaviors is in AHN, Inquisición, libro 1244, "Edicto de la fe." For purity-of-blood statutes, see Albert A. Sicroff, *Los estatutos de limpieza de sangre: Controversias entre los siglos XV y XVII* (Madrid: Taurus Ediciones, S.A., 1985).

39. Compare her palimpsestic subversion with that of women writers discussed in Gilbert and Gubar and critiqued by Moi, *Sexual/Textual Politics,* 59.

40. The quotation is from Domínguez Ortiz and Vincent, *Historia de los moriscos,* 150; for women as preservers of Muslim culture, see García Cárcel, *Herejía*

y sociedad, 229; Mary Elizabeth Perry, "Behind the Veil: Moriscas and the Politics of Resistance and Survival," in *Spanish Women in the Golden Age: Images and Realities,* ed. Alain Saint-Saëns and Magdalena Sánchez (Westport, Conn.: Greenwood Press, 1996); and Vincent, *Minorías,* 139.

41. Moi, *Sexual/Textual Politics,* 7–8, critiques this assumption about individual identity, which is also made by many Anglo-American feminists.

42. Domínguez Ortiz and Vincent, *Historia de los moriscos,* 153; see also Luce López Baralt, *San Juan de la Cruz y el Islam* (Madrid: Hiperión, 1990), and Luce López Baralt, *Islam in Spanish Literature: From the Middle Ages to the Present,* trans. Andrew Hurley (Leiden: E. J. Brill, 1992).

43. José Jiménez Lozano, *Judíos, moriscos y conversos* (Valladolid: Ambito, 1982), 97, and Anwar G. Chejne, *Islam and the West: The Moriscos* (Albany: State University of New York Press, 1983), 32.

44. *Aljamiado* literature is an especially rich source for finding examples of shared stories and traditions; see, for example, F. Guillén Robles, *Leyendas de José Hij de Jacob y de Alejandro Magna sacadas de dos manuscritos moriscos de la Biblioteca Nacional de Madrid* (Zaragoza: Hospicio Provincial, 1818); A. R. Nykel, *A Compendium of Aljamiado Literature* (New York: Macon, Protat Freres, 1929), esp. 29–30; and Antonio Vespertino Rodríguez, ed., *Leyendas aljamiadas y moriscas sobre personajes bíblicos* (Madrid: Editorial Gredos, 1983).

45. José María Delgado Gallego, "Maurofilia y maurofobia, ¿dos caras de las misma moneda?" in *Narraciones moriscas* (Seville: Editoriales Andaluzas Unidas, 1986), 21, points out that Moriscos accepted the Immaculate Conception while insisting that because Jesus was born of a human mother, he was not, himself, divine.

46. "Del nacimiento de Içe," in F. Guillen Robles, *Leyendas moriscas,* 3 vols. (Madrid: M. Tello, 1885), 1:122–28. The quoted passage reads: No hay señor sino Allah; yo soy Jesús, espíritu de Allah y su palabra. Note the similarity between this story and the syncretic statement in the leaden books: "There is no god but God, and Jesus is the spirit of God," in López Baralt, *Islam in Spanish Literature,* 200.

47. Guillen Robles, *Leyendas moriscas,* 1:29, and Vespertino Rodríguez, *Leyendas aljamiadas y moriscas,* esp. 300–325.

48. According to the legend, tall celestial women attended Aminah at the birth and sang this praise to her, as quoted in Chejne, *Islam and the West,* 99–100.

49. Ibn Khaldun, *The Muqaddimah: An Introduction to History,* 3 vols., trans. Franz Rosenthal (New York: Pantheon, 1958), 3:76.

50. Lammens, *Islam,* 117; Ibn Khaldun, *The Muqaddimah,* 100; López Baralt, *Islam in Spanish Literature,* 42–43, identifies the Shadhilites of North Africa as the Sufi sect most connected with Illuminism.

51. Carol Christ, *Diving Deep and Surfacing: Women Writers on Spiritual Quest* (Boston: Beacon, 1980), 17–18.

52. Al-Ghazzali is quoted in Ira M. Lapidus, *A History of Islamic Societies* (Cambridge: Cambridge University Press, 1988), 199; for Christian women, see Marcel Bataillon, *Erasmo y España: Estudios sobre la historia espiritual del siglo XVI*, 2 vols. (Mexico City: Fondo de Cultura Económica, 1950), 1:207.

53. Márquez, *Alumbrados*, 62. See also Perry, *Gender and Disorder*, 97–117.

54. The first quotation is from Farid al-Din 'Attar and the second is from Muhammed Zihni, both quoted in Margaret Smith, *Rab'ia the Mystic and Her Fellow-Saints in Islam: Being the Life and Teachings of Rab'ia al-'Adawiyya Al-Qaysiyya of Basra Together with Some Account of the Place of the Women Saints in Islam* (Cambridge: Cambridge University Press, 1984), 3–4.

55. Farid al-Din 'Attar, quoted in Smith, *Rab'ia the Mystic*, 3.

56. Quoted in Smith, *Rab'ia the Mystic*, 28.

57. López Baralt, *Islam in Spanish Literature*, makes a convincing argument that Islamic influences have remained powerful in Spanish mysticism and writing.

58. Giles makes these important points in "Discourse of Ecstasy," 306, 313–15, and 325, esp.

59. See, for example, the edict of grace for newly converted Muslims in Seville, in AHN, Inquisición, libro 1254, fol. 254; the "Instrucción de los moriscos valencianos," reprinted in García-Arenal, *Los moriscos*, 106–16; and *Constituciones*, 19–20. The report of Beatriz de Robles's case contains no mention of Muslim traditions and "sins."

60. "Memorial de la secta de los alumbrados de Sevilla y de sus doctrinas y delictos y de la complicidad que en ella se ha descubierto 1625," reprinted in Bernardino Llorca, "Documentos inéditos interesantes sobre los alumbrados de Sevilla de 1623–1628," *Estudios Eclesiásticos* 2 (1932): 268–84, 404–18. See also Antonio Domínguez Ortiz, "La Congregación de Granada y la Inquisición de Sevilla (un episodio de la lucha contra los alumbrados)," in *La Inquisición española: Nueva visión, nuevos horizontes*, ed. Joaquin Pérez Villanueva (Madrid: Siglo XXI, 1980), 636–46.

61. Perry, *Gender and Disorder*, 107–8. For an example of visionaries claiming to speak for God about political figures, see Kagan, "Politics, Prophecy, and the Inquisition"; for a discussion of the case of Lucrecia de León, who foretold the defeat of the Spanish Armada in 1588 as the result of the "bad government" and the personal sins of Philip II, see esp. 115.

62. For discussion of a visionary who was accused of these things, see Giles, *Book of Prayer*, esp. 21–38.

63. Gustav Henningsen, *The Witches' Advocate: Basque Witchcraft and the Spanish Inquisition* (Reno: University of Nevada Press, 1980).

64. For more on the intersection of eroticism, sexuality, and power, see Gold-berg, *Queering the Renaissance*, 10, 373.

65. Bersani, *Homos*, 12.

66. Smith, *Hispanic Body*, 25, discusses this experience in the case of Saint Teresa.

67. Bersani, *Homos*, 96–97.

68. Ibid., 32.

CHAPTER 10 · WHEN BIGAMY IS THE CHARGE

1. The majority of works on bigamy focus on male bigamists in different parts of colonial Latin America. Among others, Richard Boyer has just completed an excellent and extensive study of bigamy trials in Mexico, *Lives of the Bigamists: Marriage, Family, and Community in Colonial Mexico* (Albuquerque: University of New Mexico Press, 1995). Alexandra Parma Cook and Noble David Cook's *Good Faith and Truthful Ignorance: A Case of Transatlantic Bigamy* (Durham, N.C.: Duke University Press, 1991) is a charming and clear discussion of the is-sues involved in bigamy trials.

2. Roderick Phillips, *Putting Asunder: A History of Divorce in Western Society* (Cambridge: Cambridge University Press, 1988), 297.

3. Henry Charles Lea, *A History of the Inquisition of Spain* (New York: Mac-millan, 1907), 4:316.

4. Stephen Haliczer, *Inquisition and Society in the Kingdom of Valencia, 1478–1834* (Berkeley: University of California Press, 1990), 300.

5. For an account of this jurisdictional conflict, see Enrique Gacto, "El delito de bigamia y la Inquisición Española," *Anuario de Historia del Derecho Español* 57 (1987): 465–92.

6. See table 1 in Jaime Contreras and Gustav Henningsen, "Forty-four Thou-sand Cases of the Spanish Inquisition (1540–1700): Analysis of a Historical Data Bank," in *The Inquisition in Early Modern Europe: Studies on Sources and Methods*, ed. Gustav Henningsen and John Tedeschi (De Kalb: Northern Illinois Univer-sity Press, 1986), 114.

7. Jaime Contreras, *El Santo Oficio de la Inquisición de Galicia: Poder, sociedad y cultura* (Madrid: Akal, 1982), 17.

8. This correspondence is quoted in ibid., 461.

9. Prior to its establishment in Santiago de Compostela, the region fell under the jurisdiction of the Castilian tribunal in Valladolid. For a complete examina-tion of the tribunal, see ibid.

10. Ibid., 466. By comparison, bigamy made up only 6.3 percent of the cases in the Aragonese tribunal and 5.1 percent of those in Castile. Ibid., 455.

11. Ibid., 648. This ratio of men to women seems to have been consistent

throughout Spain. In Mexico Richard Boyer found a total of thirty-five women (16%), eleven of whom fell during the eighteenth century; see *Lives of the Bigamists*, 8. At the end of the eighteenth century in Portugal and Brazil the bigamists were almost exclusively male; see David Higgs, "Bigamia e migração no Brasil colonial no fim do século XVII," *Anais da VII Reunião da Sociedade Brasileira de Pesquisa Histórica (São Paulo)* (1988): 99–103.

12. Archivo Histórico Nacional (AHN), Sección Inquisición, legajo 2042, no. 41, fol. 25 (1604).

13. Juan Eloy Gelabert González, "Lectura y escritura en una ciudad provinciana del siglo XVI: Santiago de Compostela," *Bulletin Hispanique* 84 (July–December 1982): 268–69. Based only on signatures, his work does not take into account education that included reading only. A number of scholars have used Inquisition records to estimate literacy rates, for instance, Marie-Christine Rodríguez and Bartolomé Bennassar, "Signatures et niveau culturel des témoins et accusés dans les procès d'inquisition du ressort du tribunal de Tolède (1528–1817) et du ressort du tribunal de Cordoue (1595–1632)," *Cahiers du Monde Hispanique et Lusobrésilien* 31 (1978): 19–46.

14. AHN, Sec. Inq., legajo 2042, no. 9, fol. 14 (1582).

15. Ibid., no. 12, fol. 1 (1585).

16. Ibid., no. 34, fol. 6v (1594).

17. Ibid., no. 18, fol. 4v (1587) and no. 41, fol. 26 (1604).

18. Ibid., no. 72, fol. 1–1v (1633), and no. 83, fols. 4v–10 (1642).

19. Ibid., no. 79, fols. 1–4v (1639).

20. For more on inheritance practices in Galicia, see Carmelo Lisón Tolosana, *Antropología cultural de Galicia* (Madrid: Akal, 1979), and Marisa Rey-Henningsen, *The World of the Ploughwoman: Folklore and Reality in Matriarchal Northwest Spain* (Helsinki: Suomalainen Tiedeakatemia, 1994), esp. chaps. 3 and 4.

21. See Antonio Eiras Roel, "Mecanismos autorreguladores, evoluciön demográfica y diversificación intrarregional: El ejemplo de la población de Galicia a finales del siglo XVIII," *Boletín de la Asociación de Demografía Histórica* 8, no. 2 (1990): 51–72.

22. Caroline Brettell, *Men Who Migrate, Women Who Wait: Population and History in a Portuguese Parish* (Princeton: Princeton University Press, 1986), 95.

23. AHN, Sec. Inq., legajo 2042, no. 39, fol. 11 (1602).

24. Ibid., no. 31, fol. 9v (1593).

25. For an extensive analysis of the role of free will in marriage choice, see Patricia Seed, *To Love, Honor, and Obey in Colonial Mexico: Conflicts over Marriage Choice, 1574–1821* (Stanford: Stanford University Press, 1988), esp. 40–41.

26. AHN, Sec. Inq., legajo 2042, no. 5, fol. 1v (1579).

27. Ibid., no. 7, fol. 12v (1581).

28. James Brundage, *Law, Sex, and Marriage in Medieval Society* (Chicago: University of Chicago Press, 1987), 433–34.

29. The average age at first marriage in Galicia during the early modern period was 25.8 years for men and 25.7 for women, compared with 25.4 and 23.7 for the rest of Spain; see Eiras Roel, "Mecanismos Autorreguladores," 71.

30. AHN, Sec. Inq., legajo 2042, no. 64, fol. 12v (1625).

31. The similarities in culture and judicial systems make it easy for historians to compare cases from the Mexican Inquisition with those in Spain.

32. Quoted in Boyer, *Lives of the Bigamists*, 137.

33. For a more extensive discussion of uxorilocal residence in the region, see Brettell's study on northern Portugal, *Men Who Migrate, Women Who Wait*, 156–57.

34. This was particularly true of bigamists in colonial Mexico; see Boyer, *Lives of the Bigamists*, 122–26.

35. AHN, Sec. Inq., legajo 2042, no. 39, fol. 18v (1602).

36. Ibid., fol. 11v (1602), and no. 41, fol. 25 (1604).

37. Ibid., no. 41, fol. 23 (1604).

38. Even after the Council of Trent there was considerable confusion about whether the nuptial blessing could be conferred more than once.

39. AHN, Sec. Inq., legajo 2042, no. 40, fol. 7v (1602–3).

40. Ibid., no. 41, fol. 12 (1604).

41. Ibid., no. 38, fol. 16v (1601–2).

42. Ibid., no. 26, fol. 13v (1591).

43. Ibid., no. 34, fol. 6v (1594).

44. Ibid., no. 10, fol. 8v (1583).

45. Ibid., no. 83, fols. 4–10v (1642).

46. Although the Fifth Lateran Council (1514) had prohibited concubinage and the Council of Trent reiterated the prohibition, the act itself could not be punished by the Inquisition. Instead, the Inquisition pursued those who *said* that sex between single persons was not a sin for the crime of simple fornication. Concubinage could be punished in both civil and ecclesiastical courts but generally seems to have been tolerated.

47. Demographers estimate Galicia's illegitimacy rates at between 5 and 10 percent during the early modern period, while the rates in the rest of Europe hovered around 2 percent. For more on illegitimacy and reputation, see Heidi Kelley, "Unwed Mothers and Household Reputation in a Spanish Galician Community," *American Ethnologist* 18 (August 1991): 565–80.

48. Elizabeth Anne Kuznesof, "The Significance of Marriage among the Working Poor: Female Bigamy Trials in Colonial Mexico" (paper presented to the 1996 Berkshire Conference on the History of Women, University of North Carolina, Chapel Hill, June 6–9, 1996).

49. Unlike Mexico, anthropological studies in Galicia indicate that Castilian notions of honor and shame did not dominate there. Kelley, "Unwed Mothers and Household Reputation."

50. Dolores Enciso Rojas, "Matrimonio y bigamia en la capital del virreinato: Dos alternativas que favorecían del individuo a la vida familiar social," in *Familias novohispanas, siglos XVI al XIX*, ed. Pilar Gonzalbo Aizpuru (Mexico City: Colegio de México, 1991), 132–33.

51. AHN, Sec. Inq., legajo 2042, no. 7, fol. 2 (1581).

52. Henry Kamen, *The Inquisition and Society in Spain in the Sixteenth and Seventeenth Centuries* (Bloomington: Indiana University Press, 1985), 187.

53. Contreras, *Santo Oficio*, 565.

54. AHN, Sec. Inq., legajo 2042, no. 2, fol. IV (1567), cited in Augustin Redondo, "Les empêchements au mariage et leur transgression dans l'Espagne du XVIe siècle," in *Amours Légitimes, Amours Illégitimes en Espagne (XVIe–XVIIe siècles)*, ed. Augustin Redondo (Paris: Publications de la Sorbonne, 1985), 43.

55. For the most complete discussion of the interactions between orality, literacy, and textuality, see Brian Stock, *The Implications of Literacy: Written Language and Models of Interpretation in the Eleventh and Twelfth Centuries* (Princeton: Princeton University Press, 1983).

56. Natalie Zemon Davis has explored the way that early modern French men and women constructed their letters of remission in *Fiction in the Archives: Pardon Tales and Their Tellers in Sixteenth-Century France* (Stanford: Stanford University Press, 1987).

57. See William Monter, *Frontiers of Heresy: The Spanish Inquisition from the Basque Lands to Sicily* (Cambridge: Cambridge University Press, 1990), 32–35.

58. AHN, Sec. Inq., legajo 2042, no. 8, fol. 8v (1581).

59. Ibid., no. 9, fol. 8v (1582).

60. Ibid., no. 70, fol. IV (1631).

61. Natalie Zemon Davis, *Society and Culture in Early Modern France* (Stanford: Stanford University Press, 1975), 100.

CHAPTER 11 · "MORE SINS THAN THE QUEEN OF ENGLAND"

1. Archivo General de la Nación (hereafter AGN), México, Inquisición 210, exp. 3, fols. 307–430, 396v. Licenciado don Alonso de Peralta was then serving as sole inquisitor of the Mexican tribunal.

2. The order to imprison Marina—and to sequester her goods—was given on November 14, 1598, and appears on fol. 309.

3. ". . . poner en execucion cosas tan abominables y torpes que aun al mesmo demonio se ofenderia dellas." Marina de San Miguel, January 25, 1599, fol. 358.

4. So said Peralta during the course of Marina's eleventh confession, fol. 371.

5. See William Monter, "Women and the Italian Inquisitions," in *Women in the Middle Ages and the Renaissance: Literary and Historical Perspectives*, ed. Mary Beth Rose (Syracuse, N.Y.: Syracuse University Press, 1986), 83–85. A case with clear similarities to Marina's (aside from the question of heresy) is discussed by Luisa Ciamitti in "One Saint Less: The Story of Angela Mellini, a Bolognese Seamstress," in *Sex and Gender in Historical Perspective: Selections from "Quaderni Storici,"* ed. Edwin Muir and Guido Ruggiero (Baltimore: Johns Hopkins University Press, 1990), 141–76. For the case of three seventeenth-century *ilusas* from New Spain, see chap. 3 of Solange Alberro's *Inquisición y sociedad en México, 1571–1700* (Mexico City: Fondo de Cultura Económica, 1988).

6. The bishop Gasparo Contarini, in his *De Officio Episcopi* (1516), notes of heresy: "There is no deadlier disease nor anything which, when it destroys the foundations of faith, also suddenly overturns all public order." Quoted in and translated by John C. Olin, *The Catholic Reformation* (New York: Harper and Row, 1969), 105.

Beatas were prominent in various heretic groups of the sixteenth century and were regarded with some suspicion by its end, particularly after the Council of Trent affirmed that female religious were to be cloistered.

7. See Richard Greenleaf, *The Mexican Inquisition of the Sixteenth Century* (Albuquerque: University of New Mexico Press, 1969), 2–8 and passim. Greenleaf's study remains the outstanding work on the sixteenth century. For the general history of the Inquisition in New Spain, see José Toribio Medina, *Historia del Tribunal del Santo Oficio de la Inquisición en México* (1905; Mexico City: Consejo Nacional para la Cultura y las Artes, 1991); Julio Jiménez Rueda, *Herejías y supersticiones en la Nueva España: Los heterodoxos en México* (Mexico City: Imprenta Universitaria, 1946); Solange Alberro, *La actividad del Santo Oficio de la Inquisición en Nueva España, 1571–1700* (Mexico City: INAH, 1981); and Alberro, *Inquisición y sociedad.*

8. Greenleaf, *Mexican Inquisition*, 74–75.

9. Philip II issued the *cédula* founding the tribunal in 1569, but it was not established until the arrival of Inquisitor Pedro Moya de Contreras in September 1571. In 1574 Moya was invested as archbishop of New Spain.

10. Solange Alberro estimates that the Mexican Inquisition's territory comprised some 3 million square kilometers, compared with the 580,000 square kilometers controlled by the peninsular tribunals. See Alberro, *Actividad,* 257.

11. For the problem of jurisdiction over Amerindians, see Greenleaf, *Mexican Inquisition,* 173–74. No similar exemption from inquisitorial prosecution was granted to African slaves.

12. See Alberro, *Actividad,* 258.

13. As measured by the ratio of death penalties to total *procesos.*

14. Alberro, *Inquisición y sociedad.*

15. Alberro notes that the tribunal was founded at a time when the institution was sliding into slow irrevocable decadence on the Iberian peninsula (ibid.). For discussion of the Tridentine character of the Mexican Inquisition, see Richard Boyer, *Lives of the Bigamists: Marriage, Family, and Community in Colonial Mexico* (Albuquerque: University of New Mexico Press, 1995), 17–18, and Stafford Poole, *Pedro Moya de Contreras: Catholic Reform and Royal Power in New Spain, 1571–1591* (Berkeley: University of California Press, 1987), 35–37.

16. See Seymour B. Liebman, *The Enlightened: The Writings of Luis de Carvajal, el Mozo* (Coral Gables: University of Miami Press, 1967), and Liebman, ed., *The Great Auto de Fé of 1649* (Kansas City: Coronado Press, 1974). Alberro gives an estimate of 380 procesos for Judaism during the period 1571–1700 (of a total 2,401).

17. Evidence that the execution of heretics galvanized the city's population comes from 1598 denunciations of another beata, Doña Ana de Guillamas. Witnesses reported that she had discussed the trial and execution of Luis de Carvajal the Younger and had been tempted by the devil, who came to her saying, "poor Carvajal, killed unjustly" [pobre carvajal que lo mataron sin culpa]. See AGN, Inquisición 176, exp. 9, fol. 67.

18. Alberro, *Actividad,* 260. Alberro cites Henningsen's figures for the peninsula.

19. For example, in the seventeenth century alone there were 684 bigamy investigations. See Boyer, *Lives of the Bigamists,* 8. One would not, however, want to trivialize such investigations: a typical seventeenth-century punishment, according to Boyer, consisted of one hundred or two hundred lashes and a five- to seven-year galley term, which many did not survive (232). Ruth Behar's important studies of witchcraft and superstition, particularly among Mexican women, reinforce the notion that such crimes, rather than major heresy, were the bread and butter of inquisitorial activity. See Behar, "Sex and Sin, Witchcraft and the Devil in Late-Colonial Mexico," *American Ethnologist* 14 (1987): 34–54, and "Sexual Witchcraft, Colonialism, and Women's Powers: Views from the Mexican Inquisition," in *Sexuality and Marriage in Colonial Latin America,* ed. Asunción Lavrin (Lincoln: University of Nebraska Press, 1989), 178–206.

20. In her first audience with the inquisitor, on November 20, 1598, Marina said that she was fifty-three years old. Thus she was born either before November 20 in 1545 or between November 20 and December 31 in 1544. This and the following biographical information can be found in the information on genealogy, religious formation, education, life history, and property solicited from Marina, as was customary, during the *preguntas generales.* See fols. 347–50.

21. See Ida Altman, *Emigrants and Society: Extremadura and Spanish America in the Sixteenth Century* (Berkeley: University of California Press, 1984), 229.

22. Altman emphasizes that in the sixteenth century, "emigrating" to the Indies was perceived as similar to joining the army for a while; both were temporary. About 10 percent of emigrants did indeed return to Spain. See ibid., 85, 248.

23. . . . desde su niñez ha tenido un exercicio de oracion ynterior en el qual yba siempre sintiendo grandes regalos de nro señor. Marina neglected to mention this in the discourse of her life but introduced it during her third confession. Marina de San Miguel, November 24, 1598, fol. 351v.

24. Marina de San Miguel, January 26, 1599, fol. 364v. Marina did not mention this in the "discourse of her life" during her first confession, nor, indeed, until her ninth confession.

25. See Mary Elizabeth Perry, "Beatas and the Inquisition in Early Modern Seville," in *Inquisition and Society in Early Modern Europe*, ed. Stephen Haliczer (London: Croom Helm, 1986), 147–67. See also "Chastity and Danger," chap. 5 of Perry's *Gender and Disorder in Early Modern Seville* (Princeton: Princeton University Press, 1990), 97–117.

26. The Colegio de las Niñas was founded by royal decree in December 1552 for the protection and education of poor Spanish and mestiza girls.

27. The next two decades saw a dramatic expansion in the number of convents. For the history of feminine monasticism in New Spain, see Josefina Muriel, *Conventos de monjas en la Nueva España* (Mexico City: Editorial Santiago, 1946); Asunción Lavrin, "Female Religious," in *Cities and Society in Colonial Latin America*, ed. Louisa Schell Hoberman and Susan Migden Socolow (Albuquerque: University of New Mexico Press, 1986), 165–95; Electa Arenal and Stacey Schlau, *Untold Sisters: Hispanic Nuns in Their Own Works* (Albuquerque: University of New Mexico Press, 1989), 336–410; Manuel Ramos Medina, *Imagen de santidad en un mundo profano* (Mexico City: Universidad Iberoamericana, 1990).

28. Marina mentioned her in her fourth confession, on November 24, 1598, fol. 356.

29. Although Marina did not indicate what she taught to her charges, girls were generally taught sewing and other domestic skills.

30. Marina de San Miguel, January 25, 1599, fol. 358v.

31. Ysabel Gutiérrez, November 18, 1598, fol. 328. Cf. Luis de Valverde, November 17, 1598, fol. 326.

32. Ynés de Montesdoca, December 13, 1598, fol. 342. Ynés learned that "God was very angry with her," though he did not say the cause of his displeasure ("dios estava muy ayrado contra esta sin dezir la causa porque").

33. Such illnesses are, of course, a common leitmotif in the spiritual biographies of holy women, as they were in the life of Saint Teresa. See, for an interesting example, Concepción Torres, *Ana de Jesús, Cartas (1590–1621): Religiosidad y*

vida cotidiana en la clausura femenina del Siglo de Oro (Salamanca: Ediciones Universidad de Salamanca, 1995), 24–25 and passim.

34. María de Cárdenas, December 5, 1598, fol. 340.

35. Beatriz Gutiérrez, March 21, 1596, fol. 314.

36. Alonso describes having asked Marina to interpret a vision; she told him that she did not know what it was about but that he should not worry but should place his hope in God, fol. 333v.

37. Marina de San Miguel, January 25, 1599, fol. 359v.

38. For a discussion of how relationships between beatas and confessors, as well as other male religious, often evolved into such "inverted" teacher-disciple relationships, see Ciamitti, "One Saint Less."

39. Juana Ruiz, December 4, 1598, fol. 335.

40. See, for example, Jodi Bilinkoff, "A Spanish Prophetess and Her Patrons: The Case of María de Santo Domingo," *Sixteenth-Century Journal* 23 (Spring 1992): 21–34. Mariá de Santo Domingo was a beata who counted the three most powerful men in Spain among her patrons, offering them in turn the legitimacy brought by her spiritual endorsement. Thus, Bilinkoff argues, "an illiterate peasant woman had access to a form of spiritual authority that a duke, a king, and a cardinal of the church might only envy" (34). John Coakley makes the same point in his "Gender and the Authority of Friars: The Significance of Holy Women for Thirteenth-Century Franciscans and Dominicans" (*Church History* 60 [December 1991]: 445–60) while emphasising that the authority of medieval holy women in relation to friars was "as boundary figures," as people with privileged access to the Divine but answerable to the friars' ecclesiastical authority, therefore enhancing rather than diminishing the friars' own authority (459). For one of the few Spanish American studies, see Fernando Iwasaki Cauti, "Mujeres al borde de la perfección: Rosa de Santa María y las alumbradas de Lima," *Hispanic American Historical Review* 73 (November 1993): 590–96.

41. The phrase is Herbert Moller's, from his "Social Causes of Affective Mysticism," *Journal of Social History* 4 (Summer 1971): 333. Moller's allegation that affective mysticism thrives as a response to a sexual imbalance in favor of women certainly does not explain evidence from sixteenth-century Mexico City, but his explanation of what male clerics derived from relationships with mystic women is apt: "The men had the gripping experience of witnessing in another person a depth of feeling and an immediate contact with divine forces, of which they themselves were incapable" (334).

42. Marina de San Miguel, January 26, 1599, fol. 367.

43. Ysabel Gutiérrez, November 18, 1598, fol. 328v. *Recogimiento* is a difficult word to translate, and I have chosen the word "devotion" to convey a general sense of what Marina's neighbors might have meant, though "reclusion," "enclo-

sure," "recollection," and "concentration" would all be acceptable definitions. In Francisco de Osuna's *Tercer abecedario espiritual* of 1527, the author differentiates between a general *recogimiento* as an existence aloof from worldly matters, and a particular *recogimiento*, a specific meditative exercise based on collecting the senses and directing them toward contemplation of the Divine. See Alastair Hamilton, *Heresy and Mysticism in Sixteenth-Century Spain: The Alumbrados* (Toronto: University of Toronto Press, 1992), 14.

44. . . . la ha tenido por una santa assi por las cossas que a dicho como por los buenos consejos que dava a este. García Hernández de Castro, December 5, 1598, fol. 334. Note that this page has been improperly paginated in the original *legajo*. It belongs between fols. 338v and 339.

45. María de Cárdenas, December 5, 1598, fol. 340.

46. Ibid.

47. . . . dios le avia prometido de acordar y dar salud a las personas que la regalassen lo qual le parecio a esta cossa muy particular y menuda. Ibid., fol. 340v.

48. Juana Ruiz, December 4, 1598, fol. 335.

49. Beatriz Gutiérrez, March 21, 1596, fol. 313.

50. " . . . tomo la mano a esta y se puso sobre su coraçon, y le dixo mira hija lo que siento, y sintio esta que el coraçon le dava grandes latidos y muy a prissa." Beatriz Gutiérrez, March 21, 1596, fol. 313v.

51. Ibid. This might have aroused suspicion of heresy had the inquisitors been looking for it, suggesting a denial of transubstantiation. In the *Edicto de los alumbrados de Toledo*, published in Toledo in 1525, disdain for the host is identified as one of the principal errors of the alumbrados ("que mas enteramente venia dios en el anima del hombre que estaba en la hostia si la criatura hazia lo que devia porque la hostia era un poco de massa y el hombre era a su semejanza"). See Antonio Márquez, *Los alumbrados: Orígenes y filosofía (1525-1559)* (Madrid: Taurus Ediciones, S.A., 1972), 275.

52. Fol. 314v.

53. An excellent overview of the case is provided by Jiménez Rueda, *Herejías y supersticiones*, 139-57.

54. Hamilton, *Heresy and Mysticism*, 4. Hamilton suggests that by the 1530s, inquisitors showed a tendency to define any religious novelty as alumbradismo (91).

55. Jiménez Rueda notes that unlike *iluminismo* and alumbradismo, *ilusionismo* did not entail adherence to a general set of principles and can be simply defined as the possession of spiritual gifts, supernatural revelations, and the power to perform miracles and prophesy (*Herejías y supersticiones*, 161).

56. For more discussion of alumbradismo, see the chapters by Alcalá and Giles in this volume.

57. Jiménez Rueda notes the prevalence of *andaluzes*; see *Herejías y supersticiones*, 155.

58. Ibid., 148, 150.

59. Ibid., 149.

60. Ibid., 174–75.

61. Ibid., 175.

62. Juan Plata, August 13, 1598, fol. 318.

63. Ibid., fol. 319v.

64. . . . este dijo que le hiziese humilde y la dicha marina de sant miguel escuchaba interiormente para rresponder a este y dijo que dezia su magestad que le daria mas humildad. Ibid., fol. 320. The somewhat childlike nature suggested by Plata's report may have been what saved him from severe punishment. Though he was both a solicitant and a heretic, he was exempted from participation in the public auto-da-fé. His punishment was perpetual deprivation of administration of the sacrament of penitence, a ten-year suspension of all his orders, exile from the cities of Mexico and Puebla, and a private abjuration *de levi* in the presence of the cathedral chapter of Puebla. See Jiménez Rueda, *Herejías y supersticiones*, 153–54.

65. Juan Plata, August 13, 1598, fol. 321.

66. Marina de San Miguel, November 27, 1598, fol. 357.

67. Juan Plata, October 13, 1598, fol. 322v.

68. . . . rrespondio que dezia su magestad que quando este hizo los dichos votos no los acepto y cree le dijo que no rreparase en ellos. Ibid., fol. 324.

69. Ibid., fol. 322v. This, of course, is unoriginal. Luther had been "divined" as Antichrist seventy-five years before (Hamilton, *Heresy and Mysticism*, 19).

70. . . . le dijo a este que el spiritu santo habia encarnado en ella y otros disparates que le obligaron a dejarla y a maravillarse de el dicho gregorio lopez que a semejante muger enbiaba a que pidiese a dios lo de la nueba jerusalem. Luis de Zárate, December 20, 1598, fol. 345.

71. Marina de San Miguel, November 24, 1598, fol. 352. The ensuing description is fascinating but far too detailed to transcribe in a chapter of this length.

72. Marina de San Miguel, November 25, 1598, fols. 354v., 354v–355, 355v–356.

73. . . . una tentacion sensual de la carne la qual le obligava a esta a contactos deshonestos hechos con sus propias manos en las partes vergonçossas venia en polucion diziendo palabras deshonestas probocativas a luxuria diziendo por sus nombres propios y deshonestos muchas cossas suzias y lazivas, a lo qual le inclinava el demonio que se le aparescia interiormente en angel de luz . . . y el dicho demonio se le aparescia en figura de christo . . . y le pedia que descubriesse los pechos y que tuviesse ayuntamiento con el y assi de los dichos quinze años a esta parte ha tenido el dicho ayuntamiento carnal . . . y viendo que esta menospreci-

ava la vida de los casados estimando en mucho la virginidad le dixo el dicho demonio estando en figura de christo como quando le pintan rresucitado, en el mismo acto torpe, esta es la ley del matrimonio y me es tambien agradable, y no lo has de menospreciar. Marina de San Miguel, January 25, 1599, fol. 358.

74. Alison Weber, "Saint Teresa, Demonologist," in *Culture and Control in Counter-Reformation Spain,* ed. Mary Elizabeth Perry and Anne Cruz (Minneapolis: University of Minnesota Press, 1992), 173–74.

75. Perry, "Beatas and the Inquisition," 156–57.

76. See Judith C. Brown, *Immodest Acts: The Life of a Lesbian Nun in Renaissance Italy* (Oxford: Oxford University Press, 1986).

77. . . . y le tratava a esta de cosas de dios y de su amor y de la resignacion a su voluntad, y tratando desta platica bessava y abraçava a esta y le metia la lengua en su voca y le tentava con su mano los pechos y partes vergonçossas diziendo todo esto es tierra y una vez se acuerda le metio el dedo en sus partes vergonçossas de esta. Marina de San Miguel, January 25, 1599, fols. 358v–359.

78. Marina de San Miguel, January 26, 1599, fol. 363.

79. Marina de San Miguel, January 25, 1599, fol. 359v.

80. Marina de San Miguel, January 26, 1599, fol. 363v.

81. . . . de hordinario quando se vian se bessavan y abraçavan, y esta la metia las manos en los pechos, y . . . vino esta en polucion diez o doze vezes las dos dellas en la yglesia. Marina de San Miguel, January 28, 1599, fol. 370.

82. . . . con tocamientos interiores en sus verguenças, y las dos vezes tubo polucion. Ibid., fol. 371.

83. . . . no tubo intento de hazerlas para deleytarse en ellas, sino por estar melancolica las hazia con buen amor y limpia intencion porque como dize s. agustin que el peccado esta en la mala intencion y voluntad. Marina de San Miguel, January 26, 1599, fol. 362v.

84. Marina de San Miguel, January 28, 1599, fol. 371.

85. A terse note on fol. 346 records that Luis de Zárate could not ratify his testimony "because he was in the madhouse, deprived of his sense and understanding" [por estar en la casa de los locos, privado de su juizio y entendimiento]. This, too, could be a stratagem, of course, but insanity was certainly a credible outcome of prosecution by the Inquisition.

86. . . . e le ha mostrado en su figura de demonio y le ha visto con los ojos corporales y a muchos demonios con oçicos y malas figuras . . . sacando las lenguas y hechando fuego por las vocas aunque en poca cantidad, y levantando a esta con su cama tres o quatro vezes cada dia . . . y pidio al alcayde le diessen confessor porque la llevavan los demonios, y ha oydo esta aviendo sido arrevatada de espiritus malos un pregon que dezia, esta es la justicia que mandan hazer a marina de st miguel beata. Marina de San Miguel, January 26, 1599, fol. 360v.

87. During the course of Juan Núñez's trial, he was denounced by many women for similar sexual license. For a discussion of alumbradismo and solicitation, see Adelina Sarión Mora, *Sexualidad y confesión: La solicitatión ante el Tribunal del Santo Oficio (siglos XVI–XIX)* (Madrid: Alianza Universidad, 1994), 186–205.

88. . . . como pudo esta ignorar no peccar en las dichas cossas pues dizelas hizo incitada del demonio, *del demonio* (underlining in original). Marina de San Miguel, January 28, 1599, fol. 371.

89. Ibid., fol. 371v.

90. . . . si esta se acostara con un hombre y tuviera con el ayuntamiento carnal si peccara mortalmente aunque no consintiera con la voluntad interior." Ibid.

91. Presumably he was referring to her masturbation and her activities with the other beatas.

92. Marina de San Miguel, January 28, 1599, fol. 372.

93. Juan Núñez was disciplined in the auto-da-fé of April 20, 1603. He abjured *de vehementi,* was sentenced to serve in a hospital for six years, was perpetually exiled from Mexico City, and was fined five thousand *ducados.* Aside from the fine, Marina's punishment was arguably harsher. See Jiménez Rueda, *Herejías y supersticiones,* 147.

94. Fol. 427v.

CHAPTER 12 · BLASPHEMY AS RESISTANCE

I wish to express my sincere appreciation to Sarah Erwin, curator of Archival Collections at the Gilcrease Museum in Tulsa; to the staff of the Nettie Lee Benson Library at the University of Texas at Austin, where I completed my research for this article; and to Grinnell College for financial support.

1. "Processo contra María negra esclava de Don Antonio de Saavedra, vecino de esta ciudad de México," 1609–10, Hispanic Documents Collection, no. 20, fol. 18r, Gilcrease Museum, Tulsa.

2. Ibid., fols. 18r–20v; letters dated June 18, 1612, and July 13, 1616, Fondo Inquisición, Riva Palacio, vol. 7, fols. 96, 126, Archivo General de la Nación, Mexico, cited in Solange Alberro, "Negros y mulatos en los documentos inquisitoriales: Rechazo e integración," in *El trabajo y los trabajadores en la historia de México,* ed. Elsa Cecilia Frost et al. (Mexico City: Colegio de México, 1977), 159.

3. See *Base de datos Argena,* Archivo General de la Nación (Mexico City: Secretaría de Gobernación, 1993), CD-ROM.

4. "Processo contra Gerónima, mulata esclava de Augustín de Çevallos, vezino de el pueblo de Tulançingo," 1609, Hispanic Documents Collection, no. 18, Gilcrease Museum, Tulsa.

5. A later case also found in the Gilcrease Museum archives shows the successful negotiation of a mild punishment by a male plantation slave. See "El Señor fiscal del Santo Officio contra Lorenço de la Cruz mulato, esclabo del ingenio de Tlacomulco del Marqués del Valle, por reniegos," 1663–64, Hispanic Documents Collection, no. 47, Gilcrease Museum, Tulsa.

6. This percentage may be roughly proportionate to the number of women in the slave population, though such proportions can only be estimated by historians. Gonzalo Aguirre Beltrán estimates that one-third of all slaves imported to Mexico were women. See *Población negra de México, 1519–1810: Estudio etnohistórico*, 2d ed. expanded (Mexico City: Fondo de Cultura Económica, 1972), 217. Calculating that a male slave would live on average fifteen years under hard labor, and a female slave twice that long, Aguirre Beltrán asserts that approximately half of the slave population in any given year would be female. The assertion does not take into account the difference between urban and rural slavery. In Mexico City, slaves lived very differently than their rural counterparts, engaging in less demanding physical labor. In the city, slaves generally served a less essential economic role for their masters and enjoyed a greater flexibility and freedom in their daily movements as personal servants, street vendors, and artisans. Relative to plantation owners, urban slave owners benefited more in status than productivity from their slaves, which led them to be more concerned about the life expectancy of their slaves. Plantation owners were motivated more by the productivity and profit of their slaves and exploited labor to the fullest with less concern for the well-being of the slaves, as Douglas R. Cope asserts in *The Limits of Racial Domination: Plebeian Society in Colonial Mexico, 1660–1720* (Madison: University of Wisconsin Press, 1994), 95. Urban slaves represented a significant proportion of the slave population in New Spain: 8,000 of some 20,000 blacks—mostly slaves—lived in the capital city in the 1570s; for 1646, the numbers are 19,441 of 35,089. See Aguirre Beltrán, *Población negra*, 210, 218.

7. See Solange Alberro, "Negros y mulatos"; David M. Davidson, "Negro Slave Control and Resistance in Colonial Mexico, 1519–1650," *Hispanic American Historical Review* 46 (August 1966): 235–53; and Colin A. Palmer, *Slaves of the White God: Blacks in Mexico, 1570–1650* (Cambridge: Harvard University Press, 1976).

8. Richard E. Greenleaf, *The Mexican Inquisition of the Sixteenth Century* (Albuquerque: University of New Mexico Press, 1969), 172.

9. Henry Charles Lea, *A History of the Inquisition of Spain* (New York: Macmillan, 1907), 4:334.

10. Ibid., 328, 332.

11. Alberro, "Negros y mulatos," 160.

12. See Lea, *History of the Inquisition*, 330, and José Toribio Medina, *Historia*

del Tribunal del Santo Oficio de la Inquisición en México (Mexico City: Miguel Angel Porrúa, 1987), 51, 56, 86.

13. Palmer, *Slaves of the White God,* 152.

14. Ibid., 153.

15. Alberro, "Negros y mulatos," 140.

16. Ibid., 150–51, 156.

17. At least seventeen files in the archives of the Mexican Inquisition contain
denunciations and testimony against masters for their cruelty toward slaves,
though only in six cases does the index to the archives clearly indicate that a trial
occurred or that some action was taken against the abuser. See *Base de datos Ar-*
gena, Fondo Inquisición, 1584, vol. 139, exp. 5, fol. 12; 1611, vol. 292, exp. 2, fols. 2–4,
12–18; 1611, vol. 292, exp. 37, fols. 172–73; 1621, vol. 338, exp. 7, fol. 16; 1625, vol. 353,
exp. 6, fol. 22; 1626, vol. 303, exp. 32, fols. 224–25; 1637, vol. 384, exp. 9, fol. 47; 1643,
vol. 418, exp. 4, fols. 320–64; 1659, vol. 446, exp. 7, fols. 220–53; 1683, vol. 520, exp.
69, fol. 1; 1695, vol. 477, exp. 23, fols. 238–55; 1696, vol. 534, exp. 31, fol. 18; 1698, vol.
706, exp. 46, fols. 377–95; 1706, vol. 735, fols. 434–45; 1708, vol. 733, fols. 256–60;
1717, vol. 553, exp. 66, fol. 4; 1762, vol. 1068, exp. 13, fols. 216–63.

18. José Toribio Medina, *Historia del Tribunal del Santo Oficio de la Inquisición*
de Cartagena de Indias (Santiago de Chile, 1899), 118–19, cited in Henry Charles
Lea, *The Inquisition in the Spanish Dependencies* (New York: Macmillan, 1908),
465–66.

19. In 1570, Europeans made up scarcely two-tenths of a percent of the total
population of New Spain; see Aguirre Beltrán, *Población negra,* 210. According to
Aguirre Beltrán, more than ten thousand black slaves lived in Mexico City, far
outnumbering the fewer than three thousand whites whom they served (210). As
late as 1742, blacks still outnumbered whites in New Spain two to one; see Aguirre
Beltrán, *Población negra* (Mexico City: Ed. Fuente Cultural, 1946), 224–25.

20. Palmer, *Slaves of the White God,* 133–34.

21. Davidson, "Negro Slave Control," 238–42.

22. Palmer, *Slaves of the White God,* 121; Davidson, "Negro Slave Control," 245.

23. See Edgar Love, "Legal Restrictions on Afro-Indian Relations in Colonial
Mexico," *Journal of Negro History* 55 (1970): 131–39, and "Negro Resistance to
Spanish Rule in Colonial Mexico," *Journal of Negro History* 52 (1967): 89–103.

24. Davidson, "Negro Slave Control," 246–50; Palmer, *Slaves of the White God,*
119–44; and Love, "Negro Resistance," 94–99.

25. Aguirre Beltrán, *Población negra* (1972), 285–86; Alberro, "Negros y mulatos," 139–48; Davidson, "Negro Slave Control," 235; and Palmer, *Slaves of the*
White God, 119–66.

26. Love, "Legal Restrictions," 131.

27. Palmer, *Slaves of the White God,* 133.

28. *Población negra* (1972), 206.

29. Davidson, "Negro Slave Control," 247.

30. Love, "Negro Resistance," 97, and Davidson, "Negro Slave Control," 248–50.

31. Davidson, "Negro Slave Control," 248–50.

32. Palmer, *Slaves of the White God*, 135–40.

33. See Anthony Cascardi's discussion of the broader ideological offensive of the Counter Reformation to compel the subjects of the Spanish empire to self-control in "The Subject of Control," in *Culture and Control in Counter-Reformation Spain*, ed. Anne Cruz and Mary Elizabeth Perry (Minneapolis: University of Minnesota Press, 1992), 231–54.

34. The *Base de datos Argena* shows blasphemy to be one of the two most frequent reasons that slave women came before the Inquisition in colonial Mexico, the second being charges of sorcery or superstition. Although there are thirty-nine files corresponding to each type of offense, those relating to sorcery and superstition are distributed throughout the colonial period, whereas two-thirds, or twenty-seven, of the files relating to blasphemy are dated between 1590 and 1620. The database does not document all the Inquisition trials that were held in Mexico—the cases documented in the Gilcrease Museum collection, for example, do not appear in it—but I am working on the assumption that *Argena* is representative of the relative occurrences of various types of offenses among various populations.

35. For the first decade of the seventeenth century, the *Base de datos Argena* shows sixteen files relating to the blasphemy of slave women and thirty for male slaves. If one-third of all slaves imported to Mexico were women, as Aguirre Beltrán reports (*Población negra* [1972], 217), then these women probably used blasphemy as frequently as their male counterparts.

36. The *Base de datos Argena* holds twenty-seven files relating to cases of blasphemy by slave women which occurred between 1590 and 1620, while only a half a dozen files show slave women accused of any other crime. During the same period, only eight cases of blasphemy involved black women who are not identified as slaves and none relating to mulattas. These women are accused primarily of sorcery and superstition, which constituted almost two-thirds of their total encounters with the Inquisition during the colonial period, as represented in the database.

37. Y aviéndola amarrado para castigarla por mandado de la d[ic]ha doña Cat[alin]a de Villafañe su ama, a los primeros diez o doze açotes que le dio esta t[estig]o con una correa de cuero con que açotan a las muchachas que hazen la labor, dixo la dicha negra María que renegava de la leche que mamó y del pan que comió y del agua que bevió *y de Dios y de todos sus sanctos. Lo qual dixo dos vezes, y*

la d[ic]ha su ama, le dio con un chapín por ello, y la mandó açotar de nu[ev]o y pringar con unas velas de sebo y se hizo assí. Y se hallaron pres[en]tes qu[an]do dixo las dichas palabras esta t[estig]o, y María Mag[dale]na española que está a la portería y la d[ic]ha doña Cath[alin]a de Villafañe y que no passó otra cossa.

"Processo contra María negra," fol. 4r–v. In transcribing quotes I have left the original orthography where it represents a common phonetic usage, filling out abbreviations and adding missing letters in square brackets. In addition, for clarity, I have transcribed the original "xpiana" as [crist]iana. I have modernized punctuation and the use of written accent marks.

38. Preg[unta]da si estava en su juizio la d[ic]ha María negra quando dixo los d[ic]hos reniegos y qué presume della açerca de su christiandad. *Dixo que la d[ic]ha María negra estava en su juizio quando dixo los d[ic]hos reniegos porque nunca se emborracha y que la tienen en reputac[ió]n de bu[en]a [crist]iana porque ayuna y trae el escapulario de n[uest]ra señora.* Ibid., fol. 4v. The following parenthetical references are from the same document.

39. Prom[eti]ó de dezir verdad una muger que dixo llamarse María Magdalena, mestiza que está en servicio de Doña Catalina de Villafañe . . . de hedad que dixo ser de diez y nueve años (fol. 6r).

40. *Dixo que [María Blanca] estava en su juizio y no borracha porque* nunca se suele emborrachar. Y que la tiene por bu[en]a [crist]iana porque la ve ayunar los sábados y advientos. E que ésta es la verdad para el juram[ent]o que tiene fecho y no lo dize por lodio (fol. 6v).

41. See Cope, *Limits of Racial Domination,* for a discussion of the limited success of the dominant Spaniard's *sistema de castas* to construct a myriad of different racial categories in which each would turn against the other.

42. bell hooks, *Teaching to Transgress: Education as the Practice of Freedom* (New York: Routledge, 1994), 96.

43. "Processo contra María negra," fol. 2r. The following parenthetical references are to the same document.

44.

No supo dezir su hedad y por su aspecto paresçe de treinta años, y que su off[ici]o es servir a su amo.

Preg[unta]da, si ha sido otra vez pressa ó castigada por el s[an]to off[ici]o de la inqui[sició]n

Dixo que no.

Preg[unta]da si es christiana baptizada y confirmada, y si oye missa confiessa y comulga en los t[iem]pos que manda la sancta madre Ygl[es]ia.

Dixo que es christiana baptizada. Y que en la çiudad de Sevilla siendo esclava del Marqués de Jarifa la confirmó un ob[is]po que no sabe cómo se llamava, y que oye missa, confiessa y comulga en los t[iem]pos q[ue] manda la s[an]ta m[adr]e ygl[es]ia. Y que la quaresma pas[a]da confessó en el conv[en]to de s[an] Fran[cis]co desta çiudad con un religiosso del que no se acuerda de su n[ombr]e donde comulgó.

Signose y sanctiguosse en romançe y dixo el Pater noster, Ave María, credo, y salve Regina en romançe errando algunas palabras, y los diez mandam[ien]tos no los supo sino a pedaços. (fols. 8r–v)

45. Dixo que sospecha ha sido mandada traer porque un día de la semana s[an]ta de la quaresma próxima pas[a]da, estándola açotando dos yndios tapisques y una mestiza y una mulata con gran crueldad por mandado del d[ic]ho su amo, porque se avía huido, con un látigo de cuero, dixo ésta dos veces que la dexassen por amor de Dios, y visto que no la dexavan, con aquel dolor, dixo *otras dos vezes que renegava de Dios y de todos sus santos,* por lo qual le dieron con un chapín en la cara que le huvieron de quebrar los ojos, y la açotaron hasta que se cansaron todos quatro, y que no sabe que por otra cossa aya sido traída, y que de aver renegado le pessa mucho porque es muy devota de Nuestra Señora (fols. 8v–9r).

46. See Palmer, *Slaves of the White God,* 120–21.

47. "Processo contra María negra," fol. 10r.

48. Cope, *Limits of Racial Domination,* 96.

49. "Processo contra María negra," fols. 9r–13v. The following parenthetical references are from the same document.

50.

[P]or tanto que por reverençia de Dios nuestro Señor y de su vendita y gloriossa madre nuestra señora la virgen María se le amonesta y encarga recorra su memoria y diga y confiesse enteramente verdad de lo que se sintiere culpado o supiere de otras personas que lo sean, sin encubrir de sí ni dellas cosa alguna, ni levantar a ssí ni a otro falso testim[oni]o. Porque hazi[én]dolo assí descargará su conçiençia como cathólica [cristia]na y salvará su alma. Y su causa será despachada con la brevedad y misericordia que huviere lugar donde no se hará justicia[.] Y aviéndosele dado a entender esta mon[e]s[tació]n

Dixo que no tiene más que dezir. . . .

Y siendo pres[en]te le fue d[ic]ho si ha acordado algu[n]a cossa en su neg[oci]o la diga y la verdad so cargo del juram[ent]o que tiene fecho.

Dixo que no ha acordado más. . . .

Dixo que no. . . .

Dixo no señor. . . .

Dixo, "no tengo otra cossa que dezir." (fols. 9v, 13r, 14v)

51. [H]abiéndola mandado castigar Doña Cat[alin]a de Villafañe su Señora, porque se había huido, y estando amarrada, a los primeros diez o doçe azotes que le dieron con una correa ordinaria con que açotan a las muchachas de la labor, piadosamente y sin crueldad, dijo la d[ic]ha rea que renegaba de la leche que mamó y de el pan que comió y de el agua que bebió y de Dios y de todos sus sanctos, lo qual dijo dos veces causando escándalo a las personas que se hallaron presentes, por ser muger la q[ue] la castigaba, y por sólo que se enmendase, y por estar la d[ic]ha rea a su sano juizio y entendimiento (fol. 11r–v).

52.

C1 Al primero capítulo
Dixo que como tiene confessado es christiana bap[tiza]da y confirmada y que no ha hecho más de lo que tiene declarado.
C2 Al segundo capítulo
Dixo que no ay otra cossa fuera de lo que tiene confessado.
C3 Al terçero capítulo y último de la d[ic]ha acus[ació]n
Dixo que aquí no ay dezir mentira y que no ha hecho otra cossa.
E que ésta es la verdad para el jur[amien]to que tiene fecho. (fol. 12r)

53. Dixo que ella tiene confessada la verdad, y no se acuerda de otra cossa. Y de aver renegado le pessa. Y la causa fue averse privado de su juizio con el dolor del castigo. Y pide peni[tenci]a con misericordia (fol. 13v).

54. Dixo que se remite a lo que tiene declar[a]do, y que puede ser aya d[ic]ho assí mismo que renegava de la madre que la parió, y no lo demás (fol. 16r).

55. See, for example, the cases against Domingo Vaca, slave of Sebastián Vaca, 1609–10, and against Jusepe, "mulato criollo," slave of Don Juan de Casaus, 1609–10, Hispanic Documents Collections, Gilcrease Museum, Tulsa, nos. 19 and 21.

56. "Processo contra María negra," fol. 17r.

57. For a description of the autos, see Medina, *México*, 93–94, 125, 143.

58. Yo María Blanca, negra esclava de Don Ant[oni]o de Saavedra, vezino desta ciudad de Méx[i]co, que aquí estoy pres[en]te ante V[uestras] S[eñorías] como inqui[sidor]es que son contra la herética gravedad y apostasía en esta d[ic]ha ciudad y su partido, por authoridad app[ostóli]ca y ordinaria, puesta ante mí esta señal de la cruz y los sacro sanctos evangelios que con mis manos corporalm[en]te toco, y conoçiendo y reconoçiendo la verdadera cath[ó]lica y app[ostóli]ca fee, abjuro detesto y anathematizo toda specie de heregía que se levante contra la sancta fee cathólica y ley evang[éli]ca de n[uest]ro redemptor y salvador Jesuchristo y contra la sancta sede App[ostóli]ca Yglesia Romana, especialmente aquella de que yo ante V[uestras] S[eñorías] he sido accussada y estoy levem [en]te sospechossa. Y juro y prometo de tener y guardar siempre aquella sancta fee

catholica que tiene, guarda, y enseña la sancta m[adr]e Yglesia y seré siempre obe-
diente a nuestro señor el Papa. . . . [Y] confiesso que todos aquellos que contra
esta s[an]ta fee vinieren son dignos de condemna[çi]ón y prometo de nunca me
juntar con ellos, y que quanto en mí fuere los perseguiré y las heregías que dellos
supiere las revelaré y notificaré a qualquier inq[uisido]r. . . . [J]uro y prometo que
reçibiré humildem[en]te y con paçiençia la penitençia que me ha sido o fuere impuesta. . . . y ruego al presente secretario que me lo dé por testimonio y a los presentes que dello sean testigos. "Processo contra María negra," fols. 19r–20r.

59. "Processo contra Gerónima," fol. 5v. The following parenthetical references in the main text are to the same document.

60. Palmer, *Slaves of the White God,* 142.

61. Ibid., 133.

62. The *Base de datos Argena* records a total of 113 files related to blasphemy
between the years 1595 and 1640, when some 88,000 were brought to Mexico
(Aguirre Beltrán, *Población negra* [1972], 217).

63. Richard Konetzke, ed., *Colección de documentos para la historia de la form-
ación social de Hispanoamérica, 1493–1810* (Madrid, 1953), 2:754 ff., 3:113, quoted in
Davidson, "Negro Slave Control," 241.

CHAPTER 13 · ROSA DE ESCALANTE'S PRIVATE PARTY

This study is part of a larger work entitled "The Language of Desire: Love and
Politics in Colonial Mexico." Drawing heavily upon Inquisition sources, it an-
alyzes popular concepts of romantic love in seventeenth- and eighteenth-century
Mexico.

1. On at least one occasion, March 11, Rosa utilized the statue and scapular of
Saint Gertrude. The significance of Saint Gertrude in this context is unclear, as is
the actual identity of the saint because there are two Saint Gertrudes (Gertrude of
Nivelles and Gertrude of Helfta, the Great). Both appeared to have had a following in Spain and Mexico, although Gertrude of Nivelles, a champion of the poor
and destitute, may have had a more pronounced popular following in the early
modern period. Nonetheless, the roles of either saint within Novohispanic popular culture remain a mystery that can only be clarified by more research. See Jo
Ann McNamara and John E. Halborg, eds., *Sainted Women of the Dark Ages* (Durham, N.C.: Duke University Press, 1992), 220–34; Mary J. Finnegan, *Women of
Helfta: Scholars and Mystics* (Athens: University of Georgia Press, 1991); Jose Mar-
iano Moreira de Freitas, *Gertrudes de Helfta e Espanha: Contribucão para estudo da
historia de espiritualidade peninsular nos seculos XVI e XVII* (Porto: Instituto Nacional de Investigacão Cientifica, Centro de Literatura da Universidade do Porto,
1981); and *Novena a la esclarecida virgen Sta. Gertrudis la Magna: A quien dixo el Se-*

ñor que lo que prometiera en la tierra lo tendría por firme en el cielo . . . por un devoto de la santa (Mexico City: Francisco de Rivera Calderón, 1703).

2. Gaspar de la Cerda Sandoval Silva y Mendoza, conde de Galve, ruled from 1686 to 1696.

3. Archivo General de la Nación (henceforth AGN), Ramo Inquisición, vol. 526, exp. 24, fol. 570v.

4. Ibid., fols. 570–73.

5. Ibid., vol. 520, no. 182, fols. 288v–289.

6. See, for example, Electa Arenal and Stacey Schlau, *Untold Sisters: Hispanic Nuns in Their Own Works* (Albuquerque: University of New Mexico Press, 1989); Jean Franco, *Plotting Women: Gender and Representation in Mexico* (New York: Columbia University Press, 1989), 3–78; Kathleen A. Myers, *Word from New Spain: The Spiritual Autobiography of Madre María de San José, 1656–1719* (Liverpool: Liverpool University Press, 1993); Octavio Paz, *Sor Juana Inés de la Cruz o las trampas de la fé* (Mexico City: Fondo de Cultura Económica, 1982); Stephanie Merrim, ed., *Feminist Perspectives on Sor Juana Inés de la Cruz* (Detroit: Wayne State University Press, 1991); and Asunción Lavrin, "La vida feminina como experiencia religiosa: Biografía y hagiografía en Hispanoamerica colonial," *Colonial Latin American Historical Review* 2, nos. 1–2 (1993): 27–51.

7. Most of the contemporary scholarship, using Inquisition records, looks at those beatas who were suspected of heresy and were processed by the Holy Office. See, for example, Fernando Iwasaki Cauti, "Mujeres al borde de la perfección: Rosa de Santa María y las alumbradas de Lima," *Hispanic American Historical Review* 73 (November 1993): 581–613; Edelmira Ramírez Leyva, ed., *María Rita Vargas, María Lucía Celis: Beatas embaucadoras de la colonia* (Mexico City: UNAM, 1988); and Solange Alberro, "La licencia vestida de santidad: Teresa de Jesús, falsa beata del siglo XVIII" in *De la Santidad a la perversión o de porque no se cumplía la ley de Dios en la sociedad novohispana*, ed. Sergio Ortega (Mexico City: Editorial Grijalbo, 1986), 219–38.

8. For a good overview of the female moral code, see Asunción Lavrin, "In Search of the Colonial Woman in Mexico: The Seventeenth and Eighteenth Centuries," in *Latin American Women: Historical Perspectives*, ed. Asunción Lavrin (Westport, Conn.: Greenwood Press, 1978), 23–59.

9. See, for example, Magnus Morner, *Race Mixture in the History of Latin America* (Boston: Little, Brown, 1967); J. I. Israel, *Race, Class, and Politics in Colonial Mexico, 1610–1670* (London: Oxford University Press, 1975); and, especially, R. Douglas Cope, *The Limits of Racial Domination: Plebeian Society in Colonial Mexico City, 1660–1720* (Madison: University of Wisconsin Press, 1994).

10. See my "Saints, Sovereignty, and Spectacle in Colonial Mexico" (Ph.D. diss., Tulane University, 1993), chap. 1.

11. Solange Alberro, *Inquisición y sociedad en México, 1571–1700* (Mexico City: Fondo de Cultura Económica, 1988), graph 12, 218.

12. AGN, Ramo Inquisición, vol. 429, no. 13, fols. 391–391v.

13. Ibid., vol. 728, exp. 9, fol. 261.

14. [hicieron] en sus casas oratorios privados, de particulares devociones, poniendo en dichos altares cierto número supersticioso de candelas encendidas, y algunas retratos de personas q[ue] murieron con opinión de virtud. AGN, Ramo Inquisición, vol. 661, exp. 1, fol. 8.

15. Ibid., no. 1, fols. 8–9v.

16. Ibid., vol. 728, exp. 9, fol. 261.

17. Ibid., exp. 9, fol. 261.

18. There is increasing interest in documenting popular piety in the colonial period. Of particular interest is the two-volume set *Manifestaciones religiosas en el mundo colonial americano,* ed. Clara García Ayluardo and Manuel Ramos Medina (Mexico City: Universidad Iberoamericana, INAH, and Condumex, 1993, 1994).

19. See, for example, my "Giants and Gypsies: Corpus Christi in Colonial Mexico City," in *Rituals of Rule, Rituals of Resistance: Public Celebrations and Popular Culture in Mexico,* ed. William H. Beezley, Cheryl English Martin, and William E. French (Wilmington, Del.: Scholarly Resources, 1994), 1–26, and "Native Icon to City Protectress to Royal Patroness: Ritual, Political Symbolism, and the Virgin of Remedies," *The Americas* 52 (January 1996): 367–91.

20. See, for example, AGN, Ramo Bienes Nacionales, vol. 266, exp. 65; vol. 345, exps. 84, 87, 88, 91, 92; vol. 575, exp. 109; vol. 615, exp. 9; vol. 697, exp. 21; vol. 726, exp. 3; vol. 873, exps. 50, 51, 56, 58, 168, 171, 177; vol. 982, exp. 27; vol. 982, exps. 61, 64.

21. Rosalva Loreto López, "Familiar Religiosity and Images in the Home: Eighteenth-Century Puebla de los Angeles, Mexico," *Journal of Family History* 22 (January 1997): 26–49.

22. For native devotion to the saints during the late sixteenth and seventeenth centuries, see James Lockhart, *The Nahuas after the Conquest: A Social and Cultural History* (Stanford: Stanford University Press, 1992), 236–37, 243.

23. See Curcio-Nagy, "Giants and Gypsies" and "Native Icon."

24. All Saints' Day (November 1) and All Souls' Day (November 2) were combined into a larger festival that began in late October and lasted until November 8. Todos Santos included private altars in the home and celebrations in public at cemeteries where the dearly departed were buried. For a detailed analysis of the history and contemporary significance of Todos Santos, see Hugo Nutini, *Todos Santos in Rural Tlaxcala: A Syncretic, Expressive, and Symbolic Analysis of the Cult of the Dead* (Princeton: Princeton University Press, 1988). For a discussion of Todos Santos in colonial Mexico City, see Juan Pedro Viqueira Albán, *¿Relajados o Reprimidos? Diversiones públicas y vida social en la ciudad de México durante el Siglo*

de las Luces (Mexico City: Fondo de Cultura Económica, 1987).

25. For a contemporary description of Todos Santos *ofrendas,* see *Dos ofrendas de Día de Muertos en el estado de Tlaxcala (nahua y otomí)* (Mexico City: INAH, 1992).

26. For the specific case of New Castile, see Jean-Pierre DeDieu, "The Inquisition and Popular Culture in New Castile," in *Inquisition and Society in Early Modern Europe,* ed. Stephen Haliczer (Totowa, N.J.: Barnes and Noble Books, 1987): 129–46. This shift in emphasis from the heretical to the popular was a trend in other nations as well. See E. William Monter, *Ritual, Myth, and Magic in Early Modern Europe* (Brighton: Harvester Press, 1983), 66.

27. For a detailed description of the nature of this folk Catholicism in Spain, see William A. Christian Jr., *Local Religion in Sixteenth-Century Spain* (Princeton: Princeton University Press, 1981).

28. Pierre Sanchis, "The Portuguese Romaria," in *Saints and Their Cults: Studies in Religious Sociology, Folklore, and History,* ed. Stephen Wilson (Cambridge: Cambridge University Press, 1983), 270. The "battle" between the institutional church and popular laity regarding piety, particularly the devotion to the saints, has a long and even contemporary history. See, for example, June Macklin, "Two Faces of Sainthood: The Pious and the Popular," *Journal of Latin American Lore* 14 (Summer 1988): 67–91, esp. 67 and 68, and Thomas A. Kselman, "Ambivalence and Assumption in the Concept of Popular Religion," in *Religion and Political Conflict in Latin America,* ed. Daniel H. Levine (Chapel Hill: University of North Carolina Press, 1986), 26.

29. Mary O'Neil, "Magical Healing, Love Magic, and the Inquisition in Late Sixteenth-Century Modena," in Haliczer, *Inquisition and Society in Early Modern Europe,* 91.

30. Eventually, the relationship between the devout laity and the regular clergy was formalized with the creation of the tertiary orders.

31. *The New Catholic Encyclopedia* (New York: McGraw Hill, 1967), 12:1114–16.

32. O'Neil, "Magical Healing," 91. and Sanchis, "The Portuguese Romaria," 271.

33. *The New Catholic Encyclopedia,* 1:595–96, and Alban Butler, *Butler's Lives of the Saints* (Westminster, Md.: Christian Classics, 1990), 2:534–35. For a more official view of Saint Anthony in colonial Mexico, see José Rivera, *Patrón jurado de las aguas, grande a todos vientos, el gloriosissimo s. Antonio de Padua: Sermón panegyrico, que el día 9 de julio del año de 1758. patente el santíssimo Sacramento, predicó en el convento de* ... (Mexico City: Herederos de María de Rivera, 1759), and Juan de Torres, *Sermón panegyrico, en la festividad, que celebró la devoción al señor s. Antonio de Padua, como patrón de las benditas almas de el purgaturio, en su día* ... (Mexico City: J. de Ortega y Bonilla, 1721).

34. Sanchis, "The Portuguese Romaria," 271, 272.

35. Ruth Martin, *Witchcraft and the Inquisition in Venice, 1550–1650* (New York: Basil Blackwell, 1989), 108.

36. Padre Santo Antonio dos cativos, vós que sois um amarrador certo, amarrai, por vosso amor, quem de mim quer fugir; empenhai o vosso hábito e o vosso santo cardão, como algemas fortes e duros grilhões, para que facam impedir os passos de Fulano, que de mim quer fugir; e fazei, ó meu bem-aventurado Santo Antonio, que ele case comigo sem demora! Gastão de Bettencourt, *Os tres Santos de junho no folclore brasílico* (Rio de Janeiro: Livraria AGIR Editora, 1947), 55.

37. Ibid., 60–61.

38. Altaliba Nogueira, *Santo Antonio na tradicão brasileira* (São Paulo: Biblioteca Patria Nova, 1933), 42–49. See also Luis d'Oliveira Guimarães, *Os santos populares: Santo Antonio, São João e São Pedro* (Lisbon: Edicoẽs Patria Gaia, 1931).

39. For general information regarding the Portuguese community in seventeenth-century Mexico, see Israel, *Race, Class, and Politics,* 119, 123. A large number of Portuguese, many prominent members of the community, were tried by the Inquisition for heresy as practicing Jews from 1620 to 1650. See Alberro, *Inquisición,* 172–77.

40. Peter Boyd-Bowman, "Patterns of Spanish Immigration to the Indies until 1600," *Hispanic American Historical Review* 56 (1976): 580–604.

41. Marta Helena Sánchez Ortega, "Sorcery and Eroticism in Love Magic," in *Cultural Encounters: The Impact of the Inquisition in Spain and the New World,* ed. Mary Elizabeth Perry and Anne J. Cruz (Berkeley: University of California Press, 1991), 61; for chants to the saints requesting their intervention, see 76–78.

42. Alberrro, *Inquisición,* 207.

43. See, for example, AGN, Ramo Inquisición, vol. 1078, exp. 6, fols. 157v–158; vol. 1015, exp. 9, fols. 429–429v; caja 191, exp. 1, fols. unnumbered; vol. 1475, exp. 31 bis, fol. iv; vol. 1222, exp. 1, fol. 188 bis; vol. 760, exp. 28, fols. 320–320v; vol. 725, exp. s.n., ff 297–298; vol. 872, 1a parte, exp. 6, fol. 113; and exp. 4, fols. 80–81.

44. Exceptions to the rules existed regarding female opportunities. Financially secure widows could and did exercise more autonomy. Married women of wealth could control their dowry after their husband had signed a prenuptial contract to that effect. Nuns of wealthy conventual orders also could exercise independence in financial matters. See Luís Martín, *Daughters of the Conquistadores: Women of the Viceroyalty of Peru* (Dallas: Southern Methodist University Press, 1983), and Lavrin, "In Search of Colonial Women," 29–36.

45. Ruth Behar, "Sexual Witchcraft, Colonialism, and Women's Powers: Views from the Mexican Inquisition," in *Sexuality and Marriage in Colonial Latin America,* ed. Asunción Lavrin (Lincoln: University of Nebraska Press, 1989), 178–206, and Sánchez Ortega, "Sorcery and Eroticism," 61.

46. Fernando Cervantes, *The Devil in the New World: The Impact of Diabolism*

in New Spain (New Haven: Yale University Press, 1994), 77–97, lists a number of such cases in which men seek the assistance of the devil to procure wealth, physical prowess, and women.

47. AGN, Ramo Inquisición, vol. 526, exp. 24, fol. 573.

48. Ibid., vol. 520, no. 182, fol. 288v: siempre en los domingos, hubo fiesta donde entró un page del virrei y puso el escapulario de San Antonio.

49. See Patricia Seed, *To Love, Honor, and Obey in Colonial Mexico: Conflicts over Marriage Choice, 1574–1821* (Stanford: Stanford University Press, 1988); Carmen Castañeda, "Noviazgo, esponsales, y matrimonio" in *Comunidades domésticas en la sociedad Novohispana: Formas de unión y transmisión cultural: Seminario de Historia de las Mentalidades* (Mexico City: INAH, 1994), 117–26; and James A. Brundage, *Law, Sex, and Christian Society in Medieval Europe* (Chicago: University of Chicago Press, 1987).

50. AGN, Ramo Inquisición, vol. 520, exp. 182, fol. 288v.

51. Ibid., vol. 526, exp. 24, fol. 570v.

52. Sánchez Ortega makes this case well for Spain. See her "Sorcery and Eroticism," 83. Based upon the author's preliminary findings, this appears to apply to Mexico also, although more research is required in this regard.

53. Fernando Cervantes, when discussing native evangelization in the sixteenth century, points out that Catholicism had magical elements within it which complemented native traditions. The friars considered these indigenous rituals and concepts as suspect or believed that they were the work of the devil. See his *Devil in the New World*, 58.

54. AGN, Ramo Inquisición, vol. 429, exp. 13, fol. 391.

55. Native Americans and Africans had rich and complex magical religious traditions that combined with Spanish folk Catholic practices. See Noemí Quezada, *Amor y magia amorosa entre los aztecas* (Mexico City: UNAM, 1984), and Edward Geoffrey Parrinder, *Religion in Africa* (Baltimore: Penguin Books, 1969). See also Gonzalo Aguirre Beltrán, *Medicina y magia: El proceso de aculturación en la estructura colonial* (Mexico City: Instituto Nacional Indigenista, 1963), esp. 163–80. An illustrative case of this religious syncretism can be seen in AGN, Ramo Inquisición, vol. 303, primera parte, fols. 207–8. For specific syncretic use of Saint Anthony in a native village in Jalisco in 1776, see AGN, Ramo Inquisición, vol. 1104, exp. 2, fols. 302–4

56. Alberro, *Inquisición*, 184, and DeDieu, "Inquisition and Popular Culture," 143–44.

57. Alberro, *Inquisición*, 168.

58. O'Neil, "Magical Healing," 93.

59. AGN, Ramo Inquisición, vol. 520, exp. 182, fol. 289.

60. Ibid., vol. 526, exp. 24, fol. 573.

CHAPTER 14 · TESTIMONY FOR CANONIZATION
OR PROOF OF BLASPHEMY?

Epigraph: La Nueva España es una época en la que el arrobo de una monja, la milagrosa curación de un agonizante, el arrepentimiento de un penitenciado o los vaticinios de una beata, son más noticia que el alza en el precio de los oficios o la imposición de una alcabala; una época en que son de más momento los viajes al interior del alma que las expediciones a las Californias o a Filipinas. . . . [E]l historiador que ignore esa jerarquía en los valores vitales de la época, podrá ofrecernos un relato documentado y exhaustivo, si se quiere, de los sucesos que la llenan, pero no penetrará en la cámara secreta de su acontecer más significativo.

1. Although by no means the main focus of the Inquisition's activity, religious women, as well as books by and about them, were no strangers to the Holy Office. (According to one study, fewer than 30 percent of the people denounced and only 16 percent of those processed by the New Spanish Inquisition were women.) In sixteenth-century Spain such famous holy women as María de Santo Domingo, Saint Teresa of Avila, and Madre María Jesús de Agreda all first drew the querying eye of the Inquisition, though they were later cleared through either interviews or examinations of their writings. Others were not so fortunate, like the notorious Sor María de la Visitación and Fray Luis de Granada's reports of her stigmata. When the Inquisition determined the stigmata to be fake, Fray Luis published *Sermón de las caídas públicas* (1588), warning readers of the perils of feigning supernatural gifts. On the other side of the Atlantic, Inquisition records describe similiar cases of religious women charged with demonic possession, being alumbradas, and being false holy women, among other crimes. A famous case in Puebla dealt with the nun Agustina de Santa Clara as an alumbrada. Even New Spain's brightest literary star, Sor Juana Inés de la Cruz, discusses in her famous letter of self-defense, *Respuesta a Sor Filotea,* that she wants to avoid trouble with the Inquisition, which might judge her writings as unbefitting her status as a nun.

Studies of the New Spanish Inquisition are still relatively few in number, and none focus specifically on women. Although dated, Jiménez Rueda has added to José Toribio Medina's general history of the Inquisition in Mexico, *Historia del Tribunal del Santo Oficio de la Inquisición en México,* ed. Julio Jiménez Rueda (Mexico City: Ediciones Fuente Cultural, 1952). While Richard Greenleaf studies the sixteenth century, *The Mexican Inquisition of the Sixteenth Century* (Alburquerque: University of New Mexico Press, 1969), Solange Alberro works primarily with seventeenth-century records, *La actividad del Santo Oficio de la Inquisición en Nueva España, 1571–1700* (Mexico City: INAH, Colección Científica,

1981), and Monalisa Pérez-Marchand the eighteenth century, *Dos étapas ideológicas del siglo XVIII en México a través de los papeles de la Inquisición* (Mexico City: Colegio de México, 1945).

2. When compared with its Spanish counterpart, the New Spanish Inquisition played a more passive role—mostly receiving *denuncias* without prosecuting a large percentage of cases because of the overwhelmingly large territory it had to cover and the relatively few subjects over which it had jurisdiction. See Alberro, *Actividad*, 82–84.

3. For a general overview of the role of books and the Inquisition in New Spain, see Irving Leonard's *Books of the Brave* (New York: Gordian Press, 1964) and the work edited by Luis González Obregón, *Libros y libreros en el siglo XVI* (Mexico City: Archivo General de la Nación, 1914).

4. For a fuller discussion of these biographies and their role in New Spanish society, see Kathleen Myers, *Word from New Spain: The Spiritual Autobiography of Madre María de San José (1656–1719)* (Liverpool: TRAC, Liverpool University Press, 1993), 53, and Michael Thomas Destefano, "Miracles and Monasticism in Mid-Colonial Puebla, 1600–1750: Charismatic Religion in a Conservative Society" (diss. thesis, University of Florida, 1977).

5. Pedro Salmerón, *De la vida de la venerable Madre Isabel de la Encarnación, Carmelita Descalza, natural de la ciudad de los Ángeles* (Puebla, 1640), and Diego de Lemus (*Vida, birtudes, trabajos, fabores, y milagros de la Venerable Madre Sor Maria de Jesus angelopolitana religiosa en el insigne convento de la Limpia Concepcion de la ciudad de los Angeles* (Leon, 1685).

6. Josefina Muriel, ed., *Las indias caciques de Corpus Christi* (Mexico City: Universidad Autónoma Nacional de México, 1963).

7. That I have been able to locate in the archives in Spain and Mexico.

8. Destefano finds reference to its continued prohibition in a 1790 index of books which also includes all three volumes of Ramos's biography ("Miracles and Monasticism," 68).

9. All translations into English have been done by Peg Hausman. In the transcription of Ramos's text, I have maintained period spelling and accentuation except for *v* for *u*, *v* for *b*, and tildes that replace consonants following vowels (often for nasalized *n*) or are used to abbreviate *que*. Ramos's text reads: Cresció tanto la dissension, y porfia entre los Pyratas; que divididos en Bandos llegaron a esgrimir las espadas, y jugar las Lanzas; hasta, que uno de los Soldados, viendo tan ensagrentada la riña: dixo (hablando con sus Compañeros) muera una porque no perscamos todos: semejante voz dixo Caiphas Pontifice a los Judios en el Concilio, que formó su malicia contra Christo; pero este Soldado sin consejo, diciendo, y haciendo, arrojó un Chuzo, O Lanza a esta innocente niña con amino de quitarla la vida; para que la vida de una innocente Cordera fuesse Arco de Paz

entre tantos delinquentes. Pero no sucedió lo que pretendia el inadvertido, y cruel Pyrata; porque huyendo el cuerpo la niña, o declinando el impulso de la Lanza la superior mano, le atravesó solo un muslo; y la Sangre, que salió de la herida, bastó para que lastimados, y compassivos, cessassen en la colera, y la pendencia; y que dejando todos las armas, acudiessen a curarla; y assi fuesse lazo de union, y Concordia su innocente Sangre vertida. Volvieronse luego a los Bageles, y se quedó con la prisionera uno de los principales Captianes, que la havia ganado, con obligacion de curarla, y tratarla como a hija y no como a esclava (bk. 1, 17).

10. The referent of "she" and "her" switches back and forth without notice between the Mogul lady and Myrrha, in the original as in the translation: Determinó esta zelosa desaogar su ira con la belleza, que juzgaba causa, u occassion de su desprecio; procurando quitarle su natural hermosura; maltratabala con palabras, y con obras: pretendiendo muchas vezes consumirla, desgreñandola a repelones; arrastrabala de sus cabellos, azotabala, aporreabala, y afeaba sus mexillas, con la Sangre, que derramaba por las heridas. Procuraba que la hambre marchitasse el color, y gracias de su rostro: y finalmente fue el yunque de una muger vengativa sobre zelosa sin mas delito que ser hermosa, y amada Myrrha; y sin mas occassion que ser objepto de un aborrescimiento invidioso. Crecio este tan hasta lo summo, que no satisfaciendose bastantemente su ira, ni templandosse su rabia con la sangre de una innocente cordera; trató de quitarle muchas vezes la vida. Prevenia los cuchillos su enojo, con determinacion de matarla: pero el temor, de que la Sangre vertida diesse vozes, como la de Abel, que clamó contra el invidioso fratricida, la cortaba, y detenia. Pareciole que matandola sin Sangre, y a escondidas quedaria su maldad occulta; y asi se resolvio a otro hecho mas aleboso; que fue arrojarla al mar con el peso de una piedra, para que se atribuyesse a contingente desgracia, lo que era estudiada malicia de su rabia. Executó ayrada la traycion, pero por dicha de Myrraha tubó prevenida la Providencia Divina una Ancla en el puesto donde cayó, para que assiendose de su Cable pudiesse sacar la cabeza del agua; y pedir a vozes ayuda, favor y el Baptismo, que era ya su principal, y unico cuydado, socorriola un hidalgo Portugues que estaba cerca del mar, como prevenido instrumento de la Omnipotencia Divina, para que la librasse del naufragio, y guardasse como en otros riesgos la vida. Con esta feliz desgracia depositaron en otra casa a esta Niña; donde viendola el amante Mogor macilenta y desfigurada su hermosura, y belleza, passo su amor a la dama Mogora, que con tantas ansias le pretendia (bk. 1, 18).

11. Because of the nearly simultaneous publication of volume 3 with the Spanish prohibition of volume 1, volume 3 never had the circulation that the first two volumes enjoyed. Extant copies, therefore, are rare; I have found reference to only one in Mexico and have been unable to consult it to date.

12. Un mostruo Pez, cuya fealdad, y fiereza la causaba horror, y que no podia

explicar, llamadole ya Tiburon, ya Cayman, ya Monstruo Marino; porque su forma era extraordinaria, y abominable, y sus escamas con tales pintas, y manchas, que le hacian horrible a la vista (bk. 2, 119).

13. Lector, que era digna esta vission de mas profundas, y estendidas glosas, comparala con lo que nos dejo escrito el Evangelista San Juan en el capitulo doze de su Apocalysis, y hallaras, quan uniforme es Dios en hablar, y comunicar sus secretos en todos los tiempos a sus Siervos y escogidos, veras tambien, que como no pudo dexar de verificarse todo lo que mostro a su Sagrado Benjamin de la Catholica Iglesia, siempre perseguida, y siempre vencedora en figura de una prodigiosa muger (bk. 2, 120).

14. For example: "Sucediame algunas vezes, entre asombros, y admiraciones, ponderar conmigo mismo, la grandeza de la divina Luz, que ilustra a esta esclarecida Virgen, admirandome, de que siendo en lo natural vozal, y muy cerrada, se explicase con tanta eloquencia, con tal energia, y con expresiva tan propria en materias tan profundas, y tan varias, que parecia estaba debaxo de la Esphera de su vista todo el universo, sin que se le servasen los secretos del Cielo, ni los pensamientos, y secretos de los corazones de los hombres. Con esta admiracion, la dije un dia: 'Catharina, que necesidad ay, de que te manifieste Dios tantos, y tan desacostumbrados secretos, y mysterios?' A esta pregunta, me respondio con sinceridad, e innocencia: 'No se, que responderle, Padre y señor mio, no se si esto es malo o si es bueno; yo digo lo que me pasa, y se lo dejo a mis Confessores, para que como doctos, y esperimentados, lo apruebaen; pero lo que ahora entiendo es; que me trata, y comunica Jesus, como se pueden tratar, y comunicar aca en lo humano los dos mas tiernos amantes: y como no permite el amor, que entre dos amigos aya cosa oculta, en secreta: assi Dios se muestra Amante, comunicandome lo mas oculto de sus Mysterios.' Esta respuesta de Catharina, es el estilo, que a guardado dios con sus amigos en todos los tiempos" (bk. 2, 69).

15.

En una occasion, se le dexó ver el Señor, en la misma forma de Niño, pero casi desnudo, al modo, que solemos vestir sus Imagenes en la Solemnidad de su Resurrecion, o Natividad en el Pesebre: Andaba en aquel tiempo, muy cuydadosa Catharina de vestir a Christo desnudo en su Santissimo Nacimiento, y con la dicha apparicion parece le respondió al Señor a sus desseos, diciendole, como quien se le queria arroja a su regazo, y castos abrazos: Catharina visteme? La charidad, y amor de esta su amada, y querida Esposa, creció con esta vision, casi hasta causar excesso mental en el corazon, y la hubiera arrebatado su impulso, a coger al Niño Dios entre sus brazos, a no detenerla las prisiones de su Virginal recato, dandola temor la desnudez de su Unico, y Divino Amante: y assi le dixo, o preguntó que porque no venia vestido? Que si le faltaban Angeles, y Madre, que cu-briessen con preciosa telas la Hermosura, Y Belleza, en que se miraban, y gozaban los Cortesanos del Cielo? Respondiola, que queria fuesse ella quien lo vistiesse, y adornase. Replicó Catharina, que ella no tenia con que vestirle, ni manos para tocarle, ni aun ojos para mirarle desnudo, y procu-rando apartar la vista de aquel Dios de Pureza, Su Divino Amante, quis-iera esconderse, y rehundirse en el centro de la tierra. . . .

Pero quando mas descuydada, se hallaba otra vez con el mismo objecto, y con demostraciones, y con mas cariñosas ansias de recibir de mano de su Amada, el vestido, que la pedia. Aunque respondia Catharina, con nuevas, mayores, y mas cumplidas repugnancias de su amorosa Pureza; la dexase, que se fuesse, que se ausentarse; porque la rredraba, y acobardaba aquel desnudez de su Divinidad Humanada; y que no se hallaba con fuerzas para abrazarle; viendole tan desnudo, que la causaba no menos confusion, que Divino horror, hasta que le viesse decentemente a los ojos humanos ves-tido. Duró esta amorosa lucha, entre el Divino Amor, y su querida Esposa, mas de dos años. (bk. 1, 98–99)

16. Y él [Domingo], como hasta entonces no la entendió, quiso valerse ya de caricias, ya de amenazas, ya de rigores, pero ella sólo se valía de la verdad con que lo amonestó y se valía de las voces que a su Divino Esposo daba, y se valía de mu-chas y devotas ansias con que llamaba a la Virgen María. A estas resistencias de Catarina, si crecían en él los enfados, las irascibles y los malos tratos, en ella cre-cía más la fijeza de su prometimiento y voto (59).

17. Fue siempre esta venerable y devota mujer compuesta en sus acciones, me-dida en sus palabras, cuerda en sus respuestas, recatada en sus obras, discreta sin afectos, política sin ceremonias, silenciosa sin demasías (50).

18. Antes de pasar adelante quiero prevenir con acuerdo una pregunta que pueda pulsar con viveza a cualquiera persona, y sea el decir que por qué causa re-fiero virtudes de Catarina, que ejercitó en aquella temprana edad en que vivía? Y cómo doy razón tan por extenso de lo que yo no vi por entonces? Y además de esto si no lo vi? Luego ella me las refería cuando la comuniqué, repugnancia que hace al buen espíritu porque éste sólo dice sus faltas, no sus virtudes, pues éstas se dejan al conocimiento de quien dirige (49).

19. No averiguo de esta merced el modo con que recibió, si fue enajenada de los sentidos y potencias o si fue visión imaginaria o si la recibió visiblemente, pues queriendo yo saber de la suerte de que le pasó me solía decir (28).

20. Por contenerse en él, revelaciones, visiones y apariciones inútiles, invero-símiles, llenas de contradicciones y comparaciones impropias, indecentes y te-merarias, *que sapiunt blasphemias* (que casi son blasfemias), abusando del Miste-

rio Altísimo e Inefable de la Encarnación del Hijo de Dios, y otros lugares de la Sagrada Escritura, y doctrinas temerarias, peligrosas y contrarias al sentir de los Doctores, y práctica de la Iglesia Universal, sin más fundamento que la vana credulidad del autor. As quoted by Nicolás León, *Catarina de San Juan y la China Poblana* (1921–22; Mexico City: Ediciones Altiplano, 1971), 89–91.

21. Ramos opens with a long dedication to Bishop Fernández de Santa Cruz in which he highlights how Catarina de San Juan herself bestowed him with the authority to write her life story and he extends that privilege to the bishop, as pastor of the flock that includes Catarina (and who, of course, had the power to approve the biography). Listed in narrative order, the remaining prefatory material includes a lengthy letter by Núñez de Miranda, three *aprobaciones* by two calificadores and a theologian, a license from the viceroy Conde de Galve, four *aprobaciones* or *pareceres* written by some of the leading ecclesiastical figures in Puebla upon the request of Bishop Santa Cruz, a license by Santa Cruz himself, and, finally, the necessary license by Ramos's Jesuit superior, the provincial of the order in New Spain.

22. Two letters address more specifically what lies at the heart of the book's trial: the church's efforts to control not only heresy but also sanctity. Villa mentions Pope Urban VII's edicts in 1625, 1631, and 1640 regulating the process for canonization of holy people; from then on it was to be centralized, under the domain of Rome. Vaca also acknowledges the pope's authority for having the final word and meanwhile makes a case for the truth of Catarina's case and the need for a saint like her. Aware of the concerns about her "prodigiosa" life (that is, the abundance of miracles and visions), he enumerates evidence for its credibility.

23. The licenses include bishop of Mexico Francisco Aguiar y Sejas (not Bishop Santa Cruz, since the second volume is published in Mexico City) and the provincial of the Jesuit order—as well as two brief *pareceres* from a well-known Dominican friar and another Jesuit.

24. The material includes a long personal letter to Ramos from Ambrosio Oddon, provincial of the order and theologian, in which he responds to Ramos's inquiry about the doctrinal content in volume 2. Ostensibly a parallel to Núñez's letter in the first volume, Oddon's is not as privileged in narrative order, placed at the end of the published material, and contains none of the seriousness of tone or concern found in Núñez's. Rather, Oddon exuberantly praises the wonder of Catarina's life and the manifestation of divine grace in it.

25. Que se sepa y entienda que cuanto yo refieriere en este escrito, lo ví, lo experimenté y hice aquellas pruebas que tales materias piden para la verificación de su fidelidad, verdad y legalidad, y puesta la mano en el pecho, haciendo la señal de la santa cruz, *Iuro in verbo Sacerdoitis* decir verdad en todo (16).

26. Sólo el que aquí referiré basta para comprobarlos todos, y por haber sido

notorio a muchas personas que lo vieron, de que pueden dar fe, que yo los demás los dejo porque en materias de milagros, como son puntos de suyo tan difíciles de averiguar y tan reservados al conocimiento de la iglesia por los que tienen este ministerio de oficio, no quiero que sirvan de embarazo para el crédito de las virtudes de esta sierva de Dios, ni tampoco para alargar esta historia que sólo sirve de despertar y conmover la devoción de los fieles (199).

27. See the introductory study to Graxeda's volume for more details.

28.

[Catarina] *"En verdad ángel mío, que vuesastedes dicen el verdad, y así echen ruego a Dios no me perda."*

[Ramos] Que quiso decir: "En verdad que dicen vuestras mercedes la verdad y sienten lo que yo soy, que soy una embustera y aun por eso pido por amor de Dios rueguen por mí, no se pierda mi alma; ya conozco que soy china, ya veo que soy basura, que soy una inmundicia y que soy una perra, pero por el mismo caso, así de lo que consideráis como de lo que me decís, por eso propio os suplico hagáis especial petición para que yo tenga buen fin." (112)

29. See Peter Burke, "How to Be a Counter-Reformation Saint," in *Religion and Society in Early Modern Europe, 1500–1800,* ed. Kaspar von Greyerz (London: George Allen and Unwin, 1984), 46.

30. The concept of decorum was important to the period and is evident in other works. For example, Pedro Mercado writes a brief biography about a Philippine servant for the Jesuits and uses a direct simple style, *El Cristiano virtuoso* (Madrid, 1673); and Carlos de Sigünza y Góngora discusses the need to write in a nonflorid style because he is writing a history "de mugeres y para mugeres" in his chronicle of a Mexican convent, *Paraíso occidental* (Mexico, 1684). For a discussion of the former, see my "La influencia mediativa del clero en las vidas de religiosos y monjas" (forthcoming); for the latter, see Kathleen Ann Ross's *The Baroque Narrative of Carlos de Sigünza y Góngora: A New World Paradise* (Cambridge: Cambridge University Press, 1993), chap. 2.

31. Gwendolyn Barnes-Karol, "Religious Oratory and a Culture of Control," in *Culture and Control in Counter-Reformation Spain,* ed. Anne Cruz and Mary Elizabeth Perry (Minneapolis: University of Minnesota Press, 1992), 51–77.

32. I have been unable to locate the list of rules in effect in the 1690s, but these 1707 rules would have been similiar.

33. See Pérez-Marchand, *Dos etapas ideológicas,* for a full reproduction of the rules and an interesting study of them, and José Abel Ramos Soriano, "Critierios inquisitoriales en la prohibición de literatura relacionada con la comunidad doméstica en la Nueva España," in *El placer de pecar y el afán de normar,* ed. Semi-

nario de Historia de las Mentalidades (Mexico City: INAH, 1987), 353–76.

34. "Láminas, sellos, medallas, sortijas y las cuentas, cruzes, imagenes, retratos y otras cosas de este género, a que se atribuyen efectos, que penden de sola la voluntad de Dios o libertad humana."

35. As mentioned earlier, Palafox was another Puebla figure who had a popular following because he was considered to have died in the odor of sancity; he had also known Catarina. The edict must have been thoroughly carried out, because even the portrait of Catarina in Ramos's work has been removed from most extant copies. The edict is cited in Destefano, "Miracles and Monasticism," 72 nn. 19 and 27.

36. To date, Francisco de la Maza's *Catarina de San Juan* (1970; Mexico City: Cien de México, 1990) and León's studies of Catarina de San Juan and her biographers (*Catarina de San Juan* [1921–22]) are among the few that have worked with archival material and pieced together the series of events and edicts that help provide a fuller picture of the dynamics of religious belief, literary representation, and institutional rules.

37. December 15, 1695, letter from the Mexican Inquisition to the Spanish inquisitor general, quoted in Toribio Medina, *Historia*, 321.

38. De la Maza, *Catarina de San Juan*, 118–19.

39. Finding historical records in which Catarina is named in the late eighteenth or nineteenth century—such as the reprinting of Graxeda's biography— would support the conclusion that a cult may have not been entirely averted. According to de la Maza, a mid-eighteenth-century edition of Graxeda is noted by a bibliographer, but he has been unable to find this edition; ibid., chap. 3.

40. The Catholic Church's change in policy is seen when in the 1960s it canonized a sixteenth-century Peruvian of African descent (Martín de Porras).

41. Burke, "Counter-Reformation Saint," 49.

42. For a detailed analysis of the dynamic of clerical mediation in Sor Juana, Madre María de San José, and Catarina de San Juan, see my "The Mystic Triad in Colonial Mexican Religious Women's Discourse: Divine Author, Visionary Scribe, and Clerical Mediator" (*Colonial Latin American Research Review*, forthcoming).

Glossary

abjuration de levi. By this formal oath the accused judged guilty by the Inquisition renounced their errors and promised to return to the faith.

abjuration de vehementi. A stronger formal oath required of those found guilty of more grave offenses.

abonos. Evidence in support of the defendant.

alumbrado. An illuminist, associated with *alumbradismo*, a movement of interior spirituality that stressed illumination by the Holy Spirit.

auto-da-fé. A public or sometimes private ceremony of penitence in which those found guilty by the Inquisition had their sentences decreed.

beata. A woman who dedicated herself to God, living by herself or with other women in a community, sometimes attached to a religious order.

beaterio. A community of two or more beatas.

calificador. An official of the Inquisition whose job it was to assess the evidence against the accused to determine if there were grounds for heresy.

comisario. A commissary, or official representative of the Holy Office.

consulta de fe. A body that voted on the case; it consisted of the inquisitors, a representative of the bishop, and some graduates in theology or law.

converso. Common term for a baptized Jew or the Christian descendant of one.

cortes. A parliament of representatives from the church, aristocracy, and towns and cities.

edict of grace. The oral proclamation in church of a list of heresies and invitation to denounce oneself or others within a "period of grace," usually thirty or forty days.

ilusa. Deluded, a word disparagingly applied to a visionary woman.

indirectas. Questions asked of character witnesses whose names the defense supplied.

letrado. A university graduate in law.

licenciado. A university graduate.

limpieza de sangre. Purity of blood, meaning a genetic lineage free from non-Christian blood; it became a requirement for secular and religious offices in the sixteenth and seventeenth centuries.

Morisco. A baptized Muslim or descendant of one.

oratorio. Religious ritual organized and conducted in the privacy of one's home.

potro. The most common form of torture in the sixteenth century, in which the accused was bound on a rack by cords that were tightened around the body and limbs.

promotor. Legal counsel for the accused provided by the Inquisition.

promotor fiscal. Associated with the court, he was the prosecuting attorney.

querella. In legal terms, a complaint.

reconciliation. The step in the inquisitorial process when the guilty person had done penance and was received back into the church; also refers to a statement of contrition submitted before the trial.

relación de causa. Summary of an Inquisition trial.

sanbenito or *sambenito*. The penitential garment the penitent was required to wear, often with her family name, the crimes committed, and the insignia of the Holy Office.

Suprema. The name by which the Supreme Council of the Inquisition was known.

tachas. Lists of hostile witnesses prepared by the accused in self-defense.

toca. The water torture, applied when the victim was on the rack, with water poured slowly from a jar through a linen cloth, or *toca*, put down the throat.

Bibliography

The bibliography is arranged according to general topics that are represented in the essays. Its purpose is to provide direction for further reading.

INQUISITION STUDIES

Two works that are considered basic to the study of the Spanish Inquisition are:

Lea, Henry Charles. *A History of the Inquisition of Spain.* 4 vols. New York: Macmillan, 1906–7.

Llorente, Juan Antonio. *Historia crítica de la Inquisición de España.* 4 vols. Madrid: Ediciones Hiperión, 1980. Translation of *Histoire critique de l'Inquisition d'Espagne.* 4 vols. Paris, 1817.

More recent studies that are of a general nature include:

Alcalá, Angel, ed. *Inquisición española y mentalidad inquisitorial.* Barcelona: Editorial Ariel, S.A., 1984.

Bennassar, Bartolomé, et al. *L'Inquisition espagnole, XV–XIX siècles.* Paris: Hachette, 1979.

Contreras, Jaime, ed. *Inquisición española: Nuevas aproximaciones.* Madrid: Centro de Estudios Inquisitoriales, Ediciones Najera, 1987.

Dufour, G. *La Inquisición española: Una aproximación a la España intolerante.* Barcelona: Montesinos, 1986.

Haliczer, Stephen, ed. *Inquisition and Society in Early Modern Europe.* London: Croom Helm, 1986.

Henningsen, Gustav, and John Tedeschi, eds. *The Inquisition in Early Modern Europe: Studies on Sources and Methods.* De Kalb: Northern Illinois University Press, 1986.

Jiménez Monteserín, M. *Introducción a la Inquisición española: Documentos básicos para el estudio del Santo Oficio.* Madrid: Editora Nacional, 1980.

Kamen, Henry. *The Inquisition and Society in Spain in the Sixteenth and Seventeenth Centuries.* Bloomington: Indiana University Press, 1985.

Márquez, Antonio. *Literatura e Inquisición en España, 1478–1834.* Madrid: Taurus Ediciones, S.A., 1980.

Monter, William. *Frontiers of Heresy: The Spanish Inquisition from the Basque Lands to Sicily.* Cambridge: Cambridge University Press, 1990.

Pérez Villanueva, Joaquin, ed. *La Inquisición española: Nueva visión, nuevos horizontes.* Madrid: Siglo XXI, 1980.

Pérez Villanueva, Joaquin, and B. Escandell Bonet, eds. *Historia de la Inquisición en España y América: El conocimiento científico y el proceso histórico de la Institución (1478–1834).* Madrid: Biblioteca de Autores Cristianos, Centro de Estudios Inquisitoriales, 1984.

Perry, Mary Elizabeth, and Anne J. Cruz, eds. *Cultural Encounters: The Impact of the Inquisition in Spain and the New World.* Berkeley: University of California Press, 1991.

Pinto Crespo, Virgilio. *Inquisición y control ideológico en la España del siglo XVI.* Madrid: Taurus, 1983.

Tellechea Idígoras, J. I. *Tiempos recios: Inquisición y heterodoxos.* Salamanca: Ediciones Sígueme, 1977.

Turberville, A. S. *La Inquisición española.* Mexico City: Fondo de Cultura Económica, 1973.

REGIONAL AND GROUP STUDIES

Numerous studies exist on the Inquisition in various regions of Spain and in connection with minority groups.

Aranda Doncel, Juan. *Los moriscos en tierras de Córdoba.* Córdoba: Publicaciones del Monte de Piedad y Caja de Ahorros de Córdoba, 1984.

Blázquez Miguel, Juan. *La Inquisición en Albacete.* Albacete: Instituto de Estudios Albacetenses, 1985.

———. *La Inquisición en Castilla–La Mancha.* Madrid: Universidad de Córdoba, 1986.

———. *La Inquisición en Cataluña: El tribunal del Santo Oficio de Barcelona, 1487–1820.* Toledo: Editorial Arcano, 1990.

———. *El tribunal de la Inquisición en Murcia.* Murcia: Academia Alfonso X El Sabio, 1986.

Boronat y Barrachina, Pascual. *Los moriscos españoles y su expulsión: Estudio histórico-crítico*. 2 vols. Valencia: Francisco Vives y Mora, 1901.

Cardaillac, Louis. *Moriscos y christianos: Un enfrentamiento polémico, 1492–1640*. Madrid: Fondo de Cultura Económica, 1979.

Caro Baroja, Julio. *Los moriscos del Reino de Granada*. Madrid: Ediciones Istmo, 1976.

Chejne, Anwar G. *Islam and the West: The Moriscos*. Albany: State University of New York Press, 1983.

Contreras, Jaime. *El Santo Oficio de la Inquisición de Galicia: Poder, sociedad y cultura*. Madrid: Akal, 1982.

Domínguez Ortiz, Antonio. *Autos de la Inquisición de Sevilla (siglo XVII)*. Seville: Servicio de Publicaciones del Ayuntamiento, 1981.

Domínguez Ortiz, Antonio, and Bernard Vincent. *Historia de los moriscos: Vida y tragedia de una minoría*. Madrid: Revista de Occidente, 1978.

García Arenal, Mercedes. *Inquisición y moriscos: Los procesos del tribunal de Cuenca*. 3d ed. Madrid: Siglo XXI de España Editores, 1987.

———. *Los moriscos*. Madrid: Editora Nacional, 1975.

García Cárcel, Ricardo. *Herejía y sociedad en el siglo XVI: La Inquisición en Valencia, 1530–1609*. Barcelona: Ediciones Península, 1980.

———. *Orígines de la Inquisición española: El tribunal de Valencia, 1478–1530*. Barcelona: Ediciones Península, 1976.

García Fuentes, J. L. *La Inquisición en Granada en el siglo XVI: Fuentes para su estudio*. Granada: Universidad de Granada, 1981.

Gracia Boix, Rafael. *Autos de fe y causas de la Inquisición de Córdoba*. Córdoba: Excma. Diputación Provincial, 1983.

Haliczer, Stephen. *Inquisition and Society in the Kingdom of Valencia, 1478–1834*. Berkeley: University of California Press, 1990.

Meyerson, Mark, ed. *Christians, Muslims, and Jews in Medieval and Early Modern Spain: Interaction and Cultural Change*. Notre Dame: University Press of Notre Dame, forthcoming.

———. *The Muslims of Valencia in the Age of Fernando and Isabel: Between Coexistence and Crusade*. Berkeley: University of California Press, 1991.

Regla, Joan. *Estudios sobre los moriscos*. Barcelona: Editorial Ariel, 1974.

Vincent, Bernard. *Minorías y marginados en la España del siglo XVI*. Granada: Diputación de Granada, 1987.

CONVERSOS AND JEWS

The bibliography on the Jews and *conversos* and their treatment by the Inquisition is vast.

Amador de los Ríos, José. *Historia social, política y religiosa de los judíos de España y Portugal.* 3 vols. Madrid: Fontanet, 1875–76.

Baer, Yitzak. *History of the Jews in Christian Spain.* 2 vols. Translated by Louis Schoffman. 1966. Reprint, Philadelphia: Jewish Publication Society of America, 1992.

Beinart, Haim. *Conversos on Trial: The Inquisition in Ciudad Real.* Jerusalem: Hebrew University, 1981.

————. *Records of the Trials of the Spanish Inquisition in Ciudal Real.* 4 vols. Jerusalem: Israel Academy of Sciences and Humanities, 1974–85.

Bel Bravo, M. A. *El auto de fe de 1593: Los conversos granadinos de origen judío.* Granada: Universidad de Granada, 1988.

Blázquez Miguel, Juan. *Inquisición y criptojudaísmo.* Madrid: Ediciones Kayeda, 1988.

Caro Baroja, Julio. *Inquisición, brujería y criptojudaísmo.* 2d ed. Barcelona: Editorial Ariel, 1972.

————. *Los Judíos en la España moderna y contemporánea.* 3 vols. Madrid: Ediciones Istmo, 1978.

Cascales Ramos, A. *La Inquisición en Andalucía: Resistencia de los conversos a su implantación.* Seville: Editoriales Andaluzas Unidas, 1986.

Coronas Tejada, L. *Conversos and Inquisition in Jaén.* Jerusalem: Magnes Press, 1988.

Domínguez Ortiz, Antonio. *Los conversos de origen judío después de la Expulsión.* Madrid: Consejo Superior de Investigaciones Científicas, 1955.

————. *Los judeoconversos en España y América.* Madrid: Ediciones Istmo, 1978.

López Martínez, Nicolas. *Los judaizantes castellanos y la Inquisición en tiempo de Isabel la católica.* Burgos: Seminario Metropolitano de Burgos, 1954.

Lozano, José Jiménez. *Judíos, moriscos y conversos.* Valladolid: Ambito, 1982.

Netanyahu, Benzion. *The Marranos of Spain: From the Late Fourteenth to the Early Sixteenth Century According to the Hebrew Sources.* New York: American Academy for Jewish Research, 1966.

————. *The Origins of the Inquisition in Fifteenth Century Spain.* New York: Random House, 1995.

Roth, Norman. *Conversos, Inquisition, and the Expulsion of the Jews from Spain.* Madison: University of Wisconsin Press, 1995.

Yerushalmi, Yosef H. *From Spanish Court to Italian Ghetto: Isaac Cardoso: A Study in Seventeenth-Century Marranism and Jewish Apologetics.* New York: Columbia University Press, 1971.

ALUMBRADOS, REFORMERS, AND PROTESTANTS

Major emphasis in this section is on the alumbrados, whose influence was felt throughout the sixteenth and seventeenth centuries.

Abellan, José Luis. *El erasmismo español.* Madrid: Espasa-Calpe, 1982.

Andrés Martín, Melquíades. *El misterio de los alumbrados de Toledo, desvelado por sus contemporáneos (1525–1560).* Burgos: Facultad de Teología del Norte de España, 1976.

———. *Nueva visión de los "alumbrados" de 1525.* Madrid: Fundación Universitaria Española, 1973.

———. *Los recogidos: Nueva visión de la mística española (1500–1700).* Madrid: Fundación Universitaria Española, 1975.

———. *Reforma española y reforma Luterana: Afinidades y diferencias a la luz de los místicos españoles (1517–1536).* Madrid: Fundación Universitaria Española, 1975.

Atkinson, James. *Lutero y el nacimiento del protestantismo.* Madrid: Alianza Editorial, 1971.

Avilés, Miguel. *Erasmo y la Inquisición.* Madrid: Fundación Universitaria Española, 1980.

Bataillon, Marcel. *Erasmo y España: Estudios sobre la historia espiritual del siglo xvi.* 2d ed. Translated by Antonio Alatorre. Mexico City: Fondo de Cultura Económica, 1966.

Burgos, Jesús Alonso. *El luteranismo en Castilla durante el siglo XVI.* Madrid: Editorial Swan, 1983.

García Oro, José. *Cisneros y la reforma del clero español en tiempos de los Reyes Católicos.* Madrid: CSIC, 1971.

Hamilton, Alastair. *Heresy and Mysticism in Sixteenth-Century Spain: The Alumbrados.* Toronto: University of Toronto Press, 1992.

Huerga, Alvaro. *Historia de los alumbrados.* 5 vols. Madrid: Fundación Universitaria Española, 1972–94.

———. *Predicadores, alumbrados e inquisición en el siglo XVI.* Madrid: Fundación Universitaria Española, 1973.

Inmaculada, Román de la. "El fenómeno de los alumbrados y su interpretación." *Ephemerides Carmeliticae* 9 (1958): 49–80.

Jones, Martin D. W. *The Counter Reformation: Religion and Society in Early Modern Europe.* Cambridge: Cambridge Topics in History, 1995.

Kinder, A. Gordon. *Spanish Protestants and Reformers in the Sixteenth Century: A Bibliography.* London: Grant & Cutler, 1983.

Llorca, Bernardino. *La Inquisición española y los alumbrados (1509–1667): Según las actas originales de Madrid y de otros archivos.* Salamanca: Universidad Pontificia, 1980.

Márquez, Antonio. *Los alumbrados: Orígenes y filosofía (1525–1559).* 2d ed. Madrid: Taurus Ediciones, S.A., 1980.

Nieto, José C. *Juan de Valdés y los orígenes de la reforma en España e Italia.* Madrid: Fondo de Cultura Económica, 1979.

Sarión Mora, Adelina. *Sexualidad y confesión: La solicitación ante el Tribunal del Santo Oficio (siglos XVI–XIX).* Madrid: Alianza Universidad, 1994.

Tapia, Ralph. *The Alumbrados of Toledo: A Study in Sixteenth Century Spanish Spirituality.* Park Falls, Wis.: Weber and Sons, 1974.

THE INQUISITION IN THE NEW WORLD

Alberro, Solange. *La actividad del Santo Oficio de la Inquisición en Nueva España, 1571–1700.* Mexico City: INAH, Colección Científica, 1981.

Greenleaf, Richard. *The Mexican Inquisition of the Sixteenth Century.* Albuquerque: University of New Mexico Press, 1969.

Jiménez Rueda, Julio. *Herejías y supersticiones en la Nueva España: Los heterodoxos en México.* Mexico City: Imprenta Universitaria, 1946.

Lea, Henry Charles. *The Inquisition in the Spanish Dependencies.* New York: Macmillan, 1908.

Libro Primero de Votos de la Inquisición de México: 1573–1600. Mexico City: Imprenta Universitaria, 1949.

Liebman, Seymour B., ed. *The Great Auto de Fé of 1649.* Kansas City: Coronado Press, 1974.

Medina, José Toribio. *Historia del Tribunal del Santo Oficio de la Inquisición en México.* Ed. Julio Jiménez Rueda. Mexico City: Miguel Angel Porrúa, 1987.

Pérez-Marchand, Monelisa Lina. *Dos etapas ideológicas del siglo XVIII en México a través de los papeles de la Inquisición.* Mexico City: Colegio de México, 1945.

Poole, Stafford. *Pedro Moya de Contreras: Catholic Reform and Royal Power in New Spain, 1571–1591.* Berkeley: University of California Press, 1987.

WOMEN'S ISSUES IN SPAIN AND THE NEW WORLD

Ahlgren, Gillian T. W. *Teresa of Avila and the Politics of Sanctity.* Ithaca, N.Y.: Cornell University Press, 1996.

Alberro, Solange. *Presencia y transparencia: La mujer en la historia de México.* Mexico City: Colegio de México, 1987.

Arenal, Electa, and Stacey Schlau. *Untold Sisters: Hispanic Nuns in Their Own Works.* Translations by Amanda Powell. Albuquerque: University of New Mexico Press, 1989.

Bainton, Roland H. *Women of the Reformation: From Spain to Scandinavia.* Minneapolis, Minn.: Augsburg Publishing House, 1977.

Bilinkoff, Jodi. *The Avila of Saint Teresa: Religious Reform in a Sixteenth-Century City.* Ithaca, N.Y.: Cornell University Press, 1989.

Blásquez Miguel, Juan. *Sueños y procesos de Lucrecia de León.* Madrid: Tecnos, 1987.

Boyer, Richard. *Lives of the Bigamists: Marriage, Family, and Community in Colonial Mexico.* Albuquerque: University of New Mexico Press, 1995.

Charnon-Deutsch, Lou, ed. *Estudios sobre escritoras hispánicas en honor de Georgina Sabat-Rivers.* Madrid, 1992.

Cruz, Anne, and Mary Elizabeth Perry, eds. *Culture and Control in Counter-Reformation Spain.* Minneapolis: University of Minnesota Press, 1992.

Durán, María Angeles, ed. *La mujer en la historia de España (siglos XVI–XX).* Actas de las Segundas Jornadas de Investigación Interdisciplinaria. Madrid: Universidad Autónoma, 1984.

———. *Nuevas perspectivas sobre la mujer.* Actas de las Primeras Jornadas de Investigación Interdisciplinaria. 2 vols. Madrid: Universidad Autónoma, 1982.

Franco, Jean. *Plotting Women: Gender and Representation in Mexico.* New York: Columbia University Press, 1989.

García-Nieto París, María Carmen, ed. *Ordenamiento jurídico y realidad social de las mujeres.* Actas de las Cuartas Jornadas de Investigación Interdisciplinarias. Madrid: Universidad Autónoma, 1986.

Giles, Mary E. *The Book of Prayer of Sor María of Santo Domingo: A Study and Translation.* Albany: State University of New York Press, 1990.

Imirizaldu, Jesús. *Monjas y beatas embaucadoras.* Madrid: Editorial Nacional, 1977.

Kagan, Richard L. *Lucrecia's Dreams: Politics and Prophecy in Sixteenth-Century Spain.* Berkeley: University of California Press, 1990.

Lavrin, Asunción, ed. *Latin American Women: Historical Perspectives.* Westport, Conn.: Greenwood Press, 1978.

———, ed. *Sexuality and Marriage in Colonial Latin America.* Lincoln: University of Nebraska Press, 1989.

Martín, Luis. *Daughters of the Conquistadores: Women of the Viceroyalty of Peru.* Dallas: Southern Methodist University Press, 1981.

Melammed, Renée Levine. *Heretics or Daughters of Israel.* New York: Oxford University Press, forthcoming.

Merrim, Stephanie, ed. *Feminist Perspectives on Sor Juana Inés de la Cruz.* Detroit: Wayne State University Press, 1991.

Muñoz Fernández, Angela. *Acciones e intenciones de mujeres en la vida religiosa de los siglos XV y XVI.* Madrid: Dirección General de la Mujer, 1995.

Muriel, Josefina. *Conventos de monjas en la Nueva España.* Mexico City: Editorial Santiago, 1946.

———. *Cultura femenina novohispana.* Mexico City: Universidad Nacional Autónoma de México, 1982.

Myers, Kathleen A. *Word from New Spain: The Spiritual Autobiography of Madre María de San José (1656–1719).* Liverpool: TRAC, Liverpool University Press, 1993.

Myers, Kathleen A., and Amanda W. Powell. *A Wild Country Out in the Garden: Selections from the Spiritual Autobiography of Madre María de San José.* Bloomington: Indiana University Press, forthcoming.

Pérez Baltasar, María Dolores. *Mujeres marginadas: Las casas de recogidas en Madrid.* Madrid: Gráficas Lormo, 1984.

Perry, Mary Elizabeth. *Gender amd Disorder in Early Modern Seville.* Princeton: Princeton University Press, 1990.

Saint-Saëns, Alain, ed. *Religion, Body, and Gender in Early Modern Spain.* San Francisco: Mellen Research University Press, 1991.

Saint-Saëns, Alain, and Magdalena Sánchez, eds. *Portraits of Spanish Women in the Golden Age: Images and Realities.* Westport, Conn.: Greenwood Press, 1996.

Seed, Patricia. *To Love, Honor, and Obey in Colonial Mexico: Conflicts over Marriage Choice, 1574–1821.* Stanford: Stanford University Press, 1988.

Surtz, Ronald E. *The Guitar of God: Gender, Power, and Authority in the Visionary World of Mother Juana de la Cruz (1481–1534).* Philadelphia: University of Pennsylvania Press, 1990.

———. *Writing Women in Late Medieval and Early Modern Spain.* Philadelphia: University of Pennsylvania Press, 1995.

Vigil, Mariló. *La vida de las mujeres en los siglos XVI y XVII.* Madrid: Siglo XXI, 1986.

Weber, Alison. *Teresa of Avila and the Rhetoric of Femininity.* Princeton: Princeton University Press, 1990.

Notes on Contributors

GILLIAN T. W. AHLGREN is associate professor of theology at Xavier University. She is the author of *Teresa of Avila and the Politics of Sanctity* as well as scholarly articles on women in sixteenth-century Spain. She is currently at work on a monograph on Francisca de los Apóstoles.

ANGEL ALCALÁ is professor of modern languages and literature at Brooklyn College of the City University of New York. Among his many publications are books that focus on the Inquisition: *Inquisición española y mentalidad inquisitorial, El proceso inquisitorial de Fray Luis de León,* and, most recently, *Judíos, sefarditas, conversos: La expulsión de 1492 y sus consecuencias.*

HAIM BEINART is former director of the Institute of Judaic Studies at the Hebrew University of Jerusalem and a member or associate of prestigious intellectual academies in Israel, Spain, and Mexico, including the Real Academia de la Historia. He has written extensively on the *conversos* in numerous articles and books, including *Records of the Trials of the Spanish Inquisition,* in four volumes.

CLARK COLAHAN, professor of foreign languages and literature at Whitman College, applies his translation skills to classics, as in *The Trials of Persiles and Sigismunda,* and to television, with English renderings of the eight programs in the series *Mujeres en la historia. The Visions of Sor María de Agreda: Writing, Knowledge, and Power* demonstrates his interest in women's writing.

LINDA A. CURCIO-NAGY is assistant professor of history at the University of Nevada, Reno. Her publications include articles about politics, religion, and culture in colonial Mexico. Her book *Saints, Sovereignty, and Spectacle in Colonial Mexico* is forthcoming.

MARY E. GILES is professor emeritus of humanities and religious studies at California State University, Sacramento. The founding editor of *Studia Mystica*, she is the author of many articles and several books, including the translation, with introduction, of Francisco de Osuna's *Tercer abecedario* and *The Book of Prayer of Sor María of Santo Domingo: A Study and Translation*.

JACQUELINE HOLLER is a postdoctoral fellow at Simon Fraser University in Vancouver, Canada. Her article on Elena de la Cruz was published earlier; she is continuing research on perceptions of the body in sixteenth-century Mexico.

KATHRYN JOY MCKNIGHT taught Spanish at Grinnell College in Iowa from 1992 to 1997 and currently works for the Community Service Council in Tulsa, Oklahoma. She is the author of *The Mystic of Tunja: The Writings of Madre Castillo, 1671–1742*.

RENÉE LEVINE MELAMMED is assistant dean at the Seminar of Judaic Studies in Jerusalem, where she teaches Jewish history and women's studies. She has published numerous articles on crypto-Jewish society and medieval and early modern Sephardic women. Her book *Heretics or Daughters of Israel: The Crypto-Jewish Women of Castile* is forthcoming.

KATHLEEN MYERS, associate professor of Spanish at Indiana University, is the author of many articles and the book *Word from New Spain: The Spiritual Autobiography of Madre María de San José*. A collaborative effort, *A Wild Country Out in the Garden: The Spiritual Autobiography of Madre María de San José*, is forthcoming.

MARY ELIZABETH PERRY, professor of history at Occidental College and associated with the UCLA Center for Medieval and Renaissance Studies, is the author of many articles and books on Spanish and New World culture. Her *Gender and Disorder in Early Modern Seville* and *Cultural Encounters: The Impact of the Inquisition in Spain and the New World*, coedited with Anne J. Cruz, illustrate her interest in women and gender issues as well as the Inquisition.

ALLYSON M. POSKA is assistant professor of history at Mary Washington College. Her articles on social mores in Galicia and seventeenth-century Spain appear in the *Journal of Social History* and *Mediterranean Studies*.

ELIZABETH RHODES is associate professor of Romance languages and literatures at Boston College. She writes on Catalan as well as Spanish literature in articles and books, including *The Unrecognized Precursors of "La Diana" by Montemayor*, and is working on an extensive study of religious women's writing.

GRETCHEN STARR-LEBEAU is assistant professor of history at the University of Kentucky. She has contributed articles to *Medieval Trade, Travel, and Exploration* and currently is preparing a book on the Inquisition of Guadalupe, the subject of her dissertation.

Index

abjuration de levi, 115, 176, 229, 248, 354n.
64, 377
abjuration de vehementi, 50, 83, 227, 377
abonos: defined, 377; in María López's
case, 58, 59, 60, 62
adafinas, 28, 31
Adrian Florensz Boeyens (bishop of
Tortosa), 320n. 5
African slaves: Inquisition jurisdiction
over, 252–53, 349n. 11; rebelliousness
and suppression of, 8, 234–37, 251–53
Aguiar y Sejas, Bishop Francisco, 374n.
23
Aguilera, Francisco de: *Sermon en que se
da noticia de la vida . . . de la Venerable
Señora Chatharima de San Joan*, 276,
293
Aguilera, Luisa de, 122–23
Aguirre Beltrán, Gonzalo, 235
Agustina de Santa Clara, 220, 369–70n. 1
Aixa (wife of Muhammed), 182
Alba, duke of (Fernando Álvarez de
Toledo), 78
Alberro, Solange, 212
Alcaraz, Pedro Ruiz de, 4, 77, 92–93, 100–
101, 102, 103, 106, 107, 109, 111, 112, 117
alcazar, 47
All Saints' Day (Todos Santos), 258

Alonso, Beatriz, 51
Alonso, Margarida, 194
alumbrados (enlightened ones): as challenge to ecclesiastical authority, 11, 78,
79, 81, 99, 124, 133, 172, 173, 222; defined, 377; emergence of, 4, 78, 100,
220; as focus of Mexican Inquisition,
210, 213, 220–23; as focus of Spanish
Inquisition, 4–5, 6, 7, 11, 78, 79, 91,
98–99, 100–101, 102, 115, 171, 172–73,
185–86
Amerindians, excluded from Inquisition,
212
Aminah (mother of Muhammed),
182–83
Ana de Guillamas, 350n. 17
Andalusia: Inquisition in, 6, 172. *See also*
Seville
Andrés de la Torre, Francisco, 158, 160,
161
Angela of Foligno, 128, 332n. 19
Anne (saint), 283
Anthony of Padua (saint), veneration of,
254, 256, 259, 261–67, 269
anti-Semitism: development of, 297–98n.
2; in Spanish Inquisition, 2, 297–98n.
2, 298–99n. 5
Anton de Castillo, 39

aposentilla (little room), of Catarina de San Juan, 271, 274

Aragon: medieval inquisition in (1232), 1–2; modern Inquisition in, 2

Arrovas, Mose, 25, 36

autos-da-fé: defined, 377; in Guadalupe, 27, 40; in Mexico, 211, 212, 227; in Seville, 171; in Toledo, 71

Avila, Inquisition in, 2, 102

Baestra, Juan de, 171, 180

Bainton, Roland, 99

Balça, Isabel de, 237–38

Barcelona, Inquisition in, 2, 134–54

Barnes-Karol, Gwendolyn, 290–91

Bautista, Isabel, 120, 121–22, 123, 127, 324n. 3

Bautista, Fray Juan, 122

beata profesa, 135

beatas (holy women): defined, 377; in New World, 8, 214, 216–20, 255; in Spain, 4, 75–76, 78, 175, 214, 324n. 4

beaterios, 75, 120, 214, 299n. 10, 377

Beatriz (daughter of Rodrigo de Villa-nueva and Isabel de la Fuente), 50–51

Beatriz (orphan of Extremadura), 50

Beatriz de Robles, 7, 171–88

Bedoya, Gaspar de, 100–101

Benavides, Alonso de, 155, 158, 169, 170

bestiality, Catholic regulation of, 7

Beteta, Luis de, 91

Bible: conversos' knowledge of, 48; prohibited editions of, 5

Bichancho, Gonçalo, 44, 45

Bichancho y González, Isabel, 51

bigamy, Catholic regulation of, 7, 189–205, 213, 232

bilocations, 12; of Ana Domenge, 136–37; of Catarina de San Juan, 280; of María de Jesús de Agreda, 155–56, 157, 158, 160, 166, 167, 169

Blanca, María, 8, 229–31, 236–49, 251–53

blasphemy: among African slaves, 229–53; defined, 232–34

Blásquez, Oro, 27, 40–41

body, female: relationship to God through, 11–13

Boehmer, Edward, 94

Bohorques, Dr. Martos de, 229, 241, 247, 249

bozal, 237, 243

Burgos, Pedro de, 68

Burke, Peter, 294

Bustillo, Francisca Paz de, 264–65, 269

Busto de Villegas, Sancho, 122, 123

Cabalism, 337n. 14

Cabrera y Villareal, M., 90, 91

Calero, Antonio de, 76

calificaciones (theological assessments), 123–24

calificadores (examiners), 159–60, 272, 377

Calvin, John, 191

canonization, 156, 273, 287, 289, 294

Cárdenas, Alonso López de, 229, 247

Cárdenas, María de, 217, 218, 219

Carlini, Benedetta, 223

Carlos II (king of Spain), 280

Carmelite order, 133, 275

Carranza, Archbishop Bartolomé Miranda de, 119, 120, 123, 127, 129, 130, 133

Carrillo, Francisco, 103

Carvajal family, 212

Casas, Bartolomé de las, 157

Castile: Inquisition in, 2, 53–72; relocation of Moriscos in, 179. *See also* Extremadura; Guadalupe

Castillo, Juan del, 77, 93

Castro, Marina de, 201

Castro y Quiñones, Pedro (archbishop of Granada), 181

Catalina (neighbor of María López), 61

Catalina (wife of Fernando Cavallero), 69

Catalina (wife of Nablero), 65

Catalina de Jesús, 122, 176, 325n. 16
Catalina *la botera*, 68
Catalonia, Inquisition in, 2, 138–39. *See also* Barcelona
Catarina de San Juan, 9, 270–95
Cathar heresy, 2
Catherine of Siena (saint), 96, 128, 137, 144–45
Cazalla, Gonçalo Martínez de, 105
Cazalla, Isabel de, 105
Cazalla, Bishop Juan de, 92, 93, 101, 103, 104
Cazalla, María de: church investigation of, 4, 93, 94, 98, 101–18; clerical support for, 11; conflict with Francisca Hernández, 95, 102, 103, 107, 109; imprisonment of, 102; reputation of, 5, 92, 95
Cazalla, Pedro de, 76, 83, 93
censorship. *See* Index of Prohibited Books; Valdés Index
Cerda, Alonso de la, 59, 60, 62, 68
Cervantes, Catalina de, 68–69
Cervantes, María Ignacia, 198
Çevallos, Augustín de, 249, 250
Chacón, Pedro, 120
Charles II. *See* Carlos II (king of Spain)
Chávez, Margarita, 274
Chichimecatechuhtli, Carlos, 211, 212
children: confession, punishment, and reeducation of, 49–51; as followers of Inés of Herrera del Duque, 49–51
Christ. *See* Jesus Christ
cimarrones, 235, 251
Cisneros, Cardinal Francisco Ximénez de, 4, 78, 96, 156, 319n. 1, 320n. 5, 333n. 26
comisario, 194, 377
Conceptionist (Franciscan) order, 155, 161, 275
Consejo de la Suprema y General Inquisición (Council of the Supreme and General Inquisition): establish-

ment of (1483), 2; in María de Cazalla case, 102, 103, 111, 112; Mexican Inquisition established by, 7–8
consulta de fe, 50, 377
Contarini, Bishop Gasparo, 349n. 6
Contreras, Jaime, 203
contrition. *See* reconciliation
conversos (New Christians): communal meals of, 55; confessions by, 24, 27, 34–36, 39–40, 70–71, 315n. 75; control of, 2; defined, 2, 378; as focus of Mexican Inquisition, 212; as focus of Spanish Inquisition, 2–4, 22, 27, 41, 42, 49, 53, 72; Jewish practices of, 21, 22–23, 24–25, 28, 32, 33, 34, 37, 40, 46, 50, 54–57, 70–71; legal counsel to, 29–30; redemption of, 42–52; suspicion and blaming of, 21, 297–98n. 2; trials for deceased, 27. *See also* crypto-Judaism
Córdoba, Inquisition in, 2, 21
Cordón, Rodrigo (of Siruela), 47–48
cortes, 378
Council of the Supreme and General Inquisition. *See* Consejo de la Suprema y General Inquisición
Council of Trent (1545-63): and canonization process, 273, 287, 289; and cloistering of women religious, 136, 349n. 6; and genuineness of women's visions, 6; guidelines for literary productions, 290–92; and restrictions on women's self-expression, 10; and restrictions on women's sexuality, 12, 190–91, 347n. 46; women's gains prior to, 336n. 1
Counter Reformation: church authority during, 178, 205, 359n. 33; Inquisition under, 6, 7, 133, 156, 174; view of New World colonists, 272
Cruz, Ana de la, 197–98
Cruz, Andrés de la (Fray), 218
Cruz, Isabel de la, 4, 92, 100–101, 106, 111, 112, 117, 183

Cruz, Magdalena de la, 223
crypto-Judaism: debate over, 298–99n. 5, 301n. 1; defined, 298n. 4. *See also* conversos (New Christians)

Darnilés, Fray Antonio, 135
dejamiento (abandonment prayer), 86, 100
Delgado, Ines, 194
devotio moderna, 78
Díaz, Hernando, 116, 117
Diego de Aragón (Fray), 217
Diego de San Francisco (Fray), 215
Domenge, Ana, 6, 9, 13, 14, 134–54
Dominican order, 78, 136
Donoso, Lope, 43

Edict of Toledo (1515), 78, 81, 91
edicts of grace, 100, 104, 378
education, of women, 10, 193, 215
Eguía, Miguel de, 77, 93
Elena (saint), 263
Elias (prophet), 43, 44, 46
Elijah (prophet), 47
Elizabeth I (queen of England), 209
El-Saffar, Ruth Anthony, 159
embaucadora (fraud), 129
endemoniadas (bedeviled women), 123, 128, 223, 225–26
Erasmianism: followers of, 4, 77, 95, 99, 104, 106, 115; objections to, 5, 78
Erasmus, Desiderius, 4, 5, 77
escalera, torture on, 39, 70, 82–83, 112–14
Esteban, Juan, 42, 46
Excelencias de la fe (Excellences of the faith) (Valdés), 10
exterioridades (exterior manifestations of spirituality), 167
Extremadura, Inquisition in, 6, 42–52
Eymerich, Nicolás, 232

Felipe. *See* Philip (kings of Spain)
Ferdinand II (king of Aragon), 2

Fernández, Catalina, 189, 200–201, 205
Fernández, Pero (of Chillón), 43–44, 45
Fernández de Zamora, Diego, 28, 30, 32, 34, 36, 37
Fernando de Belalcázar, 47
Feuerbach, Ludwig, 152
Feyxoa, Margarida, 194
Fifth Lateran Council, 347n. 46
folk piety, as dangerous to orthodox Catholicism, 8–9
Follequinos, Mose, 36
Fonseca, Pedro de, 246
fornication, Catholic regulation of, 7, 196
Fraguas, Martín de, 67
Francisca de los Apóstoles, 6, 12, 13–14, 119–33
Franciscan order: missionary efforts in New World, 157; support for *beatas* and other holy women in, 77, 86, 100, 156; support for spiritual individualism in, 11
Francisco (son of María López), 55
Francisco de Bocanegra, 218
Free Spirit, heresy of, 172
Fuente, Alonso de la, 124
Fuente, Francisco de la, 160, 169

Galdo, Juan de, 254, 264–65, 269
Galicia, bigamy in, 7, 189–205
Galve, count of (Gaspar de la Cerda Sandoval Silva y Mendoza), 254, 374n. 21
Gando, Margarida de, 194–95
García, Diego (of Siruela), 48
García, Marcos, 49
García Jiménez, Inés, 49
García the redhead, 67
Gaytan, María, 60
Gerónima (mulatta slave), 230, 231, 249–51
Gerónimo (neighbor of María López), 68
Gertrude (saint), 363–64n. 1

al-Ghazzali, 183

Godínez, Miguel, 275

Golpa, Catalina, 194

Gómez, Mari (of Chillón), 46

Gómez, María (alias Maripaz), 200, 203

Goncález, Dominga, 194

González, Alvar (son of Juan González Crespo), 50

González, Elvira (aunt of Mari Sánchez), 27, 36, 40

González, Elvira (conversa of Extremadura), 51

González, Inés, 20, 22–24, 32–36, 40, 41

González, Juan (the smith), 68

González, Juan, trial documents of, 52

González, Marina, 315n. 75

González, Ysavel, 204

Gramsci, Antonio, 341n. 25

Granada, Fray Luis de, 291, 369–70n. 1

Grandín, Lucas, 161

Graxeda, José Castillo de, *Compendio de la vida y virtudes de la venerable Catarina de San Juan*, 273, 276, 282–84, 286–90, 291, 293

Greenleaf, Richard E., 8, 272

Gregory IX (pope), 289

Guadalupe, Inquisition in, 3, 19–41

Guerrero, Marcos, 247

Guinea (Franciscan friar), 77

Gutiérrez, Alonso, 224

Gutiérrez, Beatriz, 217, 219

Gutiérrez, Ysabel, 216, 218

Gutiérrez de Castro, Alonso, 217

hagiography: of Ana Domenge, 139–40; of Catarina de San Juan, 270–95; preservation of orthodox Catholicism in, 9, 333n. 26

Hamilton, Alastair, 88–89

hechicería (magic, enchantment), 256, 260–61, 263–64, 265–66, 267, 268

heresy, defined, 149

Hernández, Alonso, 116

Hernández, Catalina, 203

Hernández, Diego, 101–2, 103–4, 109

Hernández, Francisca: church investigation of, 4, 75–97; clerical (male) support for, 11, 75, 76, 79–90; conflict with María de Cazalla, 95, 102, 103, 107, 109; imprisonment of, 90–94; reputation of, 5, 90, 94–97; seven marvels of, 87

Hernández, Sebastián, 123

Hernández de Corona, García, 216, 218, 219

Herrera, Alonso de, 162

Herrera, Tomás de, 162

Hieronymite order, 120, 133

Híjar, duke of, 160–61, 162, 164

hooks, bell, 240

humanism: fostering of, 4; suspicion of, 5; waning of, 145

Hurtado, Juan, 76

Illuminism. *See alumbrados* (enlightened ones)

ilusa, 230, 378

Index of Prohibited Books, 157, 272, 273, 284, 291–92. *See also* Valdés Index

Indias caciques (Muriel, ed.), 276

indirectas, 59, 60, 62, 378

Inés (wife of Oro Blásquez), 27, 40

Inés of Herrera del Duque: children as followers of, 49–51; death of, 52; visions of, 3, 42–52

Inmaculada, Román de la, 84

Inquisition. *See* Roman Inquisition; Spanish Inquisition

Inquisition of New Spain. *See* Mexican Inquisition; Peruvian Inquisition

inteligencia ("infused knowing"), 165

interrogatorios de tachas, 109, 115, 116, 117

Irigaray, Luce, 339n. 9

Isabel (daughter of Alvaro Ortolano and Catalina López), 50, 51

Isabel de la Encarnación, 275

Isabella I (queen of Castile), 2, 21

Jaen, Inquisition in, 2
Jesuit order, 274, 277, 283, 293, 294
Jesus Christ, in visions, 140–41, 142, 143,
    144, 147–48, 151, 152, 153, 217, 222, 281–82
Jews: expulsion of (1492), 2, 42; restric-
    tions on behavior of, 25, 30, 36
Jiménez, Diego (husband of Mari Sán-
    chez), 19–20, 25, 27, 30, 40
Jiménez, Diego (son of Mari Sánchez),
    28, 32, 33, 34, 40, 41
Jiménez, Leonor, 49
Jiménez, Mari, 23, 32
John of the Cross, 150
Juan de Avila (saint), 142
Juan de Segovia, 43, 45
Juan González (son of Juan González
    Grespo), 50
Juan the tailor, 67
Juana (daughter of Juan Yague), 65
Juana (servant of María López), 61
Juana de Membrillera, 65, 66
Juana Inés de la Cruz, 78, 255, 295, 339n.
    9, 369–70n. 1
Juana la Beltraneja, 21

Kamen, Henry, 2–3
Kessell, John, 158
Kristeva, Julia, 340n. 18
Kusnesof, Elizabeth, 202

ladina, 237, 243
Lea, Henry Charles, 138
Legarda, María, 333n. 24, 335n. 37
León, Lucrecia de, 324n. 3, 344n. 61
León, Fray Luis de, 10
letrado, 378
letrado y procurador, 28
liberal humanism. See humanism
licenciado, 378
limpieza de sangre (purity of blood), 181,
    297–98n. 2, 378

Llerena, alumbrados of, 124
Llorca, Bernardino, 84, 91, 94
Llorente, Juan Antonio, 107
Loboguerrero (Mexican inquisitor), 219
Logroño, Inquisition in, 80, 159, 160, 162
Longoria, Pedro Suárez de, 247
López, Gregorio, 221, 222
López, Ina, 91
López, Inés, 51
López, Isabel (daughter of María Ló-
    pez), 53, 61, 64, 65, 68, 72, 311n. 10
López, Margarida, 189, 193–94, 201, 204,
    205
López, María, 3–4, 53–72
López de Bejar, Gil, 76, 89
López de Husillos, Diego, 77
love magic. See hechicería (magic,
    enchantment)
Luisa de los Angeles, 213, 215
Luther, Martin, 106, 191
Lutheranism, 78, 91, 92, 99, 106, 115, 214,
    220

Madalena (maidservant of María Ló-
    pez), 54, 55, 56, 65
Madalena (wife of Martin Simon), 58,
    65
Madalena of Corlo, 65
Magdalena, María, 237, 238
Malleus Malificarum, 223
Mallorca, Inquisition in, 2
Manero, Pedro, 167, 169
Manrique, Alonso (inquisitor general),
    4, 77, 100
Manrique, Jorge, 118
Manuela, Lorenca (alias de Ribas), 205
Marcilla, Sebastián, 158
Margarita de Narana, 254, 255
María (maidservant of Isabel López),
    54, 56
María Ana Agueda de San Ignacio, 295
María de Acosta, 215
María de Jesús, 122

María de Jesús de Agreda (María Coronel y Arana), 6, 9, 13, 14, 155– 70, 331n. 6, 369–70n. 1
María de la Visitación, 176, 285, 369–70n. 1
María de los Angeles, 214
María de San Jose, 255, 295
María of Carrascosa, 66
María of Santo Domingo, 13, 78–79, 96, 175, 352n. 40, 369–70n. 1
Mariana de Jesús, 220
Mariana of Austria (queen of Spain), 156
Marina de Boborques, 214
Marina de Escobar, 145
Marina de San Miguel, 8, 12, 209–28
Márquez, Antonio, 138
marriage. *See* bigamy
Marta (saint), 263
Martin, Ruth, 261
Martínez, Ana, 194, 201
Martínez, Gaspar, 114
Martínez, María, 199–200
Mary, mother of God: emulation of, 152; as Holy Mary of Monserrate (Black Madonna of Montserrat), 70, 314n. 73; María de Jesús de Agreda's *vita* of, 156–57, 161, 162, 163, 164–65, 167, 170; as Our Lady of the Pomegranate, 186; relationship to Catarina de San Juan, 274, 282; veneration of, 182, 259; as Virgin of Guadalupe, 19; in visions, 127, 137, 140, 145
masturbation, 86, 223, 225
Mayor (maidservant of María López), 54
Medina del Campo, Inquisition in, 2
medranismo, 84
Medrano, Antonio de, 76, 77, 80–85, 88, 90–91
Mena, Pedro de, 91
Mendoza, Antonio de, 234
Mendoza, Brianda de, 109
Mendoza, Leonor de, 122

Mexía, Alonso, 101
Mexican Inquisition: bigamy trials of, 198; history of, 7–8, 209, 211–13, 268, 271–72; savagery of, 229
Midrash, 46, 47
miraculous healing, 12
misogyny, 14–15
Montesdoca, Ynés de, 216, 221
Morga, Antonio de, 247
Moriscos: defined, 7, 173, 378; expulsion of (1609), 7, 173, 179–80; suspicion of, 179–84
Moya de Contreras, Pedro, 349n. 9
Murcia, Francisco de, 55, 60
Murcia, Pedro de, 64
Mystical City of God, The, 156–57, 162, 163, 164–65, 167, 170

Nájera, duke of, 84
Native Americans, excluded from Inquisition, 212
Navarrete, Catalina de, 250–51
Navas, Alonso de las, 68
New Christians. *See* conversos
New Testament, prohibited editions of, 5
Núñez, Elvira, 46
Núñez, Mari, 100, 101, 102–3, 110–12, 115–17
Núñez de León, Juan, 215, 221, 222, 224, 226, 227, 228
Núñez de Miranda, Antonio, 275, 285, 374n. 21
Nuño de Arévalo (Fray), 22

Oddon, Ambrosio, 374n. 24
Olivares, count-duke of, 156
Onofrio (saint), 263
oratorios, 9, 254, 255–61, 267–68, 292, 378
Orduña, Beatriz de, 250
Ortega-Costa, Milagros, 116
Ortiz, Francisco, 4, 77, 80, 85–90, 92, 94
Ortiz de Angulo, Diego, 101, 106, 110

palabras del futuro, 197
Palafox y Mendoza, Bishop Juan, 275, 292, 376n. 35
palenques, 235
Palmer, Colin A., 251
Pedro (son of María López), 55
Peralta, Alonso de, 209, 210, 218, 222, 223, 225, 226–27, 241, 249
Pérez, Cecilia, 201
Pérez, Ines, 202
Pérez, Juana, 197
Pérez de Montalvo (jailer of Francisca Hernández), 94
Perez Tronpeta, Juan, 67
Pérez Villanueva, Joaquín, 157, 158
Perfecta casada, La (The perfect wife) (Luis de León), 10
Perpignan: Dominican convent at, 136, 138; intercession in drought at, 146–47, 148
Perry, Mary Elizabeth, 214
Peruvian Inquisition, history of, 8
Petroff, Elizabeth, 174
Petrona (mestiza), 256, 259, 260, 266, 267
Philip II (king of Spain): New World tribunals established by, 8, 271–72, 349n. 9; petitioned by Francisca de los Apóstoles, 122; support for *beatas* and visionaries, 176; suspicion of Gallecans by, 192
Philip III (king of Spain), 139, 179
Philip IV (king of Spain), 156, 157, 160, 162, 166
Piñeda, Joseph de, 254
Plata, Juan, 220–22, 226
pornography, 15
Porras (Fray), 122
Portugal: abandoned women in, 196; emigration to New World from, 262; refuge for Jews and conversos in, 49, 51; *romaría* in, 259
potro, 378. *See also escalera*
promotor, 378

promotor fiscal, 28, 129, 378
Protestantism: Catholic alarm about, 5; as focus of Spanish Inquisition, 6. *See also* Lutheranism
pueblo (people), 48
Puente, Luis de la, 334n. 28

Quadra, Alonso Lopez de la, 122
Quemada, Gabriel de, 107
querella (complaint), 230, 378
Quirós, Gutierre Bernardo de, 229, 241, 247, 249
Quirós, Leonor de, 109

Rabi'a of Basra, 183–84
Ramírez, Beatriz, 42
Ramírez, María, 91, 107
Ramos, Alonso, *La Vida de la Venerable Sierva de Dios Catharina de S. Joan,* 272–73, 276–82, 284–86, 289, 291, 292, 293–94
rape, 15
Raymond of Capua, *Life (Vita) of Catherine of Siena,* 128, 145
recogimiento (recollection), 79, 86, 352–53n. 43
reconciliation: defined, 378; statements of, 24–26, 27, 34
relaciónes de causas, 193, 204, 378
religious orders: Carmelites, 133, 275; Conceptionists (Franciscans), 155, 161, 275; Dominicans, 78, 136; Franciscans, 11, 77, 86, 100, 156, 157; Hieronymites, 120, 133; Jesuits, 274, 277, 283, 293, 294
retablo, 258, 259
Rocha, Mencia de, 197
Rodrigo (son of Juan López), 49
Rodrigo (son of the smith Fernando Sánchez and María García, his wife), 50
Rodríguez, Ana, 193, 199
Rodríguez, María, 196
Roman Inquisition, 119

romerías, 259
Ropero, Juan, 55, 59, 60, 68
Rosa de Escalante, 9, 254–69
Royo, Eduardo, 163
Rueda, Lope de (cleric), 92
Rueda, Lope de (husband of María de Cazalla), 115–17
Rueda, Pedro de, 107, 108
Ruiz, Alonso, 32
Ruiz, Juana, 217, 219
Ruiz, Miguel, 125, 127–28

Sacromonte, leaden books from, 181, 182
Samaniego, José Ximínez, 158
sanbenito (*sambenito*), 379
Sánchez, Catalina, 37–38
Sánchez, Juan, 93
Sánchez, López, 49
Sánchez, Mari, 3, 19–41
Sanchis, Pierre, 259
Sancho de Horozco, 62
Santa Cruz, Bishop Manuel Fernández de, 275, 285, 374n. 21
Santiago de Compostela, Inquisition in, 189–205
santopan (saint's house), 258
Segovia, Inquisition in, 2
Segura, Pedro de, 91
Selke, Angela, 84, 85, 88, 89, 95
Serach (granddaughter of patriarch Jacob), 46–47
Serra, Fray Junípero, 155–56
Serrano (a vicar), 123
Serrano y Sanz, M., 84, 89, 94
Seville: Inquisition in, 2, 6, 21, 111–12, 119, 171, 172–73; relocation of Moriscos in, 179
sexual intercourse: Catholic regulation of, 7, 196; interracial, 240–41
sexuality: Catholic regulation of, 7, 12, 210; of holy women, 96, 131–32, 177. *See also* bestiality; fornication; masturbation; sexual intercourse; sodomy

Sigüenza, Inquisition in, 2
Sigüenza y Góngora, Carlos de, *Los Infortunios de Alonso Ramírez*, 290
silence, and restrictions on women, 10
Silvela, Francisco, 163
Silvestre (saint), 263
Simon, Martin, 65
Sixtus IV (pope), 2
slaves. *See* African slaves
sodomy, Catholic regulation of, 7
Sosa, Miguel, 274
Spain: expulsion of Jews from (1492), 2, 42; expulsion of Moriscos from (1609), 7, 173, 179–80; Roman Catholicism among rural population, 7. *See also names of specific cities and provinces*
Spanish Inquisition: bigamy trials of, 189–205; history of, 1–2, 4, 21; misogyny of, 14–15, 96–97, 113; purpose of, 2; savagery of, 2–3, 39, 70, 82–83, 112–14, 129, 202
spiritual individualism, 11
spontaneous bleeding, 12
Suárez de Figueroa y Mendoza, Bernardino , 117
Sufism, 183, 188
Suprema: defined, 379. *See also* Consejo de la Suprema y General Inquisición (Council of the Supreme and General Inquisition)
syncretism, 180–81, 182

tachas: defined, 379; *interrogatorios* of, 109, 115, 116, 117; in María de Cazalla case, 103; in María López case, 58, 63–70, 71
Tapia, Ralph J., 88
taqiyya (outer conformity), 179, 188
Tejeda, Juan de, 29, 30, 31, 36, 38
Tellez, Diego, 50, 51
Teresa of Avila: *avisos* attributed to, 135; canonization of, 156, 289; as Christ's daughter, 147–48; church investigation

Teresa of Avila (*continued*)
of, 6, 119, 124, 133, 369–70n. 1; emulation of, 136, 145, 289; genuineness of,
149–50, 175; opposition to, 325n. 12;
writings by, 9–10, 14, 150, 285, 333–34n.
27
texts, defined, 13–14
Thomas Aquinas (saint), 144, 145, 147
toca, 379
Toledo: Inquisition in, 2, 43, 49, 71, 75, 77,
89, 100–101, 102, 109, 111, 116, 119, 133;
poor relief in, 120–21, 326n. 18
Toledo, Edict of (1515), 78, 81, 91
Tomellín, María Jesús, 275
Toribio Medina, José, 234
Torres, Francisco de, 68
torture. *See escalera*, torture on
Tovar, Bernardino de, 76, 83, 90, 91, 92,
94, 106, 110
Trujillo, Jewish community in, 25–26, 28,
33, 34, 36

Urban VII (pope), 374n. 22
Urban VIII (pope), 289, 292
Urrutia, Joseph de, 255, 265

Vaguer (inquisitor), 88, 110
Valdés, Fernando de, 5, 10
Valdés, Juan de, 106, 115; *Diálogo de doc-
trina cristiana*, 104, 106
Valdés, Juan de Llano de, 123, 124–26
Valdés Index (1559), 5
Valencia, Inquisition in, 2
Valladolid, Inquisition in, 2, 6, 76–77
Vargas, Fulano de, 217
Vargas, García de, 104
Velasco, Pedro, 132
Velazquez, Alonso, 123
Vella, Juan de, 67–68
Vergara, Juan de, 92, 94–95, 110, 320n. 9

Vicentico (servant of María López), 66
Villaescusa, Doctor de (lawyer), 29, 35,
37, 38
Villafañe, Catalina de, 237, 239–40, 241,
246
Villaloa, Caterina de, 189, 196, 204, 205
Villareal, Diego de, 76, 91
Villarreal, Pedro de, 53, 56, 64, 65, 67–68,
71–72, 311n. 20
Virgin Mary. *See* Mary, mother of God
visions: of Ana Domenge, 134–54; of
Beatriz de Robles, 171–78, 186–88; of
Catarina de San Juan, 274, 279– 80,
283–84; as embodied experience, 11–13,
177, 184, 186–87; of Francisca de los
Apóstoles, 119, 121, 123, 124–28, 129,
130– 31; genuineness of, 6, 11, 12, 14,
124; of Inés of Herrera del Duque,
42–52; of María de Jesús de Agreda,
163; of Marina de San Miguel, 210,
217, 218, 222; as self-expressive, 174; as
self-referential, 11; of Teresa of Avila,
163, 175
Vivero, Leonor de (wife of Pedro de Cazalla), 77, 88
Vives, Juan de, 10

witnesses. *See abonos; indirectas; tachas*
women: idealized, 10; restrictions on, 10,
12, 136, 190–91, 347n. 46, 349n. 6

Ximenez, Juana, 122

Yague, Francisco, 54–55, 58, 66
Yanga (Nanga, Ñanga), 235, 236, 251
Ysabel (wife of Jerome López of Feans),
199

Zárate, Luis de, 222, 355n. 85
Zumárraga, Fray Juan de, 7, 211

.

Lightning Source UK Ltd.
Milton Keynes UK
UKHW011853220720
366985UK00001B/6